TRUST IN TROUBLED TIMES

Brett Sheehan

Trust in Troubled Times

Money, Banks, and State-Society Relations in Republican Tianjin

HARVARD UNIVERSITY PRESS
Cambridge, Massachusetts, and London, England 2003

Printed in the United States of America

Library of Congress Cataloging-in-Publication Data

Sheehan, Brett, 1960–
Trust in troubled times : money, banks, and state-society relations in republican Tianjin / Brett Sheehan.
p. cm.
Includes bibliographical references and index.
ISBN 0-674-01080-9
1. Banks and banking—China—Tianjin—History. 2. Tianjin (China)—Economic conditions. I. Title.

HG3340.T542S54 2003
332.1'0951'15409041—dc21 2002191340

To Yiyu Jiang

Contents

Acknowledgments

Many people deserve gratitude for providing the help and advice that made this book possible. Wen-hsin Yeh's unflagging support as thesis adviser for the dissertation on which the book is based included both thoughtful guidance and the ability to laugh, even when my project made undue demands on her precious time. Frederic Wakeman provided both inspiration and a practiced eye for the biases and limitations of my sources. Elizabeth Perry pushed me to bring my theoretical constructs into the realm of the greater social science discourse. Diane Lindstrom read various drafts, as well as providing the advice I needed to begin my teaching career successfully. Other colleagues and friends have read and commented on drafts or parts of drafts, including Marie-Claire Bergère, Mary Buck, Parks Coble, David MacDonald, Andrea McElderry, Julia Thomas, Thongchai Winichakul, and Jonathan Zeitlin. Two anonymous readers for the Harvard University Press, and my editors Kathleen McDermott and Amanda Heller read the manuscript with care; the result was a much-improved book. Making the acquaintance of Elaine Mei and Claire Bien, two of Bian Baimei's granddaughters, helped remind me of the humanity of the actors I had known only through documents. Claire Bien was generous with family letters and photographs.

My research in China was made possible by financial support from the Committee on Scholarly Communication in China. My time at Berkeley, as well as trips to read manuscripts at Columbia University and Yale Divinity School Library, were funded in part by grants from the University of California at Berkeley's Institute of East Asian Studies and the Center for Chinese Studies. A Mellon Foundation grant from Berkeley's Department of History supported me during one year of the time I spent writing my dissertation. Grants from the Graduate School of the University of Wisconsin–Madison provided funds for additional archival research in China in the summers of 1999 and 2000.

In China my research could not have been completed without the help of the staff and faculty of the Tianjin Academy of Social Sciences. President Wang Hui was a gracious host, and his office staff, especially, Dong Huifan, cut through much of the red tape faced by a foreigner living in China. The scholars of the academy's Institute of History were generous in sharing their time and experience. Luo Shuwei and Hu Guangmin took me under their wings, giving me needed advice and guidance; Zhang Limin and Liu Haiyan provided intellectual stimulation and companionship. Most important, Song Meiyun devoted her considerable energies and intelligence to making my research possible, spending far too much of her own valuable time dealing with the requirements and foibles of this foreign scholar. I am also grateful to the staff of the Tianjin Municipal Archive, who were unfailingly friendly and helpful, as well as to the librarians at the Tianjin Academy of Social Sciences, Nankai University, and the Tianjin Municipal Library. Fang Zhaolin shared his knowledge of Tianjin history and provided help when I needed it the most. Elsewhere in China and the United States, the staffs of the Number Two History Archive in Nanjing, the Shanghai Municipal Archive, the Shanghai Library, the University of California at Berkeley, the Butler Library at Columbia University, the Yale Divinity School library, and Martha Mitchell at Brown University all provided courteous and professional assistance.

Portions of this book draw on material previously published as "The Persistence and Limits of Localism: Paper Money and State Power in Tianjin, 1916–1937," *Special Essays on the History of the Republic of China: The Fifth Conference* (Taipei: Academia Historica, 2000), pp. 1311–86; and "Warlords, Cadres, and Bankers: Private Commercial Banking in the Republican and Post-Mao Periods," *Journal of Asian Business,* 14, no. 1 (1998): 5–22. Thanks to the editors for allowing me to use that material here.

I owe much to my friends and family, who remained supportive even when they could not quite understand why I abandoned a successful banking career to become an academic. Thanks to Kathy, Linda, and Laurie for persuading me to leave my job and go back to graduate school. My mother and father, Shirleen and William Neu, deserve credit for teaching me to aim high and believe in myself. Shelly, George, and Alexis provided shelter and emotional support during one key period. My mother-in-law and father-in-law made it possible for me to devote all of my time to writing for several months in 1997. Many classmates at Berkeley offered friendship and intellectual stimulation, especially Darren Zook, Ranjana Ariaratnam, and the members of my dissertation group: Mark Halperin, Josh Howard, and Madeline Hsu. Last, I owe an unrepayable debt to my wife, Yiyu Jiang, for providing love, companionship, and understanding, especially when I did not deserve it.

No one could have wished for a wiser or more rigorous group of teachers, readers, colleagues, family, and friends, and the resulting work could not have been completed without them. The faults of this book, of course, are my own.

A Note on Currency Values

The value of the various components of the Chinese monetary system changed from place to place and day to day, but a few rough generalizations can be made.

1 yuan = 0.667 taels (1 tael = 1.5 yuan)

1 yuan = 0.40 USD (ca. 1927)
1 yuan = 0.35 USD (ca. 1930)
1 yuan = 0.20–0.25 USD (1933)

In Tianjin in the late 1920s the income for a working-class household ranged from 14 to 20 yuan per month, bank clerks earned 40 to 80, and a bank executive like Bian Baimei earned several hundred.

TRUST IN TROUBLED TIMES

Bian Baimei (third from right), Li Guojing, his wife, (third from left), his six sons, and his daughter in the late 1910s or early 1920s. (Courtesy of Claire Bien.)

Introduction

On December 23, 1937, Bian Baimei, the manager of the Tianjin branch of the Bank of China, boarded a train to Beijing with great trepidation. Japanese troops had invaded China in July, and the war was going badly for the Chinese. The Nationalist government was retreating for a second time, now headed for Chongqing in southwest China. In North China, the Japanese occupation force engineered the formation of a new government, based in Beijing and staffed by former Chinese officials. One of those officials, Wang Kemin, had called Bian Baimei to a meeting to discuss the formation of a new central bank to issue currency on behalf of the puppet state. As Bian sat on the train during the two-hour ride to Beijing, he worried about how to protect the substantial resources of his bank from China's new masters. Such worries were not novel for him. Bian had defended the trustworthiness and institutional integrity of China's modern banks for over twenty years, weathering seven civil wars and at least nine financial crises. His banking career had started with another trip to Beijing some twenty-five years earlier. A young Bian Baimei (b. 1884) had arrived in Beijing, hoping to establish himself in the heady days of the new republic after the 1911 revolution had toppled the Qing dynasty (1644–1911). Armed with a degree in political economy from Brown University and a pedigree placing him in the highest ranks of Chinese elite families, the ambitious Bian used his foreign education and family connections to get a job in China's infant modern banking industry. As a young man, fresh from his education in the United States, Bian had no way of imagining the trials and tribulations he would have to face over the years, ending with his fateful trip to Beijing to talk to Japan's puppet rulers at the end of 1937—the day he said his spirit died.

The struggle to develop viable strategies to promote trust in banks from

1916 to 1937 and Bian Baimei's role in those processes provide the central narrative for this book. Over the course of Bian's career, the common economic good of states and citizens alike became inextricably linked to the continued viable operation of, and trust in, banks and bank-issued paper money.[1] The northern city of Tianjin, Bian Baimei's home and China's second-largest financial center after Shanghai, provides the local context. For most of this period, Bian served as manager of the Tianjin branch of the Bank of China (the largest Chinese-owned bank) and as president of the powerful Tianjin Bankers' Association. Bian's prominence as a Tianjin banker makes him a natural candidate for study. Furthermore, he left a detailed diary of his life and experiences during this time, providing one of the most important sources for this research project. Bian's thoughts and reactions, as recorded in his diary, serve as a reminder amidst discussion of groups, institutions, and patterns that the phenomena described by abstract analytical categories were produced by the complicated and often contradictory actions of individuals. In addition to Bian's diary, Tianjin offers a rich, and mostly untapped, set of primary sources on republican China, including the archives of the Tianjin Bankers' Association, the Tianjin Chamber of Commerce, and several of Tianjin's most important banks. While in Tianjin in 1994 and 1995, I supplemented these written records by interviewing a number of men (very few women worked at Chinese banks) who had worked at banks in Tianjin in the 1920s and 1930s.

China's extended political crisis during the republican period is well known. Frequent civil wars and continual political instability forced bankers to deal with a series of warlords, politicians, and political movements, each with their own agenda for the financial system. To make matters worse, interference, threats, and even military attacks from Western powers and Japan created an ongoing sense of vulnerability in the international arena. Political crises, however, did not present the only challenges to maintaining trust in banks and bank-issued money. Financial crises, little studied now, loomed large both as a challenge to the viability of the financial system and as images in the public imagination. One Tianjin resident still remembers the day he went to pay tuition at his grade school and learned that his money was no longer good because a bank run had shut down the issuing bank.[2] Stories circulated among bankers, whether true or false, demonstrate the importance of bank runs. A former banker recalled his older colleagues' story of a bank that sent its own employees to pose as customers and line up to exchange their money for silver during a bank run. These "satisfied customers" then sneaked back into the bank through the rear door to replace the silver they had just exchanged. They repeated this operation over and over, essentially exchanging the same banknotes for the same silver without reducing the bank's silver reserves at all. The real customers were so impressed by this apparent ability to exchange without limit that the run dissipated quickly.[3] Another story recounts how one banker actually spread rumors about his own bank, hoping that surviving the ensuing bank run would be a sign of his institution's solidity.[4] Bank runs also became the stuff of fiction. In Cao Yu's 1936 play *Sunrise*, a gangster threatens a banker by describing a bank run as follows:

> Tomorrow morning I'll be able to watch the rush on your bank with my own eyes, I'll see you unable to pay up, I'll see the small savers who've nine or ten dollars apiece in your bank, calling you names, cursing you—yes, they'll lynch you, they'll eat you alive! You've ruined them! You've ruined them, and they'll flay the skin off your back, they'll gouge out your heart! The only thing that can satisfy them now is your death![5]

The banker in question had made dubious loans to the gangster, and instead of repaying those loans, the gangster threatened the banker not with guns but with the specter of a loss of trust: the betrayed public would "flay the skin off [his] back and gouge out [his] heart." "Flaying" and "gouging" may have been an exaggeration, since bankers were rarely attacked personally during bank runs, but the crowds were real, and Cao Yu's hyperbole serves to illustrate the importance of trust—and the suspension of that trust during financial crises—to both the professional lives of bankers and society at large.

At least nine financial crises of varying degrees of severity wracked Tianjin between 1916 and 1937. The first seven took the form of bank runs, in which crowds gathered to cash their banknotes and withdraw their deposits in silver or copper.[6] The eighth financial crisis came as the result of the Japanese attack on Shanghai in 1932, cutting off Tianjin's banks from their close ties with their Shanghai counterparts. Finally, in 1934–35 Tianjin, and China as a whole, faced a shortage of silver, as American purchases drained huge amounts of the precious metal in a balance of payments crisis.[7]

Little agreement exists regarding either the nature of financial crises or measures for mitigation.[8] Each of the nine crises discussed in this book, however, shares a common denominator: a severe disruption in the production, regulation, circulation, or guardianship of money, specifically the paper money issued by banks. Because of the centrality of money in the historical processes studied here, a few comments on the nature of money and its relationship to trust are necessary.

In order to overcome approaches to money that see it primarily in terms of either its functions (means of payment, standard of value, etc.) or its forms (commodity money, fiat money), I draw on the theories of scholars as diverse as Georg Simmel, Joseph Schumpeter, John Maynard Keynes, and Henry Dunning Macleod. Money, in all its forms and functions, is debt.[9] Monetary economies function differently from barter economies; the ability to use money does not just facilitate exchange, as claimed by the classical and neoclassical economists, but allows fundamentally different kinds of exchange. As Simmel notes, barter is simply a relationship between two individuals, but money introduces a third factor: "The pivotal point in the interaction of the two parties recedes from the direct line of contact between them, and moves to the relationship which each of them . . . has with the economic community that accepts money . . . [which] is only a claim upon society."[10] As a result, according the nineteenth-century economic thinker Henry Dunning Macleod, "the value of currency . . . depends on the credit of the economy, that is, on the willingness and ability of members of the society to perform the services promised in exchange for units of the currency."[11] All money depends on trust that a monetary token will be accepted in exchange for goods or services at some point in the future by some member of society.

Two other factors are necessary to understand trust in money. First, money does not exist sui generis but is socially produced.[12] In the case of some monies, such as cowrie shells, production may be diffuse, but in many instances money is produced or regulated by specific organizations such as the state or, in the case of republican China, banks. Second, money circulates among a circuit or network of users.[13] These two elements, focusing on the producers and users of money, allow for the examination of trust by specifying the two sets of trust relationships involved. On the one hand, money depends on trust in the producer or, potentially, the regulator of money, and, on the other hand, money depends on trust among a network of users. Both of these sets of relationships are consistent with impersonal trust that arises "when social-control measures derived from social ties and direct contact between principal and agent are unavailable, when faceless and readily interchangeable individual or organizational agents exercise considerable delegated power and privilege on behalf of principals who can neither specify, scrutinize, evaluate, nor constrain their performance."[14] A transaction like this relies on trusting a group of individuals who are not involved in the initial transaction, and who need not be known to the initial transactors. Money that is issued by organizations such as banks or governments relies on impersonal trust in those organizations, as well as trust that society in general will accept the tokens produced by those organizations. In neither case does that trust depend on personal relations. One may rely on personal trust in an individual for assurance that a check will not bounce, that a coin has not been altered, or that a banknote has not been forged. Once the token is taken to be authentic, however (through personal trust, calling the bank to verify funds, weighing, or other examination), its value and use still depend on impersonal trust in society in general's acceptance of that token, and in the organization that produced or regulated the production of that money.

A financial crisis, then, is a suspension of impersonal trust, or a shift from *trust in* to *distrust of* either the producer/regulator of money or the likelihood that a network of users will continue to recognize a given token as money. Here the concept of thresholds, as used by Niklas Luhmann, can help illustrate the shift from trust to distrust, in which "one can remain indifferent about any distinctions until one crosses the threshold; then a small step brings great changes."[15] On one side of the threshold, trust is maintained in spite of disturbances, rumors, manipulation of the money supply, international capital flows, and so on. At some point, however, the threshold is crossed, and trust is suspended, resulting in a financial crisis. As Nigel Dodd notes, "When confidence breaks down . . . the transmission of grief through money can be penetrating and swift."[16]

The need to maintain trust in money in republican Tianjin presented a series of hard choices for Bian Baimei and other bankers, government officials, and local elites. Currency issue was a profitable activity for banks, but a financial crisis involving that currency could bankrupt even strong banks. Governments wanted to use bank resources for state projects, but abuse of those resources could instigate a crisis, undermining the stability of the financial system, the government's access to bank funds, and public order. Local elites in Tianjin, especially the businessmen who ran guilds and the Chamber of Commerce, needed a stable financial environment to function, and often took on, or were forced by government officials to take on, the role of guardians to guarantee the value of money. Such guardianship activities were expensive, however, and often threatened to overwhelm the resources of local elites. The story of negotiating among these hard choices emerges in four interrelated strands: the promotion of trusting behaviors; the institutional development of the financial system; state control over the financial system and its impact on state power; and elite roles in state-society relations.

Trust

Trust entails three essential elements: uncertainty, vulnerability, and the willingness to suspend trust under certain circumstances. First, as stated by Barbara Misztal, "to trust is to believe despite uncertainty."[17] The future uncertainty involved with money, of course, is whether or not it will hold its value between the time someone exchanges goods or services for it and the time he or she exchanges it for goods or services. Second, the trusting party is made vulnerable by the act of trusting.[18] The betrayal of trust results in some loss or cost to the trustor—financial loss, for example, in the case of money that cannot be exchanged for goods or services. Finally, current belief does not necessarily entail future belief, as such trust differs from faith. As Charles F. Sabel has noted, "trust obligates partners to behave loyally in the present, but does not obligate them to refrain from asking—out loud—whether and under what conditions they should continue to do so in the future."[19]

For our purposes here, behaviors that conform with these three characteristics—people acting as if they believe despite uncertainty, becoming vulnerable through the act of trust, and showing willingness to suspend this belief under certain conditions—are sufficient to demonstrate trust. Individual reasons for trusting may be inferred, but they are not necessary to prove the existence of trust. Thus, unlike Niklas Luhmann and Oliver Williamson, I make no distinctions between trust and "functional equivalents of trust," such as calculativeness or guarantees of authority.[20] Most money, and especially the bank-issued paper money that is the subject of this book, circulates in networks that include both elites and non-elites, and the motives of the latter are rarely reliably included in the historical record. Thus the ready acceptance of a particular token as money within a network or circuit of people shows trust, and if a guarantee by an authority leads to that acceptance, then that guarantee is considered to be a basis for trust, not its functional equivalent. Likewise, I reject the assertion that trust is a purely modern phenomenon, arising from either the differentiated complexity of modern systems or the modern subjectivity of the individual.[21] Contingency may be perceived differently at different times. For example, "human moral imperatives, natural causes, and chance" may "reign in place of religious cosmologies," but the historical record is full of premodern cases that satisfy the three characteristics of trust as defined here.[22] Finally, it is important to remember that failure to trust does not necessarily indicate "ignorance or irrationality."[23] Trust "is neither normatively good nor bad; it is neither a virtue nor a vice . . . When some fundamental interests are divergent . . . or when citizens are concerned about protecting themselves from incursions of state power or from intolerant majorities, there is good reason for the parties to be wary of each other."[24]

Studies of trust in China, and more broadly in East Asia, have usually focused on personal trust between or among individuals based on particularistic ties of kinship, identity, or networks, though opinions differ about the consequences of these forms of trust.[25] The present book expands the discussion by focusing on impersonal rather than personal trust. This is not to say that personal trust is unimportant. To the contrary, I will show how native place, educational background, and shared professional norms played key roles in elite structures and activities. Nonetheless, money, as we have seen, relies on impersonal trust from many people, not just elites, and this leads us to a line of investigation quite different from that of previous studies of trust in the Chinese context.

In this book I show how impersonal trust functioned in republican China and how the Chinese case reflects on debates in Western theory regarding the nature of trust itself. Discussion of these debates does not entail holding up the West as an ideal against which to measure China; rather, this study of China provides an important set of cases against which to measure theory. In general, strategies used by government officials, bankers, and local elites to promote impersonal trust in Tianjin fell into four categories: rhetorical appeals, reliance on authority, guardianship, and institutional arrangements. Each of these strategies corresponds to different sets of questions about the nature of trust.

In order to promote trust in Tianjin's banks, republican-period elites frequently made rhetorical appeals to various norms—including localism, nationalism, and belief in the rational workings of modern financial systems—providing an opportunity to assess the impact of shared norms on trusting behaviors. Some critics have concluded that normative explanations of trust tend to be ahistoric, without solid empirical foundation, and often underestimate the extent to which distrust and conflict can exist.[26] In contrast, the rational expectations view of the world predicts that "cooperation is the result of an accidental complementarity of maximizing strategies, and its culmination can only be a *modus vivendi,* never trust."[27] Rational views of trust, however, are hard-pressed to explain the fact that, in reality, cooperation seems to happen more often than would be predicted by the model.[28] Of course, the failure of a given rhetorical appeal, rather than providing evidence for rational actor alternatives, may simply mean that the norm in question had little resonance with the shared values of the residents of Tianjin.

During financial crises in republican Tianjin, government officials and police often issued orders mandating the normal circulation of money, which offer an opportunity to examine authority as the basis for promoting trusting behavior. Oliver Williamson and Douglass North see a role for authority in reducing transaction costs and promoting trust relationships or, in Williamson's nomenclature, their functional equivalent.[29] Other theorists emphasize the role of social relations rather than authority in creating trust, though they differ on both the relative functions of vertical and horizontal social relations and the role of norms and institutions. Prominently, Robert Putnam explicitly rejects the possibility that reliance on authority can promote trust. As he states, "A vertical network, no matter how dense and no matter how important to its participants, cannot sustain social trust and cooperation."[30] As with rhetorical appeals, the success of a given government or police order can support the notion of authority as a basis of trust, but failure of itself may indicate only that the authority in question lacks legitimacy in the eyes of the public.

Guardianship arrangements constituted a much more complex, and sometimes costly, response to financial crises by republican-period Tianjin elites. Susan Shapiro outlines three different means by which guardianship works. First, guardianship can rely on procedural norms and structural constraints, like those that regulate the professional behaviors of journalists, accountants, or scientists. The second form of guardianship focuses on the choice of reliable trustees, the selection of whom may be regulated through licensing or education. In the third form, "institutional guardians anticipate [the] possibility of normative or social control failures" through risk-spreading and insurance-like arrangements.[31] The first two kinds of guardianship, the reliance on procedural norms and the selection of trusted agents, can be either external or internal to a bank or a monetary system, while risk pooling necessitates the involvement of at least two actors.

Guardianship relationships permeate modern society, though they do not always result in trustworthy arrangements. In the literature on financial crises, guardianship often appears through the workings of a lender of last resort. Charles Kindleberger most famously advocates that a lender of last resort is necessary to promote stability in financial systems.[32] Hugh Rockoff, however, points out that no clear rules exist for the activities of lenders of last resort, and the resulting ambiguity can distort financial systems or even undermine stability.[33] Others claim that in practice the activities of lenders of last resort are always embedded in, and distorted by, political and social relations.[34] Other guardianship activities have downsides as well. Complex regulations and restrictions can "limit the efficiency, information, access, and experience that agents require to maximize their return to principals." In addition, distrust can lead to ever more layers, as when guardians are appointed to guard the guardians, exacerbating the negative effects of guardianship.[35]

In all cases guardianship relies on the successful functioning of institutions, and this leads us to the final set of strategies adopted to promote trust in money and banks in republican Tianjin: institutional arrangements. Bankers developed some of these arrangements, such as constructing impressive bank buildings, specifically to promote trust, but others, such as the stabilizing effects of branch banking, derived from institutional structures adopted for other reasons. Institutional strategies to promote trust generally fell into one of three areas: trust in the agents of institutions, trust in institutions as embodiments of expert knowledge, and arrangements to provide stable banking structures.

First, one set of theories about the institutional bases of trust focuses on the activities of the agents of organizations, postulating that organizations will be perceived as trustworthy if their agents are perceived as trustworthy. In one variation of these theories, encapsulated interest, I trust you not because it is in my best interests to do so, but because some knowledge I have indicates that it is in your best interests to be trustworthy. That is, the trusted agent will gain some benefit, or avoid some punishment, for behaving in a trustworthy manner.[36] Organizations, of course, do not always need to use constraints to ensure that their agents will behave in a trustworthy fashion, and agents can be perceived as trustworthy if they have internalized certain norms about the proper functioning of that institution, or about the virtues of being trustworthy.[37] Second, trust in institutions grows from the fact that they embody expert knowledge, a growing phenomenon in a world that increasingly relies on complex technologies.[38] Charles Goodhart concludes that the need for trust in expert knowledge arises from asymmetrical information, whereby "clients/customers know less than producers" in specialized services including banking and finance.[39] In republican Tianjin, elites attempted to engender trust in expert knowledge by establishing both external and internal guardianship arrangements to ensure adherence to professional norms; by exposing the technical workings of expert knowledge to public scrutiny in a process of openness; and, in contrast to openness, by shrouding the workings of the financial system in secrecy in order to conceal problems and promote an aura of infallibility. Third, institutional arrangements focused on trying to create stable structures of money and banking. Internally, banks used their branch structures and organizational adjustments to isolate risks. Externally, banks developed "rules of the game" to regularize their relations with the state, a major source of instability.

Like guardianship, institutional arrangements to produce trust can be problematic. The agents of institutions may be incompetent or venal. Likewise, openness has its limits, especially "when it is costly and difficult for anyone, even a specialist, to obtain such information" about the institution in question.[40] At the same time, openness and secrecy present conflicting strategies to promote belief in the expert knowledge of banking. Finally, the structures of the money and banking system were not always malleable for the purposes of promoting trust. Institutional arrangements set constraints on activities to promote trust as often as they provided solutions.

Besides increasing our understanding of the theoretical bases of trust, the relative success of each of these strategies had tremendous impact on the ease and cost of promoting trust in republican Tianjin, with consequences for the institutional development of money and banks, state power, and state-society relations.

Money and Banking as Institutions

This book examines both institutions and organizations. Following the lead of the so-called new institutionalism, I use the word "institution" to refer to systems such as the monetary system; an industry such as the banking industry; or the "rules of the game" which defined the patterns of practice, such as procedures and norms.[41] Too much focus on this abstract level of institutionalization, however, tends to understate the role of power relations and specific actors in building institutions.[42] To that end I also often refer to specific organizations, including governments, merchant associations, and business firms, especially banks.[43]

Although China had a long tradition of indigenous financial institutions, banks based on foreign models were symbols of modernity and mechanisms intended by their founders to make China strong.[44] The first of these "modern" banks was not founded until 1897, but by the mid-1930s China's modern banks had come to control more than 77 percent of the resources of financial institutions in China, with the pattern in Tianjin showing a similar growth.[45] "Modern" Chinese banks are readily identifiable because most used the word "bank" *(yinhang)* in their names.[46] Modern banks had real structural and functional differences from indigenous Chinese banks, including more capital; use of the joint-stock, limited liability form of organization; large, often nationwide branch structures; much larger customer bases; buildings that copied foreign architectural styles; and loans based on collateral rather than solely on the reputation of the borrower.[47]

Of all their operations, the new banks' impact on China's monetary system proved particularly salient. A bewildering array of different kinds of money circulated in China when elites first began to experiment with reform of the financial system in the late nineteenth century. Bank-issued paper money did not simplify the system but did transform it, as Thomas Rawski notes: "New monetary arrangements penetrated all but the most isolated regions and affected every sector of the economy . . . The first four decades of the twentieth century witnessed an unprecedented expansion of the money economy . . . [when] the money stock shifted . . . to a new structure in which bank liabilities—deposits and notes—occupied the central position."[48] Three features of this transformed monetary system had a direct bearing on the conditions for trust in this paper money and on the role of that money in state-society relations. First, prior to 1935, convertibility remained the acid test of a viable currency because holders of the paper money could ask the bank of issue to exchange it into silver or copper. Second, many different kinds of money circulated side by side, so Chinese banks that issued paper money had to compete for the trust of the public with one another and with foreign banks. Third, banks "localized" their paper money, printing each note with its place of issue (see figure). Sometimes the "Beijing" notes of a bank might be worth less than "Tianjin" notes issued by the same bank for the same face value.

The founders of China's modern banks consciously copied foreign organizational forms; this provides an excellent opportunity to study the institutional imitation that took place in non-Western countries in the late nineteenth and early twentieth centuries and continues throughout the world today.[49] Imitation rarely produces exact copies, however; we must therefore

Example of "Tianjin" money issued by the Tianjin branch of the Bank of China. On the top: Front of a five-yuan "Tianjin note" issued by the Bank of China. Note the Chinese characters for Tianjin in the side margins and Bian Baimei's signature (Z. S. Bien) in the lower right. Bottom: Back of the same note. (From the author's collection.)

examine the relationship between organizational forms and their institutional contexts. In considering this question, some scholars place predominant emphasis on the cultures or societies that provide the patterns for the institutionalization of organizations.[50] Another perspective argues that "organizations are not passive actors being imprinted by cultural templates."[51] The outcome of this debate has tremendous consequences for institution building. If, on the one hand, context is supreme, institution builders become prisoners of path-dependent conditions they cannot change. On the other hand, if organizations can change their contexts, organizational innovation can result in contextual change, though it may at the same time produce unintended consequences.

State Control and State Power

The relationship between states and financial systems has been a matter of historical study since Rondo Cameron's pioneering work, especially in regard to economic growth.[52] More recently, Richard Sylla, Richard Tilly, and Gabriel Tortella have noted the "paramount importance" of the role of the state at "most of the critical points when financial systems changed."[53] In this book I consider three aspects of state control over the system of money and banking: a monopoly over currency issue, the state's role in regulating finance, and state access to bank resources.

First, a monopoly on the control of money is often a mainstay of power in the modern state. As David Woodruff has noted, "Alongside the monopoly on legitimate violence, monopolistic control over the definition and creation of money has become one of the powers we take for granted when we speak of the sovereign nation-state."[54] Nonetheless, the path toward a monopoly over the money supply is not linear, inevitable, or irreversible. Central monopolies over money can be "unmade" by local resistance, as Woodward shows in his exploration of monetary control in Russia in the 1990s, or by regional monetary compacts like the European monetary union. In China, government officials worked to implement a monopoly of control over the issue of paper money beginning in the late Qing dynasty, but only in 1935 did the Nationalist government achieve this goal. I examine the interrelated questions of why it took so long for the Chinese state to establish a monopoly over the money supply and how the lack of that monopoly affected state power.

Second, many scholars disagree about the relationship between the state's ability to regulate financial systems and monetary stability. Free banking theorists propose that the market, not the government, should regulate banks and currency. In this view, central banks and government monopoly on currency issue are not necessary, and in fact interfere with the efficient working of banking systems. David Glasner concludes that state monopolies over money evolved not for economic reasons but to contribute "to the security of the state against internal and external threats."[55] In contrast, Anna J. Schwartz argues that "the historical evidence does not speak as loudly in favor of free banking as its proponents claim." She asserts that the evidence on the efficacy of clearinghouses, and on the stability of free banking systems in the United States, Scotland, and Sweden, shows both more regulation and more potential for instability than free banking advocates claim.[56]

Third, state access to bank resources is a major question of state-bank relations. In fact, government demands for access to the resources of banks led directly to a number of the crises in Tianjin, as loans to the government financed by the issue of paper money drained bank vaults and jeopardized exchange. The role of the financial system in government finance is a huge topic, well beyond the scope of one book. The present study concentrates on direct loans between Tianjin banks and the state at either the central or the local level.[57]

Elites and State-Society Relations

Three central processes studied in this book had an impact on elite roles in state-society relations.[58] First, studying responses to crises reflects the nature of local elite activism. In China, the late nineteenth and early twentieth centuries witnessed an increase in activism as local elites took on many functions the state was unable or unwilling to fulfill, and there exists a rich literature on this topic. Some scholars have argued that the rise in local elite activism took place in a developing public sphere or even civil society. This debate has been lively, and no consensus exists, though most public sphere theorists admit that local elite activism had its limits.[59] From a different standpoint, Marie-Claire Bergère has argued that Shanghai's bourgeoisie was hampered by a weak state in the 1920s and then "gradually swallowed up" by the state thereafter.[60] Other scholars stress the interconnected status of the state and elites. Yu Heping concludes that Chambers of Commerce—which functioned as one of the main vehicles for elite activism—depended heavily on government support and implementation to reach their goals.[61] Susan Mann, following Weber, suggests that a model of liturgical governance prevailed, in which the state entrusted certain activities, such as tax farming, to local elites, and Margaret Pearson portrays a business elite that "sat Janus-like, between state and society."[62] Similarly, in a study of business elites in Tianjin slightly before the time period treated here, Man Bun Kwan argues for an "expansive role of local mercantile elites," who could both reinforce and destabilize government authority.[63]

Second, because banks issued money locally and crises were usually dealt with at the local level, this book explores tensions between center and locality. In looking at center-locality relations, many studies of the republican period have noted a failure in state-society relations because states were unable to mobilize or reshape Chinese society.[64] Other literature on state-society relations focuses on the relative strength of the center and the locality. Frederic Wakeman argues that there was a long-term secular rise in state power, though Prasenjit Duara and Susan Mann emphasize the rise of brokers who widened the gap between center and locality. Philip Kuhn, Mary Rankin, and Joseph Esherick argue for simultaneous growth of both central and local power, and Xin Zhang for regional variation with some localities forging closer ties to the center and some becoming more distant.[65]

Third, as the banking system developed, existing elite structures had to accommodate the emergence of a powerful group of professional bankers like Bian Baimei. It is widely accepted that elite groups changed radically in the late nineteenth and early twentieth centuries, but these processes remain little understood. A long-term trend toward fusion between the traditional literati gentry (elites who either passed the imperial civil service exams or partook of the same literati culture) and merchants culminated in the nineteenth century.[66] Ma Min has argued that this merchant-gentry *(shenshang)* class of the late Qing period played a mediating role between state and society but disappeared during the republic.[67] Its disappearance coincided with increasing fragmentation of elites and the emergence of professional groups such as bankers. Marie-Claire Bergère has shown that Shanghai's bankers found strength in forms of traditional solidarity, such as native place.[68] Elsewhere, Xiaoqun Xu notes a symbiotic interdependence between professional associations in Shanghai and the state during the republican period.[69]

This book allows for a fresh look at elite roles in state-society relations. Rather than asking questions about success or failure, or looking for evidence of a Western-style public sphere or civil society, I approach the question of local elite activism, tensions between center and locality, and the emergence of a professional group of bankers by examining elite behaviors in relation to specific historical processes of institutional development and strategies to promote trust.

At times the machinations of bankers, officials, and local elites to promote trust in banks and bank-issued money in Tianjin looked like an elaborate game in which each party tried to appear to be supporting the system without actually taking financial responsibility for it. Nonetheless, the game was real and the stakes were high. Financial institutions provided a powerful tool for transforming the monetary system and promoting state power, but at the same time, the need for trust in those institutions constrained state activities, created challenges for bankers like Bian Baimei and local elites, and made China vulnerable to domestic and international disturbances during the troubled times of the republican period.

In terms of trust, Francis Fukuyama, for one, has questioned the very existence of impersonal trust in China, concluding that China is a "low-trust" society in which "the lack of trust outside the family makes it hard for unrelated people to form groups or organizations, including economic enterprises."[70] In contrast, this book shows that impersonal trust in banks and bank-issued money grew during the prewar republican period, and that the Chinese are not as culturally limited in their choice of economic forms as Fukuyama asserts. Trusting behaviors proved responsive to a variety of strategies, but in different ways at different times. Rhetorical appeals showed mixed results, doing little to restore trust during financial crises, though sometimes working in more stable times. Reliance on government authority as a regulator of the financial system was weak in the years after 1916 but increased over time. Local elite guardianship organizations had a dismal record in restoring trusting behaviors, though collective action by bankers to function as a lenders of last resort during minor financial crises had better results. In general, the most effective methods relied on institutional arrangements such as branch structures, investor support, the development of "rules of the game" to limit exposure to government extraction, and institutionalization of the expert knowledge of banking.

I also show how the use of foreign models, state fiscal needs, the influence of elite networks, and China's prolonged political crisis produced a financial system with a unique combination of properties: multiple banks of issue, branch banking by large joint-stock corporations, and issue of relatively small denomination notes, requiring trust in financial institutions from large numbers of ordinary people for the first time in modern Chinese history.

In regard to innovation, in spite of conscious attempts to copy foreign models, China's domestic conditions equally influenced the development of the money and banking system, proving that institutions both shape and are shaped by their environments. Thus, the evidence here argues for a middle road in the debates on path dependency and convergence, suggesting that organizational innovation can change economic or political systems, though not necessarily in the ways intended by their founders.

Modern banking began as a state project, and banks and bank-issued paper money generally enhanced central state power. Government supervision of the financial system waned in the 1910s and 1920s, however, as the state fragmented. State-sponsored banks achieved a degree of autonomy from their government roots, and a number of private banks, many run by managers trained at one of the state banks, joined their ranks. In spite of the coercive measures used by warlords, the need for trust forced the state to conform to "rules of the game" that determined the conditions for gaining access to bank resources. In the 1930s the Nationalist government restored old, and invented new, styles of control over the banking sector. Over the course of the entire period, the widespread impact of frequent financial crises invited supervision and regulation from the central state, local officials, and local elites, resulting in a close interpenetration of the state, society, and finance that makes a moot point of the question of free banking.

In terms of elite roles and structures, instability in the monetary system often pulled or pushed local elites into the role of regulators, and occasionally guardians, of the money supply, a situation that appears compatible with public sphere or liturgical models of elite activism. Local elite attempts to form guardianship organizations to guarantee or regulate the money supply failed repeatedly, however, in part because of the elites' ambivalence about their role and in part because the size and structure of banks outstripped the capabilities of local elites. A powerful group of bankers emerged, linked by common educational background, professional identity, native-place ties, and common experiences working in state banks. As outsiders, Tianjin's elite bankers had little interest in preserving local power. In addition, in spite of their drive for autonomy, bankers consistently demonstrated a proclivity to support state projects. The nonlocal orientation of banking elites and the inability of local elites to develop successful strategies for the promotion of trust brought about a secular decline in local elite power. Localism did not die out completely, however, and remained persistent, though limited.[71]

Study of the processes involved in promoting trust in banks and bank-issued paper money in Tianjin from 1916 to 1937 leads us to reflect on the stability of monetary arrangements that have a direct impact on both economic prosperity and the viability of social and political structures. On the train to Beijing that fateful day in 1937, Bian Baimei had to consider how to respond to state demands without destroying the public trust in his bank that he had worked so many years to build. Stability remained hard-fought and fragile in republican Tianjin, constantly subject to conflict and renegotiation. Likewise, financial crises in East Asia in 1997 and in Argentina and Turkey in 2001, and the failure of guardianship arrangements, as with the inability of accounting firms to anticipate the problems of Enron, WorldCom, and other companies, remind us that the goals of financial stability and public trust in economic institutions remain vital but elusive and hard to achieve even today.

1

Personal Networks and State Needs

> The situation is urgent. The embers only smolder now, but will eventually burst into flames. At this time, if you want to quickly raise a hundred million [dollars] and get a hundred million benefits, no method is superior to issuing paper money, [but] paper money issued without a bank will not be trustworthy.
>
> — Yiketang'a, Manchu official, 1898

When Bian Baimei was born in 1884, China's eighteenth-century prosperity, fueled in part by silver flows from abroad, was well in the past and the country had already witnessed decades of external and internal crises.[1] From abroad, foreign imperialists worked to force the Qing empire into an emerging system of nation-states with new terms and structures of international trade and international relations. Beginning with the first Opium War in 1839, China fought and lost a series of wars with the European powers, as a result of which many European countries, and later Japan, won the right to establish miniature quasi-colonies called concessions in major cities of China's eastern seaboard. These new so-called treaty ports, split between Chinese and foreign administrations and home to foreign organizations such as schools, newspapers, factories, trading companies, and banks, would provide the setting for much of the organizational and institutional innovation that would occur in the late nineteenth and early twentieth centuries. Internally, China faced unprecedented population growth, a general decline in government effectiveness, and restive populations on the frontier. At the same time, forced import of opium imposed by the European powers drained silver from the Chinese economy, and this, along with rising drug use, contributed to the sense of internal crisis and decay. External disruptions combined with these internal pressures to fuel mid-nineteenth-century rebellions of massive scale, including the famous Taiping Rebellion of 1850–1865, involving millions of people.

The other side of crisis, though, is opportunity. In the second half of the nineteenth century, many Chinese elites mobilized at the local, regional, and national levels first to defeat the rebels and then to restore China's vigor and security in the international arena. This mobilization led to the founding of new organizations—often in treaty ports—based on foreign models. At approximately the same time, local elites all over China, but especially in cities and core areas, accelerated a long-term trend of organizational activism, founding organs of local and economic administration such as water districts, fire brigades, and guilds.[2] These latter organizations had indigenous roots, but they provided important precedents for the elites who would move on to found and manage organizations based on foreign forms. Together these local administrative organizations, along with organizations based on foreign models, provided the institutional context for Bian Baimei's childhood and adult career. Organizations, however, are founded and directed by individuals, and the interaction between any given individual and any given organization depends not just on the structure of the organization and its institutional framework but also on a huge variety of personal factors, including family background, personal likes and aptitudes, and the space and time through which the individual moves.

The Bian Family and Late Qing Elite Networks

When Bian Baimei was born, his grandfather Bian Baodi (1824–1892) served as Huguang governor general, one of nine officials entrusted by the government of the Qing dynasty to oversee provincial administration in China. Bian Baodi had reached the pinnacle of a long career, climbing his way up the mandarinate ladder in the hectic years after the suppression of the mid-nineteenth-century rebellions that had almost brought down the dynasty.[3] Bian Baimei was only eight years old when Bian Baodi died, and the grandson left no record of any direct impressions of his grandfather. Nonetheless, his grandfather's place in the official hierarchy of the Qing government and in the gentry-literati networks of late-nineteenth-century China left son and grandson with a legacy of both opportunities and burdens that would shape their lives in many ways.

According to the family genealogy, the Bians had settled near the city of Yangzhou in modern-day Jiangsu Province at the time of the retreat of the

Song dynasty from North China (ca. 1126). Located at the intersection of the Grand Canal, which runs north-south, and the Yangzi River, running east-west, Yangzhou thrived as a commercial and official center, with the city's Lianghuai salt monopoly administration producing some of the richest men in China, and in the world, in the eighteenth century.[4] Although a number of Bians distinguished themselves during the Qing dynasty period, Bian Baodi was one of the most illustrious. He achieved the second-highest level in the civil service examination system, becoming a *juren* in 1851, and served at the highest levels of the Qing bureaucracy. Although Bian Baodi did not participate directly in the mid-century wars against the rebellions, he earned a reputation as a military manager during the post-rebellion mop-up.

Once the immediate threat of rebellion had been quashed, a small group of elites turned their attention to reform, and Bian Baodi circulated within the networks of those late-nineteenth-century reformers who were active at the national level.[5] In terms of marriage alliances alone, Bian Baodi's immediate family was enormous. He had four brothers, one sister, three wives, and sixteen children, thirteen of whom survived to adulthood and marriage.[6] In addition, throughout his career he served in official positions all over China, gaining the opportunity to extend his contacts and networks in directions that have been long lost to the historical record. In spite of this complexity, the important outlines of those networks can be pieced together from genealogies, biographies, and subsequent events. In terms of the impact on the life of his grandson, Bian Baimei, three families stand out with particular prominence: the Lis, the Zhous, and the Suns.

The intricate relations among these four families centered on the career of the most famous member of the Li family, Li Hongzhang (1823–1901), a towering figure in the late nineteenth century. Li Hongzhang began his career in the wars against the Taiping rebels, helping to liberate southern Jiangsu, including the Bian family hometown of Yangzhou, in 1863 and 1864.[7] The Bians and the Lis became relatives when Li Hongzhang's youngest son, Li Jingmai (1876–1938), married one of Bian Baodi's daughters.[8] Bian family lore has it that this marriage alliance was arranged to mend a rift between the two families, although the nature of the rift is left untold. Rift or not, the Bians and Lis remained closely enmeshed.[9] Two of Bian Baodi's daughters married sons of Liu Bingzhang, a general who had distinguished himself in military service under Li Hongzhang.[10]

Through the Li family, the Bians developed connections to the Zhou and

Sun families as well. Like the Lis, the Zhous and the Suns came from Anhui Province, Jiangsu's neighbor to the north. In the grandfathers' generation the most outstanding figures from each family were Zhou Fu and Sun Jia'nai. Failing to pass the government examinations, Zhou Fu found work as an assistant to Li Hongzhang, distinguishing himself as an able official. Eventually he would rise to the exalted rank of governor general. Sun Jia'nai, like Li Hongzhang and Bian Baodi, followed the more traditional route to official success by taking the exams, earning his *jinshi* degree in 1860. He too climbed to the highest ranks of the Qing bureaucracy in the late nineteenth century, though he spent most of his time in the metropolitan rather than provincial government. Like the Bians, multiple generations of the Suns married into the Li family, ensuring close family links well into the twentieth century.

As the grandfathers' generation passed into old age, China's crisis only deepened. The new navy built by Li Hongzhang was sunk in the Sino-Japanese War of 1894–95. Five years later, North China erupted in the anti-foreign Boxer Uprising. Swift military suppression by the foreign powers was followed by yet another humiliating treaty. It was during the intense first decade of the twentieth century, after the Boxer Uprising, that the generation of Bian Baimei's father came into its own. During that time elites at all levels turned their attention to reform, increasing the pace of organizational innovation in many different spheres, and increasing the diversity of elite career prospects in the process. The right family connections alone, however, did not necessarily guarantee success. None of Bian Baodi's sons reached the level of achievement of their father. The eldest son, Bian Xuchang, served as a mid-level official in the latter years of the nineteenth century, but failed to take advantage of the new opportunities offered by organizational diversification and institutional innovation.[11] When Baodi died in 1892, the thirty-one-year-old Xuchang took up the mantle of family head, including the responsibility for raising six younger half-sisters and two younger half-brothers, some of whom were actually younger than his own children. Family lore has it that Baodi had been a relatively uncorrupt official, leaving little wealth to support his large family. As a result, Xuchang's toughest responsibility was to arrange suitable marriages for his sisters. His responsibilities weighed so heavily on him that he died before the age of fifty, according to a family story, from "a severe attack of bronchial asthma brought on by the demand of one of his half-sisters for the payment of a promissory note that he had written as a part of her dowry."[12] In spite of the difficulties, Xuchang fulfilled his duty, arranging appropriate marriages for his siblings as well as for his own six children.[13] Bian Baimei's marriage in 1900 at the age of sixteen represented a landmark in his father's success at cementing networks through marriage alliances. Bian Baimei married Li Guojing, the granddaughter of Li Hanzhang, Li Hongzhang's elder brother, making the second generation of marriage between the Lis and the Bians.[14]

Like Bian Xuchang, members of the second generation of the Li family remained prominent in official circles, but without the stature of their fathers, and without a direct impact on reform of the financial system. The careers of this generation of the Zhous and the Suns tell a different story. Zhou Fu's son and Sun Jia'nai's nephews found a formula for success combining family connections, official position, and exploitation of opportunities offered by new economic organizations. In them we see the reformist-officials of the grandfathers' generation give way to official-managers of reform organizations. Their success followed closely that of Yuan Shikai (1859–1916), who came to prominence in North China at the dawn of the twentieth century, taking over Li Hongzhang's former position as governor general of Zhili Province and becoming the highest government authority in Tianjin. In order to run his administration, Yuan Shikai called on individuals from the same networks Li Hongzhang had, including Zhou Xuexi (1865–1947), Zhou Fu's son, and Sun Duoxin (1864–1907) and Sun Duosen (1867–1919), Sun Jia'nai's nephews.[15] Zhou Xuexi, Sun Duoxin, and Sun Duosen would follow very similar paths, turning their official positions into platforms for creating large business concerns. The Suns built a commercial empire that centered on flour milling, and Zhou Xuexi's companies ranged from cement to glass. Both business groups would eventually include modern banks as well. In addition, Zhou Xuexi and Sun Duosen would play pivotal roles in Bian Baimei's career.

If some members of the second generation capitalized on combining official position with commercial enterprise, many of their sons turned to foreign education as the key to success. In the aftermath of the Boxer Uprising, the Qing government founded new schools at home and sponsored large numbers of students to study in Japan, Europe, and the United States. Bian Baimei's education reflected these new trends and placed him on the cutting edge of a new generation of specialists. His foreign education actually began in treaty port Shanghai. Like many elites from southern Jiangsu and northern Zhejiang provinces, the Bians moved to Shanghai sometime in the late nineteenth or early twentieth century, probably between 1886 and 1904. In

Shanghai, Bian spent a year at Aurora College, run by French Catholic missionaries, offering a curriculum of foreign language, mathematics, and other Western subjects.[16] In 1906 or 1907 he went to study in the United States, receiving an official scholarship from the Zhili provincial government, then under Yuan Shikai's administration. Leaving his children in Shanghai, he and his wife left for America.

In the United States, Bian Baimei spent a year working on his English at Ithaca High School in New York, then in 1908 he enrolled as the first Chinese student at Brown University. He perceived his status at Brown as a distinct advantage. A few years later he would tell a local reporter in Providence, "I believed that if I could not have any Chinese to talk to I would become more quickly acquainted with the English language." Here Bian shows some of the steely determination and desire for self-improvement that would characterize much of his life. Before graduating, Bian would be joined by three more Chinese students, including Ralph Sun (Sun Yuanfang), a member of the grandsons' generation of the Sun family, Sun Duoxin's son and Bian's wife's cousin.[17]

Bian's desire to study in the United States grew from a youth spent, in part, in the treaty port culture, where China's weakness was daily displayed in contrast to foreign power:

> They [foreigners] seemed to know so much more than our well-educated men about things worth while . . . and they were vastly more alert and active. They were so practical, also, in nearly everything they did that I thought I would like to study where they had.
>
> My school work like that of any Chinese student under the old system was mainly concerned with the classics—dry and centuries old. It was all reading and writing; nothing of a live character. Why, most of us had to learn to write poetry.[18]

Bian would later temper his opinion of traditional Chinese learning. As an adult, he often would read the classics for edification and pleasure, and he would become something of a poet himself. Nonetheless, his youthful enthusiasm for the vitality and practicality of Westerners reflects both his sense of China's crisis and his own recipe for its resolution: foreign learning. Bian completed a double major in social science and political economy. In 1911, when he gave this interview, Bian intended to become a teacher on his return to China; thus, education concerned him greatly:

> We cannot begin too soon our work of putting China somewhere near the level of modern nations.
>
> I have specialized in political economy and social science and I hope to teach these subjects on my return. Our people know little about either of them. Social reform, especially, is what must be taught if we are to take our place among the nations of the world.[19]

Reform, change, and innovation loomed large in Bian's vision for his own role in improving China's place in the world, but he did not yet know that banking, not education, would provide the venue for the exercise of his expert knowledge.

At Brown, Bian Baimei and Ralph Sun studied economics, called political economy at the time, under the direction of Henry Brayton Gardner.[20] The textbook Gardner authored for the introductory class in economics provides a general sense of his approach. Gardner took the links between economics and politics quite seriously. Lecture number one begins, following Herbert Spencer, with a discussion of "social organisms" in which politics and the state loom large. Economics was the history of the progress of nations, some of which achieved economic advancement while others did not. The close relationship between politics and economics would have had great resonance with Bian, who had grown up with daily reminders that China was less strong than the foreign powers and that their strength grew, at least in part, from their economic success. Gardner did not idealize economic progress but viewed it, and its incumbent evils, as a result of the natural evolution of particular social organisms which, like amoebae, deserved study. On a matter of particular importance for the future careers of both Bian Baimei and Ralph Sun, Gardner notes the emergence in the late nineteenth century of the credit system and the joint-stock principle in industrial organization. Gardner saw credit creation and the joint-stock form of organization as twin phenomena that "increased immensely, productive power by rendering possible a more complete use of the wealth and savings of the community." At the same time, though, increased reliance on money and credit was a major contributing factor to the instability of economic life. Thus, "anything which shakes confidence, on which credit rests, acts as a check on every branch of production."[21] Little did Bian know then that he would spend much of his professional life working for a joint-stock corporation, dedicated to the cause of maintaining confidence in China's system of money and credit.

By January 1912, reverberations from the fall of the Qing dynasty in

China had reached Rhode Island. Brown's Chinese students faced an economic crisis of their own, as their government stipends and other remittances dried up in the wake of revolution. Only Ralph Sun did not feel the pinch; an uncle in Shanghai (probably Sun Duosen) had been sending him money. In fact, Ralph Sun had written to the uncle about Bian's pending financial predicament.[22] In the end, help from his wife's relatives did arrive, and Bian finished up the year at Brown, graduating in the spring of 1912.[23]

He returned to China to face an unknown future. The dynasty had fallen and his father was dead. As the eldest son of the eldest son, he knew that family responsibilities could weigh heavily, but he showed his independence and practicality by renouncing his inheritance and, and the same time, the dowry debts of his numerous aunts.[24] Perhaps to put even more distance between himself and family obligations, Bian decided not to stay in Shanghai with his mother but to pursue a career in the north, in Beijing, closer to his wife's relatives. Bian found jobs teaching and working as a newspaper reporter in Beijing.[25] But these would not last long, as he was quickly drawn, aided by family connections and his own expertise in economics, into the growing sphere of modern banking.

Late Qing Financial System Reform

The impetus for reform of China's financial system in the late nineteenth and early twentieth centuries arose from two related concerns: viability of the monetary system and the fiscal needs of the state. Prior to about the fifteenth century, China had a long tradition of government control over the monetary system, including the circulation of copper alloy (bronze) coins and the first extensive use of paper money in the world, beginning during the late Song and continuing into the Yuan and early Ming dynasties (ca. 1024–ca. 1430). At that time Chinese copper coins flowed abroad to Japan and the currency-starved countries of Southeast Asia, becoming an international monetary standard. In addition, the Chinese state's experience with paper money included an exchange standard, whereby currency was exchangeable into copper or silver, as well as a fiat standard, whereby paper money circulated with no more backing than the ruler's stamp. Gradually, however, the government lost control over the monetary system. The Ming dynasty reluctantly abandoned paper money around 1430 owing to rampant inflation.[26] At the same time, supplies of copper coins could not keep up with the demand of an increasingly commercialized and monetized economy, leading to debasement and rampant private minting. From the sixteenth to the eighteenth centuries, foreign silver from Japan and the New World flowed into China (in return for exports of silk, porcelain, and later tea), but the Chinese government never took measures to coin silver or regulate its minting and circulation as money.[27] Nonetheless, silver, minted privately in ingots or "shoes," and by the eighteenth century including large quantities of Spanish and Mexican coins, became an important monetary token, even for tax purposes.[28] By 1653, the state even began inscribing copper coins with their value in silver, acknowledging the de facto monetization of silver.[29]

At the dawn of the nineteenth century, then, China had essentially a bimetallic monetary system, consisting of copper coins (cash), mostly minted by the state and used for small transactions or larger transactions close by, and silver, used for large transactions, long-distance transactions, and the payment of taxes. In addition, indigenous banks issued a number of monetary and quasi-monetary instruments, including bills of exchange for the buying and selling of goods, drafts for the remittance of funds over long distances, and small amounts of paper money convertible into either silver or copper.

The lack of a unified market heightened the diffuse nature of the monetary system. Copper coins varied by time and place of issue, including large numbers of privately minted forgeries, and often had different values in different regions; privately minted silver ingots varied in weight and fineness. In addition, the money of account for silver, called the tael, also varied from place to place, becoming over time distinct from the actual weight of silver ingots.[30] The combination of government-minted coins, privately minted silver ingots, foreign-minted silver dollars, and monetary instruments issued by unregulated indigenous banks led to a complex and somewhat chaotic monetary system that relied on the expert knowledge of indigenous bankers to manage exchange between various monetary tokens and between monetary standards that varied from location to location.[31]

In times of peace, as in China's expansive and prosperous eighteenth century, the monetary system did not pose an urgent problem for the state. By the mid-nineteenth century, however, the Qing government found itself chronically short of the funds it needed to finance its escalating expenses. States faced with fiscal shortfalls have three sets of options: taxes, debt, or monetary expansion. Changes in China's tax structure, especially an internal customs tax called the *lijin*, did help raise funds in the long term, but revenues remained insufficient, especially when the government faced large immediate-term expenditures for war or indemnity payments.[32] In addition, the Qing state often borrowed money. The chaotic and diffuse nature of China's monetary system made it difficult, though, for the Qing state to use time-honored, if not honorable, methods of monetary expansion to meet its fiscal crisis. It could mint more copper coins; but minting depended on a steady supply of copper from mines or from abroad, and during the nineteenth-century rebellions the state was often cut off from both sources. Without means to expand the copper money supply, the government could only depreciate the copper coinage by clipping or re-minting, raise money through seignorage fees on silver used to pay taxes, or issue paper money.

About the time of the loss to Britain in the Opium Wars, Chinese officials and literati made a series of proposals about monetary reform, ranging from ideas for the Chinese state to mint silver coins to suggestions about the demonetization of silver and the issue of both convertible and inconvertible paper money.[33] The government did not take any action, though, and thus was left with little control over the monetary system when the mid-century crisis heightened with the outbreak of the Taiping Rebellion. At that time Chinese officials used all of the limited means at their disposal to expand the money supply. On the one hand, state mints began minting so-called "big" copper coins, intending that one coin should now purchase what ten coins previously had. On the other hand, the government issued paper money, though measures to enable exchange rapidly collapsed and the paper money became a de facto fiat currency. The combined effects of depreciating copper and printing paper money helped the state manage its fiscal crisis but also resulted in disastrous inflation.[34]

After the defeat of the Taipings and most of the other rebels, and another round of humiliating wars with the foreign powers, China settled into a period of relative calm, often called the Tongzhi Restoration, so named from the reign title of the emperor (r. 1861–1874). A group of reformist officials began to undertake innovations intended to restore the power and prestige of the Chinese state, resulting in the so-called self-strengthening movement. Li Hongzhang and a handful of other like-minded men led the early charge for organizational innovation. The new organizations included arsenals, military academies, foreign language schools, a telegraph administration, a steamship company, and a coal mine, with most located in or near China's treaty ports, especially in Shanghai, where Li had lived while preparing for the reconquest of Jiangsu from the Taipings, and in Tianjin, where he served as governor general of Zhili Province from 1870 to 1895 and again from 1900 to 1901.[35]

During this period of relative calm, the state retreated from its inflationary policies of the period of rebellion, withdrawing both paper money and the "big" copper coins from circulation. The rebellions and the creation of the treaty ports after the Opium Wars, however, had already changed China's financial system significantly. On the one hand, opening of the treaty ports led to the introduction of foreign banks in China, while on the other hand, China's indigenous financial institutions had expanded rapidly, performing a number of functions, including filling the void left by a state split by rebellion and preoccupied with war, financing increased commercialization in the post-rebellion peace, and acting as intermediaries between the foreign banks and Chinese borrowers. Foreign banks and two different kinds of indigenous financial institutions constituted what Linsun Cheng has called "the Three Kingdoms." Private Chinese banks called *qianzhuang* or *yinhao* controlled most of the commercial lending and domestic monetary exchange. A separate kind of indigenous financial institution, the Shanxi remittance bank *(piaohao)*, served much of the government's financial needs, including long-distance tax remittance, the selling of government offices and titles, and lending money to government officials. Foreign banks controlled foreign exchange and financed foreign companies operating in China.[36]

All three "kingdoms" loaned money to the state, especially Shanxi remittance banks and foreign banks.[37] The twin problems of monetary reform and fiscal demands remained unresolved, though; and to make matters worse, silver prices declined in international markets over the course of the last half of the nineteenth century, reducing the value of tax revenues (paid in silver) in relation to gold and making it even more difficult for China to pay foreign indemnities or purchase foreign technology.[38] These problems led a number of officials to place reform of the financial system high on their lists. By the 1880s, Li Hongzhang and other officials had had some success in minting silver dollars (yuan), called dragon dollars because of the Chinese dragon inscribed on them, and new copper coins also denominated in fractions of yuan.[39] State-sponsored reform of the financial system as a whole, however, proved much more difficult. The literati official Wei Yuan had first described the Bank of England for Chinese readers soon after the Opium Wars, but serious plans for a bank did not appear until a number of officials who promoted self-strengthening, including Li Hongzhang, offered proposals in the

1870s and 1880s.[40] In spite of such interest, early attempts by Chinese officials to found banks based on foreign models foundered on the shoals of factional infighting and special interests. For example, during the 1870s and 1880s, Li Hongzhang negotiated with a group of American financiers to found a Sino-American bank. The proposal was vehemently opposed by the other foreign powers, Chinese indigenous bankers, and conservatives at the Qing court.[41] The British-oriented *North China Herald* declared that the plan was "the most astounding transaction as regards magnitude, that has ever been made since the round world began." Opposition to the scheme from Chinese circles was just as vociferous.[42] Critics objected to the potentially powerful combination of foreign capital and Chinese official might within the framework of a modern bank.

Other Qing officials took up the idea for a modern bank to finance reform projects in the 1890s. The indemnity paid to Japan after the Sino-Japanese War was so huge that it enabled Japan to go on the gold standard.[43] The Chinese government, for its part, lacked the means to finance the indemnity, so it turned to foreign sources, creating a dramatic increase in the scale of debt owed to foreign banks.[44] At that time the impetus for reform began to shift from the generation of Bian's grandfather to that of his father. Officials such as Chen Chi and literati managers such as Zheng Guanyin who had gained experience in self-strengthening projects wrote detailed treatises on money and banking, including evaluation of the gold standard (a relatively recent phenomenon in the West), paper currency, and the operations of foreign banks, which usually emphasized the role of banking in state affairs, including currency issue.[45] Zheng Guanyin, in particular, wrote about the functions of central banking as it was then developing in the West, including lending money to the government, serving as a government treasury, and acting as a lender of last resort to stabilize the financial market.[46] Of special relevance here, Zheng noted the importance of trust in paper money, concluding that to gain the trust of the people, it was necessary to copy the methods of the foreign banks, including holding specie reserve to back the value of the paper currency.[47] By the 1890s, Chinese officials and literati had adopted the idea that reform of China's chaotic monetary system should involve issuing paper money and that trust in paper money stemmed from the banking system.

The details of financial system reform proved difficult to enact. Various officials competed for the potentially lucrative right to found and manage a Chinese bank. Finally, Li Hongzhang's protégé, the official-manager Sheng

Xuanhuai, won court approval to found the first Chinese-owned bank based on foreign models, establishing the Imperial Bank of China in Shanghai in 1897.[48] Rather than rely on foreign capital as in Li Hongzhang's earlier plan, Sheng intended to solicit capital from Lower Yangzi merchants and merchant-officials to finance China's railroad construction. In spite of receiving a central government charter, Sheng lacked the full support of the Finance Board, and the Imperial Bank of China was never given the lucrative rights to handle government deposits and tax remittances.[49] As a result, it never really achieved the status of a state bank, and it remained on the margins of the Chinese banking industry until being taken over by the gangster, opium dealer, and supporter of the Nationalist government Du Yuesheng in the 1930s.[50]

The Boxer Uprising at the turn of the century had intensified China's political and financial problems. The enormous indemnities levied by the foreign powers in the aftermath of the uprising saddled the Chinese government with a burden that would shape fiscal policy for years to come. The foreign powers forced the Chinese state to pledge some of its most important revenue sources, including customs and salt taxes, to guarantee payment.[51] At the same time, foreign demands that China reform its monetary system escalated. In the post-Boxer treaty with Britain, China agreed to "take the necessary steps to provide for a uniform national coinage," and "the English press in China was unanimous as to the need of a national bank to regulate the new currency."[52] The acute fiscal needs of the state, foreign pressure for financial reform, and a renewed sense of crisis after the Boxer humiliation all combined to prompt Chinese officials to turn in earnest to foreign banking models as a means of resolving the government's financial and monetary problems. Organizational innovation in the banking sector during the first decade of the twentieth century, the so-called New Policies period, proceeded along two lines of development—national and local.

At the national level, financial reform first centered on debates about China's monetary system. Before the post-Boxer treaties had even been completed, the Qing court sent a delegation to Japan which, on its return, recommended the founding of a central bank to regulate the currency. Subsequently, in 1903, the Qing government requested help from the United States in establishing a gold or a gold exchange standard. The resulting "Jenks plan," named after the American monetary expert Jeremiah Jenks, emphasized coinage and the need for China to go on a gold exchange standard, financed by an international loan, with provision for the issue of banknotes to add flexibility to the system.[53] Although the commission held open the possibility of multiple banks of issue, it noted that "a proper bank-note system could be best secured through the establishment of one imperial bank which should have the monopoly of bank-note issue, as is the case in Japan, France and elsewhere."[54] The Jenks report met substantial opposition, and the Qing government did not adopt its provisions on monetary reform in spite of the worldwide trend toward the gold standard.[55] Nonetheless, shortly after publication of the report in 1904, the Qing announced plans to form an imperial bank, called the Hubu Bank, under direction of the Finance Board (Hubu); its head office opened in Beijing in September 1905.[56] One Japanese critic wrote a scathing attack on the plans for the bank, saying that it simply duplicated most of the functions of Sheng Xuanhuai's Imperial Bank of China, founded ten years previously, leaving China with no clearly defined central banking institution. The Chinese translator of the article could only say that the true reason for the establishment of the Hubu Bank lay in the corruption and failure at the Imperial Bank of China.[57] China's problem with multiple state banks became even more complicated when in 1908 the Communications Ministry opened its own bank, the Bank of Communications.[58] In that same year, the Qing government issued its banking laws, creating four kinds of banks: the Hubu (now renamed Da Qing) Bank as a central bank, ordinary banks, savings banks, and banks for the cultivation of the economy *(zhiye)*.[59] Since the Bank of Communications was intended to finance railroad construction, it was apparently one of the *zhiye* banks, but it still had the right to issue money pending finalization of the government's monetary law. Since the Communications Ministry oversaw the lucrative postal, telegraph, and railway businesses, the Bank of Communications had considerable sources of revenue and significant financial power. In Beijing a clique of officials used the Communications Ministry as their base of power, and as a result, the Bank of Communications became a rival to the Da Qing Bank and a tool in factional struggles among officials.

At the local level, many provincial officials also tried their hands at financial innovation. Yuan Shikai, governor general of Zhili Province, led the pack, driven by the necessity of rebuilding prosperity in Tianjin in the post-Boxer period. When the foreign powers occupied North China, including Tianjin, in response to the Boxer Uprising, they destroyed much of the infrastructure so carefully built up during the administration of Li Hongzhang. In the looting which immediately followed the fall of the city to the foreigners, Tianjin's merchants, and especially its financial institutions, suffered massive losses.[60] On top of, and perhaps because of, the failure of many of Tianjin's financial institutions, a shortage of silver plagued the city. When Yuan Shikai took over administration of Tianjin from the foreigners in 1902, he immediately moved to prohibit the discounting of paper currency issued by indigenous banks. This resulted in a second round of failures. Between 1900 and 1902, 90 percent of Tianjin's three hundred indigenous banks closed.[61] With the indigenous bank industry in ruins, Yuan was left with the task of creating his own financial institutions. Together with Zhou Xuexi and Sun Duoxin, Yuan founded the Tianjin Mint (Yinyuan Ju), which turned out a new weight of copper coin based on the yuan, not the tael. Machine-minted, the new copper coins were difficult to forge or debase, and thus found wide acceptance, making a substantial profit. Among other projects, the mint funded a local government bank called the Tianjin Official Bank (Tianjin guan yinhao), originally the Tianjin Official Bank for Stabilization of the Market (Tianjin pingshi guan yinhao). Zhou and Sun managed the new bank, gaining valuable banking experience that would be of use in later years. The Official Bank was charged with regulating the market, making loans to merchants, and floating Zhili provincial bonds. It also handled the deposits and banking needs of local government agencies, putting one more nail in the coffin of the Shanxi remittance banks. Although its name contained the same term as that used by indigenous banks *(yinhao)*, the Official Bank also had several of the characteristics of a modern bank, including using foreign management methods and issuing paper money to, and taking deposits from, ordinary people.[62]

Thus, by about 1908, the central state had sponsored three banks—the Imperial Bank of China, the Da Qing Bank, and the Bank of Communications—and local official banks had been founded at the provincial level all over China, including the Tianjin Official Bank in Zhili Province.[63] These financial institutions dramatically reshaped China's financial system but did not simplify it. In fact, the emerging system of central and local government banks actually increased the multiplicity of currencies in China.[64] At the same time, the government gave permission for the formation of a number of private banks, some of which had currency-issue privileges. For example, the Lower Yangzi merchant Zhou Tingmi founded the Xincheng Bank in Shanghai in 1906, and a group of Zhejiang officials and elites founded the National Commercial Bank in 1907 as part of a movement to finance railway construction.[65]

With its issue of banking laws in 1908, the government began taking measures to reform the monetary system, including plans to centralize the supply of paper money at Da Qing Bank. In 1909 the government prohibited shops from issuing paper money; but the Bank of Communications started issuing paper money at the same time, showing that not all trends favored centralization.[66] Finally, in 1910 the Qing government issued its long-promised monetary regulations. The 1910 law set a standard for a silver yuan coin and gave a monopoly on note issue to Da Qing Bank, ordering the provincial banks to withdraw their paper money over a period of five years. Since this ambitious plan required financing, the Qing government negotiated a £10 million loan with a consortium of foreign banks for that purpose. While negotiations for the loan proceeded in Berlin in 1911, however, history overtook the process when the Qing government was overthrown by revolution.[67] All in all, by the time the 1911 revolution thrust Yuan Shikai and his managerial wizards, including Zhou Xuexi and Sun Duosen, onto the national stage, the seeds of China's banking system had taken root, but the monetary system remained more chaotic than ever.

Bian Baimai's Path to Banking

Yuan Shikai's local Tianjin administration had ended in 1909 when he resigned as Zhili's governor general after a dispute with the central government. When a military uprising broke out in central China in October 1911, the Qing court recalled Yuan to service, placing him at the head of the powerful northern armies which he had helped build during his Tianjin administration several years earlier. Those forces plus his control of Beijing put him in a good position to take over as president of the new republic when the last emperor abdicated in February 1912. Yuan was not alone in claiming power, however. For a brief time in early 1912, China had competing governments. In the north, Yuan Shikai set up his government in the old Qing capital of Beijing, close to the base of his military strength. In the south, Sun Yat-sen (1866–1925) established a provisional government in the old Ming capital of Nanjing, close to both centers of revolutionary fervor and to the wealth of China's most economically developed region. In the end, Yuan's military might won the day, and Sun Yat-sen agreed to cede the presidency of the new republic.

The tumult of the revolution severely affected both the Da Qing Bank and the Bank of Communications. Many branches of each had been looted during the fighting.[68] As a result, both banks suspended operations. During the brief months when Sun Yat-sen claimed the presidency, he moved to reorganize the Da Qing Bank in cooperation with a group of its Shanghai merchant shareholders.[69] They chose a returned student from Japan, and a future power in Tianjin banking, named Wu Dingchang (1884–1950) to take over the newly established Bank of China.[70] Wu's tenure at the helm of the Bank of China ended a few months after Sun Yat-sen resigned as president in favor of Yuan Shikai in the spring of 1912. At that time Yuan moved to put his own people in place as leaders of China's state financial institutions. To do so, he drew on the same networks that had provided the talent to shape the new financial institutions in Tianjin a decade earlier. He made Zhou Xuexi finance minister and tapped Sun Duosen, younger brother of Sun Duoxin, as head of the new Bank of China. In addition, he called on Liang Shiyi (1869–1932), a key man in the Communications clique, to head up the Bank of Communications.[71]

Thus, when Bian Baimei arrived in the heady atmosphere of postrevolutionary Beijing in 1912 to work as a teacher and newspaper reporter, members of the Zhou and Sun families were overseeing much of the financial direction of the new government, though the Communications clique, represented here by Liang Shiyi, presented powerful rivals. Bian used his close family connections with Zhou Xuexi and Sun Duosen, in combination with his own expert knowledge gained from studying political economy at Brown, to take the next step in his career. After hearing the news that Yuan Shikai's government planned to implement reforms of the financial system, Bian wrote a long treatise on the role of central banks in modern states based on his knowledge of the Bank of England and the plans for the Federal Reserve Bank in the United States. One morning before class he called at the house of the new finance minister, Zhou Xuexi, to deliver the essay. When Zhou saw Bian's calling card, he asked Bian to join him for breakfast. Zhou apologized for seeing Bian while eating breakfast, but as he said, Bian was the son of an old friend, and there was no need to stand on ceremony. After a lengthy discussion, Zhou left to go to the office and offered to drop Bian on the way. Bian declined and opted for a rickshaw instead, but he would later tell his children that he saw Zhou Xuexi reading the essay Bian had written as he was driven off in his carriage.[72] The essay must have made a significant impression, for soon after Bian went to work at the head office of the Bank of China in Beijing under the administration of his wife's relative Sun Duosen—the same uncle of his roommate Ralph Sun who had bailed out Bian a year or so earlier when the 1911 revolution cut off his government stipend to study at Brown. Ralph Sun himself went to work for the Bank of China at about the same time.[73]

At first Yuan Shikai's government considered either founding a central bank separate from the Bank of China or making the Bank of China entirely state owned, but in the end it adopted a structure similar to that of the Da Qing Bank, with 50 percent ownership by the state and 50 percent by private shareholders.[74] The decentralized nature of the late Qing monetary system had accelerated during the 1911 revolution, as each provincial revolutionary government issued its own paper money. Yuan Shikai's government began taking steps to centralize currency issue, inviting the Dutch banker Gerard Vissering to China to give advice on reforming the monetary system. In addition to recommending that China adopt the gold standard, Vissering advocated that the central government prohibit the circulation of provincial and foreign currency in China and gradually concentrate issue in a central bank.[75] In February 1913 the central government ordered all provincial and local government banks to cease issuing new paper money. Some provinces, including Guangdong, Hunan, and Yuan's old satrapy of Zhili, accordingly withdrew their paper money, but local authorities resisted in other provinces such as Sichuan.[76] In 1914 the government began minting silver dollars with Yuan Shikai's portrait on them (the so-called Yuan "Big-Heads" or Yuan Datou), decreeing that this would become the standard coin for the nation. Then in October 1915 the government granted the Bank of China a monopoly on note issue, requiring both modern and indigenous banks to withdraw their paper money within six months.[77] By 1915 the currency issue of the Bank of China had reached 30 million yuan, twice that of its predecessor, Da Qing Bank. Nonetheless, at the same time, the Bank of Communications had increased its issue of paper money eighteenfold, from less than 2 million yuan in 1912 to more than 37 million at the end of 1915, and 172 million yuan in provincial currencies still circulated. Currency centralization was thus only partly successful.[78]

The large issue by the Bank of Communications is especially telling. Both the Bank of China and the Bank of Communications had grown rapidly in the years after 1912—by 1916, the Bank of China had nearly 150 offices and more than a thousand employees, and the Bank of Communications had over one hundred offices—and the rivalry between the two banks continued as they competed to handle important government accounts, such as customs receipts.[79] In fact, the Bank of Communications had become a mainstay of Yuan Shikai's power; he had no interest in forcing it to discontinue currency issue. When Yuan faced rebellion in the so-called second revolution of 1913, the Communications clique, led by the official Liang Shiyi, and the Bank of Communications came to his rescue.[80] Yuan relied again on loans from the Bank of Communications, as well as from the Bank of China, when he declared himself emperor at the end of 1915. The crisis provoked by Yuan's declaration of a monarchy shook the political and economic foundations of the new republic. At the same time, it led to the end of the first stage of Bian Baimei's career as a banker.

The year 1916 had begun as one of promise for the thirty-two-year-old Bian Baimei. When the New Year dawned, Bian found himself aboard ship, returning to China from a business trip to Southeast Asia. Although he occupied himself by drafting a plan for the Bank of China to open an office in Southeast Asia, his mind was on other things as well; news had reached the ship of the Yunnan army's attack against Sichuan Province in response to Yuan Shikai's declaration of a monarchy at the end of the previous year. Landing in Shanghai, Bian spent a few days visiting some of his many relatives and attending to bank business before taking the train to Beijing. At home on the tenth of January, Bian received further disturbing news: the assistant manager of the Shanghai branch of the Bank of Communications had been assassinated, and a bomb had gone off in the Nanjing train station, which Bian had passed through only two days before.[81] Yuan Shikai's political crisis was going from bad to worse, and bankers, especially those at the Bank of China and Bank of Communications, were right in the middle of the maelstrom.

In an attempt to maintain power and stave off full-scale civil war, Yuan repealed the monarchy on March 23, 1916, but it was too late. Rumors were flying in the capital, and at the end of March, Bian moved his family to the safety of the British Concession in Tianjin. The financial crisis at the Bank of China and Bank of Communications worsened. The government had increased borrowing from the two banks at the end of 1915 in preparation for Yuan's declaration of the monarchy, with loans totaling more than 12 million yuan from the Bank of China and the astronomical sum of 47.5 million yuan from the Bank of Communications by the end of that year. In order to make these massive loans to the government, the two banks issued currency, literally printing money.[82]

In the weeks and months of early 1916, the government in Beijing began to bring all the coercive and persuasive force at its disposal to maintain order and keep its financial crisis from erupting into full-scale panic at the local level. The government relied on a three-pronged strategy to deal with the crisis at the two banks. First, it consolidated its control over the Bank of China. With the devoted Liang Shiyi at the helm, no management changes were necessary at the Bank of Communications, but the Bank of China's loyalty was less assured. The government made one of Liang's followers, Zhou Ziqi (1869–1923), supervisory official *(duban)* of the Bank of China.[83] His appointment threatened the nominal independence and professionalism of the bank. Bian remarked in his diary, "Our ability to support the situation has been completely destroyed. Very depressed. I feel that there is no resolution."[84] Second, the government ordered various of its organs—especially the railroads—to accept and use the notes of the two banks. And third, it tried to maintain consensus in the credibility of the two banks by suppressing rumors and controlling communications media.

A run on the two banks started in the beginning of April, as worried people brought in their paper money to exchange for silver. By May the government could no longer hold out, and on the twelfth it issued an order suspending exchange of the paper money of the two banks for silver. In response, Bian and a number of his Bank of China colleagues, including both the president and vice president, resigned. Bian's promising career was cut off for the moment, as he joined his family in the safety of the foreign concessions in Tianjin. Little did Bian know at the time that the events of 1916 would change China's political situation, and his life, forever. The civil war to thwart Yuan Shikai's attempt to become emperor, and Yuan's subsequent illness and death, plunged China into the throes of the so-called warlord period, when a variety of militarists maneuvered for the right to rule. Meanwhile, the financial crisis induced by Yuan's political crisis caused Bian Baimei to move to Tianjin, where he would spend the next twenty-two years, becoming the city's most prominent and powerful banker.

Foreign Models of Institutional Innovation

The Chinese banking system that emerged by about 1915 was a product of both Chinese conditions and foreign models. The former included the decentralized nature of innovation during the late Qing dynasty; the fiscal demands of the state; the networks of elites who designed, and contested the design of, the new institutions; and the extended political crisis that torpedoed attempts at centralization. The latter apparently included an eclectic mix of features from different foreign systems. It is impossible to know exactly which foreign models the founders of China's money and banking reforms had in mind, but their reliance on foreign ideas is clear. The charter of Sheng Xuanhuai's Imperial Bank of China is said to have copied that of the Hong Kong and Shanghai Banking Corporation, and the preliminary charter for the Hubu Bank explicitly stated that operations should be handled "according to the regulations of foreign banks."[85] Foreign governments applied pressure, trying to persuade China to adopt institutions that would draw it into international patterns of trade and finance. Likewise, China sent a delegation to Japan and invited the foreign experts Jeremiah Jenks and Gerard Vissering to China to act as advisers in the reform of its monetary system. Likely models for the Chinese system include the Bank of England, the Bank of Japan (and the National Bank of Belgium, on which the Bank of Japan was based), the Hong Kong and Shanghai Banking Corporation (HSBC, the most influential foreign bank in China), and the American national banking system, which existed up until the founding of the Federal Reserve in 1913. Considering these and other potential models, I will examine four specific features central to understanding the money and banking system in the two decades prior to the 1916 crisis in Tianjin: the structure of the banks, central banking, provisions for the issue of paper money, and oversight of the system.

From the beginning, all Chinese banks were structured as joint-stock, limited liability companies, and most had branch networks. Joint-stock banking had grown rapidly in the late nineteenth century in France, Belgium, Germany, and England, and had been the standard in the United States virtually from the beginning.[86] The larger capital provided by joint-stock investors enabled banks to build substantial branch networks, and the charters of the Bank of China and the Bank of Communications required them to open branches in major cities.[87] Similarly, French law required that the Bank of France open a branch in every *département* if the government so requested.[88] Not all foreign joint-stock banks opened branches, though. The Bank of England was much slower to develop a branch network, and only did so after the crisis of 1826, overcoming the opposition of some local banks.[89] In the United States, most American states prohibited branch banking, and unit bankers dominated the process of the formation of the Federal Reserve, leading to a prohibition on branching of national banks.[90] At the same time, as P. L. Cottrell and Lucy Newton caution us to remember, "major institutions possessing significant branch networks" could coexist "alongside regional or local banks."[91] This is close to the pattern that appeared in China by the 1910s. A group of large banks, both state-sponsored and private, developed significant branch networks, while provincial banks and a number of small private banks had at most one or two branches.

Contemporary observers routinely referred to the Bank of China as a central bank and similarly called the Bank of Communications a state bank. Neither the Bank of China nor the Bank of Communications was completely state-owned, but many central banks outside China had partial, or even sometimes complete, private ownership.[92] As for operations, the Bank of China and the Bank of Communications also functioned as commercial banks, although most of the world's central banks had withdrawn from the business of commercial banking by the early twentieth century.[93] Neither could own shares in or manage commercial or industrial enterprises, however.[94] In practice, both would engage in a full range of commercial banking practices, including investing in and managing commercial and industrial enterprises.

Status as a central bank generally derives not from state ownership or lack of commercial operations but from a bank's special functions. In their seminal work on central banking, Forrest Capie, Charles Goodhart, and Norbert Schnadt define the three fundamental roles of the central bank: acting as the government's bank, having a monopoly on issue of paper money, and serving as lender of last resort. Like almost all central banks, the Bank of China and the Bank of Communications each handled deposits and treasury duties for the central government; but gaining a monopoly over note issue and acting as lender of last resort presented much more complex problems. By 1900—at about the same time the Chinese government began sponsoring the formation of modern banks—at least thirteen central banks had a monopoly over note issue, and twelve of those had begun to act as lenders of last resort.[95] In many countries, centralization of issue had been a slow and contested process.[96] Similarly in China, the Bank of Communications, provincial banks, and private banks continued to issue currency in spite of plans to centralize issue at the Bank of China. As for the responsibilities of acting as lender of last resort, the 1908 regulations governing Da Qing Bank required it to act during financial crises, but nothing in the charters of its successor, the Bank of China, or the Bank of Communications gave them the same responsibility.[97] Since neither of them had a monopoly over issue, their responsibilities to act as lenders of last resort were even more ambiguous.[98] Outside of China the role of acting as lender of last resort often evolved informally in fits and starts, and even central banks were sometimes slow to adopt this function. The Bank of France did not take on the role of lender of last resort until 1914. In the United States, the need for a lender of last resort helped motivate the founding of the Federal Reserve, but not until 1913. At other times, rather than have one designated lender of last resort, banks worked together in consortiums to alleviate crises.[99] In any case, the functions of central banking evolved continuously in relation to political and economic conditions.

Arrangements for issuing currency by banks required consideration of many factors, the denomination of banknotes and reserve requirements particularly important among them. In the West, some experts argued that the poor could not get good information on the reliability of banks, while others felt that because the poor could not understand banking, their distrust of paper money would lead to instability in the banking system.[100] As a result, many governments set a minimum value for the issue of banknotes. Initially, the Bank of France could not issue notes under 250 francs; the British government outlawed notes under £5 in England and Wales in 1826 and frequently criticized the practice of the HSBC of issuing $1 notes in its colony of Hong Kong.[101] In spite of such concerns, great demand existed for small notes in many places, and their issue became more common by the late nineteenth and early twentieth centuries. Chinese banks issued small notes from the beginning, without any suggestion of controversy. As for reserve requirements, practices show great variation among banking systems. In China the charters for the Bank of China and the Bank of Communications stated that each bank would have to comply with currency regulations to be issued at some future date. Draft plans in 1913 for a commercial banking law followed American precedent, requiring banks to deposit government securities for the amount of issue with the central bank, but never became law.[102] In lieu of government-issued regulations, the Bank of China issued its own, internal rules, and the Finance Ministry ordered the Bank of Communications to comply with them. The 1915 rules of the Bank of China appear to follow the pattern of the Bank of England, with a fixed fiduciary issue (unbacked by specie) of 10 million yuan, with issue in excess of that amount to be backed 100 percent with specie.[103] At about the same time, when the Finance Ministry issued its order giving a monopoly over note issue to the Bank of China, it required other banks, including indigenous banks, to keep 50 percent specie reserves for their outstanding issues.[104] Outside of China, specie reserve requirements varied widely, though generally were below 50 percent. Prior to the adoption of a fixed fiduciary issue, Bank of England reserves ranged between 7 and 30 percent.[105] Likewise, cash reserves in Scottish banks were probably 10 percent or less of total liabilities.[106] In the United States, after 1863, all issuing banks had to maintain 100 percent reserves of treasury bonds, on deposit with the U.S. Treasury, but only a 5 percent redemption reserve of specie.[107] In Argentina, the Buenos Aires Provincial Bank initially kept extremely low reserves, even less than 1 percent of the currency; later, the reorganized National Bank was supposed to keep 25 percent reserves.[108] A few countries did advocate higher reserves. In the nineteenth century, Japan required issuing banks to keep a 40 percent specie reserve, but after the founding of the Bank of Japan, the government gave it more flexibility.[109] Even more conservative, the Prussian Bank kept 50 percent reserves.[110] Initially the Hong Kong government required the HSBC to keep a reserve of one third of its note issue in specie. Later the bank had to place an additional one third in securities on deposit with the Hong Kong government, and then a complicated formula was introduced that produced reserve requirements of 50 percent or higher.[111] Most observers agreed, however, with the U.S. congressman Edward Vreeland, who wrote in 1911 that for-profit banks in the United States could not "afford to carry great reserves of from 40 to 60 percent."[112]

State oversight of banking systems usually took one of two forms: direct control of central banks or indirect regulation of the banking system. In terms of direct control, the Chinese government appointed the president and vice president of the Bank of China, while the shareholders elected the bank's directors. Shareholders theoretically elected the top two officials of the Bank of Communications, though the charter insisted that they "obey the orders of the Communications Ministry."[113] Outside of China, by the mid to late nineteenth century, governments closely supervised most central banks, such as the National Bank of Belgium, the Bank of Prussia, and the Bank of Japan.[114] Government supervision of even the relatively independent Bank of England and the Bank of France increased over time.[115] Oversight of banking systems also took the form of regulation, especially through inspection or imposition of transparency. In China, the 1908 banking laws and the 1915 law that prohibited banks from continuing to issue money all included provisions for inspection by the Finance Ministry of those institutions that issued currency and required publication of banks' financial statements. Likewise, the Credit Office of the Russian Finance Ministry conducted inspections of banks, and in England the Bank Act of 1844 required that the accounts of the Bank of England be published weekly.[116] Other banks in the United Kingdom, however, did not have to make any reports on their financial condition as late as the early twentieth century.[117]

The emerging Chinese banking system borrowed eclectically from foreign models, though the wide variations in financial systems show that no one model existed. In terms of joint-stock, limited liability organization, China seemed to be following world trends, though allowing the Bank of China and the Bank of Communications to engage in commercial activities seemed somewhat anachronistic at the beginning of the twentieth century. Other aspects of the Chinese system developed in directions contrary to both world trends and the wishes of its founders. The central government repeatedly expressed the desire that currency issue be centralized, but multiple banks of issue remained and even thrived. Likewise, repeated assertions that reserve requirements would be established by the state fell victim to ad hoc and confusing standards, though perplexing and arbitrary arrangements for reserves were common the world over. In terms of oversight and transparency requirements, the Chinese system drew directly on foreign models, but later events would show that these existed more in intention than in fact.

In the nineteenth and early twentieth centuries, China faced a political crisis of virtually unprecedented proportions. Chinese elites responded to this crisis by working to strengthen the Chinese state, in part by adopting foreign forms of organization, including banks. Although many high-level officials advocated financial system reform from an early date, actual adoption and implementation proved difficult, and the resulting measures taken by the Chinese state appear improvised and piecemeal. The difficulties in reforming the financial system stemmed from a number of sources. Constant internal and external wars sapped the resources of the state and the energy of officials. Threatened interests also played a huge role. Externally, foreign rivalries hampered the actions of the Qing state when one foreign power feared that another would gain benefits, such as when the British and other foreign powers opposed Li Hongzhang's formation of a Sino-American Bank. Internally, factions of both merchant and official elites represented entrenched interests that either opposed change or worked to control the process of innovation. It is important to remember, however, that no single recipe for financial system reform existed for adoption by either the Qing or the republican government. In the rest of the world, as in China, financial systems grew as much out of ad hoc responses to immediate challenges as out of some master plan.

Several characteristics of the emerging Chinese financial system stand out as important. As limited liability corporations, banks could raise large amounts of capital, but shareholders had no legal obligation to assist banks in times of crisis. For the Bank of China and the Bank of Communications, the presence of both private and state shareholders raised the possibility of tension between private and public goals. The Bank of China and the Bank of Communications engaged in commercial banking activities, increasing the potential for tension between state and private interests. Branch systems facilitated the solicitation of deposits from, and the circulation of paper money among, large numbers of individuals, while increasing the size, and potentially the stability, of large banks. At the same time, local branches of banks could develop close relations with local unit banks and with one another in each locality. Multiple banks of issue created competition among banks for the acceptability of their currencies while enhancing the resources of those banks with issue privileges. Neither the Bank of China nor the Bank of Communications had a clear mission to act as lender of last resort, and the lack of a monopoly over note issue reduced the likelihood that any one bank would take on this role. The system split between establishing a fixed fiduciary reserve, in the 1915 Bank of China regulations, and a 50 percent reserve ratio for other banks. Finally, the central government exercised a high level of control over the top managers of the Bank of China and the Bank of Communications, and theoretically had the right to inspect banks and force a certain level of transparency.

In the end, the Qing state did not survive the stresses and strains of crisis and change. But the new banks survived, adapted, and even thrived in spite of the failure to achieve the state-building goals that had ignited the process of institutional innovation in the first place. The fiscal needs of the state remained paramount, however, resulting in the crisis of 1916. Bian Baimei opted to resign rather than continue to serve in ways that violated his professional principles. Balancing state needs and personal integrity would present a recurring dilemma for Bian in future years. He would cope with this dilemma by drawing on a variety of strategies and resources, including both his expert knowledge and the network of personal connections that had found him his job at the Bank of China in the first place. The 1916 crisis presented problems for more than just central government officials and bank employees, however. The actual day-to-day attempts to maintain order and restore trust in the banks took place at the local level in cities all over China. Examining these local processes is essential to understanding the question of trust in the banking and monetary systems.

2

The 1916 Moratorium on Exchange in Tianjin

> The last time the police chief had a meeting it was to advocate using banknotes instead of silver, but merchants are going one after another to exchange paper money for silver, creating a disturbance and affecting the market.
>
> — Announcement of Tianjin local elites, 1916

Located southwest of Beijing on the border between the inland portion of the North China plain and a marshy belt of land rimming the shore of the Bohai Gulf, the city of Tianjin had certain similarities to Bian Baimei's hometown of Yangzhou in the south. Both cities were at the intersection of the Grand Canal and a major river; both, as a result, had witnessed several centuries of thriving commercial life, including salt production managed under government monopoly. Here the comparison ends. The barren yellow earth of the North China plain surrounding Tianjin bore little resemblance to the lush green paddy fields and canals of the Lower Yangzi region around Yangzhou. In addition, Tianjin's Hai River, a significant waterway in the arid north, appears shallow and puny compared with the great Yangzi River.

The events that stemmed from China's late-nineteenth- and early-twentieth-century crisis served to make the differences even more stark. Tianjin stood directly in the path, either by land or up the Hai River, between the port towns of Tanggu and Dagu on the Bohai Gulf and China's capital city, Beijing. Its location near the ocean and near the capital put Tianjin much more squarely in the sights of the foreign powers than inland Yangzhou, making Tianjin an early, and frequent, recipient of foreign influence. Thus in the mid-nineteenth century, when the Taiping rebels occupied Yangzhou in the south, armies of the foreign powers marched through Tianjin on the way to a punitive expedition in Beijing. As a result, Tianjin became a treaty port, open to foreign trade and with concession areas granted to the foreign powers. Subsequently, Tianjin's population grew rapidly, and the cityscape came to be dotted with European-style buildings. Yangzhou, in contrast, tended to stagnate and even decline economically. The railroad linking North China and the Lower Yangzi region went straight through Tianjin, but to this day Yangzhou still is not accessible by rail. By the early twentieth century, Tianjin resembled other treaty ports such as Shanghai, where Bian spent his teenage years, more than it did Yangzhou, his ancestral home. Although Bian lived in Shanghai as a youth, and many of his relatives were there, he could feel perfectly at home in Tianjin. It was a treaty port with foreign bookshops and parks, which were two of his favorite haunts, and, as the course of his subsequent career would demonstrate, the cosmopolitan elite network within which Bian circulated extended to Tianjin as well as to Beijing and Shanghai.

Of all of the different forces that shaped early-twentieth-century Tianjin, the four most salient could, somewhat simplistically, be summed up as salt, commerce, foreign concessions, and reformist political administration. During the Qing dynasty the Changlu salt gabelle in Tianjin created enormous wealth. Tianjin's salt merchants lived in opulence, and, like their southern counterparts, they patronized the arts and played host to the emperor on his travels, keeping a special lodge in Tianjin for his use. In 1916 salt merchants still made up one of Tianjin's most important elite groups. As a terminal of the Grand Canal, entrepôt for both a substantial hinterland and a seaport engaged in coastal trade, Tianjin thrived on commerce. By 1916 its role as entrepôt for the seaport located a few miles down the Hai River on the coast had long superseded its role as terminal of the Grand Canal, which became increasingly impassable during the late nineteenth century. In this Tianjin differed from other Grand Canal cities, which withered as the canal declined. The presence of foreign concessions after 1860 launched Tianjin on a path of rapid growth. Foreign residents brought with them new models of institutions, lifestyles, and ways of thinking that influenced many aspects of life in the city, including banking.[1] Predominantly as a result of the foreign presence, Tianjin became the de facto capital of Zhili Province.[2] Li Hongzhang's twenty-five-year administration (1870–1895) as governor general was followed closely by that of Yuan Shikai (1901–1907), and these two powerful reformers imprinted the city with their projects. They established armies, schools, and factories, and brought large numbers of outsiders to

Tianjin to staff these institutions. It may be a truism that local administration and control deteriorated in the late Qing period, but this was definitely not true of Tianjin. The stature and energy of these two governors general ensured that Tianjin was administered both actively and effectively.[3]

The very layout of the city, from the mountains of salt piled on the banks of the Hai River to the European-style buildings in the foreign concessions, reflected these influences, though when the young Bian Baimei moved his family from Beijing to Tianjin in 1916 he wasted little effort dwelling on the city in his diary. Preoccupied with the ongoing crisis at the Bank of China, he had no time to comment on his surroundings. On April 1, still living in Beijing, he hastily noted, "Put wife and sons on the train to Tianjin at 6:30 A.M. Went on to the bank." The next day he wrote, "In the morning went to Tianjin . . . I took a house in Dunhou Li on Guangdong Road in the British Concession, very nice. In the evening returned to Beijing." Brief as they are, however, these references illustrate two important facts about Tianjin. First, with the speed of train service, the city was only about two hours away from the capital in Beijing—close enough, in fact, for Bian to come down to Tianjin for a day of house hunting then go back to the capital at night. Second, the foreign concessions represented safety and security in an otherwise chaotic and dangerous China. Paradoxically, while Tianjin existed in the shadow of Beijing's political power, at the same time the foreign parts of the city remained an island of security in an otherwise uncertain landscape.

A young American missionary, Earle H. Ballou, made Tianjin his home for many years. His description of his first glimpse of Tianjin's cityscape in 1916 illustrates the diversity of lifestyles, foreign and Chinese, as well as the potential for underlying tensions. He noted that the elegant layout of the foreign concessions differed from the broad streets of some parts of the Chinese city, which differed in turn from the small side streets of the Chinese neighborhoods. Likewise, Tianjin's residents ranged from Europeans and dignified Chinese in the foreign concessions, to fairly well-dressed Chinese in rickshaws, to yelling shopkeepers and sweating transport laborers in the Chinese city. In addition, the young missionary's frequent references to police and soldiers evoke a city in which the coercive force of the state was never far away.[4]

Unlike in Shanghai, where all the foreign concessions except the French were combined into the international settlement, eight of Tianjin's nine foreign concessions remained separate political entities. The concessions bordered both sides of the Hai River. On the west bank, moving up the Hai River from southeast to northwest, the German Concession led to the British and then the French (see map).[5] A broad street, called Zhong (Center) Street in Chinese, linked these three concessions, running roughly parallel to the River. Foreigners called it Deutschestrasse in the German Concession, Victoria Road in the British Concession, and rue de France in the French. By the 1920s, this avenue and the nearby side streets would host most of Tianjin's foreign and Chinese modern banks. From where the rue de France ended at the International Bridge, the Hai River curves first west, where the Japanese Concession bordered the French, and then north to the old Chinese city. Across the river, reached by the International Bridge at the end of

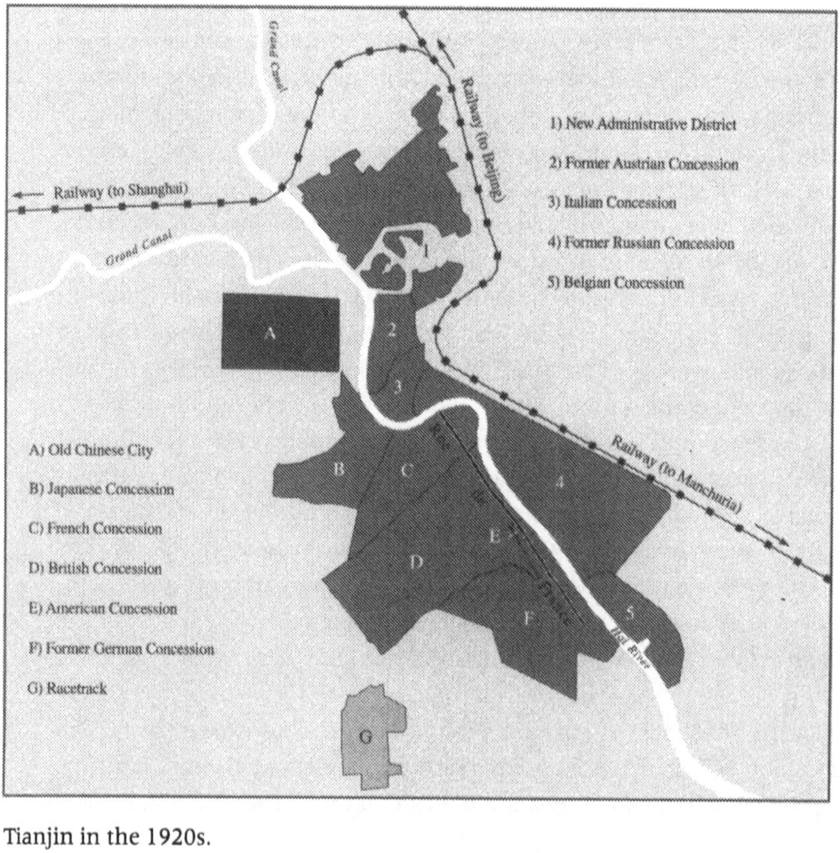

Tianjin in the 1920s.

the rue de France, the large Russian Concession dominated, with the Belgian Concession to the south and the Italian and Austrian concessions nestled within a curve of the Hai River to the northwest. Each foreign concession had its own personality. For a young foreign boy named Brian Power, styles of parks represented the differences among Tianjin's concessions. The British Concession had Victoria Park, small, neat, and almost severe in its cleanliness. More tolerant, the French authorities allowed Chinese to use their park; huge crowds thronged there every year when the authorities held a large parade in honor of Bastille Day. Across the river from the British and French concessions, the Russian park "was a stretch of wild woodland where long grass and trees of several kinds grew."[6] Later, after the 1916 crisis died down and Bian Baimei settled into his new home, a typical Sunday would include taking the family to either the French or Russian park, and then into the German Concession for tea at Kiessling and Bader's Viennese café, where you could sip hot chocolate, eat pastries, and listen to a trio play waltzes by Strauss and Weber.[7]

Whether in the foreign concessions or the Chinese city, everyday life in Tianjin reinforced a sense of diversity and division. In fact, fragmentation is a major theme of much of the English-language literature on the city. In search of evidence of a working-class consciousness, Gail Hershatter concludes that "the Tianjin working class was deeply fragmented," and Kenneth Lieberthal notes that Tianjin was bifurcated into the modern city and the older society and economy. Ruth Rogaski has shown how division of the city into nine municipal governments (one for each foreign concession and one for the Chinese areas) and "continuing social fragmentation of the city into ethnic, national, and class groups created barriers to the development of a city-wide framework for public health."[8] Fragmentation extended to the ranks of local elites as well, and the divisions among Tianjin's elites reflected the same influences of salt, commerce, foreigners, and reformist administrators that shaped the city's institutions and neighborhoods.

To begin with the political elites, Tianjin was the seat of the local county government, and of the prefect who oversaw the governance of the surrounding counties, including Tianjin. Although the city was nominally under the administration of the Tianjin prefecture and county, from 1870 on the Zhili governor general, and after 1911 the Zhili governor (or sometimes military governor), became the real government authority in Tianjin.[9] Clara Cushman, an American missionary woman who ran a girls' school in

Tianjin, aptly described the *yamen* (government office) atmosphere which still permeated the city in 1916 when her student, the daughter of Governor Zhu Jiabao, invited her to the governor's mansion for dinner:

> The carriage arrived promptly, with driver and footman. It had a glass front, so I could see the two men sitting up very straight on the high seat, with cowboy hats and four rows of brass buttons on their long, belted coats.
>
> They rushed through the streets like a fire company, sounding the bell imperatively, evidently expecting every one to clear the track for the Governor's carriage. We swept into the Yamen, through several courts, by groups of soldiers, sentinels and servants . . . [I then] followed an unforeseen guide through what seemed like endless courts with numberless turns. All along men stood in the shadows. I was glad to feel they would surely escort me out.[10]

The carriage careening through the streets without respect for life or limb, the massive and confusing *yamen* full of twists and turns and populated by guards and other hangers-on, are all extremely evocative of the power and presence of provincial administration in 1916 Tianjin. Apart from the provincial governor, the most important official in Tianjin was the police chief, who usually simultaneously held the post of police administrator for all of Zhili Province, which gave him provincial-level rank and influence. In 1916 the powerful, no-nonsense Yang Yide served as Tianjin's police chief.[11] The power of provincial governor and police chief alike, however, ended at the border between the Chinese parts of the city and Tianjin's foreign concessions; each concession had its own administrative and policing structures.

Outside of government, most of Tianjin's important elites came from the ranks of either merchants (a reflection of the importance of commerce, salt, and foreign business enterprises) or the managers of quasi-official enterprises (a reflection of the influence of the late Qing period reformist administrations). These businesspeople and their organizations mirrored Tianjin's diversity and fragmentation. Business elites and their organizations were divided by trade, with a guild representing each trade. Among these, the salt merchants' guild took its place as first among equals in Tianjin. Yet business elites were also divided by native place, and many sojourners founded native-place associations to serve as vehicles for services to compatriots and as means of enhancing their political power. Often, divisions by trade and native place were found together, as in the Indigenous Bankers' Association, which limited it membership to Tianjin natives until after 1928.[12] Unlike in Shanghai, where most elite merchants came from outside the city, the essential line of fragmentation among Tianjin's commercial elites formed between locals and outsiders. The so-called Eight Great Families most archetypically embodied Tianjin's native elite; members of one or another of these families dominated the ranks of many of Tianjin's commercial guilds.[13] At the same time, as Zhang Xiaobo notes, Tianjin hosted two main types of sojourners. The first had established a presence in Tianjin prior to its opening as a treaty port. Their main occupation was interregional trade. Shanxi remittance bankers and Jiangxi porcelain traders exemplified this type. The second type had arrived in Tianjin after its opening as a treaty port, especially after Li Hongzhang came to Tianjin in 1870. They included two main subgroups: compradors of foreign firms (mostly from Guangdong and Zhejiang) and merchant-official managers from Zhejiang, Jiangsu, and Anhui, who worked in the reform institutions founded by Li, supplemented by a group of Henan people brought to Tianjin by Yuan Shikai.[14]

Friction between sojourner and native elites played a major role in conflicts over control of the powerful Tianjin Chamber of Commerce. Governor General Yuan Shikai's first attempt to found a Chamber of Commerce in Tianjin in 1903 failed because he chose sojourners to run this citywide merchant organization. A year later a Tianjin native and salt merchant successfully headed up a newly formed Chamber of Commerce, and natives dominated thereafter.[15] At the time of the 1916 crisis, Ye Dengbang and Bian Yinchang (no relation to Bian Baimei) led the Tianjin Chamber as president and vice president, respectively. Although technically a sojourner, Ye, a Zhejiang native, had grown up in Tianjin, cutting his teeth in the financial industry as an apprentice in an indigenous bank. By 1916, though, he had turned to modern banking. He became one of the major shareholders of the Beiyang Baoshang Bank, serving as manager of its Tianjin branch. His presidency of the Chamber represented what Zhang Xiaobo notes as the increasing power of modern bankers and industrialists in Chamber politics, to the detriment of comprador and foreign goods merchants.[16] This trend, however, had only begun in 1916. The post of vice president was in the hands of Bian Yinchang, a scion of one of Tianjin's Eight Great Families.[17]

Like the city's physical layout and its elite structures, Tianjin's political economy, especially the fiscal position of the provincial government, reflected the combined influences of salt, commerce, foreigners, and reformist administrators. Taxes on land and agricultural production had constituted the traditional mainstay of the Chinese state, supplemented by other sources such as internal customs taxes and the salt and iron monopolies. In the mid-nineteenth century, more than 70 percent of Zhili's provincial revenues came from agricultural taxes; salt taxes provided 15 to 20 percent, with the remainder made up from a variety of sources. The events of China's nineteenth-century crisis, the subsequent self-strengthening and New Policies movements, and the opening of the treaty ports changed provincial finances dramatically. The Qing state had long had an internal customs tax, the *changguan*, paid at posts on major transport routes, but otherwise had taken few steps to gain revenue from the long-term increased commercialization of the economy. During the mid-nineteenth-century rebellions, however, the new *lijin* internal customs tax multiplied the number of posts, and the derived revenue from commerce, several times over. At about the same time, treaties with the foreign powers stipulated fixed customs taxes on imports and exports under a new customs administration run by a representative of the foreign powers. Although the customs administration paid its proceeds directly to the central government, during the republican period an additional 2.5 percent tax on domestic goods shipped through the treaty ports to other locations in China and on foreign goods shipped through Tianjin into the interior became a source of income for the provincial government. In addition, in Zhili Province the projects of reform officials, such as the Kailan (Kailuan) coal mine, the Tianjin mint, and other enterprises, provided new sources of both tax revenues and profits for the provincial government. As a result of these changes, by 1911 agricultural taxes accounted for only 13 percent of provincial revenues. Even though the Qing state had pledged most of its salt taxes to pay foreign indemnities, surplus salt taxes still provided 20 percent of provincial revenue. The province's share of *lijin* taxes provided 6 percent, and profits on official enterprises another 6 percent, with debt, subsidies from the central government, and miscellaneous taxes making up the balance.[18]

Finance in Tianjin was not in vigorous condition in 1916. The "three kingdoms" of the late Qing period banking world—Shanxi remittance banks, foreign banks, and indigenous banks—had changed. Although Tianjin had been the birthplace of the first of the great Shanxi remittance banks, these had withered along with the decline of the Qing state.[19] Foreign banks and indigenous banks still remained, and with the addition of modern Chinese banks such as the Bank of China and the Bank of Communications, a new three kingdoms structure had formed. Foreign banks did not arrive in Tianjin until the last quarter of the nineteenth century, but their rapid growth quickly propelled the city into becoming what was by 1905 the ninth-largest international banking center in the world, though even that distinction had declined somewhat by 1916.[20] Tianjin provided the entry point for the import of foreign goods, especially cotton cloth, for Zhili, Shanxi, Shandong, Shaanxi, and Gansu provinces, as well as Inner Mongolia. Likewise, the export of commodities such as pig bristles and hides from the same regions went through Tianjin, all financed by the foreign banks there.[21] As a result, the foreign banks thrived, and the Chinese compradors who worked for the giant foreign banks in the city became some of the most powerful merchants in Tianjin.[22] Indigenous banks made loans for domestic commerce and changed money for a diverse group of customers ranging from salt merchants, who sold salt in copper but paid taxes and other expenditures in silver, to Grand Canal workers needing money for their stay in Tianjin.[23] In 1916, though, Tianjin's indigenous financial institutions had not fully recovered from the post-Boxer financial crisis, and they had suffered again from looting in 1912 after the revolution. Individual indigenous banks still prospered, making their owners, and the Tianjin indigenous bankers' guild, quite influential, but as a whole this kingdom of Tianjin finance had yet to regain its earlier glory.[24]

The modern Chinese banking industry, the third kingdom of post-dynastic Chinese finance, was a young but rapidly growing sector. Eight modern banks had branches in Tianjin in 1916, and far and away the most important were the three banks with central or provincial government connections: the Bank of China, the Bank of Communications, and the Zhili Provincial Bank. The three government banks all worked as rivals, competing for the right to handle state funds such as from salt and customs taxes.[25] None of the state banks had much luck entering the market for local commercial transactions dominated by indigenous banks, but they did have considerably more success issuing paper money. In fact, the currencies of the Bank of China and the Bank of Communications could even compete with the paper money issued by foreign banks.[26] In 1916 the financial crisis of Yuan Shikai's government had caused a run on the Beijing branches of the Bank of China and the Bank of Communications which subsequently spread to Tianjin, creating panic in the city. The response of Tianjin bankers, other elites, and government authorities demonstrates much about money, trust, and crisis in republican Tianjin.

The Moratorium on Exchange

Rumors about the financial problems of Yuan Shikai's government and the condition of the two state-sponsored banks flew during the last weeks of 1915, as Yuan's plans for an emperorship collapsed in the midst of a civil war that threatened the very survival of his government. As early as January 1916, Yuan's cabinet ordered the military governors of the various provinces, including the Zhili military governor, Zhu Jiabao, to suppress rumors and agitation in the financial markets. Activity was stepped up a month later, when pamphlets appeared questioning the credibility of the Bank of China and the Bank of Communications. The cabinet issued an order banning the circulars and called for mobilization in support of the two banks on the local level, pointing out that the Beijing Chamber of Commerce had distributed flyers pledging to support the city's financial markets.[27]

In Tianjin, Governor Zhu Jiabao and police chief Yang Yide took up the call, asking the Chamber of Commerce to call a meeting to discuss the matter. To impress the seriousness of the situation on Tianjin's merchants, both the head of the Zhili Finance Bureau and, even more important, Yang Yide attended the meeting.[28] As a result of the meeting, Tianjin's merchants agreed not to believe rumors, not to read the subversive *Gongmin ribao* (which had been reporting the accusations of a "rebel political party"), and to support the market and help stabilize the central government.[29] By early April, Zhu Jiabao reported to his superiors that through the efforts of the police, more than three hundred circulars had been confiscated, rumors had been suppressed, and Tianjin was calm.[30]

Rumor suppression proved to be only a temporary solution, however, as the silver reserves of the Bank of China and Bank of Communications neared exhaustion. A late April order intended to bolster the credibility of the paper money of the two banks commanded that all government ministries and offices accept only paper money and not silver. This order created more confusion than credibility. Zhu Jiabao cabled the Finance Ministry and asked what to say when people wanted to know whether or not silver and copper were still legal tender. More important, he also noted that paper money did not circulate in the remote areas of Zhili Province, so asking people in those places not to use silver was akin to asking them not to buy or sell anything.[31] Zhu's response clearly illustrates the gap between the requirements of the state and the reach of its financial system. Without adequate reserves to back the ever-increasing amounts of paper money, and without the ability to demonetize silver and copper, suspending exchange of paper money for silver became the only viable option for the central government. Repeated insistence by the Finance Ministry that no plan existed to discontinue exchange, however, only exacerbated rumors.

In early May, as Bian Baimei and his colleagues at the Bank of China in Beijing struggled with the bank's problems, he and a small circle of fellow employees agreed that they would not implement an order to discontinue exchange.[32] In their view, the Bank of China and its money should be held to a standard of professional credibility and not be subject to the political fortunes of the government. At about the same time, a group calling itself the merchant shareholders of the Bank of China in Shanghai cabled the Finance Ministry, saying that exchangeability should be preserved. Central government leaders, for their part, worried about disobedience at the two banks. On May 10 they issued the completely unrealistic order that all of the branches of the banks move out of the foreign concessions and into the Chinese areas of their respective cities, an order ignored on all counts.[33] The crisis in Tianjin became acute as runs accelerated at the two banks. On May 11 the Tianjin branch of the Bank of Communications took the first step toward limiting exchange of its paper money by announcing that it would cash only paper money issued by the Tianjin branch and stamped with the Tianjin place-name. The announcement caused panic at both banks. That day the Tianjin branch of the Bank of China exchanged 500,000 yuan of paper money for silver, and the Tianjin branch of the Bank of Communications exchanged more than 400,000.[34]

On the same day, the county of Tianjin, police chief Yang Yide, and the Tianjin Chamber of Commerce took a fateful step, and announced that these local government and elite organizations would guarantee the paper money of the two banks. Their announcement declared that "the paper money of the two banks should circulate as normal, regardless of place of origin, and we will take responsibility," and ended by emphasizing that the two banks were state banks and that the military governor of Zhili and the police chief would ensure that the city's merchants would not take a loss on the notes.[35] The relative roles of Chamber leaders and local officials in instigating this move are unclear, but the later reluctance demonstrated by merchant elites indicates that the government likely played a significant role in persuading the Chamber to issue such a guarantee.

Nonetheless, the public guarantee failed to stem the crisis, and the escalating bank runs forced the central government's hand. The next day the government issued an order prohibiting exchange of the paper money of the Bank of China and the Bank of Communications for silver, signed by the new prime minister, Duan Qirui.[36] The moratorium on exchange would only serve to exacerbate the crisis, but in reality the government had little choice. The Bank of China and the Bank of Communications had issued currency far in excess of their reserves, and regular exchange had become impossible. The Bank of Communications, especially, faced an acutely thin margin of reserves. During the crisis a railway employee visited the Tianjin branch of the bank to see if an accommodation could be made to exchange banknotes in the possession of the railroad, the bank's sister agency under the Communications Ministry. The bank manager, responding that exchange was impossible, opened his account books to show that the branch had more than 7 million yuan in outstanding banknotes and meager reserves of less than 60,000 yuan.[37]

The order for a moratorium on exchange caused a spate of activity in Tianjin. Bian Baimei rushed from Beijing to Tianjin to help the Bank of China branch there deal with foreigners from the concessions who wanted to exchange their notes (Bian's foreign education and fluency in English made him the ideal man for such a task), and the Tianjin Chamber of Commerce called a meeting to be held at the police department on May 14. That night Bian drafted his letter of resignation.[38] In fact, much of the opposition to the moratorium on exchange came from the ranks of the professional managers within the Bank of China. In some parts of China—most notably Shanghai and to a lesser extent Nanjing and Hankou—Bank of China employees cooperated with local elites and officials in opposing the moratorium. In those places the Bank of China continued to exchange paper money for silver as usual, though none of the branches of the weaker Bank of Communications did so. In Tianjin, close to the center of political power in Beijing, no such opposition emerged. The Tianjin branches of the two banks, like their Beijing counterparts, complied with the moratorium, with the result that both the Tianjin and Beijing notes of the two banks became inconvertible to silver. Local officials and Tianjin's native elite mobilized to deal with the crisis.

The May 14 meeting of the Tianjin Chamber of Commerce resulted in the formation of a guardianship organization, sponsored by the local elite, called the Federated Gentry and Merchants Association (Shenshang lianhe hui), later called the All Zhili Province Gentry and Merchants Finance Provisional Maintenance Association (Zhili quansheng shenshang jinrong linshi weichi hui), hereafter simply referred to as the association.[39] The association pledged to raise 2 million yuan and obtain the guarantee of the Zhili provincial land taxes to support the paper money of the two banks. Association leaders emphasized the need to ensure the circulation of money and goods, so in essence the association stepped into the shoes of both the provincial government and the two banks to guarantee the value of the banks' paper money, using elite contributions and the provincial land tax as theoretical sources to fund its operations.[40] From the beginning the association's leaders worried about opposition from the central government, so they resolved to announce their plans in a "report" to the government, not a "request for instructions." To make their case for action more persuasive, they decided to stress that Tianjin was a large port city where Chinese and foreigners mixed. Their line of reasoning was that the central government would either have to allow establishment of the Gentry Merchant Association or find a way itself to guarantee the value of the two banks' paper money held by foreigners in Tianjin.[41]

Although the foreign presence provided a convenient cover to justify action contrary to government directives, it was not an empty threat. Foreign relations complicated central government control over the money supply in many ways. The government had pledged the customs and salt taxes as well as the revenues of the railroads to secure foreign loans and indemnities. Even if the Chinese government wanted to accept payment of taxes and railway fees in nonconvertible currency, it would still have to pay foreign creditors in silver or gold.[42] In addition, foreign banks also accepted deposits and issued paper money denominated in Chinese yuan and exchangeable for silver dollars, providing an alternative to the paper currencies issued by Chinese banks. Such foreign competition produced a situation in which the Chinese government was charged with defending the credibility of its currency not only across international borders but domestically as well. As the association undertook to assume responsibility for the government's currency, dealing with the foreign presence constantly raised problems of policy and management. Even before formation of the association, the Tianjin Chamber of Commerce had informed all nine foreign consulates in Tianjin that the goal of the association would be to ensure continued circulation of the paper money of the two banks, not to engage in full-scale exchange of the money for silver, with the exception of "a few pennies exchanged for poor people."[43]

Throwing "a few pennies" to "poor people" did not represent a realistic strategy to restore trust, nor did it prove effective in practice. Similar ambivalence informed many of the activities of the association throughout the crisis. In spite of the initial resolution to "report" to the government rather than "request instructions," it still phrased its communications to Zhu Jiabao as a "request" for approval.[44] Zhu duly forwarded the plans to the central government, apparently without any sense of irony about the fact that local officials and elites were requesting permission from the central government to violate the central government's own moratorium on exchange. In response, the cabinet, with equal blindness to the irony, and possibly sensing a way out of its predicament, approved the association's plans, subject to two qualifications: the association should not limit its guaranty to Tianjin notes and should not freeze deposits at the two banks.[45] By excluding currency of the two banks issued by nonlocal branches, the association planned to avoid financing the central government through mediation of the banks' Beijing branches, which had made the largest loans to the government, and issued the most paper money, of all the branches in China. As announced at one meeting of the association, "this is a matter of life and death for the nation, but Zhili Province does not have the strength to undertake [such a] responsibility."[46] Likewise, Tianjin's elites had no desire to take on all of the obligations of the two banks; they thus decided to "freeze" deposits at the two banks rather than allow depositors to withdraw their money in banknotes and then ask the association to guarantee the value of those notes. Possibly anticipating the government's objections, the association did not wait for cabinet instructions before announcing that its activities would be limited to local paper money of the two banks. To bolster its stand, the association sent out requests for support of its actions to Tianjin natives serving as important officials in other parts of China.[47]

Tianjin's native elites felt responsible, or else the government forced them to take responsibility, for restoring trust in the currency. In order to limit their liabilities, though, local elites needed to separate the guardianship of local money from guardianship of both the banks and the government itself. Even this limited plan of guarantee involved huge resources. The 2 million yuan pledged for association use was a substantial sum, but it amounted to less than half of the more than 5 million yuan in Tianjin and Zhili notes issued by the two banks, and an even smaller fraction of the almost 80 million yuan in paper money issued by the Beijing branches of the two banks.[48]

As part of the plan to support the currency without engaging in full-scale exchange of the paper currencies of the two banks, the association decided to set up an office at which people could request that their banknotes be stamped with the Chamber's guarantee. Association leaders quickly realized, however, that a simple guarantee would not satisfy the anxious crowds and that they would have to undertake some exchange of banknotes for silver. Paper, even when stamped with the seal of the association, did not reassure people as much as hard silver dollars. The association's leaders made plans to exchange the paper money of the two banks in limited amounts based on an elaborate schedule. From May 20 to 24, the association would stamp one-yuan bills with a guarantee, and cash a total of five one-yuan notes per person into silver dollars. From May 25 to 29, five-yuan bills would be stamped, but the limit on exchange would still be five yuan each time. From May 30 to June 3, ten-yuan bills would be stamped, and the maximum that anyone could exchange would be ten yuan each time.[49] The plan in place, the association printed flyers and enlisted the help of the police to distribute them, requesting that, in addition to twenty policemen, police chief Yang Yide himself be present at the exchange office to "lend his prestige and encourage trust among the people."[50] In spite of these precautions, some people tried to get around the daily limit on the amount of paper money that could be stamped or exchanged for silver by hiring women, children, or riffraff *(wulaizhe)* to stand in line for them. The *wulaizhe* crowded in and generally disturbed order during the exchange process.[51] As Zhang Xiaobo has pointed out, the outflow of funds increased rapidly during the later stages because people were happy to have one-yuan notes stamped for daily use, but they wanted five- and ten-yuan notes to be exchanged for silver dollars for safety. The accelerating demand for exchange contravened the original purpose of the association, which was to aid the circulation of the banks' currency, not to finance its withdrawal from the market.[52] It also threatened to exhaust the resources of the association. On May 30 alone, the first day for cashing ten-yuan notes, the association paid out 58,314 yuan in silver dollars, as nearly six thousand people lined up to exchange notes.[53]

The popularity of the currency exchange program strained the resources of the association. Fortunately, the central government, faced with rebellion at the Bank of China branches in Shanghai, Nanjing, and Hankou, and with widespread refusal to accept nonconvertible notes in Beijing and Tianjin, stepped in, acknowledging the failure of the moratorium. The government retreated from the imperatives of state power in the face of the imperatives of community trust. The crowd had triumphed over state coercion and metal had triumphed over paper. On May 31 the prime minister ordered the activities of the association in Tianjin discontinued, saying that the paper money of the two banks could be exchanged for copper if necessary and calling for the establishment of a Market Protection Bank. The association directors, with evident relief, announced the end of their mission and promptly discontinued activities.[54]

On the surface, the local mobilization in Tianjin in response to the 1916 crisis seems fairly straightforward. The state—weakened by military challenge and nearly bankrupt—tried to impose its will on two banks and a local community in order to obtain financial resources for its needs. Activist local elites banded together with local officials to maintain order and preserve the community from the harsh consequences of central state action. They accomplished this by forming an ad hoc guardianship organization to raise funds to guarantee the value of the paper money and, at the same time, closed off the locality and defined a community of interest—and a local identity—at the level of Zhili Province and the "Zhili" paper money circulating therein. To understand the implications beneath the surface of the 1916 crisis in Tianjin, it is necessary to look a little more closely at the process of mobilization to promote trust.

The Form and Structure of Guardianship

Three characteristics of the guardianship association stand out as salient. First, the association was dominated by Tianjin native merchant elites, especially leaders of the Chamber of Commerce. Second, in spite of involvement of the Tianjin Chamber, the elites formed a new, ad hoc organization rather than using the Chamber as the organizational vehicle for guardianship. Third, although its activities took place in Tianjin under the direction of local elites, the association claimed to be provincial in scope and operation. Careful examination of these three characteristics will show that the association's form and structure proved less than conducive to successful guardianship. In fact, in the end, the structure allowed local elites to avoid many of the financial costs of guardianship.

So who were the gentry and merchants who rushed to Tianjin's aid? Three overlapping groups of elites composed the All Zhili Province Gentry and Merchants Finance Provisional Maintenance Association. A core group of twenty or so people signed the initial announcements and served in many officer positions in the association. A larger mid-level group of seventy to ninety people served as "directors" and signed later declarations. A third, larger group of more than one thousand gentry and merchants attended at least some of the meetings.[55] Most of the people who participated in the association have fallen out of the historical record, but membership lists include a healthy sprinkling of the surnames of the Eight Great Families, the Bians (no relation to Bian Baimei), Huas, Gaos, and Lis in particular. In spite of the association's own charter requiring that it include both local and sojourning gentry and merchants, locals dominated both the core leadership and the general membership. Sojourners accounted for only five of the twenty-three members of the mid-level group who can be identified, and two of those five were from families that had been in Tianjin for generations.[56] The absence of sojourners from the association can be attributed in part to the fact that many of Tianjin's sojourner merchant-official managers had followed Yuan Shikai to Beijing when he became president, and they held posts in his central administration. Nonetheless, other factors came into play as well. Sojourning elites had kept their distance from local crises in the past, as in the post-Boxer crisis, and they did so again in 1916. The dominance of natives brings into question the extent to which sojourners identified with Tianjin—or were allowed to identify with Tianjin—as anything more than a temporary residence. Unlike in nineteenth-century Hankou, where "in terms of functional participation, at least, the city's leading sojourner merchants represented themselves as fully integrated members of a Hankow [Hankou] community," in Tianjin elites were divided between locals and sojourners in their organizations.[57]

In addition to being locals, the leaders of the association are more appropriately described as merchants than as gentry. Merchants dominated the membership of the association, especially the core group of twenty, nine of whom had commercial backgrounds. None of them had higher imperial degrees, and only one had a purchased degree. Five of them had trained as apprentices, four of those five in indigenous banks. The mid-level group of seventy to ninety did include several people who would be considered gentry by any definition of the term. The most prominent was Yan Xiu, a Qing period *jinshi* who had held several official positions and who would go on to found Nankai University. Yan's gentry status was not his only qualification to participate in the association's activities. He too was a son of Tianjin, and came from a prominent salt merchant family.[58] Yan Xiu's gentry status aside, Zhang Xiaobo rightly sees management of the 1916 crisis as primarily the work of the Tianjin Chamber of Commerce.[59] Chamber president Ye

Dengbang and vice president Bian Yinchang played the most active roles in the association. They attended all of the meetings, public and private, and drafted association documents. Their presence was so dominating that Bian Yinchang actually apologized at the May 18 meeting for the speed and secrecy with which the association's charter had been written.[60] Clearly a small group of activists, led by Ye and Bian, planned out the structure of the association, wrote up the documents, and then presented them to the larger group for approval. This does not mean that the other directors had no input. On the contrary, many of their board meetings were quite lively, but Ye and Bian took the roles of principal leaders.

Given that the Chamber of Commerce was the key player in organizing the association, the question remains as to why Chamber leaders decided to form such an ad hoc organization. Using a provisional association as its form of organization had several advantages for Tianjin's local elites. First, an ad hoc form of organization allowed the Tianjin Chamber leaders to conform to the provincial structural requirements of both the local government and the two banks. In 1916, Tianjin still had no separate political identity, and provincial-level officials remained its most important local authorities. Throughout the crisis all communication between the association and the central government went through the province, and the support of the provincial military governor was essential to the successful functioning of the association. The fact that the province pledged its land taxes to support the activities of the association also indicates that the gentry and merchants were acting on behalf of the province, which would, in theory, eventually step in and reimburse them. In addition, the organization of the two banks also made the province a logical unit of activity. The Tianjin branch of the Bank of China supervised thirty-four sub-branches and offices in Zhili Province, each of which issued paper money stamped with the local place-name. Likewise, the Tianjin branch of the Bank of Communications administered four sub-branches which issued local money. Thus the internal structure of the two banks linked Tianjin paper money with the paper money issued in other places in Zhili Province. In fact, Dezhou sub-branch of the Bank of Communications was in Shandong Province, but because it was under the administration of the Bank's Tianjin branch, this Shandong money also became the responsibility of the association.[61]

Second, the provisional association promoted the illusion of inclusiveness, making its backing seem broader than it really was. The "gentry and merchants of Zhili Province" has the resonance of a much higher status than the

"Tianjin Chamber of Commerce." It connotes the complete body of local elites, regardless of profession, including literati and businessmen, with both strength and depth, united in the purpose at hand. In fact, the "Zhili" gentry and merchants who served as directors of the 1916 association worked in Tianjin, held their meetings in Tianjin, lived in Tianjin, and conducted their activities to support the paper money of the two banks exclusively in Tianjin.[62] Claims of territorial inclusiveness, like those regarding native place, were a fraud.

A third advantage of using a provisional form of organization was that it limited the liability of the Chamber by creating a temporary organization that could be disbanded at any time. This ad hoc nature worked more to protect association members from loss than to ensure circulation of the paper money of the two banks. If the problems of the two banks proved beyond the capabilities of the association, then it could simply disband and there would be no remaining exposure to legal liability. The Chamber of Commerce, by contrast, was a permanent organization, and it could not escape its obligations so easily; dissolution was not a viable option for the Chamber. An ad hoc organization gave Tianjin's native elites the structural precondition for avoiding full financial responsibility for the 1916 crisis.

Association leaders planned to obtain the 2 million yuan funding for the organization in four 500,000 yuan lots from (1) the Zhili Provincial Bank, (2) the Tianjin branches of the Bank of China and Bank of Communications, (3) the gentry and merchants of Zhili, and (4) the Changlu salt merchants. In theory this allocation of funds indicated a unity of interest among the two central state banks, the province, the salt merchants, and the other elites of Zhili Province. In this equation the state and non-state sides balanced equally. Three state institutions—the two central state banks and the Zhili Provincial Bank—pledged 1 million yuan. Non-state elites, salt merchants, and other gentry and merchants pledged the other half of the funds. In reality, however, much of the funding for the association never materialized, and fulfillment of funding pledges preoccupied the association's directors, taking up the agenda of many of their meetings. In the end, the bulk of the association's money by far came from the three banks, which put up the 1 million yuan they had pledged, but the gentry and merchant elites contributed only a little more than 18,000 yuan, and that came from the indigenous bankers. The salt merchants—who had so often been the mainstay in meeting challenges in the past—provided not a penny. In all, merchant elites raised less than 2 percent of the amount they had pledged. On top of that, the provincial structure of the organization did little to help the financial position of the association, since the head of the Zhili Provincial Bank admitted at a meeting of association directors that there were no available provincial land tax funds to use as a guarantee.[63]

The failure of the salt merchants to fulfill their traditional role in local crisis management is telling. Zhang Xiaobo has noted that "in times of local crises such as the 1853 Taiping assault and the 1858 and 1860 foreign invasions, the Lugang Gongsuo (the Changlu salt merchant guild), the leading common-trade guild in Tianjin, emerged as an interim municipal government, taking on the responsibilities of defending and administering the city and dealing with the foreign invaders."[64] The fact that the association initially tapped salt merchants to provide one fourth of the funding for its activities amply demonstrates the continuing expectation for them to fulfill their traditional role. Although individual motivations are difficult to assess, the reluctance of Tianjin's salt merchants to fund the association might stem from the nature of the threat in 1916, which involved the rescue of two state institutions, as opposed to the kind of danger that the Taiping and foreign invading armies had presented in the past. The 1916 crisis thus had more in common with the post-Boxer financial crisis. In 1903, when the new Zhili governor general, Yuan Shikai, was forced to invent his own financial institutions in order to deal with the problems, local elites proved hesitant to fund a planned commercial bank.[65] The implicit message in both 1903 and 1916 was that regulation of money and finance was a problem for the state, not local elites. In part, too, this reluctance stemmed from the close relationship between local financial problems and state revenues. While local elites proved willing to take activist roles in maintaining local order, philanthropy, and defense, they were not prepared to contribute to state coffers without some sort of quid pro quo.[66] When it came to matters of state revenue, Tianjin's native elites could, and did, often block actions of the central state, as with the successful 1908 protest against a stamp tax, led by salt merchants.[67] Likewise in 1916, when support of the local currency of the Bank of China and the Bank of Communications meant de facto support for the revenues of the state, Tianjin's local elites kept their pocketbooks shut.

In the absence of full-scale financial support for the two banks, the association had to rely on exhortation to persuade people to continue to accept the paper money of the two banks. But the nature of its rhetoric proved no more conducive to guardianship than the form and structure of the organization.

The Rhetoric of Guardianship

On May 22, 1916, at the height of the crisis in Tianjin, more than one thousand local elites—identified as gentry and merchants in the newspapers—gathered to hear the leaders of the association speak about plans to deal with the financial crisis. The key speaker was not an association leader but police chief Yang Yide. In his speech, later published in the newspapers, Yang took special pains to point out the significance of his native-place origins. After reporting on the activities of the association, he stated that he was neither a stockholder nor an employee of either the Bank of China or the Bank of Communications. He went on to say that his brother Tianjiners [*tongfu laoxiang*] would certainly understand that he had not stinted in his efforts since the beginning of the crisis. Yang concluded, "I am after all a Tianjiner [*ben jin renmin*] and that makes me different from other officials. I came today, in spite of illness, because I would not dare to shirk my duty."[68]

Yang made it clear that his local identity gave him special status and proved his interest—or more specifically his disinterest—in supporting the two banks. Throughout the 1916 crisis, references to a local identity often accompanied the declaration that the speaker had no hidden personal agenda. Yang used the device again in a rhyming speech he gave urging support for the banks: "Police matters are my responsibility. I protect the locality and pay no attention to money. When it comes to one's home locality [*sangzi*], it is difficult to shirk responsibility. Elders and brothers: Enthusiastically commence."[69] The same reasoning came up again in the controversy regarding the plan to establish a Market Protection Bank in the wake of the 1916 crisis. In connection with this matter, a member of the local elite, Wang Zhilong, responded to criticism from the Chamber of Commerce's newspaper [*Shang Bao*] by writing a scathing letter declaring that the Market Protection Bank was needed for the good of local finance, and that he himself was very concerned with his home locality [*sangzi*].[70] The implication, of course, was that a local person would work for the local good, and his motives should not be impugned. The local man was a man to be trusted.

In addition to this common usage of native place or hometown as proof of the purity of one's motives, it was also used to appeal for the support of famous Tianjiners in other parts of China. Association elites sent a circular cable to luminaries such as Xu Shichang, former prime minister, and Feng Guozhang, military governor of Jiangsu. The telegram read in part: "The main purpose of the association is to ensure the circulation of Zhili and

Tianjin paper money. Beijing and other provinces are excluded . . . This is a matter of the safety of [our] home locality [*sangzi*]." Tianjin's newspapers then published a collection of responses to show that Tianjiners serving in official positions all over China had approved of the activities of the association. Some, such as Feng Guozhang, expressed unreserved approval, writing, "Support of Zhili depends on you gentlemen who have implemented a plan to turn danger into safety for the hometown [*zixiang*]." Others, especially Xu Shichang, were more discreet. Xu, who had recently been ousted as prime minister by Duan Qirui, did not even reply directly to the association. Instead he addressed his response as a personal communication to Yan Xiu, saying that the association's efforts were admirable, but the task was "extremely difficult and would require official support at every step." The list of those notable Tianjiners contacted by the association reads like a who's who of the Beiyang Army. All owed their success in some measure to Yuan Shikai.[71] In supporting the association, then, they opposed the wishes of their old patron. On the one hand, their willingness to do so clearly indicates the extent to which Yuan had already lost his hold on the reins of power. On the other hand, the fact that the association had solicited their support indicates the extent to which its leaders feared reprisals from the central state for their actions. It was no coincidence that they sent out the cables soliciting support on the same day (May 19) that they announced the scope of their operations and asked for approval to limit themselves to Tianjin and Zhili paper money. Thus, their need for the approval of these powerful Tianjin natives was both a matter of self-defense against government reprisals and part of the local publicity campaign to restore trust.

The concept of localism, then, functioned in two ways. It was a badge of purity, certifying the holder as trustworthy to place the interests of the community above his own, and it was a call for elites to unite in the face of potential censure from the state. Localism did not stand alone as a principle of action; elites, however, also justified even the most localizing actions in terms of the good of the country and the nation.

In Tianjin, the issue of nationalism did not come up much in the private meetings and communications of the association. In public, though, nationalism was another matter, as seen most clearly at the May 22 rally of more than one thousand of Tianjin's elites. At the same time Yang Yide took such pains to point out his local identity, he linked localism to nationalism by declaring that he was "expending all of [his] efforts to fulfill [his] responsibility of supporting the locality [*weichi difang*] and preserving the reputation of the state [*baoquan guojia zhi lianmian*]."[72] In this view locality and central state were linked, and preservation of one entailed preservation of the other. At the same meeting representatives of the association spoke in a similar manner. According to one, "the level of the people's patriotism, as seen in the active response of the gentry and merchants in raising money [to manage the crisis], was reaching a higher level every day and was much stronger than in recent years." This statement is interesting in two respects. First, the speaker equated local elite activism with the good of the nation, conveniently ignoring the fact that he referred to a local activism which was exercising disobedience to state policy. More important, he was constructing a public vision of an activist and nationalist elite. Since merchant contributions to the association represented a dismal failure, his description of a high tide of nationalism that buoyed the credibility and strength of the association was pure fiction. Whether he intended this fiction to spur contributions by urging merchants to jump onto the bandwagon on the road to Chinese nationalism or simply as a public relations gimmick to convince the public of the financial wherewithal of the association is unknown. Another association leader at the mass rally decried the "shame of mistreatment of the people of a subjugated nation [*wang guo*] by strong nations." In its way, this statement was also a construction. Little in the 1916 crisis could be attributed to foreign instigation, but foreigners made a convenient scapegoat, deflecting distrust away from both the central government and local elite motives.[73]

Broaching the subject of the nation may have been a standard justification for elite actions, but it posed the risk of focusing attention on the fact that the Bank of China and the Bank of Communications were state banks and their problems the result of state actions. This risk did not seem to worry the Tianjin elites, however. At the May 22 meeting, one association speaker even declared that the "two banks are state banks and would not fail unless the country was lost. As long as there is the nation, then [the banks] cannot lose credibility [*xinyong*]."[74] In contrast to all of the localizing tendencies of the association, this statement portrays a fundamental level of trust in the ability of the central government to survive and protect the banks, regardless of its policies.

Thus the elites spun an intricate web of inconsistent reasoning to justify their actions and reassure the public. The banks had to be protected in order to protect both the locality and the central state. If the motives of governments and government officials were suspect, local elites (native Tianjiners) could be trusted to protect local interests. The nation should be protected because it was the nationalist thing to do. Nationalists should give money to protect local interests. The banks were government banks and were not endangered as long as the nation existed. The convolutions of this scattershot approach to creating credibility and trust serve to highlight the difficult position in which the Tianjin elites found themselves. Unlike in Nanjing, Shanghai, and Hankou, Tianjin's elites did not have the luxury of simply asking the two banks to continue exchanging paper money for silver. Disobedience to the moratorium on exchange in Shanghai, Nanjing, and Hankou was made possible, in part, by the very health of the banks there.[75] In Tianjin, the elites could not overcome the central fact that rescuing the banks entailed a massive outlay of funds. Defiance of the state, in terms of either localism or nationalism, was easy enough, but support for the currency proved much harder to achieve.

In the end, all of the speeches and appeals had little effect. The people of Tianjin continued to line up by the thousands to exchange their paper money for silver, straining the resources of the association. The holders of the banknotes of the Bank of China and the Bank of Communications rejected the rhetorical calls of elite leaders to equate the two state banks and the paper money they issued with either the local parochial or the national patriotic good. The 1916 crisis grew from state problems and could not be solved without fundamentally addressing the relationships among the banks, the local community, and the state.

Authority and Trust

If anything, state policy regarding the moratorium was even more ambivalent and confused than the actions of Tianjin's elites. State leaders did not think through the details of such a moratorium, and the order looked more like a desperate attempt at crisis management than a considered effort to rewrite the rules governing the bases of trust for bank-issued paper money. Contradictions and inconsistencies within the government exacerbated the problems of implementing the moratorium, and the nation's top leadership began backpedaling almost as soon as the order was issued.

When it gave the order for a moratorium on exchange of the paper money of the two banks, the central state justified its action in terms of the imperatives of state power. In fact the Chinese government cited a European precedent to explain the need for a moratorium on exchange. As the text of the order states: "A custom prevails in foreign countries at a time of extraordinary financial stringency for notes issued by the Government banks to be rendered temporarily inconvertible . . . Such an excellent practice of the West being of far-reaching benefit should speedily be imitated in China." Aware that the government would be accused of improper administration, officials took the initiative of justifying the moratorium in terms of the only model of proper administration accepted by both the government and its critics: the European state. In case this argument was not persuasive, the government added a measure of coercive threat, advising local officials to "station adequate troops and police at the branch banks to see that these branches do not violate the order by secretly exchanging notes or paying money to depositors."[76]

In spite of the lofty declaration of European precedent, the central government did not think through the technical details of the moratorium. Inconsistent application within government agencies constantly undermined its own efforts. The most blatant inconsistency arose from confusion within the Communications Ministry. Shortly after the crisis began, the Beijing-Fengtian Railroad issued new regulations for purchasing tickets and shipping goods, requiring 30 percent of payments in silver or copper. The remainder could be paid in Bank of Communications paper money, not Bank of China money, and only in notes stamped with the Tianjin or Beijing place-names. Without this kind of paper money, the customer would have to pay in full in silver or copper. When Yuan Shikai's secret police promptly moved to investigate the matter, the railroad responded that it needed hard money to pay foreign employees and foreign loans and to buy foreign equipment. Even more stringent, the Tianjin Telegraph Office, in the French Concession, refused to take any paper money, even that issued by the Bank of Communications.[77] The foreign powers lost no time in protesting such inconsistency. A letter from the French ambassador to the Chinese Foreign Ministry asked why the moratorium declared that paper money of the two banks would be accepted but the telegraph administration accepted only silver and copper cash. The Foreign Ministry could only cite the telegraph administration's foreign obligations, requiring the demand for payment for services in silver.[78] With such conflicting signals, it is not surprising that the people of Tianjin remained suspicious of claims made in the name of the nation or government. As a letter from a group of merchants to the association read, "The association's plans [to support the paper money of the two banks] are insufficient to cope with the secret calculations of officials."[79]

Inconsistency in government action was not limited to the Communications Ministry. Duan Qirui himself, signatory of the moratorium on exchange, began backpedaling within days of the order. Duan first issued the moratorium on May 12, and it went into effect in Tianjin on May 13. On the seventeenth the cabinet issued another order to military governor Zhu Jiabao stating that silver needed to be preserved to pay foreign reparations and insisting that the moratorium must be implemented.[80] Three days later, on May 20, Duan Qirui actually sent a telegram to the association of Shanghai shareholders of the Bank of China saying that the moratorium was only a temporary measure and congratulating the Shanghai Bank of China for continuing exchange. For Duan not only to sanction but to praise the rebellious actions of the Shanghai branch of the bank and its Jiangnan shareholders demonstrates how quickly he came to realize the futility of the order. Predictably, Duan phrased his telegram to the Shanghai shareholders in nationalist terms: "The central banks are the arteries of the nation . . . [F]ortunately through the sincere support of you gentlemen the merchants and people have been blessed with fortune and [you have] my deepest gratitude."[81] This from the same man who only a week before had proclaimed that soldiers and police would be stationed at each bank branch to prevent continued exchange!

Unfortunately for Duan, the Beijing and Tianjin branches of the two banks were in no condition to resume exchanging notes immediately. He was especially worried about the situation in the capital, where most of the unbacked paper money circulated. When it became apparent that the moratorium on exchange had failed and the government would have to find some other way of financing its deficit, Duan scrambled to control the damage. In desperation he turned to Tianjin's elites for help. First he wrote to Zhu Jiabao, asking him to delay the start of the activities of the association for a couple of days, claiming that "the stagnation of finance is not the sickness of just one place."[82] Having failed to come up with a solution, two days later the cabinet ordered the association to included Beijing notes in its scope of operations, but the association had already announced its plans to limit support to Tianjin and Zhili notes. Duan's plan for the elites of Tianjin to bail out the central government failed before it even started. Had he known that the association had raised only half of its announced goal, he might not have bothered.

With open disobedience in South China and the association stepping in to supplant the government's credibility with its own in Tianjin, Duan Qirui needed to find a face-saving way out. The government came up with an organizational solution, asking elites in each locality to establish and fund a Market Protection Bank *(baoshi yinhang)* to issue money. Since each province already had a provincial bank, the only reason to establish new local banks would be to tap new sources of funds. In essence, this was another variation on the theme of having local elites raise money to bail out the state banks. The shareholders of the new banks would be local gentry and merchants, and the alleged 2 million yuan already raised by Tianjin elites was specifically cited as a start. Three weeks previously, Duan had said that only the moratorium would save the country. Now his change of mind was complete, and he asserted that beginning exchange quickly would benefit both the nation and the people's livelihood.[83] If Duan Qirui and the government saw the Market Protection Banks as an escape route, so did the association in Tianjin. As one of its directors said at a board meeting, "If the Market Protection Bank is formed, we can get out."[84] The association disbanded shortly thereafter, before any real resolution to the crisis had been found. The central government could not rely on the Tianjin elites any more than local elites could rely on the central government. In the end, no Market Protection Bank appeared in Tianjin or anywhere else in China.

With the bankruptcy of the central state apparent, Tianjin's elites turned to the local government to begin issuing money to take the place of the currency of the central state banks. The comprador Du Kechen suggested that the Zhili Provincial Bank issue 3 million yuan in paper money, to be used to withdraw the Tianjin and Zhili paper money of the Bank of China and the Bank of Communications from circulation. The other directors immediately approved his suggestion. Finally, the Tianjin Chamber of Commerce asked Zhu Jiabao to issue through the Zhili Provincial Bank 300,000 to 500,000 yuan, much less than the 3 million which had originally been envisioned. Although a small amount, this represented a significant retreat from the centralization of the money supply—and state power—which had been the hallmark of Yuan Shikai's presidency. Only a little more than a year earlier, the Tianjin County magistrate had issued an order prohibiting all kinds of paper money issued by public and private banks and *yinhao* from circulating in Tianjin. In light of the current crisis, Zhu Jiabao agreed to issue the provincial money, but only as a temporary measure. In fact, Zhu did his best later to obey repeated orders from the Finance Ministry to withdraw the notes from the market. Although future warlords would eagerly use the Zhili Provincial Bank to issue money to finance their regimes, Zhu Jiabao had no such intentions. The Tianjin Chamber of Commerce, however, opposed all moves to eliminate the provincial currency as harmful to Tianjin business.[85] This important step in the devolution of state power came not from a local militarist expanding his empire but from elite pressure to maintain the local currency supply.

The small amount of money issued by the Zhili Provincial Bank may have injected needed liquidity into Tianjin's financial markets, but it fell far short of replacing the currency of the Bank of China and the Bank of Communications. After Yuan Shikai died, a group of Tianjin elites petitioned the new president, Li Yuanhong, to cancel the moratorium on exchange. Once again it was not the Chamber itself which made the appeal but an ad hoc group set up for the purpose. Li Yuanhong responded that he would ask the cabinet to consider the matter.[86] In the end, Tianjin's local elites thrust the problems of the two banks back on the central state in demanding that the two banks reestablish exchange, and on the province in demanding that the Zhili Provincial Bank provide an infusion of liquidity into the local market. For Tianjin's native elite, monetary control and government financing were problems of the state. For the state's part, neither the central nor local governments had the ability to resolve the situation, and the two banks were left largely to their own devices.

In fits and starts over the course of several months, the Tianjin branches of the Bank of China and the Bank of Communications began to reinstitute first limited then full exchange of Tianjin and Zhili money. Resolution of the crisis in Beijing proved more difficult. The supply of Beijing notes on the market continued to balloon in order to finance central government deficits, eventually approaching 100 million yuan. Unexchangeable for silver, the Beijing notes became a commodity, bought and sold based on the level of speculators' belief that the government would eventually find a solution. Prices of Beijing notes eventually fell as low as fifty cents on the dollar, and five years would pass before the problem of the Beijing notes was completely resolved. In the meantime, the exchangeable notes of the Tianjin branches of the two banks gradually expanded in circulation, becoming an accepted currency of exchange in most of North China, including the capital. A new role for Tianjin—as a stable financial center and producer of a trustworthy paper currency in the midst of the chaos of republican politics—had begun.[87]

In 1916, at the urging of local authorities, Tianjin's native elite, led by the heads of the Chamber of Commerce, formed an ad hoc guardianship organization to guarantee the value of the Tianjin notes of the two banks. In forming this organization, Tianjin's native elites adopted a three-pronged strategy. First, they tried to insulate Tianjin and the local branches of the Bank of China and the Bank of Communications from events in the capital by refusing to support paper money issued by the Beijing branches of the banks. Second, they publicly pledged millions of silver yuan to support the association's activities and guarantee the value of the Tianjin notes of the two banks. Third, they appealed to broad, and fuzzily defined, notions of local native place, community loyalty, and even patriotism as the bases for rebuilding trust in the paper money of the two state banks. Their actions entailed constructing a local identity predicated on the assumption that city residents were willing to trust fellow Tianjin natives; but the local identity they constructed was ambiguously defined, centered sometimes on the city of Tianjin and sometimes on the province of Zhili. This ambiguity lay in the fact that native elites had to adjust to the structural conditions provided by the organization of the two banks and the provincial authorities with whom they cooperated. As Emily Honig has asserted, "Native place identity—no matter where and when in China—must be understood as a social and historical construct."[88] In addition, contrary to their public pronouncements, the native elites refused to provide significant funds for the effort, and the city's fledgling modern banks ended up standing alone in fact, if not in name. Ultimately, the most effective result of the elite mobilization was the assertion that the merchants and people of Tianjin would not take responsibility for Beijing paper currency. "Native place" and "locality" thus served as effective rallying cries in Tianjin to defy the central government, assert local prerogatives, and facilitate relations among elite leaders, but they could not serve as an effective basis for guardianship of trust in the medium of paper money.

The crisis of 1916 grew directly from the central government's financial problems, demonstrating the close links between the financial sector and government funding. Suspension of convertibility itself was not necessarily a problem; historical evidence shows frequent occurrences of suspension in Western countries in the eighteenth and nineteenth centuries.[89] The failure to enforce the suspension in China in 1916 exposed the inability of the state to use its authority to promote trust, a failure of both legitimacy and state power. The 1916 crisis also resulted in an important reversal of the trend toward centralizing the money supply, and thus a diminution of state power, when, after 1916, the Zhili Provincial Bank was back in the business of printing money. This devolution of power from the center to the locality as a result of the 1916 crisis, however, represented neither a simple rise in provincial militarism nor a claim to local government by an activist elite. Both elites and governments worked within the constraints of a financial system they could not completely control.

At the same time, central and local responses to the crisis demonstrate much about state-society relations. On the one hand, by stepping in to take over exchange operations of the Tianjin branches of the Bank of China and the Bank of Communications, Tianjin's native elite appeared to be following a time-honored pattern, dating back at least to the Taiping threat, of stepping in to protect the city when the central government failed. On the other hand, attempts by Zhili provincial and central government officials to push responsibility for guardianship onto local elites followed the traditional pattern of what Susan Mann, following Weber, calls liturgical governance, whereby local elite organizations undertake governance activities under state direction and supervision. In reality, the elites' actions in meeting the 1916 crisis conformed to yet another well-worn tradition of refusing to increase state revenues at local expense without something in return. These actions tended to reinforce the notion that guardianship of paper money was a state rather than a local responsibility. The uneasy balance of state-society relations seen during and after the crisis could best be described as a compromise between the inability of the central state to accomplish its goals and the unwillingness, or inability, of local native elites to step into the breach. The need for trust in bank money limited the state's ability to manipulate banking institutions, but at the same time, modern banks were too big, and their paper money circulated too widely, to allow localism or native place to substitute for the expert knowledge of professional bankers or adequate reserves as a basis for trust in bank currency.

Professional bankers, though, played little active role in the resolution of the 1916 crisis in Tianjin. The Tianjin banking industry was in its infancy at that time; it even lacked a trade association to coordinate local interests. Professionals at the Bank of China and the Bank of Communications continued to garner internal financial resources to recommence exchange of Tianjin paper money, but they worked mostly behind the scenes. Even Bian Baimei, who had resigned from the Bank of China after the moratorium was issued, continued to confer closely with the manager of the Tianjin branch and kept in contact with many of his former colleagues in Beijing, Tianjin, and Shanghai.[90] If 1916 marked a crisis for the state banks, it also marked an opening for new competition in the banking industry. In the years that followed, a large number of new private banks would make their homes in Tianjin. Bian Baimei himself would be working for one of these new banks within months of his resignation. Expansion of the banking industry in Tianjin would not forestall further financial crises, however.

3

Local Regulators, Paper Tigers, and Good Citizens

> The bank [of China] has become a "paper tiger," which looks good from the outside but is actually weak on the inside.
>
> — Bian Baimei, 1921

Between 1916 and 1921, the Chinese state fragmented as various warlords vied for control in the wake of Yuan Shikai's death. The military units of the old Beiyang Army began the process of breaking into what would become the Anhui clique under Duan Qirui, the Zhili clique under Feng Guozhang and Cao Kun, and the Fengtian clique under Zhang Zuolin. Although a central government continued to exist in Beijing, its hold over the rest of China varied over time, locality, and sector. Between 1916 and 1919, Duan Qirui and the Anhui clique wielded the predominant military and political power in Beijing, supported in part by the New Communications clique, headed by Cao Rulin after Liang Shiyi fled Beijing to avoid arrest.[1] Cao arranged for the Nishihara loans from Japan, which played an important part in government finances, but political fortunes could change rapidly during this period.[2] In 1918, Liang Shiyi returned to Beijing, where he served as head of the Bank of Communications under Cao as minister of communications.[3] Likewise, Duan Qirui's Anhui faction weakened over time, and in 1920 the Zhili clique defeated the Anhui forces in the Anhui-Zhili war. Jin Yunpeng became prime minister, marking an uneasy balance in North China between the Zhili and Fengtian factions.[4]

In comparison to national politics, the provincial administration of Zhili Province remained relatively stable under the control of the Zhili clique. Cao Kun replaced Zhu Jiabao as military governor in 1916, and he kept that position until 1922. He simultaneously held the civil governorship until 1918, when he decided to pursue national politics in Beijing, passing the civil governorship on to his brother Cao Rui. During this period Tianjin also began to acquire a new identity unique among Chinese cities. Tianjin's many foreign concessions provided a safe haven for warlords and officials who had fallen, or been forced, from power. Hidden behind the walls of their villas, wealthy retired militarists and other officials managed their investments, helping to launch enterprises ranging from cotton mills to banks, and planned their comebacks.[5]

The warlord period also saw a major expansion of the economy, brought about in part by the First World War.[6] During these years, China's modern banking industry grew rapidly, becoming one of the most dynamic sectors of the economy. The circulation of bank-issued paper money increased accordingly, making the issue of trust in currency more important for more people. As a result of this growth, Tianjin became a major domestic financial center.

The Institutionalization and Growth of Banking after 1916

As the 1916 crisis slowly wound down in the summer and early fall, Bian Baimei found himself unemployed and living in Tianjin. Once again, though, his skills and connections would come to the rescue. His old patron and his wife's relative, Sun Duosen, opened a private bank, the Zhongfu Bank, in Tianjin, and Bian found employment there. In fact, the end of Yuan Shikai's regime and the monetary crisis which hastened its passing in 1916 marked a dramatic rise in private modern Chinese banking in Tianjin. At the time of the 1916 crisis, only one private bank had its headquarters in Tianjin, but in the four years from 1916 to 1919, six more banks joined that one.[7] Five of these six banks became some of the largest and most successful private banks in the republic. Sun Duosen (Zhongfu Bank) and Zhou Xuexi (the National Industrial Bank) both founded banks in Tianjin as part of the expanding business groups that each managed.[8] The mix of backers for the latter represents a combination of older and newer factions, including Cao Rulin (head of the New Communications clique), Liang Shiyi (head of the Old Communications clique), Li Shiwei (a backer of Duan Qirui and former president of the Bank of China), Wang Kemin (a backer of Feng Guozhang and president of the Bank of China), and the professional banker Hu Bijiang (a former employee of the Bank of Communications). Tan Danya, a former manager at the Bank of China, opened the Continental Bank with backing from Feng Guozhang, a group of Yangzhou salt merchants, and a number of professional bankers. Lest Continental Bank seem simply a project of the emerging Zhili clique, though, it should be noted that the Anhui native and

Duan Qirui supporter Gong Xinzhan and Feng Guozhang's enemy Zhang Xun were also co-founders.[9] Another professional banker and former Bank of Communications employee, Zhou Zuomin, opened Jincheng Bank with backing from the Anhui military governor Ni Sichong in 1917.[10]

Of all of Tianjin's new private banks, Jincheng had the closest affiliation with a single political faction. The list of its founders reads like a who's who of Duan Qirui's Anhui clique in power in Beijing at the time. The relationship between bank and faction never had time to develop, however, because the Anhui clique quickly fell from power. Zhou Zuomin, for his part, managed to survive the decline in the fortunes of the Anhui clique. He proved to be a master at issuing new stock in order to expand his bank's capital base and ensure its continuity in the face of political change.[11] Finally, Wei Changyuan established Dasheng Bank with a group of Beijing officials in 1919. Unlike the other professional bankers who founded banks, Wei did not study abroad, but began his training as an apprentice at an indigenous bank in Tianjin before working for the Hubu Bank, Da Qing Bank, and the Bank of China. Dasheng's backers were just as eclectic as those of most other Tianjin banks.[12]

The remarkable expansion of Chinese banking in Tianjin after 1916 resulted from China's economic growth combined with political and institutional developments. The 1916 crisis had brought into question the stability of the two central state banks, undermining their dominant position, and providing a window of opportunity for potential competitors. As civil and military leaders competed for power and wealth, they began to invest in and found banks as part of their long-term strategy. Former officials from Yuan Shikai's administration, now unemployed, and militarists, feeling newly independent, were especially prominent. To manage the banks, a number of young, often foreign-educated bankers who had been trained at the Bank of China and the Bank of Communications left state service and entered the private sector. In many cases these two state banks had provided the venue where officials and professional bankers made the connections with one another that would enable them to cooperate in founding private banks in Tianjin after 1916.[13]

Although many of the backers of the new banks were either civil or military officials, Tianjin's banks were less closely identified with factional politics than one would expect. As Andrew Nathan has noted, the boards of directors of Beijing and Tianjin banks were usually balanced between professional bankers and men from more than one political faction.[14] In addition, the leading private banks in North China came into existence between 1916 and 1919, but the political changes of 1919 and 1920 completely changed the lines of patronage and political affiliation in North China. Most important, as joint-stock organizations, banks were structurally incompatible with factional affiliation. By their nature, joint-stock corporations have an institutional life of their own and continuity beyond the whims of any one stockholder or group of stockholders. Officials and militarists invested in Tianjin's banks as individuals, and though their political and private interests could not be completely separated, they had a vested interest in the strength and continuity of these banks beyond their own potentially short official careers. Planning and opening a modern bank took as much as a year or two—sometimes longer—and any bank which made it through the planning stages had most likely already outlasted at least one factional shift before it opened its doors. Because of their large capital requirements and reliance on trust, banks differed from newspapers, which could sprout up quickly to support particular factional interests.[15] Their requirements for capital and management simply made banks too big to be the products or supporters of any one faction, and these conditions gave considerable power to their professional managers.[16]

The managers who staffed Tianjin's new banks came from three distinct groups. First, men who had worked as official-managers during the late Qing and early republican period, such as Sun Duosen and Zhou Xuexi, founded and managed banks as part of their enterprise groups. Second, there were members of Bian Baimei's generation, such as Tan Danya and Zhou Zuomin, who had studied business or economics abroad then gained experience at the Bank of China and Bank of Communications before moving on to the private sector. Third, men from both generations who had apprenticed at Tianjin's indigenous banks, such as Wei Changyuan, also moved into the modern banking sector. Former indigenous bank employees were mainly Tianjin or Zhili natives, but the other two groups consisted of outsiders, especially natives of Zhejiang, Jiangsu, and Anhui provinces, who dominated the upper ranks of bank management. These outsiders had close ties to professional bankers in Beijing, Shanghai, and other cities which provided a basis for cooperation and communal action.

As the Bank of China tried to adjust to the aftermath of the 1916 crisis, a new management team came to Beijing, including Zhang Jia'ao (Gongquan, 1888–1979), a Japanese-educated Jiangsu native. Zhang, who had served as assistant manager of the Shanghai branch during its epic stand against Yuan

Shikai's moratorium on exchange in 1916, was brought to Beijing as chief vice president of the bank in 1918. Zhang was from a prominent family; his older brother Zhang Jia'sen (Carson Chang) was a close associate of Liang Qichao, who became finance minister for a brief time in 1917, facilitating Zhang Jia'ao's rise within the Bank of China. Zhang serves as one of the best-known models of the professional banker from the republican period.[17] His close links to the state and his own political ambitions should not be overlooked, however. He first reestablished his family's declining fortunes by becoming secretary to the provincial governor of Jiangsu and then moved on to work for the Bank of China.[18] One need not accept the post-1949 assessment of Zhang's former boss at the Bank of China, Feng Gengguang, that Zhang was a "political manipulator and fast talker" to understand that Zhang was less independent from political affairs than he later claimed.[19] Zhang himself admitted that he had to make a lot of compromises with the political authorities.[20] As vice president, he provided managerial continuity during the frequent changes of political regimes in warlord China. From 1917 to 1923, the presidency of the Bank of China alternated between the Japanese-educated Guangdong native Feng Gengguang and the former Qing period official Wang Kemin. When Wang had a government position, Feng Gengguang would be Bank of China president, but when Wang was out of office, he would serve as Bank of China president himself. In and out of office, he took responsibility for managing the relations between the Bank of China and the central government in Beijing during the warlord period.[21]

Revision of the Bank of China's charter in 1917 gave new power to the bank's private shareholders and professional managers.[22] Under the new charter, the government still appointed the bank's president and vice president, but they had to be chosen from among the members of the board of directors, themselves elected by the stockholders. At the time, "as the government controlled about half of the bank's shares as well as the power to appoint the governor and deputy governor, there was no fear that the bank would try to be independent from it."[23] In 1921 the Bank of China issued additional shares, providing a chance to dilute the government's influence. Bian Baimei, who had left Zhongfu Bank to serve as manager of the Tianjin branch of the Bank of China, noted in his diary, "In truth, the Ministry intends to control the bank . . . If bank operations are controlled for the purpose of political struggles, that would truly be a misfortune for the country."[24] Bian's words proved prophetic. The bank's lack of independence quickly became apparent a few months later when massive loans to the central government in Beijing threatened the stability of the bank.

Unlike the Bank of China, whose managers struggled with competing professional and political demands, the Bank of Communications remained much more a tool of factional struggles. Liang Shiyi had helped engineer the financial legerdemain that supported Yuan Shikai, and his return from exile in Japan did not help morale at the bank. In January 1921, Bian Baimei observed that "the internal fights at the Bank of Communications are extreme" since Liang Shiyi had recently taken over authority over personnel.[25] In general, the Bank of Communications had even closer financial ties to the state, and as a result less financial stability, than the Bank of China. The precariousness of its position would come to the fore again in 1921.

With the institutional growth of banking, the years after 1916 witnessed a dramatic increase in the collective activities of bankers, most visibly with the establishment of bankers' associations. First in Shanghai and then in cities all over China, managers at private and state banks banded together to form these professional associations. As Marie-Claire Bergère has noted for Shanghai, existing networks of acquaintance and native-place affiliation helped facilitate formation of the bankers' associations.[26] Likewise, in spite of rivalries among banks, most of the professionals who staffed the upper levels of Tianjin's private and state banks came from one of four provinces: Zhili, Zhejiang, Jiangsu, and Anhui. In addition, many of them had studied together in Japan or the United States, and most of them had worked together at either the Bank of China or the Bank of Communications.[27] These traditional forms of solidarity facilitated the formation of bankers' associations but did not define them. Unlike many of Tianjin's traditional guilds, all banks that met minimum criteria could join the bankers' association, regardless of the native place of their owners or managers.[28] Within a year of its founding, the Tianjin Bankers' Association had eighteen members, representing every major bank with an office in Tianjin.[29] Bian Baimei became chairman of the association in March 1920, beginning a fifteen-year administration. Initially the new bankers' associations were founded under the Finance Ministry regulations published in 1915 covering both modern and indigenous banks under one set of rules, but no indigenous banks joined the Tianjin Bankers' Association. Indigenous bankers had their own professional association in Tianjin, and there was no question of mixing with modern banks in a combined organization. The Finance Ministry issued new regulations in August 1918 that covered only modern banks, recognizing the reality that modern and indigenous banks had distinct identities.[30]

The problem of paper money provided China's bankers with ample opportunity to work together. In the wake of the 1916 crisis, Beijing paper money of the Bank of China and the Bank of Communications remained unexchangeable for silver. The Beijing government continued to force the two banks to issue money stamped with the Beijing place-name—to pay bills and government employees' salaries—but the paper money declined in value, fetching as little as fifty cents on the dollar in exchange for silver or other currencies. At its high point in 1917, the Beijing government owed the Bank of China and the Bank of Communications a total of more than 90 million yuan, and the outstanding Beijing paper money of the two banks equaled a like amount. Initial attempts to begin exchange for this massive amount of paper money failed, but in 1918 a group of Chinese banks acting collectively persuaded the government to issue more than 60 million yuan in new government bonds; the proceeds were used to buy back some of the Beijing notes. In 1920 the government issued additional bonds, and most of the remaining Beijing notes were withdrawn from the market.[31]

Even without resolution of the Beijing note problem, trust in the Tianjin notes of the Bank of China and the Bank of Communications had recovered. As Beijing notes became less viable, Tianjin notes became the standard currency of the two banks in the Tianjin-Beijing area. The Tianjin branch of the Bank of China even set up a Tianjin currency exchange office in the capital in order to promote circulation of its paper money there.[32] The patriotic movements of the 1910s also helped the recovery of credibility. As early as 1916, Tianjin residents were asked to boycott money issued by French banks in China as part of the protest against plans to build a church at Laoxikai in the French Concession. At that time, Tianjin shopkeepers posted notices at the doorways of their shops reading, "No French money accepted."[33] On the national level, during the May Fourth Movement, activists sponsored a boycott of the currency issued by the Yokohama Specie Bank, resulting in a drop in circulation from more than 22 million yen in 1918 to just over 3 million yen in 1923.[34] Although the Japanese compensated by replacing Yokohama Specie paper money with gold notes issued by the Japanese-controlled Bank of Korea (Chaoxian Bank), the association of foreign money with foreign imperialism had become a potentially potent weapon for promoting the currency of the Chinese state banks by the 1920s.

The strength of the state bank currencies also resulted in another kind of bank cooperation: the widespread practice of issuing so-called adopted *(lingyong)* banknotes. Many of China's new private banks that did not issue money themselves contracted to issue money through a bank that did, especially the Bank of China. The adopting bank would place a reserve of silver on deposit with the issuing bank, and it would be allocated a certain number of banknotes. To the average user of currency, these "adopted" banknotes appeared no different from any other paper money of the issuing bank. Only the two banks in question knew the identity of the real issuer, keeping track by use of special serial numbers and other secret marks.[35] This practice also provided a certain level of risk sharing. In the case of a bank run, covering at least some of the notes brought in for exchange to silver would be the responsibility of the adopting bank. Of course, banks that wanted to adopt banknotes sought out issuers with the most trustworthy reputations in order to minimize the risk.

Government finance provided the most fertile field for cooperation, as banks desired to participate in this lucrative business while at the same time sharing risks with other banks. Foreign bank consortiums, which had been making loans to the Chinese government since the late nineteenth century, offered ample precedent for this kind of cooperation.[36] Formation of a new foreign bank consortium in 1919 and 1920 even prompted the first national meeting of Chinese bankers' associations in Shanghai in 1920.[37] The foreign consortiums, however, usually broke down in internecine fighting in only a short time—often before the loan was even made—and the new consortium came together in 1920 only with great difficulty.[38] Chinese bank cooperation in government financing proved more durable, though ad hoc and flexible arrangements far outnumbered formal consortiums. Over time, banks would develop methods of limiting risks on government loans. The period between 1916 and 1921 provided a testing ground for learning how to deal with warlord governments. In their most successful, and most formal, arrangement, a group of Chinese bankers forced the central government to sign a consolidated loan agreement in March 1921. The agreement placed customs surpluses in the hands of the inspector general of customs, Sir Frances Aglen, to create a sinking fund for the repayment of certain government bonds.[39]

Fresh from their success with the consolidated loan agreement, China's bankers faced another challenge when in July the Sino-French Banque Industrielle de Chine (Zhongfa Shiye Yinhang) failed, leaving holders of its paper money stranded. Bankers' Associations in Beijing and Tianjin worked together to alleviate public distress by acting as guardians and cashing outstanding notes of the defunct Sino-French bank for silver. The rescue operation succeeded admirably, and the affairs of the Banque Industrielle concluded without any undue social unrest. The Bank of China and the Tianjin and Beijing Bankers' Associations stepped in to help the Banque Industrielle de Chine partly because Wang Kemin—on-again/off-again head of the Bank of China and former finance minister—was a major investor in the bank. Bian Baimei met with Wang many times over the course of 1921 about Banque Industrielle's troubles, and Wang repeatedly urged him (and others at the Bank of China) to help. Bian even remarked in his diary that the manager of the Banque Industrielle was "very cunning. No wonder people without any learning, like Wang Kemin, etc., were fooled by him."[40] Professional managers may have been gaining strength, but they still had to bow to the wishes of "unlearned" politicians like Wang Kemin.

Much bank involvement in government finance walked the same fine line between professional practice and the behind-the-scenes machinations of warlord politics. Hardly a day went by that Bian Baimei, as manager of the Tianjin branch of the Bank of China, did not deal with government finance in one way or another, and rarely did government finance appear as neat and tidy as in the consolidated loan agreement of 1921. For example, in January 1921 the Finance Ministry tried to borrow 6 million yuan from a foreign bank, using 1912 bonds issued by the Chinese government as security. A Finance Ministry official called Bian's house in the middle of the night to ask him to vouch for the value of the bonds in case the foreign bank made inquiries. Bian's servant refused to wake up his master; but hearing about the phone call the next day, Bian, after conferring with colleagues at the Bank of China, concluded that he could say only that since the bonds "are issued by the Finance Ministry, then they have value." Caught between their duty to help the government and their duty not to lie about the questionable value of the bonds, Bian and his colleagues chose a middle ground of diplomatic doublespeak. At the same time, Wang Kemin heard that the Beijing Bankers' Association opposed issuing new bonds to act as collateral for loans. Not bound by any such scruples, he decided to ask Zhou Ziqi to intercede as a personal favor.[41] Although the Bank of China had a new charter and a new independence, its ties to the Finance Ministry and the Beiyang government in Beijing remained strong.

To all outside appearances, though, by 1921 the institutionalization of bank professionalism had triumphed over government interference. Rapid expansion of the banking industry, the rise to prominence of a group of foreign-trained professional bankers, success in forcing the government to deal with the Beijing notes left over from the crisis of 1916, the consolidated loan agreement, and formation of bankers' associations all over China gave the impression that the banking sector made for a powerful and independent force in China. The tiger of Chinese modern banking appeared to be both healthy and strong. For Bian Baimei in particular, 1921 started out as a promising year. In February he successfully mediated between a group of Tianjin cloth merchants and a group of foreign bankers to whom they owed money, thereby increasing his stature in both the Chinese and foreign communities in Tianjin, reflecting the importance and strength of the banking industry.[42] The Bank of China and the Bank of Communications were still loaning massive amounts of money to the Beijing government, however, and by October 1921, rumors again began circulating that the banks would default on exchange of currency for silver. No sooner had the last of the Beijing notes, inconvertible since 1916, been withdrawn from the market than bank runs began again on the Tianjin notes of the two banks, threatening to prove that the tiger was indeed made of paper.

The 1921 Bank Run

In the early fall of 1921 the central government engaged in a mad scramble for money. The Communications Ministry sought a loan of 2.8 million yuan and the Finance Ministry a loan of 2 million. The Tianjin and Beijing Bankers' Associations met individually, and bankers in the two cities conferred as proposals and counterproposals passed along the telegraph cables and telephone lines. Under a risk-sharing formula, a group of five banks, including the Bank of China and the Bank of Communications, agreed to come up with 450,000 yuan for the Ministry of Communications, but this fell far short of the ministry's demand. Likewise, the Finance Ministry's demand that the Bank of China and the Bank of Communications each take 500,000 yuan of the Finance Ministry loan and then underwrite the balance remained unsettled.[43] As negotiations dragged on, the government's financial crisis became increasingly public. It was common knowledge that the government was in arrears in paying salaries, and that the employees of the Finance Ministry, the Judiciary Ministry, and the Education Ministry had all threatened to strike.[44] The common perception portrayed in the press in both Beijing and Tianjin was that the government was in desperate straits. These problems had an immediate impact on both the Bank of China and the Bank of Communications because each had large outstanding debts to the central government.[45] With the discontinuance of Beijing notes after 1916, the Beijing branches of the Bank of China and Bank of Communications could not freely issue currency in order to finance loans to the government. Instead, they turned to their healthier Tianjin counterparts for funds. The Tianjin Bank of Communications financed its Beijing counterpart by making a special currency issue designated for the Beijing branch. The Tianjin Bank of China simply loaned large amounts of money to its Beijing counterpart. In fact, Bian Baimei had worried about loans from the Tianjin branch to the Beijing branch as early as January, and in August he wrote to the Beijing branch again asking that the loans be repaid as soon as possible.[46]

The catalyst that turned rumor into bank run is a matter of some dispute. In Tianjin, initial reports on the crisis attributed the cause to a combination of financial difficulties on the part of the government and a few wicked people *(jianren)* who spread rumors.[47] The Tianjin police department blamed the entire crisis on evil merchants *(jianshang)* who fabricated rumors for their own personal benefit. In fact, the police went so far as to imply that the banks were sound.[48] Many would later claim that the general inspector of customs, Sir Francis Aglen, issued an order that the paper currency of the Bank of China and the Bank of Communications would not be accepted for customs payments. Bian Baimei, however, made no indication in his diary that such an order had been issued, and neither the archives of the Tianjin Bankers' Association nor those of the Tianjin branch of the Bank of China contain any reference to such an order or a foreign conspiracy. In fact, it was five days into the bank run before there was any suggestion of a foreign conspiracy in Tianjin's press. On that day *Dagong Bao* printed a Shanghai cable claiming that an unnamed person had intentionally disrupted the market by proposing that the foreign powers take joint control of China's finances. Although none of the sources named Aglen directly, he was the only foreign individual in a position to issue the alleged order. Students in Beijing immediately took up the cry, distributing flyers asking people to support the two banks for patriotic reasons.[49] On all sides there were calls for Aglen to disburse surplus customs funds to save the two banks. He refused, claiming that he was bound by the consolidated loan agreement signed by the government and by foreign and Chinese bankers to reserve customs surplus funds to repay government debts.[50] Aglen's refusal added fuel to the fire, making claims of both a foreign plot and his involvement more believable. From a contractual standpoint, Aglen certainly had little leeway to bail out the two banks. He was in fact bound by the 1921 consolidated loan agreement to use the funds in his hands to repay specified bond issues. Nonetheless, charges of a foreign plot deflected attention from the bankruptcy of the central government.

The ongoing Washington Conference on the Pacific lent credence to rumors that foreigners were planning to intervene in China's chaotic financial situation. The conference was one of the most important events affecting China in 1921, and it served as an integral part of the background to the November bank run. Organizers of the conference intended to resolve unsettled issues in the Far East, including Japan's position in Shandong. All of the major European powers with interests in the Far East, as well as the United States, Japan, and China, sent delegations to the conference. In China there was a perception that the nation's fate would be decided at the conference.[51] Coming one year after the formation of the new foreign banking consortium and its announcement about conditions for future loans to China, the Washington Conference raised suspicions in China that the foreign powers wanted increased interference in China's finances. "From the standpoint of China's financial circles, much of China's revenues were in the control of the foreign consortium. If the foreigners had taken control of the currency system, then China's financial power and influence would have been completely lost."[52] In 1921 the conference lent credibility to claims that foreign rumors had started the bank run as a means to discredit the state banks and as an excuse for more foreign interference in China's financial affairs.[53]

Regardless of Aglen's culpability, the ultimate cause of the crisis lay with the financial demands of the central government on the two banks. The internal report prepared by the Tianjin branch of the Bank of China blamed loans by the Beijing branch to the government, and years later Lin Xisheng, the manager of the Tianjin branch of the Bank of Communications, confessed to Bian that his bank's financial condition had been strong in 1921 prior to a sudden 4 million yuan loan to the Finance Ministry.[54] People began lining up at branches of the Bank of China and the Bank of Communications in Beijing to withdraw their savings and exchange their paper money for silver on November 15, 1921. The next day the bank run spread to Tianjin. Both banks began limiting exchange of paper money for silver to 10 yuan per person. Ten policemen were sent to keep order at the Bank of Communications branch in the Chinese part of the city. More than one thousand people were gathered outside the branch's doors. The crush even overcame the usually intimidating presence of police chief Yang Yide, who had to retreat from the crowd and find safety inside the bank. In the French Concession, authorities reputedly dispatched four hundred policemen to control the crowds at the main branch of the Bank of China. In one day the branch cashed about 1 million yuan in paper money, or one quarter of its total circulation, for silver.[55]

Chamber of Commerce leaders called a special meeting and summoned the Tianjin managers of the two banks, who agreed to take responsibility for paper money used to purchase rice and flour in the city. That same night the Tianjin Bankers' Association held an emergency meeting to pass such a resolution. The following day three hundred people attended another special meeting of the Chamber of Commerce, and a delegation was selected to go with Yang Yide to the provincial governor, Cao Rui, and reaffirm the measures already in effect. More police were dispatched, and Yang Yide reprised his role as the keeper of order in a time of financial crisis. Local elites publicized the guarantee of banknotes used to purchase rice and flour, and other businesses were ordered to accept the paper money of the two banks. Most important, Yang Yide, in concert with the Chamber of Commerce, ordered the Tianjin branches of the banks to report on their financial condition. Rather than repeat the ill-fated 1916 attempt to act as lender of last resort, local political and commercial elites took on the role of regulators, supervising audits and guaranteeing not the value of the banks' currency but the overall financial condition of the banks, seeing that they adhered to the standards of the expert knowledge of banking. Their report was later summarized at a public meeting and even published in the newspapers. Tianjin's *Dagong Bao* reported a few days later that the two banks had collateral goods to guarantee the value of their paper money to the sum of more than 10 million yuan. In truth, the public reports about the financial condition of the two banks were quite euphemistic. For example, the Tianjin branch of the Bank of China had loaned 2,123,938 yuan (nearly 20 percent of its total assets) to the Beijing branch of the bank, and the Tianjin branch had only 254,238 yuan in silver to cover outstanding paper money of 4.45 million yuan.[56] Instead of using their reputations (though not their pocketbooks) in an ill-conceived move to cash paper money, as in 1916, in 1921 the local elites used their reputations to *re-represent* the financial condition of the banks to the Tianjin public.

The most disturbing result of the audit was the discovery that a large portion of the "Tianjin" paper money issued by the Bank of Communications was actually Beijing money in disguise. In an interesting twist on the practice of "adopting" currency, it turned out that some of the banknotes, which were clearly stamped "Tianjin," also had an unobtrusive "H," indicating that they were instead the responsibility of the Bank of Communications' Beijing branch. In fact, more than 4.7 million yuan in these masquerading notes was in circulation at the time of the 1921 bank run. The underlying assumption behind local currency stipulated that the silver reserves backing the paper money be in the issuing branch. Therefore, the silver reserves backing Tianjin currency should have been in Tianjin, under the responsibility of the Tianjin manager and, at least theoretically, one step removed from interference by the Beijing government. The fact that the silver reserves for and the management of the so-called "H" Tianjin notes lay not in Tianjin but in Beijing represented a serious breach of trust. Not only had the Tianjin Bank of Communications violated the tenets of local trust by lending money to its Beijing counterpart, but also, even worse, it had openly deceived the public by passing Beijing money off as Tianjin money. This fraud would catalyze Tianjin's local elites into a flurry of activity and rhetorical excess. In the meantime, however, the bank run continued, and, as in 1916, the two banks were left to their own devices to resolve the situation.

The banks responded by limiting exchange while they tried to raise funds. The more stable Bank of China could rely on its extensive branch system. The bank simply transferred funds from its southern branches to Tianjin, and full exchange began on December 1. The Tianjin Bank of Communications was in more desperate straits. Because of the bank's weak financial condition, the leaders of the Tianjin Chamber of Commerce were not content with merely inspecting the books; they actually sealed up securities (mostly government bonds) owned by the bank as collateral to guarantee the bank's outstanding paper currency. Although this may have put the minds of the Chamber leaders at rest, it still did not provide a way for the Bank of Communications to restore unlimited exchange of its paper money for silver. Eventually the Fengtian militarist Zhang Zuolin stepped in and loaned 4 million yuan to the Bank of Communications through the provincial bank which he controlled.[57] With this loan the Bank of Communications began exchanging its paper money, thus setting a precedent whereby Chinese bankers initiated direct negotiations with militarists. Tianjin banks and bank money soon became the object of competition among warlords outside the central government.[58]

Local Elite Regulation

The choice by local elites to opt for regulation instead of direct guardianship during the 1921 crisis reflected prudence in light of the failure of guardianship in 1916 as well as recognition of the growth and institutionalization of the banking sector. The size of banks and the scope of bank-issued paper money left no illusions that local elites could, or would want to, simply step into the shoes of the banks and take responsibility for guaranteeing the value of the money supply. Local elite regulation worked best, however, when elites faced immediate threats to local economic stability. Ongoing regulation and supervision of bank activities proved more difficult, and, as with guardianship in 1916, the motivation to continue faded along with the urgency of the crisis.

Localism remained a potent motivating force in elite regulation of banks prompted by the 1921 crisis, but this time "localism" referred simply to the city of Tianjin, losing the connections with both native place and Zhili Province that had made it such an ambiguous concept in 1916. Since 1916, Bian Yinchang had become chairman of the Tianjin Chamber of Commerce, but he was sick and could not attend the first meeting of the expanded Chamber on November 17. Sun Junqing, another Chamber leader and Tianjin native, took his place and spoke about the close link between the health of the two banks and that of the city of Tianjin: "The Tianjin banks of China and Communications are the arteries of all of Tianjin. If there is a change in the rudder, Tianjin will follow it under. Therefore, it is necessary that the two banks support themselves, that the government authorities support them, that the Chamber of Commerce, the Bankers' Association, and the Native Bankers' Association together support them. Supporting the banks of China and Communications is like supporting yourself."[59] Unlike the Chamber leaders and local officials who had spoken at similar meetings in 1916, Sun made no reference to native Tianjiners, either as a badge of purity or as a call for unity. In addition, since this time elites had not formed an organization to act as lender of last resort, there was no need to include the rest of Zhili Province. Sun's localism referred simply to the city of Tianjin. His appeal focused on equating the interests of the community with the interests of the banks; thus he specifically excluded other branches of the banks by referring to "the Tianjin banks of China and Communications." In adding that the Chamber of Commerce, the Bankers' Association, and the Indigenous Bankers' Association, all local organizations, had agreed to support the two banks, he conveniently left the meaning of "support" vague. This kind of empty rhetoric probably did little to stem the bank run, but it did make the position of the Chamber clear. Local elite responsibilities began and ended at the city limits.[60]

Discovery of the Beijing "H" notes issued by the Bank of Communications under the Tianjin place-name inspired more stirring rhetoric and more concrete action. As newspapers reported that one could distinguish these false "Tianjin" notes by looking for "English writing" on them (a reference to the "H" mark), Bian Yinchang, recovered from his illness, wrote an outraged letter to the Beijing office of the Bank of Communications:

> These secretly marked paper bills circulated in Tianjin absorbing our cash, deceiving merchants and the people. Where is the credibility of the nation [*guojia*]? . . . Your bank should make up the deficit with a good heart quickly in order to preserve popular trust in the state.
>
> Even more painful are the men and women who recently brought their paper money to cash [for silver]. [They] stood waiting in the street all night, lined up in single file. The army and the police suppressed [harassed] them and they did not dare disturb order. The north wind was piercingly cold, the winter chill pushed them to the limit. In comparison with them, those who printed banknotes under a false [place] name sucked up silver. [Their] tall buildings were warm. [They] enjoyed [their] good fortune. They are as different [from those people who waited in the cold to cash their paper money] as heaven and earth . . . We insist that the 2 million in silver be provided within two weeks.[61]

Bian Yinchang's indictment is clear. Outsiders had deceived the people of Tianjin and sucked up the resources, the vital essence, of Tianjin's local community by passing off Beijing notes as Tianjin money. He even asks, "Where is the credibility of the nation?" implying that local distrust of a state bank could easily translate into a local lack of legitimacy for the country.

In the end, the Bank of Communications agreed to withdraw the "H" notes and end its improper use of the Tianjin place-name. As the Bank of Communications used its newfound funds from the warlord Zhang Zuolin to withdraw its "H" notes from the market, the Tianjin Chamber even sent a representative to Beijing to witness the destruction of the offending paper. Newspapers duly published reports on the destruction of these notes for the benefit of Tianjin readers.[62] This bit of political theater is an extraordinary example of the reach of regulation of the money supply and protection of the locality by Tianjin's elites.

In addition to their rhetorical use of localism and nationalism, the local elites' response to the crisis in 1921 also included auditing the books of the two banks to assert the primacy of local trust over bank secrecy. As the crisis wound down, Chamber leaders took steps to institute regular supervision of bank currency and reserves. In a letter to the Tianjin Bankers' Association, Chamber leaders stated that "banks are the fulcrum of finance and control the economy. All of the trades and industries are concerned and regulation of society's financial profits and losses depends on them. When it is a matter of public interest, the state's laws [*guofa*] can impose limits." The letter goes on to require that all banks which issue money "make timely reports to the Chamber." The Chamber, in turn, would examine the reports and "make them public in the market to increase credibility, eliminate suspicions, and stabilize finance."[63] It is interesting to note that the Chamber imposed limits on the operations of banks not in the name of the locality but in the name of the state's laws. Leaders of the Tianjin Chamber may have been willing to act as a regulatory organization for banks and bank money, but they wanted to do so within a larger and more legitimate framework than just that of local prerogative. By asking banks to report on and publicize their currency and reserve statistics, the Chamber leaders flatly rejected the idea that secrecy should be a basis for trust, and they worked hard to publicize their efforts at policing the bank. At one point in early 1922, Tianjin's newspapers published a letter from the Chamber of Commerce to the Tianjin Bankers' Association notifying the bankers of the Chamber's intent to examine currency reserves before the bankers received it.[64] This kind of public exposure was a key part of Chamber strategy. Openness worked to guarantee bank professionalism only when public pressure for trust, or the threat of public disorder in the absence of trust, backed Chamber supervision. More fundamentally, the Chamber's moves to publicize bank reserves represented an implicit acceptance of the rules of the game for modern banking. In this particular case, those rules stipulated that banks had to keep a certain percentage of their currency issue in silver reserves. The underlying message of public supervision, then, worked to reinforce the idea that the safety of modern financial institutions depended on the application of particular forms of expert knowledge.

Bankers themselves were of two minds about secrecy. On the one hand, secrecy coincided with one view of the relationship between expert knowledge and impersonal trust which relied on the reputation of banks and bankers to engender trust. If nothing else, secrecy also provided flexibility in managing bank reserves so bankers could deal with government demands for loans without unnecessarily alarming the public. On the other hand, disclosure coincided with a contrary view which relied on openness and transparency to create trust. Bankers, too, could use public disclosure of currency and reserve figures to put pressure on the government not to abuse bank lending practices.

The relative advantages and disadvantages of secrecy and disclosure confronted Tianjin's bankers with a very real dilemma. As the crisis developed in 1921, the Bank of China's main office repeatedly ordered Bian Baimei, then manager of the Tianjin branch of the Bank of China and protector of the credibility of Tianjin notes, to lend money to the Beijing branch for government use. In one scathing letter Bian refused, threatening to resign if forced to endanger the viability of the Tianjin branch. The bank, he wrote, has become a "paper tiger," which looks good from the outside but is actually weak on the inside. Bian Baimei was caught between government demands for loans and the need to maintain public faith in the Bank of China. His contact in Beijing, in the same predicament, concluded that the job of China's professional bankers was to ensure that the public not realize that this tiger was in fact made of paper. He responded when Bian threatened to resign:

> As for the situation of our bank and your reference to a paper tiger, keeping the people in the dark is our general goal. The important employees of our bank [referring to Bian Baimei himself] should remain determined and forceful in order to give outsiders the impression that we have good backing and nothing to fear. Then the rumors will cease of themselves.
>
> If outsiders knew that an important employee of the bank had requested to resign, they would either think that the bank's operations were in trouble or that the general office was not willing to take care of matters at the Tianjin branch . . . I request that you don't mention it again, either inside or outside the bank. Otherwise outsiders will become suspicious, especially for someone as strong and direct as you. Without people like you, we couldn't get outsiders to trust us [*qu xin yu wairen*].[65]

According to this reasoning, the bank needed strong and upright agents to inspire confidence, and those professionals had the unpleasant duty of lying in order to keep the bank's internal condition a secret, since government borrowing had created a situation in which the bank truly was weak. In other words, the public (here the people of Beijing and Tianjin) had to be fooled into believing that the tiger was flesh and bone by means of the assumption that honest bankers would not lie. Finally, people in local areas had to be certain that nonlocal priorities would not threaten their interests. Appearances had to be kept up that the main office was "taking care of" the Tianjin branch, and that regional or national concerns would not violate the tenets of local trust.

In the end, local elites' demands for disclosure won out over bankers' desires for secrecy, at least for a time. In accordance with Chamber of Commerce wishes, the Bank of China and the Bank of Communications in Tianjin began regularly disclosing their reserve statistics. Tianjin was the only city where the banks implemented the open reserves policy as early as 1921, thus demonstrating the strength of demands for local credibility. Reserves of the other branches of the two banks would not be opened to public inspection until 1928. Tianjin's precociousness resulted from two factors. First, propinquity to Beijing heightened the potential threat of central government interference in Tianjin's banks, forcing local elites to look for ways to protect local interests from the state. Second, the entrenched local elite was suspicious of outsiders, and the public pressure for making bank reserves open served as an effective weapon to ensure that supra-local banks and their cosmopolitan managers would not violate the tenets of local trust. Local zeal for bank supervision faded along with memories of the crisis in the 1920s, but the principle of openness as a means of engendering trust would persist until it was codified into law by the Nationalist government.

Another vision of trust, this one involving the responsibilities of patriotic citizens to understand and have faith in modern institutions such as banks, emerged during the 1921 crisis. The scholar Ma Yinchu lectured Beijing University students on the nature of banking and paper money in a version of the real bills doctrine.[66] In his view paper money represented not silver but the goods financed by bank loans. As a result, the amount of paper money expands and contracts with the circulation of goods, and bank runs are completely unnecessary.[67] Ma overlooked the point that the Bank of China and the Bank of Communications had financed the government, not goods, in 1921, buying into the mistaken argument that banks financed commerce rather than state building. In a similar vein, localism, nationalism, and reliance on the expert knowledge of banking all came together when the provincial bureaucrats who ran the Zhili Social Education Bureau enunciated this public duty in the "Money Scare Vernacular Song."[68] Intended to educate Tianjin's residents in the technical details of bank-issued paper money, the song expressed an implicit assumption that the workings of modern banks were transparent and needed no further disclosure. The song provides a fascinating glimpse into an emerging vision of the relationship between banks and a responsible citizenry, and is worth quoting at length.[69] It opens by describing the financial crisis, placing the Bank of China and the Bank of Communications in their context as "state" banks which are vital to the health of the nation:

> Recently a money scare, Beijing, Tianjin, Shanghai, Hankou all involved.
> Bonds fell, currency ran, the two banks almost went under.
> Half merchant–half government, as the state treasury [the banks] still part of the center
> If a bank run really puts them under, the country's markets will stagnate.

By referring to the money scare as a nationwide phenomenon, the writer tried to make Tianjin's case seem nothing out of the ordinary. In this version of the events, Tianjin's crisis was portrayed as part of a general phenomenon striking the major cities of China. This portrayal sets up the background for the primary argument, that the bank run was the result of a misunderstanding of economic principles by the Chinese people, not the result of government mismanagement of finances.

To present this financial principle, the writer first calls on a foreign example to show that China's situation is no different, and that all countries are subject to the same economic rules:

> Using paper money is a good thing, easy to carry and easy to save
> All of the countries of the world are like this and all have national banks.
> If reserves are sufficient, credit is good and people use currency without fear
> Paper money is not a silver substitute, it is a vehicle for the circulation of goods.
> No country in the world has a dollar of reserves for every dollar of currency
> [Economists can attest to this principle][70]

> If currency were all cashed at the same time, any bank would be hard-pressed.

The principle is that paper money, like silver, is a circulating medium. Although this argument denies the entire rationale for a convertible currency, the writer does not go so far as to advocate an inconvertible paper money. Instead, he discusses the principle of bank reserves, pointing out that only a portion of paper money in circulation is backed by silver reserves at any given time. Once again, he calls on the authority of universal economic principles, stating that all banks in all countries are the same. With the economic principles established, the lyrics shift to the crux of the argument. The Chinese people do not understand these economic principles:

> Too bad our country's people don't understand this principle, all say silver is sweetest
> If the wind blows or the grass moves, everyone rushes to cash in paper for silver.

The premise, then, is that misunderstanding of economic principles caused the crisis. No mention is made of heavy government borrowing from the banks or their inadequate reserves.

To make the obfuscation complete, the writer, like the Tianjin press, shifts attention to foreigners:

> Another important matter, don't have superstitious belief in foreign banks
> Foreign banks are not completely reliable, sometimes they're empty shells.
> For example: the Bank of the Philippines and the Banque Industrielle
> Draining your own blood is like helping a fat man gain weight.
> If our money flows to foreign banks, blue-eyed fat-stomached merchants will think it great
> When our country has trouble, foreigners will be happy to eat our last bit of grain.
> The Boxer Uprising is a good example, could it be that you are not moved?

Unlike the press accounts during the crisis itself, which focused on foreigners spreading rumors and the threat of joint foreign control of China's finances, the song lyrics emphasize the fact that foreign banks have no magic.

The recent failure of the Banque Industrielle de Chine would have had particular resonance with the people of Tianjin since only a few months earlier, they had witnessed the Tianjin Bankers' Association step in to bail out the foreigners. The songwriter did not completely ignore the threat of foreign intervention, as shown by his reference to the most traumatic foreign intervention in Tianjin in recent memory: suppression of the Boxer Uprising and the occupation of Tianjin by foreign troops for almost two years.

Having shifted attention to foreigners, the song concludes with its vision of the good citizen:

> Although our country is poor to the point of starvation, we still have some strengths
> America cannot compare, we're stronger than Austria, Germany, France.
> If only everyone could understand, unity of the will is our impregnable stronghold
> If the country is lost, where will you hoard your silver then?

Hyperbole aside, the vision is clear. The power to make China strong exists in the unity and will of the people. By 1921, Tianjin's residents had been subjected to at least fifteen years of such rhetoric of populist patriotism.[71] Nonetheless, there were several special elements in 1921. First, the vision of the "modern" participating and patriotic citizen had been appropriated by the government authorities. This vision had been used not to protest government actions but to promote the institutions of government banks, and thus obfuscate government wrongdoing in the process. In addition, the good citizen was asked not just to be patriotic but to understand complex economic principles—principles which are universally applied throughout the world.[72] The good citizen, as portrayed in this song, is someone who understands and accepts the principles of modern banking and who accepts and welcomes the presence of modern banks—and bank instruments such as paper money—in their daily lives. In this song, written in the vernacular to be comprehensible to a large number of Tianjin's residents, the bureaucrats of the Zhili Provincial Social Education Bureau portrayed a conscious vision of a direct relationship between individuals and modern institutions such as banks and, by extension, the state itself.

During the 1921 crisis, Tianjin's local elites and local government authorities forced the two banks to submit to audits of their internal financial condition and their currency reserves. Spurred by the discovery that the Bank of Communications had falsely issued Beijing paper money under the Tianjin place-name, leaders of the Tianjin Chamber of Commerce tried to institute a system of regular reporting by banks and regular audits by Chamber representatives. Although they did not try to reprise their failed role as guardians from the 1916 crisis, in 1921 local elites assumed the role of regulatory institution for bank money. Chamber supervision of bank-issued money was sporadic, however, and eventually fizzled out as memory of the crisis faded. In the absence of continuous and credible supervision by regulators, users of bank money had no guarantee that currency reserves were truly adequate, or that the central state would not force the Bank of China and the Bank of Communications to make additional, unreasonable loans.

Nonetheless, the 1921 crisis saw the enunciation of two other visions of the bases of trust in banks and bank-issued paper money. Bankers, like the executive at the Bank of China in Beijing who corresponded with Bian Baimei, realized that maintaining trust through secrecy and reliance on the upright reputation of bankers might provide just enough flexibility to allow the bank to satisfy both government demands for loans and public demands for exchange. If the public found out about the true condition of the banks, however, the decline in trust and the resulting bank run would upset the whole arrangement, possibly even leading to bank failure. The intellectual Ma Yinchu and bureaucrats at the Zhili Social Education Department became complicit in the plan for trust based on secrecy when they enunciated the idea that good citizens should trust banks and bank-issued money as both a patriotic duty and a result of understanding proper economic principles. They ignored the fact that banks played an important role in state building and developed the fiction that China's banks financed only commerce. Making this fiction transparent by explaining how banks worked served to make the true nature of banks opaque.

In addition to all of these efforts, restoration of exchange also made a major contribution to the creation of trust. The jury remained out, however, on the usefulness of extensive branch systems in contributing to bank stability. The existence of a well-developed branch system provided some stability for the Bank of China, since its Tianjin branch could call on funds from sister branches, but undermined trust in the Bank of Communications, whose managers had used the branch system to issue Beijing money under the Tianjin place-name. In addition, the other branches of the Bank of Communications were not strong enough to provide funds for the restoration of exchange. A branch system alone proved insufficient to ensure stability when not combined with appropriate practice of the expert knowledge of banking. In the end, the Bank of Communications restored exchange by receiving a loan from, and perhaps selling its soul to, the militarist Zhang Zuolin.

By 1921, the growth of banking in the preceding years had already clearly established that banks had a vital role in state-society relations. That role depended on trust in banks, though, providing proof that the tiger was simultaneously both powerful flesh and weak paper. All attempts to restore trust —public audits, banker secrecy, good citizens' understanding of banking principles, the restoration of exchange—brought the importance of bankers and their expert knowledge to the fore. What these methods share is a common belief in or reliance on the efficacy of bank professionalism, even if that professionalism had to be regulated by local elites, in the Chamber of Commerce version, or was subject to abuse, as in the case of the Bank of Communications. The balance among the various strategies for creating trust had tremendous implications for the nature of the role of banks in state-society relations. If banks kept their inner workings secret, then the government would have more latitude to arrange for bank loans to increase state strength. Likewise, if bank trust could be predicated on patriotic duty, then the trust in the workings of modern institutions could potentially be transferred from banks to the institution of the nation-state. Alternatively, publication of bank reserves and local regulation might fend off government demands for loans, weakening the power of the central state. Similarly, if the restoration of exchange relied on deals with warlords rather than help from expertly managed sister branches, then banks would be in no position to resist pressure from their saviors.

All parties agreed that trust in banking was a fundamental concern, but choosing among the multiple scenarios for the creation of trust had tremendous implications for the role of banks and bank-issued money in state-society relations. To what extent would bankers bow to regulation by local elites or control by the government, or would Tianjin's bankers assume leadership roles for themselves? Which vision of local trust would win the day, and which would be the basis for the relationship between citizens and the state? The continued devolution of power in the 1920s shifted the focus from the relationship between Tianjin's banks and the central state to the banks' relationship with the local provincial government.

4

The Rules of the Game under Warlord Governments

> Whenever the authorities talk about military expenses, the plans are many. They always look at the ledgers from the business community before making decisions, and businesspeople are simply afraid, for they cannot withstand the military. [In the end] all the plans come to nothing, and the authorities just have to make new ones.
>
> — Bian Baimei, *Diary,* June 11, 1922

During the 1920s, Tianjin's banks and bankers had to deal with frequent changes in regimes and an increasingly fragmented state; these altered the environment in which the banks functioned by shortening the life of governments and decreasing the importance of the central state in favor of local authorities. Between 1922 and 1928, warlords fought over Zhili Province almost every other year.[1] Bian's disdain grew with each successive change of government. From cavalier comments that Jin Yunpeng, prime minister of the republic for most of the period from 1919 to 1921, was a scoundrel *(wulaizhe),* to poems written on China's contemporary plight, Bian sprinkled his diary with derogatory references to warlords throughout the 1920s. Part of his dislike of them stemmed from their ignorance of modern finance. After a meeting with Cao Kun, then president of the republic, Bian commented that Cao "doesn't understand Finance Ministry matters. Acts like he knows, but he really doesn't."[2] As warlords vied for power, the central government in Beijing, the provincial government in Zhili, various temporary military commands, and competing army groups all vied for access to bank-controlled financial resources. A confidential internal report from the Tianjin branch of Beijing's Salt Bank stated, "If [we] open a branch in a particular place, then the possibility arises of making loans to the local government."[3] In Tianjin, of course, "local government" meant Zhili Province, and provincial finances, following the general trend of the times, became increasingly strained in the 1920s.

Straitened finances increased the influence of banks but also made warlords more predatory.[4] This odd mix of power and vulnerability shaped bank-warlord relations during this period as bankers walked a fine line between safety and danger, often having to make deals with men they despised. Tianjin's banks and bankers took shelter in the foreign concessions of the city, but their responsibilities also included trips into the Chinese parts of Tianjin and to other cities as well—all under the control of warlord governments. Bankers took threats of coercion seriously, but there is little evidence that their lives were often in real danger. In fact, both sides seem to have realized that coercion played just one more part in the mix of variables that determined the amount and terms of bank financing for warlord governments. For example, in 1926 the Shandong warlord Zhang Zongchang placed the manager of the Jinan branch of the Bank of China under house arrest. When the Bank of China agreed to lend the Shandong government 500,000 yuan, the threats against the Jinan manager ceased. Bian noted in his diary, "Actually, if we had persevered some, the amount might have decreased a little."[5] Banks did not exist at the complete mercy of warlord coercion, even if such coercion played a role in the relationship between banks and the many local governments in China.

The demands of government authorities for bank financing often threatened to disturb trust in banks and the money they issued. In response, bankers developed a number of strategies to promote trust, most involving institutional arrangements.

Promoting Trust in Warlord Tianjin

The ownership and organizational structures of the Bank of China and the Bank of Communications changed dramatically in the 1920s. As the central state weakened, stock ownership in both banks became predominantly private.[6] In addition, after the 1921 crisis the Bank of China underwent yet another reorganization. The other branches stepped in to rescue its beleaguered office in Beijing, which was demoted from the status of a branch to that of a sub-branch under the supervision of the Tianjin office.[7] The bank divided China into five currency zones, with treaty ports designated as the centers of four of them. The Tianjin branch became head of Zone 2, including Zhili, Shanxi, Shaanxi, Suiyuan, and Shandong provinces.[8] Thus by the mid-1920s, Bian Baimei, as Tianjin branch manager, supervised the bank's Beijing office and controlled the bank's paper money in all of North China. The system was far from completely institutionalized, however. Once in 1924, Zhang Jia'ao forced the Beijing exchange office for Tianjin currency to make a 400,000 yuan loan directly to the Beijing branch without Bian Baimei's approval. Bian objected because this weakened reserves for the bank's paper money, but he could do little since his own superior at the bank had arranged the loan.[9]

After the 1921 crisis Cao Rulin resigned from his position and the Bank of Communications underwent reorganization, engineered by a group of Jiangnan bankers. In 1922 the bank's shareholders elected Zhang Jian (1853–1926) to head the bank, with Qian Yongming (1885–1958), a Japanese-trained professional banker, in the number two position. At the same time, the bank's directors agreed to become more independent, refuse future military loans to the government, and concentrate on commercial business. In an extension of the new networks arising from the modern banking sector, a number of professional bankers, including Zhou Zuomin and Tan Danya, also became directors.[10] Like the Bank of China, the Bank of Communications reorganized its money issue, setting up five currency zones, making Tianjin the center of Zone 1, in charge of issue in the North China plain, including Beijing, Hebei, and Shandong. The new regulations also required specie reserves of 60 percent, with the remaining 40 percent in marketable securities.[11]

Privatization and reorganization succeeded to some extent. During the 1920s neither the Bank of China nor the Bank of Communications incurred any bank runs as serious as those of 1916 and 1921. Even after ownership of the banks became almost completely private, however, the banks' activities still linked them closely to the state. At the Bank of China, the Finance Ministry still appointed the president of the bank, even if he was chosen from the board of directors elected by shareholders. From 1923 to the end of 1926, when Zhang Zuolin's Fengtian regime had the upper hand in Beijing, the Jiangsu native Jin Rengzhu (Huan) held the position. He was Fengtian's man at the bank, but he generally kept a low profile, leaving day-to-day management with Zhang Jia'ao. Feng Gengguang and Wang Kemin continued to take an active hand in the bank as well. At the beginning of 1927, Feng Gengguang took the helm again, this time as acting president. Control of the Bank of Communications remained more unsettled, and more closely linked to political struggle. In 1924 three private banks floated a plan to purchase the remaining shares of the Bank of Communications still in the hands of the Communications Ministry.[12] In 1925 another plan was floated to convert to stock the 4 million yuan that Zhang Zuolin had loaned the Bank of Communications during the 1921 crisis and to make Zhang's son Zhang Xueliang president of the bank.[13] After the Zhili-Fengtian war in the fall of 1924, the victorious Fengtian alliance made Duan Qirui head of the government. Duan, in turn, brought Liang Shiyi back from exile, and Liang, in a remarkable comeback, took control of the Bank of Communications in 1925, forcing Zhang Jian and Qian Yongming to resign.[14] Liang ran the bank until he fled to Hong Kong in 1928 to avoid capture by the Nationalists.[15] Privatization also did not mean that the banks stopped funding government operations. Throughout the 1920s, loans to the central and local governments consistently accounted for 30 to 40 percent of all loans made by the Bank of China.[16]

As the state banks reorganized, four private banks in Tianjin worked together in an innovative risk-pooling arrangement, the Four Bank Joint Treasury (commonly referred to as the Four Banks or the Northern Four). The new organization became a force in the Tianjin money market shortly after its founding in 1922. Three of the four banks which combined in the joint treasury are already familiar: Zhou Zuomin's Jincheng Bank, Tan Danya's Continental Bank, and the Salt Bank, now in the control of Wu Dingchang. Prior to 1922, each of these three banks had a separate agreement to "adopt" and use the paper money of either the Bank of China or the Bank of Communications. The 1921 crisis provided a window of opportunity, and the three banks decided to go into the currency business. To increase credibility, they combined their resources.[17] Because of political problems, none was in a position to apply to the central government for permission to issue currency, however. After the Anhui-Zhili war in 1920, an arrest order was issued for Wu Dingchang, who took shelter in Tianjin's Japanese Concession until he could bribe his way out. Wang Zhilong, one of the main investors in Jincheng Bank, fled to Japan, and in the same year the National Assembly forced Tan Danya to resign from his concurrent position with the Bank of China.[18] The three banks invited Shanghai's China and Southsea Bank, which already had the right to issue money, to join them. The bank was managed by Hu Bijiang, a fellow Jiangsu native of Zhou Zuomin and Tan Danya and a former colleague of Zhou's at the Bank of Communications.[19] The four banks maintained independent operations, but they established a well-publicized joint treasury of reserves to back China and Southsea's currency. A few years later they founded the Four Bank Savings Society to accept small deposits from individuals, called *chuxu*. The managers of the Four Banks realized that attracting small savings from private individuals, like the issue of paper money, required impeccable credibility—credibility which came from the strength of their combined operations.[20]

In spite of the success of the Four Banks, their operation remained unique in China. Risk pooling required a solid basis for personal trust among the bankers involved. The common native places, educational backgrounds, and longtime associations of Wu Dingchang, Zhou Zuomin, Tan Danya, and Hu Bijiang provided the basis for such an arrangement, and it was not easily replicated.[21] As a result, most smaller banks and Tianjin's indigenous banks that wished to issue money continued to use adoption agreements with the Bank of China, the Bank of Communications, or even the Four Banks.[22]

As Tianjin's Chinese banks grew, they joined the city's foreign banks in transforming the area along the rue de France/Victoria Road into North China's Wall Street. The bank buildings along that street and on nearby side streets, constructed in neoclassical style—mostly Greek Revival—still dominate that part of Tianjin today. In the space of a few years in the early to mid-1920s, the granite fronts and polished brass doors of these giants came to embody the presence and meaning of modern banking in the Tianjin cityscape. In quick succession, the foreign bankers built their temples of finance, with the two giants—and rivals—of foreign banking in China, the British Hong Kong and Shanghai Banking Corporation and the Japanese Yokohama Specie Bank, next door to each other on Victoria Road. The marble lobby of the HSBC covered 670 square meters.[23] Tianjin's banks mirrored the activities of their foreign counterparts, but Chinese banks, for the most part, were barred from the rue de France/Victoria Road. Only Jincheng Bank managed to move onto the section of the road which ran through the former German Concession.[24] In addition, the Four Bank Savings Society found a home on Victoria Road in a large building fronted with Greek columns. For the most part, though, the Chinese banks were relegated to the side streets. These secondary locations, however, did not keep Tianjin's modern Chinese bankers from copying their foreign counterparts, if on a smaller scale.[25] Most spectacular was Wu Dingchang's Salt Bank, which built a new Tianjin branch building in 1929. The building's edifice is faced with granite and fronted with columns running down both sides of the building that face the street (it is on a corner). The floor of the lobby and the counter were made of imported Italian marble and the walls lined with a row of black marble columns.[26] With concrete, granite, and marble, the management of the Salt Bank tried to demonstrate the reliability and credibility of their bank.[27]

The transformation of Tianjin's cityscape at this time was similar to what happened in many American cities when "banks, churches, courthouses, firehouses, and railroad stations . . . asserted as if by right a predominant architectural presence . . . with the cocky air of those who, not without reason, regard themselves as indispensable."[28] Unlike Chinese indigenous bank buildings, which were hardly distinguishable from other shops or even from residences, modern banks built large and readily identifiable buildings, creating an unprecedented public presence and leaving an architectural footprint on Tianjin visible to this day. These buildings must have seemed immense at the time, impressing all of the residents of Tianjin, not just those who frequented these banks.

Bank architecture served a dual purpose. On the one hand, these impressive facades created a very open and public presence. As Robert Nesbit notes, "Bank architecture thus communicates the importance of banks as institutions, assuring us of their stability, prosperity, and permanence and inviting us inside to do business."[29] The link between this impressive public presence and trust was quite explicit in the minds of Tianjin's bankers. As one old banker told me, "In the past Zuo Junmo [his teacher at business school] and Zhou Zuomin both said that if you build a big building, then deposits will come in."[30] On the other hand, banks were constructed so that customers were confined to impressive lobbies, the "front stage" for the performance of bank professionalism. A similar distinction could be found in traditional indigenous banks in Tianjin, which had a "front counter," where loan and deposit transactions were handled, and a "back counter," which smelted and exchanged silver.[31] That distinction represented as much a division of labor as control over the threshold of access, however. In modern banks, controlling access became predominant. Zuo Junmo told his business classes in Tianjin that "the best bank design was to have the manager's office on the second floor with a small window from which he could see activity in the lobby, but through which customers could not see."[32] The manager's hidden gaze from his second-floor office on customers in the lobby below represented perfectly the need to control the threshold between the "front stage" and backstage, and the need to keep backstage activities secret.[33] Bank architecture both embodied and concealed expert knowledge.

Impressive architecture could not shield banks from the demands of warlords, however. Tianjin's banks continued to make government loans throughout the warlord period. A partial list of loans to various levels of the government made by the Tianjin branch of the Bank of China during 1927 shows loans to at least three entities of the Zhili provincial government and three army commands. The bank routinely loaned funds amounting to hundreds of thousands, and sometimes millions of yuan.[34] By 1927 the Bank of China had been privatized for several years, but as this list of loans shows, the bank had not cut off its relations with the government. The bank had simply redefined that relationship to a number of power centers, especially at the provincial level.

Constantly changing and often dangerous political regimes created a potential nightmare for bankers. If each new regime disavowed loans made to the previous government, then the banks that had made those loans stood to lose large amounts of money. By developing a set of practices—rules of the game—banks maintained cordial relations, for the most part, with the warlord governments which ruled Tianjin, and regularly loaned money to those governments without significant losses. The rules that governed bank-warlord relations can be summarized in four points. First, the primary tenet was that organizations dealt with organizations. Banks dealt with various agencies of the Zhili provincial or central government rather than with the warlord or warlord army which controlled that government. These provincial government agencies exhibited a surprising continuity over the course of the republican period, giving banks a more secure foothold in the ever-shifting political landscape. Second, banks based their loans on reliable collateral and verifiable sources of repayment. Government institutions like the Zhili Finance Bureau or the Zhili Provincial Bank had their own assets and revenue sources which provided the collateral and repayment for bank loans. Foreigners even controlled some of those revenue sources, such as the customs and salt taxes, giving bankers an extra level of security. Third, banks dealt with warlord governments by negotiating collectively, usually through the Tianjin Bankers' Association, and by sharing the risks of each loan. Finally, banks tried to minimize loans to faltering regimes. Bankers became expert at delaying tactics as they waited to see which way the political situation would shift.

Risk sharing and continuity provided the keys to the rules of the game for lending money to warlord governments. When making government loans, banks usually tried to find two or three partners to share the risk. Most commonly, when the Tianjin Bankers' Association coordinated loan negotiations, a three-tiered formula determined the amounts of each bank's share. The Bank of China and the Bank of Communications took the lion's share of the loan. Next, the Four Banks took substantial portions. Finally, the other twelve member banks divided up the remainder. Beyond pooling their risk, banks needed to know that their loans would be repaid even if the political regime changed during the term of the loan, so they ensured continuity by following the rule that organizations deal with organizations. For example, the 1922 Zhili-Fengtian war provided an occasion for the Bank of China to lend money to the central government. Through the intercession of two members of the bank's board of directors, the bank had loaned money to the Zhili army rather than the Finance Ministry. Bian noted in his diary: "This matter is very suspicious. Not that you can't lend, but there should truly be surplus funds, and procedures should be complete. The Zhili army should get its funds from the Finance Ministry, and the ministry can negotiate borrowing money [from the bank]. The bank can approve [loans] based on the ability to repay."[35]

Bian objected not to making a loan to the government, but to doing so without following the rules of the game as defined by his expert knowledge as a banker. Toward the end of this period, as the victorious troops of the Nationalists' Northern Expedition swept into Zhili Province, a friend told Bian that people admired him for the way he had handled the outside world. Bian responded that he "simply used one organization [*jiguan*] to handle [other] organizations, without personal feelings or political party opinions mixed up in between them. As a result [he] could keep things in perspective, and thus could avoid blame somewhat."[36] In Bian's idealized formulation, banks, as organizations, dealt with government organs, as organizations; personal feelings and ideology did not get in the way. Although the militarist in control of Zhili Province changed often, the basic institutional structure of the provincial government, including the Provincial Finance Bureau, the Salt Transport Controller, and the Zhili Provincial Bank, exhibited remarkable continuity.

These agencies also had valuable assets to pledge to Tianjin's banks in return for loans. Stock in one or another provincial enterprise, such as the Kailan Mining Administration (jointly run with foreigners), the Hengyuan Cotton Mill, and the Zhili Provincial Bank, could be used as collateral to get bank loans.[37] The other primary asset of the Zhili government was land, especially land that it inherited in the former Russian, German, and Austrian concessions when they were returned to Chinese control.[38] Unlike stocks and bonds, though, land could not be put in the banks' vaults, safely locked away from militarists' hands. Once, Tianjin's bankers made a 200,000 yuan loan to the Zhili Provincial Bank secured by land in the former Russian Concession. After the Fengtian army took Tianjin, it appropriated the land and sold it without consulting the bankers. In a rather wounded letter to Marshal Zhang Zuolin of the Fengtian army, the Tianjin Bankers' Association stated that Tianjin's banks had only been trying to help the Provincial Bank.[39] Whether or not the marshal was sympathetic to the bankers remains unknown, but Tianjin's bankers did not lend money to the local government secured on land again. Nonetheless, the Zhili Provincial Bank continued to be a preferred customer of the Tianjin banks, and later that year, when a 2.5 million yuan loan to the Provincial Bank secured by stock in the Kailan Mining Administration came up for renegotiation, Bian noted in his diary that he "did not want to lose this nice piece of business."[40]

In addition to these assets, two of the most reliable sources of income for the Zhili provincial government were a 2.5 percent surcharge on customs duties and salt taxes. The foreign-controlled Customs Administration, or the foreign banks that received customs and salt taxes to pay foreign loans, could send surplus amounts directly to Tianjin's Chinese banks without risk that Chinese officials would divert the funds. Only when the loan was paid in full could the provincial government receive the customs or salt taxes for its own use. Often by that time the province needed money again, and Tianjin's bankers would make a new loan. In contrast, banks had little control over land taxes, and rarely loaned money based on Zhili's agricultural tax revenues.

In the mid-1920s, the Tianjin branch of the Salt Bank prepared a partial list of the collateral it held for loans to various organs of the Zhili provincial government. This list demonstrates the variety of assets the local government used to borrow money. It includes a 300,000 yuan loan to the Mining Bureau secured by paper money of the Zhili Provincial Bank, a 600,000 yuan loan made to the Zhili Provincial Finance Bureau secured by postdated checks drawn on the Zhili Provincial Bank, a 600,000 yuan loan to the Zhili Provincial Finance Bureau secured by stock in the Kailan Mining Administration, a 40,000 yuan loan secured by a contract on real estate in Hankou, and a loan of unstated amount secured by shares in the Hengyuan Cotton Mill.[41]

The government loans made under the supervision of the Tianjin branch of the Bank of China in 1927 also show the rules of the game at work. The bank made its largest loans to agencies of the Zhili government, including the Zhili Provincial Bank, the Zhili Finance Bureau, and the Zhili Salt Controller. In some cases the Beijing sub-branch still loaned money to army commands, though large amounts had collateral guarantees. In most cases several banks shared risks by making the loan together. Preferred collateral included the 2.5 percent customs surcharge or transit tax receipts in Beijing.[42]

Evidence for the Existence of Impersonal Trust

Bankers intended that reorganizing state banks, pooling risk, constructing impressive bank buildings, and following the rules of the game for government loans would ensure the stability of their banks and promote trusting behaviors among the members of the public. The extent of that trust in the 1920s can be gauged by examining the performance of those two banking products which required the greatest amount of trust from customers: savings deposits and circulation of paper money.

Chinese indigenous financial institutions had long taken deposits *(cunkuan)* from customers.[43] Deposits, however, usually came from wealthy individuals, officials, or government agencies. During the early republican period, deposits by individuals usually ranged from 500 to 2,000 yuan, well beyond the means of the average person.[44] Modern banks took such deposits, but they also offered another kind of service for ordinary savers called *chuxu,* whereby deposits could be as low as one yuan. In the 1920s, banks escalated a campaign to increase *chuxu* deposits, and in the process expanded both the number of bank customers and the need for impersonal trust in the banking system.[45] In terms of absolute dollars of accumulated savings, *chuxu* did not really take off until after the establishment of the Nationalist government in 1928, but all of my informants in Tianjin remembered the 1920s as the time when *chuxu* became a fixture of the urban landscape.

Those people who deposited money in modern bank *chuxu* accounts did so not because they personally knew and trusted professional bankers, but because they had impersonal trust in the bankers' professionalism and in the banking system itself. Their contact with banks was fairly direct, however. They had to walk into branches, entering the polished lobbies, the "front stages" of Tianjin's banks, where they had personal contact with the low-level staff members who took their deposits. Users of bank-issued paper money did not necessarily have this kind of contact, and their trust in banks was even more impersonal.

More and more residents acquired a stake in the viability of Tianjin's banking as the circulation of bank-issued paper money increased, reaching levels never even imagined by indigenous banks, and not seen in China since the Ming dynasty. For example, all of Tianjin's indigenous banks combined had issued only 127,000 yuan in paper money in 1914.[46] By comparison, the Tianjin branches of the Bank of China and the Bank of Communications had combined currency issue of over 5 million yuan in 1916. Indigenous banks were simply too small either individually or in the aggregate to develop the widespread credibility among strangers needed to issue large amounts of paper money. In spite of setbacks in 1916 and 1921, circulation of the Tianjin paper money of the Bank of China and the Bank of Communications increased rapidly, augmented by the banknotes of the Four Banks, the Zhili Provincial Bank, and a number of other modern banks. By 1923, the total currency issue of Tianjin's banks exceeded 13 million yuan, and by 1925, the Bank of China and the Bank of Communications alone had more than 19 million yuan in circulation, 18 yuan in paper money for every man, woman, and child living in Tianjin. Much of this paper money circulated outside of Tianjin, especially in Beijing, but the general trend was clear.[47] When paper money was trustworthy, the convenience made it greatly preferable to silver, and it was not unusual for individuals to bring silver into banks to exchange for banknotes.[48]

The increasing acceptability of savings deposits in, and paper money issued by, Chinese banks in Tianjin also stemmed from several well-publicized problems with foreign money and banks. Early in the twentieth century, Russian rubles had wide circulation among merchants in Tianjin, but their value declined after the Bolsheviks toppled the tsarist government.[49] Boycotts of French money in Tianjin in 1916 and of Japanese money in all of China after the May Fourth Incident, plus the 1921 failure of the Sino-French Banque Industrielle de Chine, further tainted the reputation of paper money issued by foreign banks in China. Finally, in 1925, the May Thirtieth Incident in Shanghai, when foreign police opened fire on demonstrating students and workers, led to a new mobilization in favor of Chinese money and banks. Since demonstrators blamed the British and the Japanese for the incident, the HSBC and Yokohama Specie Bank bore the brunt of people's ire. In early June, bank runs erupted on the Shanghai branches of the two foreign banks. Ten thousand students surrounded the Beijing

Bankers' Association until they received a promise that Beijing's Chinese banks would boycott British and Japanese money.[50] Events in Tianjin were less dramatic, but the Tianjin Bankers' Association met and issued a statement deploring the incident and expressing sympathy with bankers in Shanghai and Beijing who had agreed to the boycott.[51] Likewise, in the year after the May Thirtieth Incident, Chinese bank deposits increased by 67 percent.[52] By the 1920s, it was clear that foreign banks and foreign money had no special intrinsic magic.

The breadth of the customer base of Tianjin's Chinese banks is hard to gauge. *Chuxu* did not encompass every sector of Tianjin society, and traditional "rotation" savings societies thrived well into the 1930s.[53] All of my informants agreed that workers, for example, would not have had savings accounts, and certainly not in the 1920s. Instead, *chuxu* appealed mainly to the many small merchant families and the growing body of salaried white-collar employees who made Tianjin their home. The potential customer base was still substantial. The commercial class, about 15 percent of the population, outnumbered workers throughout the 1930s and 1940s, and the disparity was probably even greater in the 1920s.[54] Currency circulated among a much wider group. There are no reliable statistics, but some anecdotal evidence demonstrates that paper money was widely held. For example, in 1924, during a short run on Zhou Xuexi's National Industrial Bank, the *Peking and Tientsin Times* described the crowd of about one hundred people who crowded into the bank to exchange paper money for silver: "In the queue were coolies with two or three $1 notes, and shroffs [clerks, especially those with experience in money exchange] with thick wads of $5 and $10 denomination, and there was even a fair proportion of women of all classes. Some of the shroffs were accompanied by coolies with sacks, and these coolies would later emerge from a side-door staggering under the weight of silver dollars."[55]

Not every laborer in Tianjin had bank-issued paper money, but at least some of them did. In fact the reporter made a point of the fact that people of all classes were present. In terms of dollars, however, merchants of one sort or another clearly held the largest amounts of paper currency. Their shroffs brought laborers to carry the heavy sacks of silver from the bank—a different matter of scale altogether from the "coolies with two or three $1 notes." By the 1920s, savings deposits and increased circulation of paper money had extended the network of individuals who needed to trust banks to almost every sector of society. An extended crisis at the Zhili Provincial Bank would once again test that trust, as well as the ability of Tianjin's local elites to act as guardians or regulators of the money supply.

The 1927–28 Zhili Provincial Bank Crisis

After the run on the Bank of China and the Bank of Communications in 1921, the Zhili Provincial Bank had lost no time in announcing plans to promote its own currency. The Zhili provincial governor's office issued an order to all of its subsidiary organs stating that "since the bank run and suspension of exchange at the Bank of China and the Bank of Communications, only the Zhili Provincial Bank has not been affected because its reserves are fully adequate and its credit obvious. As society has long known, the bank acts as a provincial treasury accepting taxes paid by the people to the counties and other organs [of government]. Now, in addition to cash, only Zhili Provincial Bank paper money will be accepted for the payment of taxes."[56]

In spite of such grand plans, the paper money of the Zhili Provincial Bank remained of only secondary importance in Tianjin during the early 1920s. Each time the province changed hands, bank runs erupted on the Provincial Bank. Tianjin residents had well-founded suspicions about the likelihood that exiting regimes would plunder the bank's silver reserves. The bank maintained institutional continuity from regime to regime, but moveable liquid assets, such as silver currency reserves, were a weakness. At the time of the first Zhili-Fengtian war in 1922, the Provincial Bank had a currency issue of about 1.2 million yuan, with reserves of only 300,000 yuan. In a pattern which would be repeated often, representatives of Tianjin's Chamber of Commerce and the Tianjin Indigenous Bankers' Association came to the city's modern banks to arrange a loan on behalf of the Zhili government. The first plan involved using the cotton cloth inventory at the Hengyuan Cotton Mill as collateral to borrow money. The bankers rejected this plan because of the small amount and poor quality of the cloth. In the end, the banks issued a loan of 160,000 yuan based on 200,000 yuan in 1914 central government bonds owned by the province. Two years later, in 1924, the second Zhili-Fengtian war led to another run on the Zhili Provincial Bank. This time the modern Bankers' Association helped the Provincial Bank with a 200,000 yuan loan secured on land in the former Russian Concession.[57]

With the imposition of the Fengtian-sponsored regime in 1924, Zhili Province began printing money as a major means of financial support.[58] As its currency circulated in greater amounts and more widely in Tianjin and

Zhili Province, problems at the Bank resulted in ever more serious crises, beginning in early 1926 with the crisis atmosphere accompanying Feng Yuxiang's retreating forces and the Fengtian recapture of Tianjin. At that time, the military currency issued by the incoming forces exacerbated the sense of crisis:

> Armed with various lethal weapons, and supplies of these notes, the benevolent protectors of the Chinese Republic have indulged in an orgy of reckless expenditure since their arrival. A Soldier will visit, say, a tobacconist, fling down a five-dollar note on the counter, and ask for a packet of cigarettes, and four dollars in change . . . Chinese merchants are showing considerable reluctance to part with silver in exchange for Chihli [Zhili] Military Notes. Consequently many shops have put up their shutters, and, it is reported, the Chinese Chamber of Commerce has temporarily closed its doors.[59]

As this article points out, the Chamber of Commerce leaders were reluctant to help the government. Bian Yinchang even suggested that the circulation of military currency be implemented by force, rather than have the Chamber put up the money. Separately, two Chamber leaders came to Bian Baimei and asked for money to support the military currency.[60] Bian found the suggestion laughable. Military currency issued by an army lacking solid assets or revenues to pledge as collateral had little or no credibility because it lacked the backing of an organization with a continuous and stable presence.

In contrast to their attitude toward the military currency, Bian and Tianjin's other bankers expressed a willingness to help the Zhili Provincial Bank, even though it was in dire financial straits. The provincial bank negotiated a small loan from the members of the Tianjin Bankers' Association in April 1926, at the height of the provincial government's transition crisis. Negotiations with the banks revolved not around whether or not to make a loan, but around collateral for the loan, terms of repayment, and other technical details. In the end, Tianjin's banks made an advance against future salt tax revenues.[61] That small loan, however, did not suffice to save the Zhili Provincial Bank. Occasional bank runs erupted on and off for the next several months, and Tianjin's banks made a series of stopgap loans to various organs of the provincial government.[62] In September, negotiations came to a head over a 1 million yuan loan to the Zhili Salt Transport Controller. The Tianjin Bankers' Association remained divided. Finally, at a contentious meeting Bian convinced his colleagues that the time for hesitation was over, pointing out that the foreign concessions provided only limited protection: "As for [asking for] protection from the concession authorities, I do not approve because our bank and other banks have offices outside the concessions and they would be difficult to protect from danger." Tianjin's modern banks had extended themselves too far into the city and into the lives of its residents to be completely shielded from the long arm of government coercion. That afternoon the Bankers' Association met again and decided to make the loan. In the evening, Chu Yupu gave a banquet for Tianjin's merchants. The deal was as good as done, sealed by a combination of technical financial details regarding collateral and repayment and cultivation of old-fashioned personal connections.[63]

Zhili Province mortgaged its future revenues as fast as it could. By the early months of 1927, Tianjin's bankers were busy making arrangements for provincial finances, including the purchase of provincial bonds and loans to buy foreign weapons.[64] When bank loans proved insufficient for the regime's voracious appetite, the province resorted to printing money. Currency issued by the Provincial Bank had hovered around 1 million yuan for most of the early and mid-1920s, but by June 1927, the figure had shot up to 5.6 million yuan.[65] This rapid increase came without corresponding increases in the bank's silver reserves, spelling trouble. A run on the Provincial Bank in February 1927 prompted the Zhili provincial government "on the one hand to extend exchange hours and on the other to execute two people for joining in the bank run."[66] The government proclaimed that the Provincial Bank's reserves were more than adequate and blamed the bank run on the actions of a few "evil merchants fishing for profit."[67] More concretely, in May the Zhili Provincial Finance Bureau concluded a 1.2 million yuan loan with the eighteen banks of the Tianjin Bankers' Association secured on the 2.5 percent customs tax surcharge to help the Provincial Bank out of its insolvency.[68]

Nothing, however, seemed to stop the run on the Zhili Provincial Bank. Government exhortations about the credibility of the bank fell on deaf ears, and even the execution of two people who had speculated in Zhili notes did not stop desperate people from lining up to exchange their Zhili Provincial Bank notes for silver. Finally, in June 1927, Chu Yupu decided that coercion, exhortation, and mortgaging future provincial revenues in return for stopgap bank loans would not salvage the weakened credibility of the bank's paper money. In a letter to the Tianjin Chamber of Commerce, he ordered additional salt taxes to be levied for the use of the Provincial Bank and demanded that the modern banks, merchants, and indigenous banks of Tianjin make a loan based on that new salt tax to support the more than 5 million yuan in outstanding currency.[69]

Tianjin's elites would spend the next six months passing this hot potato back and forth, knowing that the one who got stuck with it might be asked to pay more than 5 million yuan. The revenues from the added salt taxes would bring in at most only 200,000 to 300,000 yuan a month, and in the meantime, there was no guarantee that the province would stop printing money. In a letter to the general office of the Bank of China, Bian Baimei noted that "illicit discounts [of provincial money] have reached 30 percent. The [provincial currency] does not circulate in the foreign concessions, and does so in the Chinese part of the city only under the threat of coercion from the authorities . . . Many small merchants have closed down, some of them sell rice and flour [and thus] concern the food of the people."[70] In more dramatic terms, a local newspaper reporter described one day of the bank run:

> In the last few days, large numbers of people have been cashing notes at the Gujia Bridge Exchange Office [of the Zhili Provincial Bank]. Yesterday [July 31] the morning was [designated as] women's note-cashing time, and although it was raining hard, there were still two to three hundred people waiting outside the door, clothes all wet.
>
> The office did not open its doors until it stopped raining, and then all the women, struggling to be the first and fearing to be the last, exerted their utmost strength to crowd in. Although there were soldiers and police to keep order, there were too many people. Some people were pushed down, some lost the banknotes they were holding, some people had their clothing torn, some people had run through the gutter and their clothing was covered with mud. People were yelling and screaming in anguish. [It was] difficult to describe. In the end, because the [exchange] office's funds were limited, more than one hundred people had made the effort for nothing, and [they] were all moaning endlessly.[71]

In response to Chu Yupu's order, the Chamber of Commerce organized the Zhili Provincial Currency Support Association, casting its net wide among official and non-official Tianjin elite groups. In all, nine groups were eventually asked to send representatives: the modern Bankers' Association, the Indigenous Bankers' Association, the Salt Merchants' Guild, the Tianjin Chamber of Commerce, the Association of United Chambers of Commerce of Zhili Province, the Zhili Provincial Assembly, the Zhili Agriculture Association, the Zhili Provincial Finance Bureau, and the Zhili Provincial Bank.[72] Bian Baimei participated prominently in the Support Association from the beginning, and was eventually elected its chairman.[73] After its formation, however, the association did little. As June stretched into July, Chu Yupu became increasingly desperate to raise money. His desperation, in turn, spelled danger for Tianjin's bankers. Wanting to expropriate money owed to the Finance Ministry in Beijing by Beiyang Baoshang Bank, Chu had the assistant manager of the Tianjin branch of the bank lured to a hotel and arrested. Two days later, with the banker still in custody, Chu Yupu called the leaders of the Chamber of Commerce and the Bankers' Association to his office. Chu's "words [at the meeting were] coercive and full of invective. [He] also set a week as the deadline to come up with something or else he would use extreme methods." In a version of "good cop, bad cop," one of Chu's subordinates came to Bian Baimei a couple of days later to say that "there need be no hard feelings over Chu Yupu's impolite words the other day, and Zheng Shaotang [the assistant manager] can be set free."[74] The imprisoned banker was released, but in return the Support Association met and decided to take action.

The association agreed to take responsibility for only 2 million yuan in provincial currency, asking the outlying counties of Zhili Province to take responsibility for another 2 million with surcharged grain taxes as collateral.[75] Later the 4 million yuan total was increased to 5.6 million, of which 2.8 million yuan became the responsibility of the Support Association, with the rest farmed out to the rural counties. From the beginning the Support Association did not plan to cash notes directly. Instead, it hoped to stamp 2.8 million in notes with the statement that if the Provincial Bank could not exchange the notes for silver, the Support Association would. As in 1916, this plan was fraught with dangers. Bian Baimei pointed out, "As soon as word spreads that the Support Association is guaranteeing provincial currency, provincial banknotes will pour into Tianjin from the whole province."[76] A guarantee of only half of the amount in circulation was doomed to fail. Stamped and unstamped currency would circulate side by side, creating confusion and further financial chaos. Bian noted in his diary that the people in the association "support with empty words, but are not willing to put up the least amount of real help."[77] Bian's analysis proved prophetic. Throughout its life, infighting and disingenuousness plagued the operations of the Support Association. Once again, the weeks dragged on with no action. Technical problems of implementation proved difficult, and no one had provided the silver needed to back the association's guarantee.[78]

At the same time, Bian heard that Chu Yupu had threatened to arrest Chamber leaders who had privately opposed the guardianship plan. Probing for a soft spot, Chu also ordered an official audit of the currency reserves of all of Tianjin's banks, intending to scare the banks into action. A provincial official came to see Bian and told him that if the province could borrow another 2 million yuan for the Provincial Bank based on the customs tax surcharge, the matter of the audit of bank reserves could be "arranged." Bian responded that "the banks were very willing to have their reserves examined and there was nothing to 'arrange.'" Nonetheless, the customs surcharge provided a reliable source of repayment, and the banks continued to negotiate a loan.[79]

While the members of the Support Association argued about what to do, the Zhili Provincial Bank continued to issue money. An accountant, hired by the Support Association to examine the books of the Provincial Bank, reported in November that the amount of currency in circulation had ballooned to 8,493,100 yuan.[80] The 2.8 million yuan promised by the Support Association, but still not raised in full, now appeared a pittance compared to the massive amount of paper money floating around Tianjin and the rest of Zhili Province. As the situation became increasingly untenable, Bian resigned his positions as chairman of the Support Association and chairman of the Tianjin Bankers' Association. Soon after his announcement, the chairman of the Chamber of Commerce, Zhang Pinti, and of the Indigenous Bankers' Association, Wang Xiaoyan, asked Bian to stay on as head of the Support Association, and he agreed. Likewise, the other members of the Bankers' Association persuaded Bian to continue as chairman. The next day, the Support Association began stamping banknotes of the Zhili Provincial Bank. Commitments to fund its operation still fell well short of the 2.8 million yuan goal, but the Provincial Finance Bureau allocated 1 million yuan from a new 1.3 million yuan loan from the members of the Tianjin Bankers' Association secured on the customs surcharge for Support Association activities.[81]

No sooner had the association finally commenced action, however, than problems arose. The five hundred shops of the local guild of rice and flour merchants, which had pledged as a group to participate in the Support Association to the amount of only 10,000 yuan, reported that they already had 100,000 yuan in Zhili currency in their possession.[82] The rice and flour merchants were later accused of buying up Zhili provincial currency at a discount in order to have it guaranteed at full value by the Support Association.[83] Whether this was true or not, the episode pointed up the inherent weaknesses in half-measure guardianship plans. As long as the Support Association could stamp and guarantee only a portion of the notes, the danger existed that people would try to make money off the difference in value between stamped and unstamped notes. As a result, the Support Association had a built-in conflict of interest; there was always the risk that some members would use their insider position to act in their own interests rather than the public's. A guarantee of half the money created as many problems as it solved. On November 28, the Zhili Finance Bureau wrote the Support Association, complaining that the value of Zhili provincial currency was continuing to fall. Seeing the ineffectiveness of Support Association activities, the cash-starved provincial government demanded the return of its 1 million yuan deposit. The Support Association called an emergency meeting at which it decided to abandon its efforts. Finally, a little more than two weeks after the association had begun to stamp notes, Chu Yupu issued an order to suspend all exchange of the provincial currency and to disband the association.[84]

The finances of the Support Association tell us much about the dynamics of elite action in 1927 Tianjin. The table shows the relative weight of the different merchant groups in Tianjin in terms of financial if not political power. At the top sat the modern bankers, in command of financial resources far and above those of any other group—having taken over this role from the salt merchants. Between their pledge to the Support Association and their loan to the province, Tianjin's modern banks shouldered 2.4 million yuan, or almost half the 5.6 million yuan total.[85] Next came two of Tianjin's traditionally most powerful guilds: indigenous bankers and salt merchants. The newly rising industries of cotton and flour milling claimed third place, and below these groups ranked the bean sellers, rice and flour shops, shoe guild, and the dozens of other trades. None of these smaller groups committed more than 30,000 yuan to the effort, and some had shares as low as 1,000 yuan. Notably absent from this list are the provincial government institutions, such as the Zhili Provincial Assembly and the Zhili Agriculture Association, which were also technically members of the Support Association. In fact, the Zhili Provincial Finance Bureau and the Zhili Provincial Bank could contribute on behalf of the province only because they had obtained a bank loan under the rules of the game.

Table 1 Sources of funding for the rescue of the provincial currency in 1927 (yuan)

Support Association Commitment		Provincial Commitment	
Source	Amount	Source	Amount
Modern banks	1,400,000	Bank loan	1,000,000
Indigenous banks	400,000		
Salt merchants	300,000		
Cotton mills	100,000		
Flour mills	80,000		
54 other guilds	520,000		
		Rural land taxes	1,800,000
Total	2,800,000		2,800,000

Source: Chamber Collection, 1912–1928, pp. 1139–47.

Financial strength did not always translate into power, however. The negotiations over funding the Support Association in 1927 show that merchant groups made up of Tianjin natives carried more weight in Tianjin elite circles than the nonnative modern bankers. The three largest contributors to the Support the Currency Association in 1927, the modern banks, indigenous banks, and salt merchants, all asked for reductions in their shares. Only the indigenous bankers and salt merchants, all Tianjin natives, had their shares reduced.[86] Modern banks dominated by outsiders like Bian Baimei did not.

Changes in Tianjin's elite structures had reduced but not eliminated the influence of natives, as demonstrated by the composition of Chamber of Commerce leadership. After the First World War, industrialists and bankers gained increasing prominence in the Chamber. Concurrently, the proportion of Chamber directors who were Tianjin natives fell from 94 percent in the 1910s to 75 percent in the 1920s.[87] Nonetheless, in spite of these changes, natives still dominated. By 1927, however, even Tianjin's native elites were far from united. Bian Yinchang, longtime stalwart of Chamber activities, had died in late 1926, leaving something of a power vacuum during the tumultuous years of Chu Yupu's regime. In fact, the Chamber of Commerce was leaderless for most of the period of the 1927–28 crisis. In spite of repeated urging by Governor Chu, the Chamber continued to procrastinate over choosing a chairman.[88] An exasperated Chu eventually appointed Zhang Pinti, a modern industrialist and head of the weavers' and dyers' association, as chairman and Wang Junzhi, a salt merchant and head of the salt merchants' guild, as vice chairman. Both were Tianjin natives.[89]

Since even before the 1916 crisis, Tianjin's elites had shown themselves to be a divisive and fragmented lot. Changes in the economic relations in the city during the 1910s and 1920s had begun to alter the relative balance of power among elite groups, creating even more instability. This instability combined with the particularly vicious Fengtian regime to create a volatile mixture in 1927. Given this potential for division and fragmentation, Bian Baimei's acceptance of the job as chairman of the Support Association was fraught with difficulty. In his diary he notes that he "refused stridently . . . Clearly [I] know it is full of difficulty and danger, [but I was] forced to deal with it, and make a sacrifice on behalf of society."[90] Bian had been elected a director of the Chamber of Commerce in 1920, and his status as the head of the Tianjin Bankers' Association and a recognized mediator in local disputes placed him in a unique position in Tianjin. Even Bian, however, could not unify local elites behind the cause of saving the provincial currency.

The 1927–28 crisis also shows a certain change in elite guardianship practices. There were no mass meetings in 1927, no invocations of common native place, no appeals to patriotic duty, and no attempts to compose poems or songs to convince the public of the reliability of the currency. Publicly, the provincial government simply made repeated announcements that the crisis would soon be resolved. Privately, and sometimes not so privately, the government put tremendous pressure on local elites to come up with a solution.[91] A Shandong-born provincial governor and an indispensable modern Bankers' Association led by the Jiangsu native Bian Baimei precluded the use of native place as a rallying cry. The days when Tianjin's native elites could explicitly make an appeal to localism based on native place were over, ended by the vagaries of warlord politics and the rise of a powerful modern banking industry.

The lack of patriotic appeals in 1927 is harder to explain. Local elites made no attempts to reprise Yang Yide's patriotic poem from 1916 or the "Money Scare Vernacular Song" from 1921. Perhaps the ongoing "Nationalist" revolution in South China precluded the use of patriotic discourse in support of the Fengtian regime.[92] In addition, the lack of mass meetings or mass public relations campaigns in 1927 indicates an implicit belief that the provincial money, and by extension Chu Yupu's provincial regime, was somehow not eligible for such rhetorical support. Rather than using patriotic or native-place appeals, throughout the many months of 1927, elite speeches and documents contained only vague references to an ill-defined notion of local community. In his tirade at local elites, Chu Yupu criticized Chamber leaders by saying that their "unwillingness to help the locality [*difang*] made people angry."[93] Similarly, in their appeals to have their obligations reduced, the modern Bankers' Association and the Salt Merchants' Guild used nearly identical language to describe their role in the local community. As Bian Baimei stated in his letter on behalf of the banks, "the banks are a part of commerce and industry [*shangye zhi yi fenzi*], and so of course approve" of the effort to support the currency. Likewise, the salt merchants wrote that "our guild is a part of the business world [*shangjie yi fenzi*], and so it should completely approve [of the effort to support the currency] and strives to do its duty."[94] Both organizations described themselves as being part of the local business community, but that community was divided and mutually suspicious.

The 1927 crisis did instigate two other separate and contradictory attempts to promote trust. On the one hand, the members of the Support Association prepared the "front stage" for their activities with all of the luxury and grandeur associated with modern banking. The association refurbished the former building of the Bank of Communications in the French Concession and prepared to receive the public for the operation of stamping bank money with the association's guarantee. "The interior was glowing and new. Although work on the sidewalk and yard was not yet complete, the five-color flag was flying at the corner [of the building] yesterday. All the employees had arrived at work, and the place was buzzing."[95] On the other hand, when a "certain accountant" submitted reports to the newspaper suggesting that the circulation and reserves of the Provincial Bank be made public, he wrote, "If circulation is not open [*gongkai*], then reserves are not independent and people don't dare use [the paper money of the bank]."[96] In a reprise of the contradictory measures to restore trust in 1921, the Support Association tried to hide the fundamental flaws in its structure behind a glowing and impressive facade, while the professional accountant who made anonymous suggestions to the newspaper called for openness and disclosure to restore trust.

Neither of these approaches proved to be a viable strategy. In the absence of full reserves, a united elite, and a responsible government, the carefully prepared "front stage" simply could not support the weight of the association's responsibility as guardian organization. By the time the association opened its office, the bank run had been going on for months. Not only had two "speculators" been executed, but also a customer had been killed in the crush at one office. In addition, the run had witnessed numerous fistfights and arguments over dropped notes and attempts at cheating.[97] In the presence of such obvious and public problems, the association needed much more than a pretty building to restore trust. Similarly, openness was not an alternative. Full disclosure and adequate reserves would only require local elites to put up more money, a step they were not willing to take.

As in 1916, the 1927 ad hoc organization of local elites formed to guarantee the exchange of paper money issued by a state bank failed almost as soon as it started. Funds raised by local elites once again remained totally inadequate for the purpose at hand, and a guarantee of only half of the outstanding currency was no real guarantee at all. The scope of operations of modern banks and the amount of bank-issued currency were simply too great, and local elites too parsimonious, for success. In addition, ad hoc operations had little hope of fulfilling the role of guardian organization. The creation of impersonal trust in the currency required ongoing efforts, and provisional organizations were structurally mismatched for the job. Vague promises of guarantee on the part of a provisional association did little to convince people that they should use and accept the paper money of the Provincial Bank. In addition, the Zhili Provincial Bank continued to issue currency at an alarming rate, undermining even these incomplete and poorly conceived guardianship efforts.

In the wake of the failure of the Support Association, the hard-pressed Zhili government turned to one of its most reliable sources of funds: bank loans secured by future tax revenues. In January 1928, the Zhili provincial government concluded an 800,000 yuan loan with the Tianjin Bankers' Association. Far from adequate to rescue the provincial currency, this loan simply went to support the Fengtian clique's efforts to stay in power and stop the advance of the Northern Expedition. Loans between ongoing institutions, playing by the rules of the game regarding collateral and repayment, proved more effective than ad hoc efforts to mobilize elites on behalf of the creation of impersonal trust in paper money. Banks as institutions served as effective vehicles for the concentration of financial resources, and the rules of the game allowed those resources to be used by the local state.

One of the rules of the game stipulated that bankers limit loans to exiting regimes. By the end of 1927, the Northern Expedition was threatening the survival of the Fengtian warlords. Tianjin's banks continued to make loans to the Zhili provincial government, but only reluctantly, and they tried to limit the amounts as far as possible.[98] Deprived of the ability to print money and limited by the amount of tax revenues which could be mortgaged to the banks, the Zhili government had little hope of halting the Nationalist advance. The bankers knew this to be the case, and they had no incentive to lend any more money than necessary. As the prospects of defeat became more real, the Zhili government's demands grew more desperate. In May 1928 the Tianjin Bankers' Association refused a demand for a 10 million yuan loan, saying that "when news of this loan spread, depositors began lining up to withdraw their funds."[99] The threat of the loss of trust in banks became a weapon to enforce the rules of the game. Government officials, who only months before had succeeded in borrowing large amounts of money, now got short shrift from the Tianjin Bankers' Association.[100]

In early June, Zhang Zuolin left Beijing for Manchuria. He was killed en route when the Japanese bombed his train. As Chu Yupu and the Shandong warlord Zhang Zongchang settled in to make a last-ditch fight against the Nationalists in Shandong and Zhili provinces, the Tianjin bankers settled in to wait for the transition to the new government. During the first two weeks of June, Bian claimed illness and stayed home in order to avoid further contact with government officials. His lieutenants at the bank approached the authorities in the French and British concessions for protection. The Bankers' Association simply ignored repeated demands for loans, and threats from Chu Yupu did little. Some Tianjin banks even balked at making contributions to a fund to "reward" the retreating troops—a tradition of the warlord period meant to limit looting and chaos in times of transition.[101]

The 1927–28 financial crisis revealed the weakness of both warlord authority and ad hoc local elite guardianship in promoting impersonal trust in money. Government orders and coercion failed either to stem the bank run or to force complete elite cooperation. Chu Yupu's regime lacked the necessary legitimacy and strength to enforce its will. The rules of the game limited the government's ability to borrow directly from banks, and the need for trust in the currency of the Provincial Bank limited its ability to print money. Tianjin's local elites, for their part, proved unwilling or unable to dig into their own pockets to bail out the provincial government. The elites continually fought among themselves, and the continued domination of Tianjin natives placed the Chamber of Commerce in opposition to the nonnative bankers. A temporary organization was unsuited to act as trustee for the long-term process of trust creation, and guaranteeing only half of the paper money in circulation set the stage for conflict and insider abuse. In addition, guaranteeing a fixed sum did little to promote trust when the amount of money in circulation kept increasing.

In the end, the growing power and importance of modern banks came to the fore. Bankers commanded greater amounts of financial resources than any other merchant group in Tianjin, and they were willing, if not always happy, to put those resources at the service of the state when certain rules of the game applied. Continuous and stable organizations dealt with other continuous and stable organizations; loans required collateral and confirmed sources of repayment; banks negotiated collectively; and loans were withheld from faltering regimes. In addition to the rules of the game, Tianjin's bankers initiated a number of other institutional arrangements to promote trusting behaviors during this period. These arrangements included a drive to increase the autonomy of the Bank of China and the Bank of Communications; reorganization of the internal structures of the two banks to isolate risks and centralize currency issue in treaty ports; risk pooling by the Four Banks; and the construction of elaborate bank buildings to embody, and conceal, the expert knowledge of banking. Increases in bank deposits, including *chuxu* deposits from small savers, and the rapid growth in the circulation of bank-issued money provide evidence that the banks had succeeded in promoting trusting behaviors, though the shared norm of nationalism also played a role.

Fragmentation of the state under the warlords had given bankers an opportunity to achieve a certain amount of independence, but it also increased the number of political centers with which the banks had to deal. Using their expert knowledge, and following certain rules of the game, banks survived and even prospered in the 1920s. Nonetheless, bankers had no admiration for the warlords; they wanted an atmosphere in which the actions of government officials matched their own sense of professionalism. Once Bian described a job at the Bank of China's Beijing branch by saying that it required someone willing to "endure humiliation in order to carry out an important mission."[102] Bian saw his mission as in part following the centuries-long line of Chinese scholar-officials who served the state with virtue on behalf of the people, in part Buddhist vocation to save living beings, and in part a modern and Western vocation of building society through economic prosperity. As he began a new diary on the first day of 1928, he named it the "Pulling up from Hardship Diary," and stamped it with a chop which read, "the monk who pulls the masses up from hardship." He explained the name as follows:

> If a great man wants to save people from bad conditions, then [he should] work and worry and never relax like Yu [the mythical emperor] who had calluses on his hands and feet [from his hard work] and like Confucius and Mozi who did not rest.
>
> Last year when I went to the Biyun temple in the Western Hills [near Beijing] I counted five hundred statues. I got to one with white eyebrows [*baimei*—a play on Bian's own name] and gray hair called the Monk who Pulls the Masses up from Hardship. From that time, I took this as my inspiration.[103]

If "enduring humiliation to carry out an important mission" marked the years before 1928, Bian still had hopes that he would be able to "pull the masses up from hardship" in the future. That future would take place under the rule of the Nationalist government, and with the direction of the Nationalist (Guomindang) Party. The Nationalists, however, had their own ideas about the role of banks in state building and the role of the party in elite organization.

5

Early Nationalist Rule and a New Environment

I would like to see a thorough break.

— Bian Baimei, *Diary*, February 28, 1927

By the summer of 1928, much of the open conflict within the Guomindang (GMD), or Nationalist Party, and government had already diminished. Chiang Kai-shek's bloody purge of communists and labor activists was already more than a year in the past, and Sun Fo's attempt to lead a leftist coalition regime in late 1927 had collapsed under financial strain. In January 1928 supporters called Chiang Kai-shek back into power, and he successfully directed the second half of the Northern Expedition, taking the North China plain, including Tianjin, in June. A "reign of terror" against Shanghai capitalists financed the huge military expenditures of 1928, helping to fuel Chiang's success.[1]

The early Nationalist regime in North China was an alliance with two northern warlords: Yan Xishan and Feng Yuxiang. The members of this coalition divided up government posts among their followers, creating a fragmented state apparatus. Among all the various claimants to power, Tianjin's banks and bankers struggled to identify those government institutions with the requisite continuity and staying power to play by the rules of the game of modern banking and provide a secure environment for the creation of impersonal trust. The Nationalist government in Nanjing held out the most promise for such an institutional framework, and in many ways, Tianjin's modern bankers made natural allies for the Nationalist state. As outsiders, the bankers had little interest in protecting local power from central state intrusion. At the same time, GMD activism still existed, and Tianjin's native elites, government officials, and modern bankers shared a fear of party domination. In a Leninist system, the party reserves the right to set the institutional rules of the game for all other organizations. Party rule threatened merchant associations, government organs, and banks alike.

Tianjin under Early Nationalist Rule

Bian Baimei started preparing for the advent of Nationalist government rule long before the Fengtian regime limped to defeat and retreated to temporary safety north of the Great Wall. As early as October 1926, Bian discussed with Feng Gengguang how to handle the rising Nationalist power in the south. Two days later, he began reading Sun Yat-sen's *Three People's Principles.*[2] In 1926, however, the actual arrival of the Northern Expedition in Tianjin was still a distant prospect. The much more immediate impact of the Nationalist movement came from labor unrest. The massive increase in labor agitation, much of it organized by the Communist Party, which cooperated with the Nationalists during the first stage of the Northern Expedition, had repercussions as far north as Beijing and Tianjin. As a preliminary measure to deal with potential worker unrest, the head of the Salt Bank, Wu Dingchang, organized a Producers' Association *(shengchan xiehui)* in Tianjin along with several of the city's modern industrialists.[3] Wu's leadership of this group indicates the fragmented nature of the Nationalist movement from its beginning. Wu, an early member of Sun Yat-sen's Tongmeng Hui, was a longtime follower of Sun and a natural ally of the Nationalists, but as a banker and capitalist, he balked at the more radical side of party activism. The presence of Bian Baimei as one of the Producers' Association's six founding members also seems surprising. Bank employees were few in number and had traditionally benefited from relatively good pay and working conditions, certainly in comparison with the armies of laborers who kept Tianjin's cotton mills, chemical factories, mines, flour mills, and transport system running. Nonetheless, labor unrest presented a real threat to banking elites in 1926. After the Nationalists occupied Hankou, the bank employees there organized a union, and modern bankers in the north feared similar activism from their own workers.[4]

At the same time that Bian and his colleagues in Tianjin were preparing for the more radical elements inherent in a potential Nationalist victory, China's modern banks prepared for an accommodation with the Nationalist government. The vice president of the Bank of China, Zhang Jia'ao, left Beijing in 1926 for Shanghai, where he directed the coming rapprochement between the bank and the Nationalist government, including secret loans to the Nationalists even before they reached Shanghai.[5] In the north, Bian Baimei alternately longed for and feared the Nationalists' approach. Completely disillusioned with warlord government, he was ready to welcome change, even if that change included with labor activism and anticapitalist rhetoric. Bian's major worry was not that the Guomindang would be too radical, but that it would not be radical enough to break China loose from the torpor of the preceding years:

> I would like to see a thorough break [*chedi zhi pohuai*], and don't want to see an incomplete getting-by. Even though there would be great chaos with a complete break, the mutual stimulation and mixing together amidst the chaos could create real stability. Otherwise, [if there is no thorough break], after a few months of calm, chaos will rise again and there will never be hope for stability. In chaos some people, unfortunately, will be sacrificed, but if we can achieve stability for those who come after us, then this sacrifice would certainly be worth it.[6]

Bian's almost mystical faith in the regenerative force of chaos shows the lengths to which warlord misrule had driven him.

His professional actions, however, were much more pragmatic than these musings confided to his diary. The "complete break" he envisioned clearly did not include a break with the institutional integrity of the Bank of China. During the transition to Nationalist rule, he worked assiduously toward the goal of preserving the bank. On the labor front, he preached appeasement and peaceful resolution; in dealing with Chu Yupu's Fengtian-sponsored regime, he tried to limit bank loans to a bare minimum, anticipating its imminent collapse; and in anticipating a new Nanjing regime, he prepared to cooperate. As he noted in his diary: "We only recognize government offices and don't ask who is the official in charge. No single political party can get special services just because it is a party army. Also there is no need to think of it as illegitimate just because it is a party army. Just as long as [demands] are reasonable and we have the ability, we can do it."[7] Reasonable demands, however, did not characterize the Nationalist movement during the period of the Northern Expedition. Two months later, the Nationalists forced the Shanghai branch of the Bank of China to lend the government 2 million yuan after the branch had refused a loan of 1.5 million.[8]

As the Northern Expedition approached Tianjin in the summer of 1928, members of Tianjin's native elite tried to gain a greater voice in the outcome of the struggle for their city. A Committee for Public Safety, formed by a group of native elites, colluded with one of Zhang Zongchang's subordinate military officers to take over the city and then run negotiations for turnover to the Nationalist faction of their choice. Incensed by the perfidy of his underling, Zhang Zongchang literally handed over power to the Shanxi commander and withdrew from the city. The acerbic Zhang—whose corruption and cruelty during his rule of Shandong are legendary—preferred to give Tianjin to his opponent than to a rebellious subordinate.[9] External forces thwarted this attempt by native elites to gain a greater say in the fate of the city, and its defeat made for an unpromising omen for the protection of local elite power in the coming years.

The Nationalist coalition partners reorganized administration in Zhili Province. They made Beijing, renamed Beiping, the capital of the province, now renamed Hebei. In addition, they created a municipal government for the city of Tianjin and removed it from the control of the province, making it a special city that reported directly to the central government.[10] Initially, though, it was not entirely clear if the central government meant the Nationalists in Nanjing or Yan Xishan in Shanxi. Shanxi appointees staffed much of the new Tianjin bureaucracy, including the new office of mayor. Confusion plagued the new government in Tianjin. "Sometimes as many as four individuals . . . appeared as appointees to certain positions," variously claiming appointment from General Yan, the Nationalist government, the GMD, or local officials.[11] All of the factions maneuvering for power wanted access to the city's substantial financial resources. Yan Xishan and the Nationalists divided up Tianjin's revenue sources, though fair division remained a matter of contention. In November 1928, General Bai Chongxi, a Nanjing representative, protested to Nanjing that Yan was sending the lion's portion of the revenues of the Tianjin-Beiping area to Shanxi. Later, when the local salt commissioner refused to deliver salt on which Nanjing taxes had been paid, the Nanjing authorities ordered the storehouses of the salt gabelle occupied and locked in an attempt to ensure central control over salt taxes. From the standpoint of Tianjin's bankers, however, certain sources of taxes were more important than others. Nanjing claimed control of the important 2.5 percent customs surcharge that had previously played such a large role in loans to the provincial government.[12]

Even before Chu Yupu and Zhang Zongchang's troops had retreated from Tianjin, Wu Dingchang, who had close ties to individuals in the Nationalist government, told Bian that the Nationalist Finance Ministry wanted a loan. Then on June 15, only two weeks after Tianjin's bankers had told Chu Yupu that they "did not have the strength" to make any more loans, the Tianjin Bankers' Association met with representatives of the new Nationalist government about a 5 million yuan loan to be made by the Beijing and Tianjin banks. Tianjin's bankers alternately negotiated that day between Shanxi militarists and Nationalist bureaucrats in the fragmented pattern that would characterize Nationalist rule over Tianjin in its early years.[13] Tianjin's bankers proceeded cautiously in trying to sort out the new lines of power. They pledged cooperation with the Shanxi commander but gave their serious attention to negotiating with the Finance Ministry in Nanjing. Their experience told them that established government institutions like the Finance Ministry would have greater continuity and greater reliability for playing by the rules of the game than the ever-shifting "army groups" and "commands" which made up military governments.[14] In addition, Tianjin's bankers had more in common with the southern bureaucrats of the Nanjing government than they did with the Shanxi militarists. For example, Qian Junkui, the representative sent by the Nanjing Finance Ministry to speak to Bian Baimei, was a Jiangsu native who had studied in the United States at the same time as Bian and who had previously worked for the Bank of China.[15] The Finance Ministry concluded a provisional 5 million yuan loan from the Tianjin and Beiping Bankers' Associations in early July, and then appointed several northern bankers, including Bian Baimei, to a committee which would oversee the issue of government bonds secured by the 2.5 percent customs surcharge taxes.[16] Tianjin's bankers politely declined ad hoc requests for loans from less legitimate government agencies, though.[17] In contrast to his self-professed desire for a complete break, Bian still wanted to abide by the rules of the game, in which institutional legitimacy played a key role.

The composition of the Tianjin association appointed by the Finance Ministry to sell an upcoming issue of 2.5 percent customs surcharge tax treasury notes nicely illustrates the coalition of interests which came together in the early days of Nationalist rule in Tianjin. The standing committee of the association had eleven members: three modern bankers who were all natives of Jiangsu, including Bian Baimei; two Shanxi military officials, one of whom was a native of Shanxi and one a native of Hubei; and six local businessmen, including the chairman of the Chamber of Commerce, all but one of whom were Tianjin natives.[18] Significantly, the Tianjin association for the sale of the treasury notes worked closely with its Beiping counterpart.[19] During the 1910s and 1920s, Beijing was the seat of the government, from which

Tianjin's bankers and native elites tried to shield their resources. After the success of the Northern Expedition, Tianjin and Beiping simply became sister cities, objects of extraction from distant governments in Nanjing and Shanxi.

Elite Organizations in Crisis

At the same time that the Nanjing Finance Ministry was patching together this makeshift elite coalition to sell treasury notes, the Tianjin GMD branch tried to reorganize local groups under party leadership. Radical activities of the GMD in Tianjin were somewhat problematic from the beginning, however.[20] Although the previous year's purge of the communists did not end party activism, it certainly left open the possibility that such activism could easily be painted by its opponents with the "communist" brush. More than that, Yan Xishan's alliance of convenience with the Nationalists had little to do with party-led revolution. Shanxi-appointed government authorities in Tianjin had even less in common with the party activists there than the state did with the party in Shanghai.[21] For example, in the realm of labor relations, the local government and the GMD did not see eye to eye. Chu Yupu's regime had severely suppressed Tianjin's union movement, but shortly after the GMD arrived in the city, it attempted to reorganize labor unions under party sponsorship. The officials running the government in Tianjin, representing the Shanxi faction, quickly ordered the dissolution of all unions, and the GMD reluctantly complied. Labor agitation did not cease completely, however, and many labor disputes cropped up over the next few months, leading the American consul general to observe that "the local authorities have asserted that they can probably control the labor unions but if the Kuomintang [Guomindang] becomes interested they are powerless beyond good offices."[22] In other words, Shanxi officials would do their best to keep party activism in check, but they could not always expect to succeed.

In addition to its labor activities, the GMD launched an all-out offensive on the entrenched interests of Tianjin's local elites. In a pattern similar to that in Shanghai in the previous year, this was a two-part offensive. First, it began with the organization of small shopkeepers, artisans, and shop employees into a Merchants' Union *(shamgmin xiehui)*. Party organization of such unions was part of a nationwide attempt to dissolve preexisting elite organizations like the Chambers of Commerce and replace them with a broader based party-led group.[23] Second, also as part of a national movement, the party sponsored an anti–Japanese goods movement for the purpose of registering and taxing imports from Japan. Anti-foreign boycotts had a long history in China, but this movement conveniently also served as a way of raising money for the Tianjin branch of the GMD.[24]

Attempts by the Nationalist Party to reorganize and undermine elite business structures date back to the Nationalists' experiences in Guangdong in the mid-1920s.[25] In 1927, after the Northern Expedition reached Shanghai, and even after the purge of the communists, the party declared that Merchants' Unions would take the place of elitist Chambers of Commerce. By mid-1928, however, the party had moderated its stance, declaring that Chambers of Commerce and Merchants' Unions could coexist.[26] The leaders of the Tianjin Merchants' Union toed the party line and initially adopted a semi-cooperative attitude toward the Chamber. One Merchants' Union leader told reporters that "although the Chamber of Commerce represents 'imperialist-type' capitalists, I have hopes that it will awaken and not oppress the class of small and medium merchants . . . Both organizations can exist without conflict."[27] In a similar spirit of cooperation, the Tianjin Chamber of Commerce wrote to the local party branch approving the formation of the Merchants' Union and asking the party to lead it. Like the leaders of the Merchants' Union, Chamber leaders had quickly adopted the rhetoric of the Nationalist revolution. Their letter to the party stated, "The period of military revolution will conclude and the period of political tutelage will begin. All undertakings will undergo renewal."[28] Perhaps Chamber leaders even believed that "renewal" of local elite organizations would allow the Chamber to continue functioning as before. In any case, they had little time to worry about the Merchants' Union, as the anti–Japanese goods movement began to heat up.

In August 1928 the GMD committee in Tianjin organized an anti–Japanese goods association, and in September and October it and other related organizations, including the Merchants' Union, dispatched teams to discover and register Japanese goods at shops all over the Chinese areas of Tianjin. The Merchants' Union organized car and bicycle teams to patrol the city; activists even set up stations to examine goods entering and leaving the foreign concessions.[29] The anti–Japanese goods movement threatened to damage some of Tianjin's largest and most prosperous businesses. Tianjin merchants imported large amounts of flour, paper, woolen yarn, sugar, matches, and other goods from Japan, totaling approximately 75 million yuan in 1928. The movement to register, boycott, and tax Japanese goods in

Tianjin simmered for the next couple of months throughout the summer of 1928, but before it came to a boil in the fall, Tianjin's elite faced yet another challenge.

The next shock came from Chiang Kai-shek himself. In mid-October 1928, amidst circumstances still shrouded in mystery, Chiang ordered the arrest of four of the leaders of the Tianjin salt guild, including the head of the guild and the vice chairman of the Tianjin Chamber of Commerce, Wang Junzhi. The arrest of such prominent members of the native elite sent shock waves throughout Tianjin. Regardless of the exact circumstances, the desire for revenue certainly lay at the heart of the conflict.[30] It is also likely that Chiang was trying to ensure his control over salt revenues to the detriment of Yan Xishan. Fearful that the arrests signaled the beginning of an extortion campaign like that in Shanghai during the previous year, Tianjin's elite groups scrambled to ask for the release of the salt merchants. Even the Tianjin Bankers' Association sent a telegram asking that they be released on bail, pending further investigation.[31] Regardless of their willingness to cooperate with the Nationalist government, secret arrest orders based on unexplained reasons did not fit the rules of the game of government-elite relations as seen by Tianjin's bankers. Nonetheless, the Nanjing government remained deaf to all protests and proceeded with plans to take the four arrested salt merchants to Nanjing for "investigation." Chiang Kai-shek's only response to the many inquiries he received about the incident was a curt telegram saying that their arrest was related to the payment of two categories of taxes.[32] The salt merchants would remain in Nanjing for twenty-eight months; Wang Junzhi died in captivity in early 1931. Eventually, the remaining four merchants returned to Tianjin, and the Salt Merchants' Guild paid a fine of 500,000 yuan to the Nanjing government.[33]

At the same time the Chamber was trying to obtain the release of the salt merchants, the anti–Japanese goods movement came to a head. In late October the Tianjin merchants who sold Japanese goods wrote to the Bankers' Association saying that the anti-Japanese movement might endanger their solvency. After a meeting at the party office to discuss the matter, Bian Baimei noted that "there was a lot of criticism of the Chamber of Commerce, and if the Chamber does not have an appropriate solution, it will be very dangerous." From the beginning the Tianjin GMD branch made it clear that the anti–Japanese goods campaign was as much an attack on the elites as it was a boycott of Japan. The officials told Bian Baimei that their strategy was to be "strict with large merchants and lenient with small." City authorities, however, wanted the matter to be resolved as quickly and in as orderly a fashion as possible. In November the mayor proposed a 100,000 yuan payment in lieu of the inspection and registration of goods.[34] Since the anti–Japanese goods association had proposed a 9 percent fine, or "national salvation fund," on all Japanese goods, a mere 100,000 yuan payment appeared to be a complete sellout.[35] The association did not accept this proposal, and plans went ahead for inspection and registration. In response, more than two hundred shops closed their doors, and five merchants were arrested and placed in custody on the premises of the association, as the conflict threatened to bring commerce in Tianjin to a halt. Over the next few days, Chamber leaders came to see Bian almost daily, though for the most part he tried to stay out of the fray. Within a few days the anti–Japanese goods association, the Chamber, the city government, Japanese goods dealers, and the local party branch reached an accommodation. The Japanese goods shops reopened for business, and the Chamber leaders went back to work.[36] The total payment to the national salvation fund was slightly over 150,000 yuan. Long-run damage to the Japanese goods merchants proved greater, however; in 1929 imports of Japanese goods into Tianjin declined by approximately 28 million yuan from the year before.[37]

The quick resolution resulted in part from the capitulation of the Japanese goods merchants who agreed to register their goods, and in part from reorganization of the Guomindang district committee. As the American consul general in Tianjin noted, the anti-Japanese movement "lacks the impetus and direction given it while the Kuomintang [Guomindang] district committee was in power."[38] The reasons why the central party committee replaced the personnel of the Tianjin and Beijing party branches at this time remain obscure. An editorial in Wu Dingchang's *Dagong Bao* simply says that the internal workings of the party were of no concern to outsiders and that the important thing was to understand that the party branches had to observe party discipline and obey the center.[39] This would not be the last time the Tianjin party committee had troubles; committee operations would be suspended, reorganized, and revamped many times over the next decade.

Resolution of the Japanese goods crisis did not mean the end of challenges to elite organizations, either. Someone wrote to the government alleging that Zhang Pinti had not been fairly elected chairman of the Chamber of Commerce in 1927 and had subsequently abused his position for economic gain. Zhang fired off a defense to the newspapers asking for a thorough investigation, but he could not hold out and two months later submitted his resignation.[40] For the Chamber leaders the writing was on the wall. Their vice chairman was in custody in Nanjing, the anti–Japanese goods movement had damaged an important commercial sector, and the organization of the Merchants' Union threatened the Chamber's very existence. Chamber leaders wrote to the All-China Federation of Chambers of Commerce to urge the Nanjing government to resolve the legal ambiguity of the coexistence of the Chambers of Commerce and Merchants' Unions.[41] Shortly thereafter, Bian noted in his diary that "the operations of the Chamber of Commerce have ceased, the president resigned, and all of the members of the discussion committee are in hiding." Bian, a member of the discussion committee himself, invited the committee members to dinner at the Bankers' Association and decided "to ask the city government if we can [have an election] under the old Chamber of Commerce law."[42] In 1928, Bian was one of only ten nonnative directors of the Tianjin Chamber of Commerce (out of a total of fifty-four), but his position at the head of the Tianjin Bankers' Association and his stature in the city placed him in a position to act as an organizer of elite activities.[43] Much had changed in the twelve years since Bian had resigned his position as middle manager at the Bank of China and come to Tianjin in the midst of the 1916 crisis.

In fact, the mayor of Tianjin actually wanted Bian to take over as chairman of the Chamber of Commerce and named Wang Wendian to take over as vice chairman. Wang, a Zhejiang native and chief representative of the Nanyang cigarette company in Tianjin, also served as manager of the Sino-American Huiye Bank. As a modern industrialist, banker, and southerner, Wang shared with Bian many of the qualities which appealed to the government authorities, who needed a functioning merchant organization in order to raise funds and institute new laws. Bian balked at the suggestion and advised the mayor to proceed cautiously.[44] He had good reason to be concerned. No nonnative Tianjiner had headed the Chamber since Yuan Shikai's ill-fated and short-lived attempt to found a business organization run by Zhejiang and Guangdong compradors in 1902.[45] In addition, the challenges the Chamber faced in late 1928 made direction of that organization a thankless, and possibly dangerous, job.

The spring and summer of 1929 saw the resurgence of the national movement to abolish Chambers of Commerce in favor of Merchants' Unions.[46] In May the Merchants' Union in Tianjin asked that the city government rescind the seals of the Chamber of Commerce. The call to revoke the seals accompanied allegations that the Chamber was run by "local bullies and compradors" and had "cooperated with the warlords." The city government pragmatically replied that "the question of the survival of the Chambers of Commerce has not yet been decided."[47] In the end, the national GMD lost its battle to overturn the Chambers. Promulgation of a new Chamber of Commerce law in the summer of 1929 abandoned revolutionary rhetoric, and the trade associations—the existing *tongye gonghui,* not the newly organized Merchants' Unions—continued as the basis for the Chambers of Commerce. At the same time, the Tianjin GMD party branch was once again shut down for reorganization.[48] In spite of this fundamental victory, the Tianjin Chamber of Commerce would never be the same again. Organization of a large number of small stores and artisan shops brought a new segment of Tianjin's merchant class into the political realm. These newcomers may not have had their own separate organization after the summer of 1929, but neither would they be easily ignored by the elites who ran the Tianjin Chamber of Commerce in the years to come.

The newly activist small- and medium-sized merchants contested the process of Chamber reorganization under the new Chamber of Commerce law at every turn. The most immediate challenge to the status quo came over a dispute as to whether merchant firms could join the Chamber as individual shops or whether they would first be forced to organize trade associations. The dispute involved the ability to control the Chamber because, according to the new law, guilds could appoint one representative to the Chamber for every fifteen member firms up to a maximum of twenty-one representatives. Businesses which joined as individual firms, however, could send one representative for every five employees up to a total of three representatives.[49] For trades with many small shops, the difference could be dramatic. For example, if two hundred firms composed a given trade, then as a trade association member the group could appoint thirteen representatives to the Chamber of Commerce. But if each of those firms joined the Chamber of Commerce as individual members, then each could appoint from one to three representatives, for a minimum of two hundred representatives and a potential total of six hundred. In contrast, trades such as banking and cotton manufacture, which had a small number of very large firms, would be able to appoint only a fraction of that number of representatives. The Tianjin Banking Association had only eighteen members, qualifying it for only one representative to the Chamber of Commerce if it joined as a trade association or a maximum of fifty-four representatives if banks joined as individual firms.

Before this dispute could be resolved, though, the political situation in North China changed once again, as Yan Xishan took steps to declare independence from the Nanjing government. As early as May 1930, he tried to tell the Tianjin banks how and to whom they should disburse salt tax funds in their possession. As a next step, he set up a "national bank" in the Shanxi capital of Taiyuan. He tried to entice Bian to come and run the bank, with no luck. In Tianjin, Yan disbanded the local GMD party committee and the next month took control of the Tianjin customs administration.[50] A group of Shanxi military officers gave a banquet at city hall for Bian and a group of modern bankers, demanding a loan of 9 million yuan over three months, which could not be "reduced in amount." Even though their attitude was "almost threatening," Bian declined "politely, but righteously," pointing out that the proposed collateral for the loans, the Shandong salt tax, was unacceptable. The next day several bankers met and decided to propose that the government borrow money on the 2.5 percent customs surplus, but with the caveat that funds had to be set aside to repay the Nationalist government treasury notes issued two years previously. In addition, the bankers decided to wait until "a so-called formal government has been established in Beiping." As with previous regimes, Tianjin's bankers fought to uphold the rules of the game and make loans to formally structured government institutions secured by viable collateral. As negotiations continued, the banks managed to delay a decision. Within a month Zhang Xueliang weighed in on Nanjing's side, and Yan Xishan retreated to Shanxi.[51]

During Yan's brief takeover of Tianjin, the ongoing work of reorganizing the trade associations and preparing for election of Chamber leaders came to a complete halt. In truth, Chamber leaders had no reason to rush to reorganize. A functioning and legitimate Chamber would only have given Yan Xishan that much more leverage in extracting financial resources from the local community. In fact, Yan's officials repeatedly inquired about the delays in reorganization.[52] The defeat of Yan Xishan brought a revival of the local GMD party committee, a new mayor and official bureaucracy for the city government, and a renewed effort to reorganize merchant groups. More than forty trade associations quickly reorganized, elected directors, and appointed representatives to the Chamber of Commerce. In a victory for elite forces, individual firms were not allowed to join the Chamber, and none of the merchants and artisans who had joined the Tianjin Merchants' Union formed trade associations, excluding small- and medium-sized merchants from the Chamber election.[53] The Chamber held an election to choose a new board of directors in February 1931. After a brief behind-the-scenes contest with the indigenous banker Wang Xiaoyan, Zhang Pinti was reelected chairman.[54] Of the twenty-two people elected as standing, administrative, and supervisory committee members, seven worked for modern industries and only six were nonnative Tianjiners, including Bian Baimei and one other modern banker. Otherwise, the vast majority of committee members were Tianjin natives from the city's traditional trades. In spite of the three years of struggle since the arrival of the Guomindang in 1928, the native elite managed to preserve the status quo to a remarkable extent.[55]

Even with the continued dominance of the traditional trade associations, subtle changes in elite organizations began to appear. For example, the Tianjin Bankers' Association elected new officers on March 8, two days before the Chamber election. Instead of meeting in private, as in the past, the Tianjin GMD branch and the city's Social Affairs Bureau both sent representatives to observe and deliver speeches. In addition, the symbolic presence of the state was greater than ever before; at the inauguration ceremony of the newly elected officers, all of the participants bowed three times to a picture of the late leader Sun Yat-sen, listened to a recitation of his will, and then stood in silence for three minutes. Structurally, the requirement that half of a trade association's directors needed to be reelected every two years and could serve at most two terms ensured that although Bian Baimei was again elected chairman, he would be able to continue in the post for only another two, or at most four, years.[56]

The new physical and symbolic presence of the party and state demonstrated the activist nature of the Nationalist government. That same activism combined with attempts by bankers to maintain the institutional integrity of their banks to create a new regulatory environment for both banking and bank-issued money.

Transparency and Trust

As had become the pattern with government transitions, financial crises marked the Northern Expedition's arrival in Tianjin. In addition to the extended crisis at the Zhili Provincial Bank at the end of the Fengtian regime, a number of smaller bank runs on less prominent banks followed the establishment of the Nationalist government in 1928, 1929, and 1930. These bank runs, and the more serious problem of oceans of worthless provincial banknotes flowing all over China, created an atmosphere in which the very nature of the money supply came into question. Ongoing issues involving trust in paper money and an activist Nationalist state prompted considerable activity regarding the transparency, regulation, and control of banks and bank-issued money.

As early as 1910, the Qing government's ill-fated monetary law required the regular publication of figures on currency issue and reserves.[57] Transparency as a means of creating trust came to the fore again in the 1920s in debates on the pros and cons of keeping bank reserves secret. Bank of China vice president Zhang Jia'ao had actually floated the idea of making currency reserves open in the spring of 1921, several months before the financial crisis broke out. Bian Baimei opposed the notion, saying that it was a good idea in principle but difficult to implement.[58] Bian knew that regular disclosure would limit the bank's flexibility to respond to problems such as those posed by government demands for loans. Within a few months of their discussion, the November bank run prompted demands for openness from local elites. As a result, the Tianjin branches of the Bank of China and the Bank of Communications became the first banks in China to regularly publish their currency reserve status. The banks stopped publishing currency reserve reports after a year or two, though, as Chamber supervision faded. Afterwards, bankers intermittently discussed making reserves open among themselves but took no further action.[59] Then, in the summer of 1924, a run on the National Industrial Bank of China in Tianjin prompted the Chamber leader Sun Junqing to advocate making currency issue open and sending people to audit the banks. Bian commented in his diary that "Sun really did not know the seriousness involved, and wanted to arbitrarily exercise power." Sun eventually agreed that the Chamber was unable to take on too much responsibility in auditing the banks' books, and the plan was dropped.[60]

Transparency, or openness, in currency issue and reserves provided a number of advantages and disadvantages for bankers, state officials, and would-be regulators. From the standpoint of bankers, openness was a two-edged sword. On the one hand, transparency was a useful means of promoting trust by convincing the public of the reliability with which they practiced their expert knowledge and managed the money supply. On the other hand, prudence dictated that the bank try to leave some room for flexibility. With secrecy, a bank could temporarily reduce the amount of silver in its currency reserve if it faced difficulties. As long as no one on the outside found out, no harm would come. For government officials, secrecy allowed bankers to finance loans to the government by adjusting currency reserves—or by issuing new money without increasing reserves. As a result, government officials during the warlord period made little effort to force banks to become more transparent. In contrast, if banks routinely published reserve information, they could use the threat of public panic to resist government loan demands and force the government to respect the rules of the game. For would-be regulators like Tianjin elites, openness could be a powerful tool to force banks to comply with the standards set by their own expert knowledge, but it could also place the regulators in a position of taking responsibility when reserves were found to be wanting. As Bian Baimei told Sun Junqing in 1924, the Chamber simply did not have the resources to make up any shortfalls that audits of the banks might discover.[61] In fact, an audit would actually do more to destroy trust than to create it if shortfalls were made public without any corresponding ameliorative action. As a result, with the exception of a brief period after the 1921 crisis, bankers, government officials, and local elites all colluded throughout the warlord years, tacitly accepting secrecy, and the flexibility it allowed, as the best means of maintaining trust.

The rise of the Nationalists revived discussion of making reserves open. By 1927 and 1928, a broad consensus had emerged among bankers, local elites, and Nationalist officials on the importance of making currency reserves public. Zhang Jia'ao at the Bank of China, Chen Guangfu of the Shanghai Commercial and Savings Bank, Li Ming of the Zhejiang Industrial Bank in Shanghai, and Wang Kemin, still closely tied to the Bank of China in the north, all advocated making their banks' reserves public. After the Northern Expedition arrived in Tianjin in 1928, the Chamber of Commerce dispatched a team to audit and make public the reserves of the Bank of China and the Bank of Communications. A few months later the Nanjing Finance Ministry followed up this initial effort and required regular reports on the currency reserves of Tianjin banks.[62]

This consensus for openness grew from three sources. First, Zhili was hardly the only province in which local authorities had abused currency-issuing privileges during the warlord period. Fengtian, Henan, Hubei, and Shandong all had large amounts of worthless currency issued by government banks controlled by warlords.[63] If the Nationalists wanted to prove that they differed from warlords, then, among other things, they needed to refrain from taking actions that hurt trust in currency. As the Northern Expedition force moved north in 1928, one of its promises included rectification of the money supply. In Shandong, Nationalists often celebrated victories by staging bonfires of the worthless local paper money.[64] Second, concern about Nationalist policies toward banks and bank money caused bankers to consider some preemptive actions to preserve the integrity of their banks. Nationalist plans for a central bank included provisions for making reserves public, thus providing China's other banks with new and unprecedented competition for trust from users of paper money. At the same time, the Nationalist government had tried to inspect the reserves of the Bank of China in Shanghai as early as November 1927. Zhang Jia'ao refused to open the bank's books, but he could not resist such moves forever.[65] Third, Nationalist demands for loans raised the specter, once again, of the need to issue paper money to finance government activities. As Zhang Jia'ao wrote to Bian Baimei in 1927, making currency reserves public provided a way of "resisting outside forces."[66] In the end, however, the consensus for transparency was easier to achieve than implement, and only the Bank of China's Shanghai branch and the new Central Bank made their currency reserves open as early as 1928. Most other Chinese banks followed over the next few years, and by 1931 the Nationalist government had codified transparency of currency issue into law.[67] In the early Nationalist period, however, banks implemented openness only in fits and starts. Powerful forces for secrecy still remained, as shown by the events surrounding a number of small bank runs, especially a run at the Quanye Bank in Tianjin in late 1930 and early 1931.

In 1928 a number of bank runs involved small-denomination paper money of less than one yuan, so-called dime *(jiaopiao)* notes. Because this paper money circulated most widely among low-income groups, these bank runs hit the lower levels of Tianjin society hard.[68] Preoccupied with other matters, neither the government nor local elites in Tianjin did much to alleviate the runs. Instead, the Tianjin Bankers' Association coordinated help from other Tianjin banks, but only when the banks in trouble could play by the rules of the game and provide reliable collateral for loans.[69] Unlike the ill-fated attempts at elite guardianship in 1916 and 1927–28, actions by the Tianjin Bankers' Associations represented more limited, and more effective, measures to extend liquidity to banks based on the value of their assets. The actions of Tianjin's bankers at the time demonstrate the truth of Charles Goodhart's claim that "despite the manifold problems of agreeing on common action, and how to share the (potential) costs of such support actions, historical experience suggests that groupings of major commercial banks—even in the absence of leadership from a Central Bank—can still on occasion mount partial support and relief operations during crises."[70] The small size of the banks helped make possible the success of this kind of guardianship, as did the consensus among professional bankers on the standards of expert knowledge with which to judge collateral and extend loans. Interestingly, the guardianship activities of the Tianjin Bankers' Association did not extend to the provincial currency issued to finance Chu Yupu's former Fengtian regime. The Nationalist government dissolved the Zhili Provincial Bank in 1928, and Tianjin's residents had to absorb about 6 million yuan in losses.[71] Likewise, the Tianjin Bankers' Association initially disclaimed any responsibility for the Shanxi Provincial Bank's debts, including its currency, incurred during the short period of Shanxi rule in 1930.[72] When it turned out that the Shanxi Provincial Bank had left substantial deposits at the Tianjin branches of the Four Banks, then the Bankers' Association did step in and arranged for liquidating the deposits and paying off holders of Shanxi paper money.[73]

The most intractable bank run came in late 1930, when a crisis caught the managers of the Tianjin branch of the Quanye bank by surprise. The branch had incurred bank runs on its notes in 1928 and 1929, but both times the crises died down without seriously affecting the bank.[74] Founded in 1921, the Quanye (Catalyzing Industry and Commerce) Bank was founded by a combination of Lower Yangzi merchants and Beiyang officials.[75] On September 23, 1930, only one day after Zhang Xueliang had retaken Tianjin for the Nationalists, runs on the local offices of the Shanxi Provincial Bank and the Hebei Provincial Bank spread to Quanye as well.[76] The next day, when anxious note holders showed up at the bank, they found the doors closed and a note promising that exchange would continue when the bank's main office in Shanghai sent additional funds. After the first hectic day of exchanging money during the bank run, Quanye had only about 90,000 yuan in outstanding currency. Since dime notes made up the vast majority of the bank's paper money, the impact on ordinary people was particularly severe. The bank manager's repeated statements that the Shanghai office would shortly be sending money started to ring hollow after two months of delays. Finally, money did arrive from Shanghai, and exchange began on December 1 under supervision of representatives of the finance and social departments of the city government, the police department, and a recently reconstituted Chamber of Commerce. By December 13, virtually all of the bank's paper money had been withdrawn from the market.[77] Resolution of the crisis relied on Quanye's ability to access funds from its branch system, but the constant delays in the arrival of those funds also demonstrates the importance of pressure from local regulatory activities.

In mid-October the Finance Bureau of the Tianjin municipal government had ordered an audit of the books of the Tianjin branch of the bank. We thus have an opportunity to examine exactly how regulation and transparency worked in early Nationalist Tianjin.[78] The Finance Bureau took responsibility for oversight of the audit and hired an outside accountant to examine Quanye's books. Time and again the bank's managers refused access to their account ledgers, often saying that the ledgers had been sent to Shanghai for review by the general office. The exasperated accountant wrote to the Finance Bureau to complain about the lack of cooperation. As he stated in one letter in March 1931, "With this kind of attitude it is difficult to implement my legal responsibilities." A month later, after another round with the bank's managers, he wrote, "Without complete proof [the bank] cannot gain the trust of the people." In addition, this audit "was originally the idea of the Chamber of Commerce and the Bankers' Association, and the implications for my reputation as an accountant are serious." Repeatedly, the Finance Bureau ordered the bank to comply with the accountant's wishes. Quanye finally produced some ledgers, but still the accountant was not satisfied. At last in May, almost eight months after the bank run began, the Finance Bureau sent an investigator to both the Chamber and the Bankers' Association to find out what was going on. To his surprise, he discovered that all of the bank's currency had been withdrawn from the market. Acting on Bian Baimei's recommendation, the Finance Bureau ordered that the audit cease until such time as the bank decided to begin issuing currency again. The bill for the auditing fees was sent to Quanye Bank.[79]

The resolution of the Quanye Bank crisis of 1930 differed from that of the earlier bank runs in several ways. First, although local regulators had examined the books of banks in crisis in 1921, this time a certified expert—an accountant much concerned about his professional reputation—took on the task that Chamber leaders and police had handled in 1921. Second, although the government consulted the Chamber of Commerce and Bankers' Association, the municipal Finance Bureau assumed primary authority for bank regulation. Local elites played only a supporting role. Third, although the audit certainly applied pressure on the bank's general office to find a solution, there was no suggestion that the Chamber or Bankers' Association take financial responsibility for the paper money issued by the Quanye Bank. Resolution of the crisis focused on regulation, not acting as lender of last resort. Fourth, the city government had no interest in regulation for regulation's sake. State enforcement of proper practice based on the expert knowledge of banking stemmed from the need to maintain trust in the money supply. When that need disappeared, so did the local government's interest in full transparency. Fifth, and most important, the resolution of the crisis indicates a remarkable consensus on all parts that trust in the money supply should stem from the correct application of the principles of banking. Considerations of native place, nationalism, and locality had completely disappeared from the repertoire of crisis management techniques used by local officials and elites. The institutionalization of banking and bank money had changed the very basis by which local officials and elites approached the creation of trust in bank-issued paper money. In addition, even though the bank's managers resisted the audit at every step, the municipal government asserted its right "to see the ledgers whether or not the banks' main office or board of directors agreed."[80]

The local government may have had little interest in transparency for transparency's sake. But the central state had a much more generalized interest in the regulation of banks, and it took steps to codify its regulation of the expert knowledge of banking in a series of laws promulgated a few months after the Quanye audit ended in 1931.

The Banking Laws of 1931

By 1931, Tianjin's political situation had stabilized significantly, but its economy still suffered and residents began to turn their attention to the future of the city. Nearby Beijing witnessed a significant depression during the early Nationalist period because the former central government had been one of the largest employers, and spenders, in the city. In Tianjin, the warlord capital that had fueled economic expansion during and after World War I had dried up, and, like the rest of China, the city began to feel the effects of the worldwide depression. Decline in the price of silver increased the prices of imports into China at the same time that declines in world commodity prices prevented Chinese exports from growing.[81] On New Year's Day 1931, Tianjin's *Dagong Bao* published interviews with an unnamed "leading local banker" (perhaps Wu Dingchang, who controlled the newspaper) and Bian Baimei about the future of the city's economy. Both bankers observed that Tianjin lacked investment outlets, and so local banks tended to invest in the Shanghai government bond market instead of in Tianjin. T. V. Soong's financial policies had successfully created a lively bond market in Shanghai, and the voracious appetite of the Nationalist government for funds combined with the economic slowdown in the north to draw funds south from Tianjin. Bian Baimei went on to say that "banks the world over are all undergoing rationalization [*helihua*], and our country's financial world should follow the trend."[82] Bian, as always, was interested in the institutionalization and perfection of the expert knowledge of banking, and by 1931 the central government was in step with his thinking as well. Nationalist officials took a serious interest in the institutionalization of banking, though their regulation and control of the banking system took two separate forms: controlling specific banks and regulating the entire financial system.

After completing the unification of the north under Nationalist rule in 1928, the Nanjing government increased the capital of both the Bank of China and the Bank of Communications, raised government ownership to 20 percent, moved their headquarters from Beijing to Shanghai, and arranged for three government-appointed directors to sit on their boards. In addition, the government reserved the right to appoint the chairman of the board.[83] Parks Coble claims that the two banks were semiofficial in "form only" and were free to operate as commercial banks, though as we saw in chapters 3 and 4, even as "private" commercial banks they had hardly been free from government interference in the 1920s.[84] In addition, in 1926, Bian had still referred to the Bank of China as a "state bank," complaining that most managers of the bank "don't know what it means to be a central bank and make molehills into mountains, struggling with other bankers over little things."[85]

Bankers themselves were ambivalent about state control. At least twice during the 1920s, new warlord governments in Beijing had proposed the formation of a central bank. Bian received these proposals with mixed feelings, though he even admitted that dissolution of the Bank of China and the Bank of Communications would be worth it if a new central bank could "help credibility." Nonetheless, a few days later he lamented that existing conditions did not allow for the establishment of a real central bank.[86] As for Nationalist proposals to create a central bank, Zhang Jia'ao later recalled that he valued independence and the right to guarantee "the integrity of banking personnel from government interference." Nevertheless, state-sponsored status gave banks a certain prestige and special privileges, and Zhang seriously considered T. V. Soong's suggestion that the Bank of China become the Nationalist Central Bank.[87] In June 1928, Wang Kemin wrote to

Bian Baimei that Zhang Jia'ao was in the south trying to obtain the status of "state bank" *(guojia yinhang)* for the Bank of China from the Nationalist Government. Wang himself hoped that the Bank of China would either become the new government's central reserve bank or have some form of "statification without partification" *(zhengfuhua er bu danghua)*.[88] In the end, T. V. Soong formed a separate Central Bank, remaining content with increased stock ownership and board representation as means to control the Bank of China and the Bank of Communications. Although the government was the only shareholder of the new Central Bank, loans from the Bank of China and the Bank of Communications funded a portion of its capital.[89]

In addition to these direct steps to take more control over China's two largest banks, the Nanjing government instituted a series of laws and regulations to increase state control of banks and bank money, extract revenue from banks, enhance their perceived credibility, and make the expert knowledge of banking more transparent. In 1927 it created a Financial Supervision Bureau to oversee and inspect banks; in 1928 it stipulated that the Central Bank would work to unify the monetary system and assist during financial crises; and in 1929 it prohibited indigenous banks from issuing paper money.[90] None of these laws had much effect on the money and banking system in Tianjin, though, and, following a decades-old pattern, reform seemed difficult. In 1929 the Ministry of Finance invited E. W. Kemmerer from the United States to investigate the possibilities of reforming and unifying the Chinese monetary system. Kemmerer's commission recommended that China gradually convert to the gold standard in order to be in step with the rules of the game of world trade.[91] The world decline in silver prices made implementation of Kemmerer's suggestion difficult, however, so the government focused on regulation of the existing system, promulgating in 1931 the Banking Law, the Bank Tax Law, and the Currency Tax Law. Many of the requirements of the new laws, especially the Banking Law, had been included in previous banking regulations, though remaining virtually unenforced during the warlord period. In addition, the tenor of the new laws followed the trend toward professionalism established by earlier laws and bankers themselves in the 1910s and 1920s.[92] Nonetheless, the laws provoked a storm of protest among both modern and indigenous bankers.

The government announced the Banking Law first, which led to wide discussion among modern bankers, indigenous bankers, officials, and intellectuals about the very nature of banking. The law stipulated that banks follow strict procedures in formation and registration, established minimum capital requirements, restricted the legal activities of banks, made provisions for publication of financial information on banks, and allowed for government regulation and examination.[93] "Protests against the Banking Law centered on two points: the definition of a bank and bank capital requirements."[94] Under the language of the law, all institutions which took deposits, made loans, or remitted money, including indigenous banks, were defined as banks. Most indigenous banks, however, were not large enough to meet the capital requirements of the law. Even though the definition of a bank and the capital requirements were almost identical to those of the 1924 Banking Law, the intent of the Nanjing government to enforce the provisions of the new law brought the issue to the fore and created a vivid contrast between modern and indigenous banks.[95]

In the debates over the 1931 Banking Law, those contrasts boiled down to size, nature of lending, and transparency.[96] The size differences between modern and indigenous banks had been apparent since the beginning of modern banking in China. An estimate of the comparative financial strength of Tianjin's modern and indigenous banks would conclude in 1933 that the city's twenty-nine modern banks controlled more than 320 million yuan, whereas Tianjin's ninety-nine indigenous banks controlled less than one tenth that amount, a little more than 30 million yuan.[97] In addition, indigenous banks focused on people rather than organizations. A small number of owners had unlimited liability for the operations of their firm, and relations with customers relied on personal knowledge of the creditworthiness of borrowers. Modern banks, in contrast, focused on organizations as their institutional basis. They had a large number of shareholders who did not personally guarantee the liabilities of the banks and loaned money based on collateral, not personal relations. As early as 1928, an article in a modern bank journal had criticized Tianjin's indigenous banks for their "unfounded belief in people without investigating the true nature of institutions [*jiguan zhi shizhi*]."[98] Indigenous banks also worked under strict secrecy, while modern banks, at least in theory, worked to promote transparency as a way of creating trust. Modern banks in China had a long history of publishing their annual financial statements, and publication was a requirement of both the 1924 and 1931 Banking Laws. At the time the Northern Expedition reached Tianjin, currency reserves were added to the list of items on which they should make information available. The means of acquisition and propagation of the expert knowledge of modern banking also reflected openness. Notable bankers often gave lectures on their trade to public groups; Bian

Baimei did so in Tianjin at least once a year. Modern bankers had long published journals, such as the Shanghai-based *Bankers' Weekly*, and in the early to mid-1930s the bank publishing business expanded rapidly, including yearbooks, directories of bankers, and monographs on specific technical topics. In contrast, financial information on indigenous banks was secret and difficult to obtain, though one observer argued on the question of secrecy that indigenous banks "will have to change in the future in the name of establishing trust [*xinyong*] . . . even if not forced to do so by law."[99] In fact, some of the larger indigenous banks began to publish reports on their financial condition in the 1930s.[100] Nonetheless, China's indigenous banks demanded a separate law, the drafting of which was still in process in 1934.

In line with the need for transparency, the Banking Law of 1931 also included provisions about the government's right to examine banks and punish bankers who had concealed the true condition of their institution. The law appointed the Finance Ministry of the central government as primary bank regulator with a broad range of powers to dispatch auditors for examination of banks' records; to require changes in bank operations or bank management; and, in the case of problems, to seize assets, suspend operations, or even liquidate the bank. Bankers who falsified the financial statements of their banks or who lied to government examiners faced a minimum of one year in prison and a 1,000 yuan fine. In his analysis of the Banking Law, Zhu Qinglai concludes that the law erred by placing too much authority for regulatory power in the hands of the state. Zhu cites the example of the openness of the currency issue of the Shanghai branch of the Bank of China, where representatives of the Shanghai Chamber of Commerce, Shanghai Bankers' Association, and Shanghai Indigenous Bankers' Association examined and then published reserve information under the overall supervision of the Finance Ministry. In his view, examination of banks should be conducted under similar conditions. Zhu goes on to decry the fact that "self-regulation by trade associations is a good precedent, and it is unfortunate that the new law does not acknowledge [this example]."[101] Tianjin's experience with regulation by local elites in past crises shows, however, that local regulation often failed to live up to its promise. As with the Quanye bank run of 1930, Chamber and Bankers' Association leaders were quite content to allow the municipal government to oversee the examination of banks and the regulation of transparency.

In contrast to discussion of the Banking Law, which continued for years, response to the operating and currency tax laws, especially on the part of

China's modern bankers, proved much more urgent. The government announced the new laws on August 1, 1931, and two days later the Shanghai Bankers' Association circulated a letter to Bankers' Associations in Hankou, Beiping, and Tianjin asking for their responses. Beiping and Hankou replied that a meeting should be called of all of China's Bankers' Associations, and Tianjin, led by the studious Bian Baimei, responded by sending a long opinion paper making specific recommendations on revisions in the law and strategies for persuading the Nationalist government to make changes. The Shanghai Bankers' Association vetoed the idea of calling a meeting of all Bankers' Associations, using the excuse that flooding made travel difficult. Reading between the lines, the Beiping Bankers' Association wrote to Shanghai saying that the meeting had been intended to promote discussion, not to give the impression of trying to organize united opposition to the government's plans. Three years into Nationalist rule, elites of all kinds, including powerful bankers, were still walking on eggshells when dealing with the government, as memories of arrests and other attacks on local elite power remained fresh. In the end, after much correspondence, China's bankers did not meet as a group, but the Shanghai Bankers' Association summarized bankers' objections in a letter to the Finance Ministry. Many of the objections focused on the new taxes: a 2.5 percent tax on non-specie currency reserves (at the same time requiring that specie be at least 60 percent of issue) and an operating tax. The bankers argued, on the one hand, that the currency tax was too high and, on the other, that in foreign countries currency taxes provided for the regulation of the money supply, not the raising of government revenues. As for the new operating tax, bankers argued that it placed an unfair burden on banks by imposing higher taxes on them than on other businesses. Moreover, the bankers argued that foreign banks in China should have to pay the same taxes, for otherwise they would have an unfair advantage over Chinese banks. Eventually, in response to the bankers, the government reduced the tax on non-cash currency reserves from 2.5 to 1.25 percent.[102] The Nationalist government's right to regulate and tax banks, however, remained unchallenged and tacitly accepted.

Fragmented political authority and disunity within the government itself handicapped Nationalist rule of Tianjin. As a result, attempts to regulate and reshape the institutions of Tianjin society had mixed results. At the beginning of the Nationalist period, Bian Baimei had looked forward with longing to a "complete break" from the vicissitudes of warlord China, but in many ways the three years from 1928 to 1931 presented just more of the same. In quick succession Tianjin's bankers had to negotiate with Chu Yupu's Fengtian regime, with the Finance Ministry of the split Nanjing/Shanxi regime, with Shanxi alone as Yan Xishan broke with Chiang Kai-shek, and then with a reconstituted Nationalist regime. Throughout, Tianjin's modern bankers sought stable government institutions with the legitimacy to commit verifiable sources of revenue to the banks in return for loans. Temporary military governments and faltering regimes were given short shrift. Their support went for the most part to the Finance Ministry in Nanjing. For Tianjin's native elite and the Tianjin Chamber of Commerce, the years between 1928 and 1931 initially presented a much greater, and much more frightening, potential for a complete break. Under attack from both local party activists and Chiang Kai-shek in Nanjing, Chamber leaders faced a complete reversal of their entrenched power. After Yan Xishan's rebellion, and perhaps because of it, Tianjin's native elites rallied and quickly reconsolidated their pre-1928 position and leadership structure. The ability of Tianjin's elites to defend their turf and resist opening the leadership of the Chamber of Commerce to merchants of all classes demonstrates the substantial continuity of institutions under the early Nationalist regime.

In the creation of a new regulatory environment for banking, we see the emergence of a consensus on the importance of transparency in creating trust, though bankers could take as much credit as officials for this development. This consensus was evident in guardianship activities coordinated by the Tianjin Bankers' Association, as well as in the audit of Quanye Bank, supervised by the Tianjin city government, though the latter faced obstruction and obfuscation in its attempt to regulate, examine, and impose transparency. In the end, the state prevailed, though with less thoroughness than its hired professional accountant would have preferred. The bank runs of the early Nationalist period show that Tianjin's native elite had become much less active as either guardian or regulator of trust in bank money. At the same time, a division of labor appeared where lender of last resort activities fell to the banking industry itself, but regulation became the province of the state. At the national level, the government took a series of measures to reinstitute lapsed state control over the Bank of China and the Bank of Communications, China's two largest banks. Likewise, the state asserted its right to regulate and tax banks, and vigorous protests by bankers resulted in only a slight reduction in their tax burden. Nonetheless, although China's banks came under increased state control, they maintained their institutional continuity to a considerable extent, including their active role in supporting state finances. As indicated by bankers' ambivalence about having the status of a "state" bank, the nation still loomed large as a source of power and legitimacy.

In the end there was no "complete break" for either Tianjin's bankers or the city's native elite. The break that 1928 signaled was not a sudden or revolutionary one. Actions by the Nationalist Party to organize new merchant groups and the state's creation of a new regulatory environment met with setbacks and compromise. At the same time, the new regulatory environment for banking was built on the foundation of the expert knowledge of banking, which had considerable continuity before and after the Nationalists came to power. The changes set in place between 1928 and 1931 would have long-term effects, however, eventually bringing about fundamental changes in local elite organizations, banks, and the money supply. To cite just one example already apparent in the period of early Nationalist rule, the move of the capital to Nanjing, as well as the move of the head offices of the Bank of China and the Bank of Communications to Shanghai, shifted the center of gravity of bank-state relations in China. In the 1920s, the Beijing branches of the two banks had the most intimate connections with the central state, and nearby in Tianjin bankers, especially Bian Baimei, became deeply involved in negotiations with both the central and provincial governments. The early Nationalist period witnessed a decline in state activities of Tianjin's bankers, however, and after the initial loan on the 2.5 percent customs surcharge, Shanghai took the lead in negotiating future loans to the Nationalist government. Likewise, debate on the banking laws of 1931 deferred to the leadership of the Shanghai Bankers' Association. Tianjin remained China's second-largest financial center, though a more distant second, and Shanghai moved well beyond being first among equals.

The coming transformation of elite organizations and financial institutions would take place in a new international political environment. In fact, in September 1931, seven months after the Nanjing government promulgated the new banking laws, the Japanese army occupied Northeast China, also known as Manchuria, and committed the first of a series of dramatic actions which challenged the rule of the Nationalist government in Nanjing and reminded Tianjin's bankers and native elites that they lived in an uncertain world.

6

Trust at a Time of International Crisis

> The goal of Chiang [Kai-shek] and those around him is to resist [Japan] in a small way and lose ground, hoping that Europe and America will intervene. To run the country like this breaks your heart.
>
> — Bian Baimei, *Diary,* March 23, 1933

From 1931 to 1937, international concerns became the most important challenges to maintaining trust in money and banks in Tianjin. Japanese aggression, the effects of the worldwide economic depression, and American silver purchases created a new institutional environment and prompted innovative strategies to promote trust.

Trust under Japanese Aggression

During the 1920s and early Nationalist period, Bian Baimei sprinkled his diary with the myriad concerns of Chinese government finance at both the central and local levels. During the late summer and early fall of 1931, however, events regarding Japan's activities in Manchuria and elsewhere preoccupied his jottings. His entries ranged from rumors that the Japanese had instigated Shi Yousan's rebellion against Chiang Kai-shek to the observation that Duan Qirui, the head of the discredited Anhui clique, had become active in trying to mediate connections between the Japanese and opponents of the Nationalist regime.[1] Others in Tianjin felt a sense of impending crisis as well; in July, *Dagong Bao* printed an editorial about increased tensions with Japan, declaring that East Asia rested "on the cusp between peace and chaos."[2] Then on September 19, Bian records his initial reaction to the Manchurian incident, when a rogue Japanese army began its seizure of China's Northeast: "Cabled each branch and office to be careful with loans, and to use little cash . . . Cabled Shanghai to send 1,000,000 yuan . . . The City government sent Shen and Miao over because the Frontier Bank's notes are dropping in value, they asked that a method be found to support it." This diary entry reflects Bian's multiple responsibilities. Since he supervised bank branches all over North China, he telegraphed his subordinates to advise caution. At the same time, as protector of impersonal trust in the Tianjin branch, he asked the Shanghai branch of the bank to send funds north in anticipation of a possible bank run. Finally, city officials looked to him as leader of the Tianjin Bankers' Association to direct lender of last resort activities for the Frontier Bank. Apart from his obvious concern for trust in his and other banks, Bian had personal reasons to worry as well. His younger brother, Bian Fusun, lived and worked in the Northeast as manager of the Fengtian branch of the Bank of China.[3]

The Japanese takeover of the three northern provinces of Manchuria proved surprisingly easy, and Nationalist forces put up little resistance. The civil war with Yan Xishan the previous year had taken a huge toll on the Nanjing government, and a separatist movement in Guangdong Province further weakened Chiang Kai-shek's position, as did his dispatching 130,000 troops in Jiangxi to fight the communists.[4] As with the fight against Yan Xishan in 1930, Zhang Xueliang held the key to Nationalist power in North China in September 1931, though the Japanese had returned Yan to Shanxi in August as a means of weakening the Nationalist hold on the north.[5] In the end Chiang Kai-shek adopted a policy of nonresistance to Japan, and Zhang Xueliang complied.

The "Manchurian incident" shocked the residents of Tianjin. In addition to the political implications, there was the fact that the city of Tianjin had well-established trading ties with the Northeast, and the sense of crisis created a liquidity crunch in the city. As a result, Shanghai bankers prepared to ship 3 million silver dollars to Tianjin to relieve the situation.[6] The greatest trouble, however, struck the Tianjin branches of two banks, the Frontier Bank and the Northeast Three Provinces Bank, which had originally been sponsored by the northeastern militarist and Zhang Xueliang's father, Zhang Zuolin. Runs on the paper money issued by those two banks grew worse as news of Japanese military success spread. Nationalist soldiers who retreated from Manchuria carried large amounts of the notes of the two banks into Hebei Province, taxing the ability of their Tianjin branches to exchange the paper money for silver. As with the bank runs in 1928 and 1929 after the Northern Expedition, the 1931 crisis elicited no native elite mobilization in Tianjin. Instead, following the precedent set in the early Nationalist period, local government officials in Tianjin and Beiping arranged for emergency loans from the Tianjin and Beiping Bankers' Associations.[7] The banking industry acted as lender of last resort under the regulatory supervision of the government.

No sooner had the markets calmed down in Tianjin than the "plainclothes troops incidents" erupted to disturb local order. On the night of November 8, 1931, armed Japanese and Chinese men poured out of the Japanese Concession in Tianjin and attacked the police station and telephone office and the Tianjin municipal government buildings. Bian heard gunfire all night. The next day, none of the bank employees who lived in the Chinese part of the city made it to work.[8] During the warlord period, Tianjin's foreign concessions had provided protection from China's domestic political turmoil. Now the Japanese Concession there served as a base to foment turmoil in the Chinese sections of the city. The Japanese succeeded in using the fighting as a diversion to spirit the former Qing emperor Puyi out of his house in the Japanese Concession and take him to Manchuria. Rioting began again on the night of November 26, allowing the Japanese to move Puyi's wife out of the city and providing a pretext to demand the removal of Chinese troops from Tianjin, the stationing of additional Japanese troops in the city, and the suppression of anti-Japanese activities.[9] The riots increased the sense of tension and crisis in the city. The Tianjin Bankers' Association sent a public letter to local and central government officials asking for alleviation of the crisis and noting labor unrest and disruptions in transportation.[10]

A little more than two months after the "plainclothes troops incidents," news reached Tianjin that the Japanese had attacked Shanghai. Although Nanjing had initially conceded to Japanese demands to remove troops from Shanghai and suppress anti-Japanese activity there, slow compliance on the Chinese side and overly eager commanders on the Japanese side led to a Japanese attack on the night of January 28, 1932. Unlike in the Japanese occupation of Manchuria the previous year, Chinese forces in Shanghai put up stiff resistance, leading to thirty-three days of "intense, brutal war in the midst of a densely populated city."[11] The fighting closed down financial markets, and because Shanghai was the financial center of the country, this distant threat had a greater impact on Tianjin in many ways than the street fighting in the city itself a few months before. During crises the Shanghai branches of China's modern banks provided funds for their Tianjin counterparts. In addition, Tianjin's banks often relied on drafts drawn on Shanghai banks, called *shenhui*, to clear accounts with one another. The fighting in

Shanghai cut off transactions between that city and Tianjin, instigating yet another crisis in Tianjin's financial markets. The approaching lunar New Year, which traditionally required Chinese merchants to settle their accounts, made the situation even worse.[12]

The tense situation caused a run on the National Industrial Bank of China. Rumors that the Shanghai branch was in trouble caused hundreds of people in Tianjin to line up to cash in paper money issued by the bank. The Tianjin branches of the Bank of China, the Bank of Communications, and the Four Banks arranged an emergency loan for the National Industrial Bank of 800,000 yuan, though Bian Baimei worried that the amount still might not be enough. Loans to the National Industrial Bank depended on reliable collateral, though, and guardian activities by Tianjin's banks conformed with the rules of the game. A few weeks later, although the bank run was over, the National Industrial Bank still had not solved all of its problems. When bank managers came to Bian Baimei for a loan, he told them not to depend "completely on other banks." Bian urged them to think what they might do themselves and noted in his diary that the bank's managers had caused the problems because of their own incompetence.[13] Tianjin's bankers took guardianship and the protection of financial markets seriously, but they ultimately upheld the principle that trust still relied on the proper practice of the expert knowledge of banking.

Concerned about the reliability of Tianjin's modern banks, Wang Xiaoyan, a leader of the Chamber of Commerce and head of the Indigenous Bankers' Association, came to Bian to suggest an audit of currency reserves. Not all of Tianjin's banks had made their currency reserves public, and members of the local elite were concerned about hidden problems. Bian responded that the Bank of China and the Bank of Communications would have no problem with such an action, but other banks might indeed have less than the necessary reserves. An audit by the Chamber of Commerce, though, might cause more harm than good. As Bian pointed out to Wang, "if problems surfaced, would the official authorities or the Chamber of Commerce have the strength needed to support [the banks]? In the present political situation, the advantages or disadvantages of [an audit] are quite serious."[14] Thus Tianjin's local elites faced a familiar problem. They wished to regulate banks and bank money as a means of preserving local order but did not have the financial resources to remedy crisis situations. Modern banks were too large and they issued paper money in too great a quantity to be handled at the local level. Transparency was a viable way of creating trust, but only when guardians stood by to step into the breach. Without that kind of backup, secrecy was preferable, allowing for the possibility that banks could muddle through without a public crisis.

Even though the Japanese eventually withdrew from Shanghai, the attack exposed the potential weakness of Tianjin's dependency on Shanghai both as a means of clearing accounts and as a source of guardian funds in times of crisis. Even before the attack, the general sense of crisis in China had caused silver dollars to flow into the major urban areas of China's eastern seaboard, creating the odd situation of a decline in the value of silver dollars in comparison with silver taels (loose or bar silver) and bank drafts drawn on banks in yuan. As a result, Tianjin's banks could not get checks from foreign banks for clearing without selling drafts on Shanghai, and when Shanghai was cut off, clearing became impossible.[15] Bankers at both modern and indigenous banks in Tianjin revived the idea of forming a joint treasury *(gongku)* to act as clearinghouse for bank transactions, as a repository for the unneeded silver dollars, and as a potential guardianship organ. Bankers had discussed the idea for a joint treasury on and off for many years. In early 1921, Continental Bank's Tan Danya had proposed a joint treasury, but Bian objected that "the Bank of China needs to be healthy before it can run a joint treasury for the rest of the banking establishment."[16] The idea came up again amidst the financial crisis that marked the end of the Fengtian regime in Tianjin in 1927.[17] Establishment of a joint treasury posed three primary problems for bankers, making them hesitate each time the proposal came up. First, it involved a certain level of transparency, because each participating bank would need to deposit at least some of its silver reserves in a jointly managed vault. Thus, creating a joint treasury created problems similar to those of making currency issue transparent by reducing a bank's ability to adjust silver reserves secretly. Second, a joint treasury would work as a means of risk pooling, requiring a high degree of cooperation among bankers and of the financial health of the banks involved. A weak link would force the joint treasury into guardianship activities too often. As Bian noted, "The important point is in allowing [banks] to survive or die together."[18] Third, in order to work, a joint treasury required highly institutionalized and commonly acknowledged procedures. Without common agreement on the appropriate principles of expert knowledge to be implemented, the treasury could not effectively fulfill its functions. Determining a set of rules acceptable to both modern and indigenous bankers proved especially difficult since practices in the two sectors differed greatly.[19]

In spite of these potential problems, China's political crisis of 1931–32 forced Tianjin's modern and indigenous bankers to take matters into their own hands in order to provide an institutional solution to the city's financial difficulties. After several months of preparatory work, the Tianjin joint treasury opened for business in October 1932. In the interests of transparency, Bian proudly announced that the treasury would be subject to monthly audits by foreign and Chinese accountants, with the results published in Tianjin's newspapers.[20] On its first day of business, the joint treasury received deposits of silver dollars totaling more than 3.4 million yuan.[21] By February 1933, Bian noted that "foreign businessmen strongly approve of the work of the joint treasury. The silver taken in by them has shrunk, reducing their losses by not a little."[22]

The events of the last half of 1931 and the beginning of 1932 cut Tianjin off from the Northeast and showed that it was possible to cut the city off from Shanghai as well. Formation of the joint treasury only heightened the sense of isolation. The Tianjin Joint Public Treasury provided a means of establishing trust through transparency and risk sharing, but it was a local response to a local problem, brought on by the need to increase the self-sufficiency of Tianjin's financial markets in the wake of Japanese aggression. At the same time, Tianjin's modern bankers also began to hedge their bets by shifting control of the banks and resources to the south, exacerbating Tianjin's isolation even more. In May 1932, Bian Baimei even discussed with Zhang Jia'ao making the Tianjin branch of the Bank of China a subbranch of Shanghai. Although the Bank of China did not take such a drastic step, in subsequent years funds at the Tianjin branch were kept at minimum levels.[23] In addition, a number of Tianjin's banks, including two of the largest private banks—the Salt Bank and Jincheng Bank—moved their headquarters to Shanghai.[24] The sense of isolation, which went much further than the financial circles in Tianjin, represented one aspect of the growing lack of faith in the Nanjing government. At a dinner party one businessman even suggested to Bian Baimei that industrialists organize a "backup" government. It would not be easy, but with the help of the bankers they thought it might be possible.[25] The idea came to nothing, but it would arise again when Japanese aggression was rekindled in the first part of 1933.

On New Year's Day 1933, Japanese troops began a broad series of attacks along the Great Wall. Eventually they would take Rehe (Jehol) Province north of the Great Wall and drive deep into Hebei, within striking distance of Beiping and Tianjin. The central government in Nanjing contributed to "popular apprehension that Nanking [Nanjing] would abandon Hopei [Hebei] Province" by beginning shipment to the south of the treasures of the National Palace Museum and the archives of the Foreign Ministry in Beijing. At the same time, Chiang Kai-shek and Zhang Xueliang put up only token resistance in fighting, and Chiang dispatched Huang Fu to negotiate a truce with the Japanese, causing an outcry among Chinese inside and outside the Nationalist Party and government.[26] In May, Nanjing and Japan concluded the Tanggu Truce, establishing a demilitarized zone in Hebei, and requiring the establishment of rail and postal links between China and Manchuria.[27] The events of 1933 radically changed the balance of power in North China. With the resignation of Zhang Xueliang and the defeat of Feng Yuxiang, troops more loyal to Chiang were now in Hebei. In addition, the Nanjing government created a supposedly semi-autonomous committee, called the Beiping Political Affairs Council, to oversee North China.[28]

The events of the first half of 1933 exacerbated the sense of crisis in Tianjin and provoked emotional responses from many residents. After a visit from Zhang Pinti and Wang Xiaoyan, Bian Baimei criticized them and other native elites who wanted peace and order, noting, "Tianjin people see living and producing as more important than anything else. They don't know that circumstances exist where peace is not possible."[29] A month later, at the height of the crisis, one Ji Yunong came to Bian Baimei advocating that local gentry and elders endorse a military commander to oppose the Japanese in defiance of Nanjing.[30] While some local elites wanted to sue for peace, others endorsed local opposition to the Japanese. Kong Xiangxi, minister of commerce at the time, told Bian Baimei's younger brother, "Beiping and Tianjin will sooner or later fall into other [Japanese] hands." Bian noted in his diary, "The goal of Chiang and those around him is to resist in a small way and lose ground, hoping that Europe and America will intervene. To run the country like this breaks your heart."[31]

In spite of emotions running high on all sides, unlike the events of 1931 and 1932, the intense fighting of 1933, even reaching within miles of Tianjin, failed to provoke a major financial crisis. In April the Tianjin Bankers' Association met on schedule and reelected its officers, with Bian Baimei continuing as chairman. At the meeting the bankers agreed that "members of the association should help each other every day. If one member comes up short, then it should be made up with drafts on the joint treasury." Beyond this, the financial crises did not even appear on the agenda for the meeting.[32] In fact, in January and February, Tianjin and Beiping bankers concentrated their efforts on government finances, not on the question of local trust. As disillusioned as Bian and other Tianjiners were, he and the other bankers in Beiping and Tianjin subscribed, somewhat reluctantly, to a new issue of "patriotic bonds" issued by Nanjing, in the amount of 9 million yuan.[33] Even at the time there was little hope that these funds would go to defending the north. Japanese aggression had become an accepted reality, and Tianjin's bankers dealt with that reality by reaffirming their commitment to self-regulation and guardianship through the joint treasury and, at the same time, by continuing their traditional support of the state's finances.

Tianjin's Elites in Crisis while Banks Thrive

The Tanggu truce ended overt Japanese military action, at least for a while, and in late 1933 Chiang Kai-shek easily defeated a rebellion in Fujian Province. As a result, "Chiang Kai-shek entered 1934 in a stronger political position than at any point since the Manchurian Incident."[34] The problem of North China remained, however, with the Japanese firmly entrenched in Manchuria and a demilitarized zone in Hebei Province that began just north of Beiping and Tianjin. In Tianjin the Nationalist presence remained strong, as seen in the state's ability to regulate elite organizations in the city.

Reorganization of the Tianjin Chamber of Commerce under the Nationalist government had resulted, after much struggle, in a restoration of the pre-Nationalist status quo in early 1931. Nonetheless, the new Chamber of Commerce and Trade Association laws passed by the Nationalist government had created a new regulatory environment, and the establishment's victory proved to be only temporary.[35] The laws required that all trades with seven or more firms in a given city had to form guilds, or trade associations *(tongye gonghui)*. In Tianjin, most of the newly organized trades of the Merchants' Union did not organize as trade associations in time for the 1931 Chamber elections, but in the following years, the number of trade associations in Tianjin grew enormously. In 1930 there had been approximately 60, and at most 70, but by the mid-1930s, the number had ballooned to more than 130.[36] Each of these new associations had the right to appoint representatives to the Chamber of Commerce, and their influence would be felt in 1934.

According to the 1929 Chamber of Commerce Law, the Tianjin Chamber should have reelected half of its executive committee in March 1933. In fact, no election was held, and in 1934, fifty-three trade associations accused

Chamber leaders of purposely delaying reelection of its administrative committee and unfairly disqualifying a number of trade associations from participating in a planned Chamber election.[37] After the controversy erupted, two members of the Chamber's executive committee resigned "on a pretext."[38] Tianjin government and party leaders rushed to ask Nanjing for instructions; in the meantime, the dissatisfied trade associations leveled new accusations, implying that the financial affairs of the Chamber were not in order and that the leaders had refused outside inspection of the books, thereby "keeping secrets from the Party and the public." In addition, they accused the Chamber leaders of hiding in the foreign concessions and refusing to help Tianjin in the aftermath of the Manchurian incident in 1931.[39] Eventually all attempts to reconcile the two sides and hold an election failed. The city government and party bureau ordered that a "reorganization committee," with Bian Baimei as chairman, be established to supervise a Chamber reelection. After several months of work, the Tianjin Chamber of Commerce elected a new leadership on January 1, 1935.[40] An American-educated financier and trader named Ji Hua, the representative of silk, cotton, and woolen goods merchants, became the first new chairman in nearly a decade. The Chamber's new executive committee of fifteen people included representatives of eight trade associations from the old faction, five from the new, and two from a group of neutral associations. Ji himself came from the old faction.[41]

A few months later, the Tianjin Bankers' Association held an election of officers on schedule. Under Nationalist rules, leaders of trade associations could serve no more than two consecutive terms, so Bian Baimei was ineligible to continue. Instead, Zhong Bingfeng (Zhong E, 1890–?) became the new chairman and representative to the Chamber of Commerce, serving on the Chamber's executive committee. Zhong, a graduate of the University of Wisconsin and a Guangdong native, was a newcomer who had recently been made the Tianjin manager of the Bank of Communications.[42]

The events set in motion in 1928 with the arrival of the Nationalists in Tianjin had ultimately reshaped the face of merchant organizations in the city. The compromise ticket of Chamber leaders was hardly a recipe for success, however, and the Chamber functioned only with difficulty. Internecine conflict would break out again a year and a half later. Zhong Bingfeng would prove to be inept in dealing with Tianjin's volatile politics, and he soon came into conflict with local government officials. The reorganization of local elite organizations under the Nationalist legal structure combined with the residual effects of the mobilization of small merchants and artisans by the left wing of the GMD to produce unpredictable and unstable results. State and party actions had broken much of the power of the entrenched local elite but failed to fill the vacuum with strong, government-directed elite organizations.

The development of banking and bank-issued currency fared much better than the merchant organizations. In spite of the fact that the first half of the Nanjing decade in Tianjin more often than not resembled the chaos of the warlord period, Tianjin's banks survived and even flourished from 1928 to 1934. The number of bank offices in Tianjin expanded, and banking became an ever more important part of people's lives. By 1934, thirty banks had opened sixty-three offices in Tianjin, thirty-eight of them in the six years between 1928 and 1934.[43] The growth of bank-issued paper money continued as well. Although Tianjin's population dipped slightly between 1928 and 1933, the Tianjin currency of the Bank of China and the Bank of Communications increased by 22 percent. The Four Banks showed slower but still significant growth, increasing its currency issue by slightly less than 10 percent over the same period.[44] All three of these major issuers had made their currency reserves open by 1930, promoting the growth and stability of their currencies. Zhang Jia'ao later observed that "following the practice of opening currency reserves to public inspection, public confidence in the bank increased tremendously, and the volume of issuance increased steadily."[45] Tianjin witnessed two bank runs in 1934, one on Dazhong Bank and one on the beleaguered National Industrial Bank. Neither lasted more than a couple of days, however, demonstrating an essential stability in trust in Tianjin's bank-issued paper money.[46]

In spite of, and in some ways because of, the growth of banks and bank-issued currency, by the mid-1930s government officials and intellectuals had begun to turn their attention to reform of the financial system. Some, such as the economist Yao Qingsan, made scathing critiques of the Chinese financial system. Yao insisted that China needed to regulate its monetary system, especially flows of foreign exchange, to deal with continued drops in the world price of silver. He decried the fact that China did not even have a standard unit of account for its money supply, stating that "without elimination of the tael [in favor of the yuan], all discussion of [financial] reform is empty." Yao went on to say that all of China's banks, including the Central Bank, functioned as speculative commercial banks with no division of labor or means of cooperation among them. According to him, banks were investing in government bonds and real estate instead of in commerce and industry, creating the odd situation that the circulation of paper money increased even as the economy slumped.[47] From another standpoint, Li Zixiang published an article in late 1933 claiming that China's banks functioned as tools for foreign control of the economy. He too pointed to speculative real estate investments as a weakness of China's banks, and here he could rely on none other than Zhang Jia'ao, whom he cites as stating that the bursting of the real estate bubble after the Manchurian incident saved China's banks from continuing their speculative trend.[48] Banks had their defenders, though. The educator and editor of the *Bankers' Weekly,* Xu Baohe, published two articles in 1933 in support of China's banks. Noting that many people had recently criticized banks, he cites Chen Gaoyong's assertion that "the abnormal growth of Chinese banking makes one pessimistic, not optimistic, about the future of Chinese capitalism." Chen also quoted the criticism, previously published in Shanghai's *Shenbao,* that "banks absorb huge amounts of capital, but use it for real estate speculation and purchase of government bonds, instead of for the development of industry and the advancement of agriculture." In contrast, Xu concluded that more than half of bank investments went to business, with only 17 percent in government bonds and 3 percent in real estate.[49]

In spite of such defenders, criticism worried China's bankers. At a meeting of bank managers in Shanghai in April 1933, Zhang Jia'ao stated that "the Bank of China faced four challenges: (1) exorbitant demands of the authorities, (2) criticism from the scholastic community, (3) competition from other banks, and (4) jealousy from the foreign banking community." Zhang proposed that the bank deal with these problems, especially criticism, by "obtaining sympathy from society." Bian Baimei later noted in his diary that Zhang meant that the bank should emphasize "the rural economy and other matters."[50] A few months later Bian and a group of Bank of China executives took a trip through rural areas to investigate means of increasing bank investments in the countryside.[51] Bankers also took the offensive in public relations, turning out a huge volume of publications in the mid-1930s, ranging from bankers' annuals to the results of essay contests about savings.[52]

The international environment, especially the decline in the price of silver and the impact of the worldwide depression, stood at the center of many calls for reform. Many observers claimed that China's economic problems stemmed from imperialist nations' pushing their crisis off onto other, less developed countries.[53] The impact of external economic decline on China may not have been that simple, and the silver standard may have helped shield China from direct transmission of the depression.[54] Nonetheless, China did not remain immune to worldwide problems. Exports declined, as discussed earlier, and American economic problems directly caused a small financial crisis in Tianjin. In 1933, when the United States went off the gold standard, a bank run ensued on the Tianjin branch of the National City Bank (now Citicorp).[55] In any case, "China's urban economy slid into a depression in 1933–36, idling textile mills and causing prices of finished products to tumble."[56] At the end of 1934, however, China did not face any difficulties as a result of low silver prices; in fact, the case was exactly the opposite.

The Financial Reforms of 1935

On June 19, 1934, the U.S. Congress passed the Silver Purchase Act, intended to raise silver prices by requiring that the government buy large amounts of silver. That year, the flow of silver out of China increased twentyfold over the previous year, and within six months, more than 230 million yuan in silver left China.[57] Opinions about the impact of this silver drain vary. Milton Friedman and Anna Jacobson Schwartz argue that American silver purchases imposed "several years of drastic deflation on China." In contrast, revisionist work by Loren Brandt and Thomas Sargent asserts that the Chinese money supply did not decline, "Chinese aggregate economic activity did not suffer marked or prolonged depression," and "there was no wide-spread contagion of banking panics." Instead, the authors conclude that "China was forced off silver by its own government, which wanted to make itself beneficiary of the capital gain associated with the appreciation of silver and to relieve itself of the restrictions that are imposed on government financed by a commodity standard."[58] More recent work by Cheng-chung Lai and Joshua Jr-shian Gau, using additional data, takes a middle road between the two views, concluding that American silver purchases created "a shock that caused panic" but did not generate "a depth bomb effect."[59] A large increase in the circulation of paper money issued by Chinese banks did offset the silver drain and kept China's money supply relatively stable.[60] In any case, for the purposes of analysis here, perception of crisis is as important in generating trust-promoting strategies as actual crisis. Nationalist officials used the crisis, and panic about the crisis, to tighten state control over the money supply and make reliance on government authority the basis for trust in Chinese money.

Although the immediate threat came from the United States, Japanese aggression set the stage for, and continued to play a major role in, Nanjing's response to the crisis. Bowing to Japanese pressure, Chiang Kai-shek had removed the actively anti-Japanese T. V. Soong as finance minister in October 1933.[61] The appointment of Kong Xiangxi as finance minister in his place ended the relative restraint toward banks seen under Soong, and the government began to increase its demand that banks absorb bond issues.[62] In North China in mid-1935, under instructions from Nanjing, a Nationalist military commander negotiated the so-called He-Umezu Agreement with the Japanese.[63] As a result, Song Zheyuan became governor of Hebei Province and Shang Zhen mayor of Tianjin.[64] At that time Song was best known for his stand against the Japanese after the Manchurian incident, so his appointment signaled a fairly firm response to Japanese aggression. Nonetheless, some Japanese military leaders still hoped to include him in a pro-Japanese "autonomous government."[65] These political developments alarmed local elites in Tianjin. Ji Hua and other leaders of the Tianjin Chamber of Commerce came to the Tianjin Bankers' Association to discuss the tense political situation. Bian and Zhong Bingfeng decided that "in the future no matter what the [kind of] organization [local elites formed], regarding politics and foreign relations [they] would not participate."[66] Once again, Tianjin's modern bankers demonstrated that their interests lay not with the protection of the locality but with the central government. Likewise, when in August, Chiang Kai-shek ordered well-known members of the Beiping and Tianjin Chambers of Commerce and Bankers' Associations to start an economic cooperation association with the Japanese, bankers such as Wu Dingchang and Zhou Zuomin were heavily represented.[67] As a result of Japanese pressure, China faced the 1934–35 financial crisis with a finance minister who had little sympathy for bankers, an unpredictable Song Zheyuan as the most important Chinese political leader in North China, local elites in Tianjin who were suspicious of central government plans, and a group of professional bankers in Beiping and Tianjin willing to cooperate with central policies.

As banks in China, especially foreign banks, reaped profits by shipping cheap Chinese silver abroad, silver reserves became tight in Chinese cities. A year earlier bankers had worried about having too many silver dollars on hand, but by the end of 1934 they faced the opposite problem. In October, Bian drafted a policy to try to balance demand for silver in the interior with demand in the cities, while at the same time trying to use paper money instead of silver whenever possible.[68] Finally, in October 1934, Kong Xiangxi instituted a customs tax on the export of silver in order to stem the flow. Bian Baimei noted in his diary:

> Du Yuesheng happened to be short in British pounds the day of the order about silver export taxes, and he lost as much as 2,000,000. Also hear that Kong's wife and T. L. Soong [T. V. Soong's brother] had first purchased gold futures, and made a lot of money. Du, according to the custom of Shanghai gangsters, sent a coffin to Kong's house. Kong et al. were very frightened, and to repay Du, the Central and Guohuo banks will accommodate him with a large loan. If this is the way people control the monetary system, what good can come of it?[69]

Relations with Du undermined the Nationalists' claim to the role of rationalist regulators but would be useful later in facing down China's bankers.

In spite of the tax on exports of the metal, silver still continued to flow out of China. Combined with China's existing economic problems, the silver flight brought on a severe panic, potentially jeopardizing the ability of the Nanjing government to finance its deficits. In response, at the end of February 1935, Kong Xiangxi and Chiang Kai-shek developed a secret plan to nationalize the Bank of China and the Bank of Communications. Even Wang Jingwei, then head of the Executive Yuan, did not know about the plans to take over control of the banks. He sent a worried confidential cable to Chiang Kai-shek urging government officials to meet with Zhang Jia'ao as soon as possible to forestall his possible resignation. Chiang Kai-shek, however, had decided that the Bank of China and the Bank of Communications needed to be tamed. In a confidential message to Kong Xiangxi, Chiang wrote: "The nation and society are facing bankruptcy, and the crucial reason is the inability to unify the money supply. The key lies with the Bank of China and the Bank of Communications who stubbornly suck out the nation's blood and the people's vital fluids and defy the orthodox policies of the times, [and] without a care for the nation or society . . . carry out [this plan] in order to save the party state which is on the verge of extinction."[70] On March 20 the executive committee of the Nationalist Party passed a resolution to issue 100 million yuan in new bonds, to be exchanged for shares in the Bank of China and the Bank of Communications, thus ensuring effective government control.[71]

The ensuing drama took place primarily in Shanghai, where the government prepared the ground with a combination of a public relations campaign and coercive threats against the bankers. As in Tianjin, Shanghai's modern banks were located in the foreign concessions. But Du Yuesheng's gangster organization recognized no boundaries, and he played a key role in coercing bankers to comply with the government takeover. Zhang Jia'ao later recalled that not only did Chiang's secret police watch and intimidate him throughout the ordeal, but also Du Yuesheng warned him not to oppose the government actions "for the sake of [his] health."[72] The board of directors of the Bank of China wanted to object to Nanjing's plans, on four sets of grounds: first, the state's new capital came from bonds which had no market; second, they felt that private shareholders should have a chance to invest if the bank increased its capital; third, according to the bank's charter, shareholders had to agree to changes; and fourth, the bank was not short of capital.[73] In other words, the board members wanted to play by the rules of the game within the established institutional context. In the end, Du Yuesheng's coercive power and the severity of the silver crisis, for which the bankers themselves had no resolution, altered the rules of the game in the state's favor. A few months later, Chiang and Kong went even farther and, in the "little coup" of June 1935, took over three private banks, including the National Industrial Bank of China. By 1936, the group of banks controlled either directly or indirectly by the government held 72.8 percent of the assets of all Chinese banks.[74]

The sense of professionalism of the modern bankers and the institutional loyalties so carefully cultivated in the 1920s and 1930s facilitated Nanjing's nationalization of the banks.[75] Kong had removed Zhang Jia'ao as head of the bank, and was looking for a replacement. The new power of the bank lay in the hands of T. V. Soong, who took over as chairman of the board, but for the position of president, Kong wanted a professional banker with a good reputation in order to instill confidence among outsiders. For a brief time in 1935 he considered Bian Baimei for the job. Bian told Kong that "bank employees only know to pledge loyalty to the organization [*xiaozhong yu jiguan*], and do not change with individual [changes] . . . If it is necessary to fill in, then I would not dare shirk [the responsibility]." Later that same day Bian had a long talk with Zhang Jia'ao, whom he self-servingly described as "overly resentful and angry."[76] Although Bian's comments likely masked a certain amount of ambition on his part, they also have the ring of truth. In fact, at the last minute Zhang Jia'ao himself had tried to negotiate a compromise whereby he could stay on at the Bank of China, but Chiang Kai-shek insisted that Zhang be completely cut off from connection with the bank.[77]

Assertion of control over the bulk of China's banking sector still did nothing to stem the drain of silver from China, and by May 1935 the crisis had become untenable. The high price of silver had begun to jeopardize the ability of Chinese banks to maintain adequate reserves for the paper money which they had issued. Bian Baimei told T. V. Soong, "If you want adequate [currency] reserves, then it will be difficult to plan on profit. If you want profit, then reserves will soon weaken."[78] Although most silver shipped abroad originated in Shanghai, the drain caused shortages all over China, including Tianjin. In April the Tianjin managers of the Bank of China, the Bank of Communications, and the Central Bank met to discuss a resolution to the problem.[79] This crisis was not amenable to local solutions, however, since, according to statistics compiled at the time by the Bank of Communications, from April 14 to May 25 the Tianjin branches of the Central Bank, Bank of China, Bank of Communications, and Four Bank Joint Treasury faced a silver drain of more than 1.6 million yuan. Branches in Shanghai, Beiping, and other major cities faced similar runs.[80]

In Tianjin the monetary crisis heightened the general sense of tension over Japanese aggression. An unusual number of Japanese and Korean people started coming to the local branches of the Bank of China in Beiping and Tianjin to exchange paper money for silver beginning in May 1935.[81] The run did not create a major crisis, but it certainly reinforced the impression that the Japanese and Koreans, with Japanese protection, were smuggling silver out of China. In fact, Japanese smuggling was a well-known phenomenon at this time. Statistics are not available for Tianjin, but in May 1935 the Nationalist government estimated that Japanese smuggled 200,000 yuan of silver out of China every day.[82] The American missionary Earle Ballou described the scene a friend had witnessed on a train in Tianjin in November 1935: "Five or six Koreans in their 3rd class car took off their outer garments, took pocket-lined vests from their luggage, and put them on. These vests were loaded so heavily with silver dollars that one man had to be helped to his feet and helped off the car . . . Each man must have been carrying between one and two thousand dollars—to smuggle out of the country, as no police, customs officer or soldier dares interfere with the person of a Jap or Korean."[83] Such smuggling contributed to the general impression that the Nationalist government had lost control over North China. One periodical in Tianjin even ran a story about "new methods for smuggling silver," describing clever ways the Japanese had of avoiding Chinese police and customs officials.[84]

As the silver drain continued unchecked into the fall of 1935, rumors abounded about government plans to reorganize the monetary system. Bian remarked in his diary that bankers "should demand reorganization of the Finance Ministry's old debt in return for giving up the right to issue currency."[85] In spite of the nationalization of much of the Chinese banking industry earlier that year, Bian still thought that government-bank relations could be played according to the rules of the game. The nature of the financial crisis in 1935, however, went well beyond the framework established in previous negotiations over monetary matters. Nationalist officials, realizing that China could not solve a balance-of-payments crisis on its own, began simultaneously and secretly to negotiate with both the British and the Americans for help with the currency reforms. The British wanted China to link its new currency to sterling and the Americans wanted it linked to the dollar. The British even dispatched a financial adviser, Sir Frederick Leith-Ross, who first went to Japan, trying in vain to gain cooperation for Chinese monetary reform, and then to China. Simultaneously the United States agreed to purchase a huge amount of silver from China to finance the reform, but set conditions, including linking the new currency to the dollar.[86] Chinese officials preferred not to accept these conditions, however, and when Kong Xiangxi announced the nationalization of the monetary supply on November 3, 1935, the Chinese state made no provisions to link the new currency to the dollar. The order ended convertibility of paper money to silver, making it illegal for any Chinese except the government to own silver, and canceling the rights of all banks except the Central Bank, the Bank of China, and the Bank of Communications to issue paper money. From then on, the country's new currency, called the *fabi,* or legal currency, was intended to be under strict central control.[87]

The reaction to the *fabi* reform proved surprisingly tame. In 1916, almost twenty years earlier, the moratorium on exchange issued by Yuan Shikai's government had engendered a storm of protest from bankers, local officials, and other elites. Many branches of the Bank of China outside of Beijing and Tianjin did not even institute Yuan's order. In contrast, when the Nationalist government suspended exchange in 1935, bankers, local officials, and other elites all cooperated. Bian Baimei, who had resigned rather than work to implement the 1916 moratorium, promptly went to the Central Bank to discuss how to proceed.[88] Likewise, in Tianjin there were no crowds in the streets demanding exchange, nor did the native elites form an ad hoc organization to take over exchange as they had in their ill-fated attempt in 1916. Rather than telegrams of condemnation, as in 1916, local elite groups in

Shanghai, Tianjin, and other major cities sent telegrams pledging cooperation. The Tianjin Bankers' and Indigenous Bankers' associations held a special combined meeting at which they agreed to obey the government's order. They composed a message, to be sent to all the local banks and indigenous banks, declaring that "the *fabi* reform is completely different from the 1916 moratorium on exchange. If customers are suspicious, the banks and indigenous banks should explain [the situation]."[89] Some people in Tianjin even saw a certain ironic humor in the switch from silver dollars to paper money. A local pictorial, the *Beiyang Huabao,* ran an amusing story about how inappropriate it had been previously to refer to all silver dollars as foreign *(yang),* even if minted in China, as most silver dollars were by 1935. "At last," the author exulted, "nobody will call [Chinese money] 'foreign' again!"[90]

There were many reasons for the success of the 1935 monetary reforms. First, the British and American governments backed the reforms instead of opposing them as in 1916. Initial American anger over apparent links between the new Chinese currency and sterling gave way when China sent the American-educated banker Chen Guangfu to the United States to reach agreement for the Americans to buy Chinese silver. In addition, most foreign banks in China cooperated with the reform, with the exception of the Japanese-controlled banks: the Yokohama Specie Bank, the Chaoxian (Korean) Bank, and the Bank of Taiwan.[91] In fact Leith-Ross had the British government "issue a king's command to all British subjects in China to accept the *fa-pi* [*fabi*] policy."[92] Second, the nationalization of much of the banking industry had, in the words of Parks Coble, "politically emasculated" the Shanghai bankers.[93] Without the leadership of the Bank of China and the Bank of Communications, the two largest issuers of paper money, bank opposition to government monetary policies was impossible, and by the fall of 1935, the government firmly controlled the management of those two banks. Third, the sense of economic crisis in 1935 was widespread. Many firms had gone bankrupt, prices continued to decline, and the continued flow of silver abroad jeopardized the financial stability of the country.[94] In contrast, as real as Yuan Shikai's political crisis was in 1916, the concurrent fiscal crisis of the government was seen as the result of Yuan's ill-considered attempt to misuse bank funds to restore a monarchy, not as a fundamental economic problem. Since Yuan's government had already lost legitimacy, so had its monetary policies. The Nationalist government in 1935 had not come to that stage, in spite of the worried plotting of Tianjin's native elites. Fourth,

China faced a balance-of-payments crisis in 1935 that neither local guardianship, bank association–coordinated guardianship, risk pooling, transparency, regulation, or any of the other means for creating trust that had been perfected over the years could solve. Resolution of the 1935 crisis required both international diplomacy and unified domestic action, and this led to a preference for state initiative. Fifth and finally, the modern bankers' long years of preparing the public for impersonal trust in paper money played an important role in facilitating the 1935 *fabi* reform. In thinking about the success of the reform, Zhang Jia'ao later recalled that "public confidence in banknotes had been established firmly, especially the banknotes of the Bank of China which were circulated in remote and far-flung places in the interior."[95] In addition, the Bank of China and the Bank of Communications still issued much of the new *fabi* currency, providing continuity for trust in the mind of the public.

To understand the role of public confidence in the 1935 *fabi* reform, however, we need to consider one crucial fact about the new monetary system. China did not go off the silver standard in 1935; in fact, the government still pledged to keep silver reserves and foreign exchange equal to 60 percent of issue.[96] Prior to 1935, most banks also kept, or claimed to keep, 60 percent silver reserves, a standard benchmark which implied safety. The *fabi* reform did not mean that silver reserves no longer backed the currency, only that individuals no longer had the right to exchange paper for silver. Instead they would have to trust the government to keep its word and maintain adequate reserves. The publication of currency reserves by banks in the years prior to 1935 had set an important precedent in developing this kind of trust. Since some reserves had become public at the beginning of the Nanjing decade, bank reserves were no longer the subject of rumor and speculation. Instead, banks published the amounts of their reserves regularly in the newspapers, and committees of accountants periodically audited the reserves to assure people that the bankers were not lying. On the national level, the *fabi* reforms copied that precedent by providing for a Reserve Management Board to oversee silver reserves. In North China, however, the Japanese had other plans for currency regulation.

Japanese opposition to the *fabi* plan emerged only a few days after Kong Xiangxi announced the monetary reform. Over the space of several days the Japanese military demanded that Song Zheyuan prohibit silver in North China from being shipped south, ordered that Japanese financial advisers be attached to local governments in North China, prohibited *fabi* from circulating, and issued a statement saying that the currency reform "threatens the basis for lasting peace in Asia built up in recent years." The Japanese even made currency a major item in their drive for a "North China autonomy movement."[97] The Japanese proved unable to stop implementation of the *fabi* monetary system in North China, but their demand that silver reserves stay in North China and not be shipped south did come to fruition—in part because of additional pressure applied by local elites.

Initially, the government planned to ship Tianjin's silver to Shanghai, but this plan, unlike the idea of a nonconvertible currency itself, provoked a strong protest from local officials and local elites, as well as the Japanese. Doihara Kenji pressured officials in Hebei and Shandong provinces not to ship silver south.[98] In Tianjin, Cheng Zhongyu (Cheng Ke), then the mayor of Tianjin, emphasized to Bian Baimei that the silver should not be shipped out of Tianjin, and that a local management board should be formed to oversee reserves. Likewise, local elites seemed genuinely worried that shipping silver south would be tantamount to abandonment of the north by the Nationalists. Wang Xiaoyan, head of the Indigenous Bankers' Association, and Ji Hua, head of the Chamber of Commerce, both wanted the silver to stay in Tianjin.[99] As a result of the pressure from local officials and elites, Tianjin's modern and indigenous bankers' associations sent a combined request to the Finance Ministry to allow the formation of a local currency reserve management board.[100]

About a week later, the Beiping and Tianjin Reserve Management board held its founding meeting. Modern bankers predominated on the board, accounting for at least twelve of the nineteen members, and of those twelve at least nine came from native places other that Tianjin or Beiping. Ji Hua, Wang Xiaoyan, and Bian Shucheng (no relation of Bian Baimei's, but from the Tianjin Bian family and a classmate of Kong Xiangxi's in the United States) represented the Tianjin native elite.[101] Wang Kemin, bureaucrat, former president of the Bank of China, and Beiyang period finance minister, also sat on the Reserve Board and was even elected to its standing committee, an indication that his career had revived with the rise of Japanese power in North China. Zhou Zuomin, president of Jincheng Bank, was chairman, but he rarely came to meetings. Instead, the standing committee, led by Bian Baimei, took over the day-to-day operations of the board. The board sealed up the currency reserves of the various banks and conducted frequent audits.[102] Tianjin had its guardianship organization to provide a guarantee that the *fabi* silver currency reserves would remain local. The keepers of that guarantee included a large number of professional bankers and a few of the leaders of the native elite. The leap from "public reserves" of the pre-1935 period to the Reserve Management Board after 1935 was not such a very long jump after all.

Keeping silver reserves in North China fell far short of Japanese demands that *fabi* currency not circulate, and for the most part the monetary reform proved successful. Nonetheless, the Japanese continued applying pressure to advance "autonomy" in the region. After a series of complicated maneuvers, Nanjing and Japanese officials reached a compromise agreement in December, creating the Hebei-Chahar Political Council *(jicha zhengwu weiyuanhui)* to oversee administration in those two provinces as well as cooperation with the Japanese.[103] Song Zheyuan became head of the council, and Xiao Zhenying, another military officer, former chairman of Chahar and a native of Jilin whom Bian described as "straightforward, simple, and uneducated," became mayor of Tianjin.[104] The council also included Zhou Zuomin, a professional banker, and many former officials in the Beiyang government considered sympathetic to the Japanese, Wang Kemin prominent among them.[105] To many, the Nanjing government seemed to be capitulating to the Japanese plan to establish an "autonomous" region in North China. In Beiping, more than a thousand students took to the streets to protest the autonomy movement, and when their petition fell on deaf ears, they called for a strike to close down Beiping's colleges.[106] The Nationalist policy of nonresistance provoked a storm of protest all over China.[107] Nonetheless, plans for the Hebei-Chahar Political Council went ahead essentially unimpeded. For Bian Baimei in Tianjin, the political outlook was not good. One of his subordinates returned from a meeting in Shanghai to report that "T. V. Soong et al. are very dispirited and are thinking of giving up on North China."[108] More immediately, however, Bian faced the demands of Japanese officials in Beiping and Tianjin for the right to supervise regulation of the *fabi* currency.

In November 1935 the Japanese military police informed the Tianjin Bankers' Association that they intended to examine the vaults of the city's banks. Zhong Bingfeng and Bian Baimei dismissed the suggestion as ridiculous, but the Japanese were serious. The dispute led to a series of meetings in Tianjin between bankers, local officials, and Japanese representatives.[109] As with the earlier demand that silver reserves remain in North China, the Japanese found allies among local officials and Tianjin's native elites who also worried about Nationalist government designs on North China's silver. Wang Xiaoyan came to tell Bian Baimei that Song Zheyuan had "heard slanderous talk saying the Central Bank, the Bank of China, and the Bank of Communications recently have been shipping silver south. He is very unhappy." Bian also got a letter from the Beiping branch of the Bank of China suggesting that the "Reserve Management Board quickly examine and seal silver treasuries because Song [Zheyuan] and Xiao [Zhenying] had been instigated by the Japanese and were going to organize a so-called Support Finance Association."[110] Not all local officials in North China had bowed to Japanese demands, however. The mayor of Beiping sent word that he would cooperate only with the Beiping-Tianjin Reserve Management Board.[111] Nonetheless, the board's right to act as primary guardian and regulator of the monetary system in North China faced challenges on all sides.

By mid-1936, the Hebei-Chahar Council had plans to take control of currency issue in North China.[112] Since the Nationalist government had authorized formation of the council, Bian could not ignore its demands as easily as other, less orthodox would-be regulatory bodies. The council even issued an order to the effect that the only institution empowered to issue new paper money in Hebei Province was the Hebei Provincial Bank, directly contradicting the Finance Ministry's *fabi* policy.[113] This new provincial currency never came to be. But when the council informed the Reserve Management Board that it would like to audit silver reserves, there was little Bian and his colleagues could do. From that time on the council sent auditors to accompany board members in their work, and the two organizations published their reports jointly.[114] As a result, the Nanjing Finance Ministry's control over the money supply in North China had been undermined one additional degree.

As the Hebei-Chahar Political Council attempted to take control of supervising the money supply, the patchwork solution which had been imposed on local elite organizations in Tianjin the previous year fell apart. First, Xiao Zhenying, the new mayor of Tianjin, took a perverse dislike to Zhong Bingfeng, chairman of the Tianjin Bankers' Association. In spite of all efforts by Bian Baimei and others to mediate, Zhong was forced to flee Tianjin.[115] The Bankers' Association met and elected the Sichuan native Wang Yiling, manager of the Tianjin branch of Jincheng Bank and a returned student from Japan, as chairman.[116] Zhou Zuomin had brought Wang to Tianjin from the bank's Hankou branch specifically to deal with the Japanese presence in North China. In addition, Wang's ascension to the helm of the Bankers' Association came only a few months after his boss, Zhou Zuomin, had become a member of the Hebei-Chahar Political Council.[117] The problems of the Tianjin Bankers' Association, however, paled in comparison to those of the Tianjin Chamber of Commerce. Conflicts between the "new" and "old" factions had persisted after the 1935 election, and by the end of the year the Chamber had virtually ceased to function again.[118] Finally, the city government simply ordered the two factions to stop meeting and set up a committee to reorganize the Chamber completely. The reorganization committee found that the Chamber was "short of talent," "short of funds," and "had a flawed structure," and its accounts had not been straightened out "in decades." The committee decided to revamp the entire organization.[119] After a few minor changes to the Chamber's regulations, in December 1936 the membership elected yet another set of leaders, including Bian Baimei as a member of the executive committee. The election represented a triumph for the so-called old faction, which won all but three of the fifteen executive committee memberships and all of the standing committee memberships.[120]

A reconstituted Chamber could do little to provide security for the city in the face of foreign aggression, however. Seven months later the Japanese launched an invasion of China south of the Great Wall. Less than ten days after the beginning of the invasion, Bian shipped 25 million yuan in un-issued *fabi* paper money south for protection. Both he and the Nanjing government worried that if these unused notes fell into Japanese hands, that could spell disaster by giving the Japanese the opportunity to issue currency and spend money in Nanjing's name. At the same time, the Japanese began to spread rumors that silver was being shipped south. Finally, the Beiping-Tianjin Reserve Management Board asked the Hebei-Chahar Political Council to audit silver reserves and publish the results in order to reassure the public.[121] Only a year before, Bian Baimei had resisted interference by the Hebei-Chahar Political Council in the management of silver reserves, but in the face of Japanese invasion, it was the only government entity in North China with enough legitimacy left to act as guardian and regulator to create trust in the money supply.

After Tianjin fell to the Japanese, the situation became a little calmer. In fact, the Japanese invasion had been anticipated in Tianjin for so long that many people faced the transition with equanimity.[122] Bian's worries were hardly over, though. By the end of August, the Tianjin Bankers' Association had begun negotiations with a Japanese general over a 3 million yuan loan, in a pattern reminiscent of both the warlord and early Nanjing periods.[123] Once the Japanese had formed a "provisional" puppet government in Beiping, they also started making plans to set up their own central bank in North China. At the head of the new government, and a moving force behind the plans for a new central bank, sat Bian Baimei's former boss at the Bank of China, Wang Kemin. On December 19, Wang invited Bian to a meeting about forming the puppet regime's central bank. Although Bian told Wang that the Bank of China would not become a stockholder in the central bank or hand over its reserves, he had little power to back up his words.[124] In fact, by the end of 1937, the only leverage Bian had left to use against the Japanese lay in the continued existence of the foreign concessions, where most of Tianjin's banks had their main offices. Past experience had proven, however, that the protection of the foreign concessions was incomplete at best. A few days later Bian took his fateful train trip to Beijing. His entry for the day of that meeting is headed simply "The day Bian Baimei's spirit [*jingshen*] died." In Beijing, Wang Kemin presented all of the bankers with prepared pledges to buy stock in the new central bank:

> The Bank of China, 4,500,000, the Bank of Communications, 3,500,000, the Four Banks and Hebei Provincial Bank each 800,000, Jidong Bank 500,000, all together 12,500,000. The attendees were asked to sign the stock participation agreements.
>
> I do not have the authority as a branch manager to purchase stock [on behalf of the Bank of China], and so I refused to sign. After going back and forth, Wang Kemin came up with the four words "Raise with best efforts." I had no choice. I signed with the seven words "Bian Baimei will raise with best efforts" to show that I was not representing the bank's authority [but my own].
>
> After signing, I was very distressed. The old me died today, I am only a walking corpse, only a living dead person.[125]

At his worst moment, when foreign invaders had taken control of Tianjin and the rest of North China, when the puppets of those invaders forced Bian into the humiliating move of appearing to collaborate—the day his "spirit died"—he expressed his anguish in terms of the violation of the institutional integrity of the Bank of China. After a lifetime of playing by the rules of the game of modern banking, he even tried to finesse the situation by claiming that bank regulations did not give him the authority to invest on behalf of the Bank of China in the new central bank. Ultimately, he preferred to humiliate himself personally rather than compromise the bank, so he signed the agreement as Bian Baimei the individual, not Bian Baimei the manager of the Tianjin branch of the Bank of China. His extraordinary commitment to the Bank of China as an organization and to modern banking as an institution may have been exceptionally strong, but his attitude is also representative of the growing importance of institutions in Chinese society during the republican period.

Banker-led guardianship worked to maintain trust during the crises that resulted from Japanese aggression in 1931 and 1932 but proved impotent in the face of the balance of payments crisis of late 1934 and early 1935. Throughout this period the Chamber of Commerce fell prey to infighting that grew out of earlier Nationalist policies, making it even less able to take on guardianship duties. Bankers and local elites alike had to rely on state power, and the Nationalist state rose to the challenge with unexpected facility, taking control of the banking industry and instituting a unified, government-controlled currency for the first time in modern history.

Continued Japanese pressure for influence in North China could not stop implementation of the *fabi* currency reform, but it did undermine Nanjing's ability to act as sole guardian and regulator. Pressure from the Japanese, local officials, and local elites forced the Nationalist government to leave silver reserves in North China, under the supervision of the newly created Beiping-Tianjin Reserve Management Board. Although this board, under the day-to-day administration of Bian Baimei, remained faithful to Nationalist control, the Japanese became joint regulators of the reserves by using the power of the Hebei-Chahar Political Council to audit those reserves. In the final analysis, banks and bank money were vital to state power, but without support and regulation by a stable and strong government, a modern and thriving banking system acting on its own was not powerful enough either to help the Nanjing government defeat the Japanese or to help bankers stand alone. In the end, Tianjin's bankers had to accept Nationalist state control in 1935 and bow to the power of the puppet state after the Japanese invasion in 1937. Thus, although banks and the state enjoyed a symbiotic relationship, the state played the primary role in creating the institutional environment for the rules of the game.

Conclusion

> If [you] want to protect [the nation's] sovereignty, then [you] cannot talk about destroying the [new currency] system.
>
> — Bian Baimei, *Diary*, 1935

Bian Baimei left Tianjin shortly after his humiliating confrontation with Wang Kemin over the puppet government's central bank. In January 1938 the upper management of the Bank of China called Bian to Hong Kong for a meeting from which he never returned. In spite of the fact that Bian intended to "ask the general office for punishment and disciplinary action," no one blamed him for the Tianjin Bank of China's role in founding the Japanese puppet regime's central bank. He continued his distinguished career at the bank, eventually working his way up to the post of vice president.[1] When the communist revolution swept through China after the war with Japan, Bian left China for the United States, returning to the country of his education. He died in Valejo, California, in 1968.

Bian had arrived in Tianjin in 1916 during a financial crisis and he left in 1938 in the midst of war. Over the course of his twenty-two years in Tianjin, Bian endured almost constant political turmoil and frequent financial crises. In spite of such troubled times, trust in Chinese-owned and operated banks spread among ever larger numbers of Tianjin residents, as evidenced by growth in bank deposits and paper money. In spite of these successes, the financial system remained vulnerable to government abuse, rumor, and the impact of foreign and domestic political events, which induced officials, local elites, and bankers to undertake a variety of strategies to promote trusting behaviors.

Throughout this period, two types of events caused elites to make public proclamations about money and its use: patriotic political movements and financial crises. During the former, the rhetorical appeals to support Chinese rather than foreign banks had some success, providing evidence that shared norms can sometimes promote impersonal trusting behaviors, especially in times of financial stability. By contrast, patriotic rhetoric had little effect during financial crises, an indication that self-interest could trump shared values when individuals perceived that their financial well-being was at stake. The use of rhetoric during financial crises followed a kind of reverse arc over the period, starting strong in 1916 and 1921, dying out almost completely after more than a decade of warlord depredations in 1927–28, and then reviving briefly during the balance of payments crisis of 1934–35. The content of rhetorical appeals changed with time as well. Invocations of the good of the local community and patriotic duty remained fairly constant, but 1916 witnessed a one-time attempt to rally Tianjiners through the mention of common native place. In later years the presence of large numbers of nonnative professional bankers, and by 1927 nonnative warlords, made such appeals difficult. In addition, in 1921 elites made a special attempt to invoke belief in the expert knowledge of banking, though the rational functioning of banks as they explained it had little to do with the reality of the conditions of the Bank of China and the Bank of Communications at the time. Ultimately, guardianship, impressive bank buildings, and the employment of trustworthy agents linked trusting behaviors to the expert knowledge of banking more effectively than rhetorical appeals.

Many strategies to promote trust involved guardianship structures of one kind or another, especially third-party guarantees (lenders of last resort), third-party oversight, and risk pooling. Officials and local elites in Tianjin demonstrated over and over again that they felt some responsibility to regulate, and even guarantee, the viability of the money supply. Under the leadership of the Tianjin Chamber of Commerce, in 1916 and 1927–28 local elites tried to form ad hoc organizations to raise funds to guarantee the value of paper money, and in 1921, 1924, and 1930–31, local elites took an active role in trying to regulate the currency issue by making the operations of banks more transparent. The organizations formed in 1916 and 1927–28 failed miserably, receiving little real financial support and operating as virtually empty shells, in part because banks issued too much money to be easily covered by local resources. In the end, holders of paper money proved justifiably suspicious of both elite motives and commitments. Local elites' attempts at regulation through promoting transparency proved more successful, especially in 1921, but oversight was spotty and faded along with the memory of the crisis. In addition, their demands for transparency became problematic when the elites could not provide financial support if audits uncovered problems. All in all, local elite guardianship did little more than suggest that regulation and openness might be useful strategies for promoting trust if conducted by organizations with both the will to maintain continuity and the financial strength to follow through.

Banker-initiated guardianship activities had a better record of achievement. Banks' lender of last resort activities resolved a number of crises, though these successes derived in part from the fact that they involved relatively minor crises (1924, 1928, 1929), and in part from the ability of bankers to make loans based on collateral. Risk pooling by the Four Banks proved quite effective, but other banks lacked the mutual personal trust among managers necessary for such cooperation. The disruption of financial markets caused by the Japanese aggression led to the formation of two guardianship organizations. The attack on Shanghai in 1932 led to the formation of the Tianjin clearinghouse and joint treasury, a banker-initiated guardianship organization combining transparency, lender of last resort, and risk-pooling functions. After the *fabi* reforms in 1935, fear that the Nationalists planned to abandon Tianjin to the Japanese caused local elites, officials, and bankers alike to demand the formation of the Beiping-Tianjin Reserve Management Board, a guardianship organization intended to provide oversight and transparency.

In addition to guardianship activities, banks engaged in a variety of other institutional arrangements to promote trust. The biggest banks, like the Bank of China and the Bank of Communications, had large branch structures, allowing for the isolation of problem branches and assistance from stronger branches for weaker ones, as in both 1916 and 1921.[2] In addition, since government interference often lay at the root of local problems, banks adjusted their internal structures to isolate problem branches and centralize currency issue in the relative safety of the treaty ports. Bankers also tried to minimize risk by maintaining high reserves, coming to consider 60 percent silver and 40 percent securities as standard. The Bank of Communications solicited additional investment in 1921, though the warlord source of that money carried a high price in terms of autonomy. Most important, during the warlord period, bankers developed rules of the game for dealing with government demands: emphasizing relations between organizations, not individuals; lending on collateral; negotiating collectively; and limiting loans to faltering regimes. Although some aspects of the rules of the game, such as collateral-based lending, were borrowed from foreign models, most of these rules developed over time. From the 1910s through 1921, the Bank of China, the Bank of Communications, and the Zhili Provincial Bank routinely violated these rules in their dealings with the state. As captive institutions created for financing state activities, they had little choice. Nonetheless, the phenomenal success of bank organizations in attracting deposits and issuing paper money gave them great leverage to enforce the rules of the game as time went on. In addition, banks implemented many of the agreements with the state by riding on the back of foreign prerogatives in China, as with the customs and salt taxes.

Bankers also worked hard to establish belief in the stability and institutional integrity of their banks. They worried about their personal reputations as representatives of their organizations, with Bian Baimei as the sterling example of the effort to encourage trust through the probity of agents. In addition, bankers worked to encourage trust in their own expert knowledge, relying on both secrecy and openness to do so. In the 1920s, following the lead of foreign banks, Tianjin's Chinese banks built elaborate offices to represent their strength and provide a "front stage" to conceal their inner workings backstage. At the same time, some consciously tried to hide the internal financial condition of their banks, as in 1921, under the assumption that the appearance of having the strength of a tiger was a workable substitute in the absence of actual strength. In contrast to this secrecy, bankers also debated and experimented with the idea of transparency by publishing currency issue and reserve figures, usually in the newspaper, or by allowing outside audits. The impetus for openness came alternatively from external demands of government officials or local elites and internally from bankers themselves. In the end, by about 1928, a combination of external and internal pressure had led to a consensus on openness, although transparency remained incomplete.

The use of state authority as a basis for promoting trust showed the greatest change over the course of this period. During bank runs in the 1910s and 1920s, the state often tried to enforce the circulation of bank-issued paper money by command. But government edicts, the dispatch of police to maintain order, arrests, and even executions (in 1927–28) did not stem financial crises. In the 1930s, the Nationalist government changed the rules of the game and institutionalized its authority over the financial system by issuing regulations, undermining local elite structures, and—taking advantage of the balance of payments crisis in 1934–35—nationalizing much of the banking system and the money supply. The result was a smooth transition to a nonconvertible currency in 1935, which proved that authority could be effective in promoting trust under the right conditions, such as government control of the banking sector.

Nigel Dodd has argued that "contemporary monetary networks are remarkable for the complexity of technological, institutional and social mechanisms necessary for them to operate at all. But they are also compelling for their fragility."[3] Noting similar complexity, Susan Shapiro concludes, in contrast, that "impersonal social exchange and agency relationships persist, principals still willingly trust strangers, and the engine of social complexity presses onward."[4] The historical record in Tianjin between 1916 and 1937 shows both views to be correct. Complex arrangements resulted in the secular growth of impersonal trust, punctuated by episodes of crisis that shook the very fabric of society. Financial structures were simultaneously resilient and fragile.

The fact that those financial structures centered on modern banks provides an opportunity to examine the nature of the institutional development of this sector, especially in regard to organizational imitation and the relationship between institutions and their environment. The adoption of foreign models of bank organization fell far short of completely replicating foreign monetary systems. In fact, given the variation and complexity of financial systems in the West and Japan, no single foreign model existed. The joint-stock corporation was the most important foreign import. In contrast with most kinds of firms during this period, in which "the notion that one's money be put into the pocket of some strangers for them to run a business was . . . unthinkable," modern banks raised large amounts of capital from large numbers of investors.[5] The structure and operations of these joint-stock banks, however, reflected the Chinese context as much as foreign models. At a time when the world trend favored central banks with a monopoly over note issue, the new Chinese monetary system relied on multiple banks of issue. The mutual interactions of fiscal penury and political weakness constrained institutional innovation by hindering government control over the money supply prior to the 1930s. Although the lack of a monopoly on currency issue weakened the power of republican governments, the unintended consequences of "failed" institutional innovation did not always have results that the architects of the system would have found negative. For example, although foreign experts all advised China to go on a gold or gold exchange standard, a recent study concludes that China's continued adherence to the silver standard "seems not to have been a mistake" because it protected China from price instability.[6] These variations from international models reflect the mutual influence of organizations and their environments.

In China this was seen most clearly in the relationship between networks and the rules of hierarchical organizations. In the late nineteenth and early twentieth centuries, infighting and mutual suspicion among various cliques within the Chinese bureaucracy, as well as opposition from both foreign and Chinese indigenous bankers, caused numerous delays and digressions in the formation of state-sponsored banks based on foreign models. In the end, to satisfy various factional demands, the state either withheld important government privileges from some banks, such as in refusing to give Sheng Xuanhuai's Imperial Bank of China the right to handle government funds, or created multiple banks with similar privileges, such as the Da Qing Bank (later the Bank of China) and the Bank of Communications. By the republican period, many factions had founded banks, including the National Industrial Bank of Zhou Xuexi and the Jincheng Bank of the Anhui faction. Most private banks did not represent any one faction, however; their backers usually included a mix of individuals with different political affiliations, professions, and native places. Furthermore, by the 1920s, many bank managers had managed to distance their corporations from their original patron-client networks. The banks did not exist as completely independent corporate hierarchies, though, and bankers forged new professionally based networks that allowed for collective action. Common age, educational background, and native place assisted cooperation among professional bankers, but their networks also reflected the new institutional environment produced by the banks themselves. The impact of state-sponsored banks as training grounds for professional bankers who later worked in the private sector was particularly salient. The evidence here supports Sherman Cochran's conclusion that, although a significant literature argues that in Chinese culture networks take primacy over hierarchies in commercial organization, "in one way or another, corporations and networks all engaged in long-term dynamic interaction."[7] Organizations were not prisoners of their environment. Organizations and their environment existed in a mutually interactive relationship.[8]

From the beginning, state needs drove innovation in the Chinese financial system. The central government founded some modern banks, with the Bank of China and the Bank of Communications as two of the more important examples. In addition, provincial governments also established banks.

The Zhili Provincial Bank played an important role in Tianjin's financial system. In the 1920s, the Bank of China and the Bank of Communications achieved a measure of autonomy. Under the Nationalist regime (1928–1937), however, the government curtailed the autonomy of both banks, as well as a few of the smaller private banks, and this resulted in a state-dominated banking system by 1935. The *fabi* reforms a few months later represented a significant increase in central state power for the Nationalist government since, among other things, stabilization of the monetary system allowed for a large increase in foreign lending to the government.[9]

For the most part, the experience in republican Tianjin shows that the phrase "free banking" is meaningless. Banks in China arose from state needs, and frequent crises and instability invited regulation and supervision from all sides. Even at the height of their independence in the 1920s, banks remained closely tied to the state, and local elites persisted in their attempts to regulate them. Free banking theorists might argue that an independent banking system, free from state claims on bank resources, could have achieved stability, but the close links among banks, the monetary system, and the state made such a possibility simply unthinkable in China. In addition, independence from the state would not have preserved the banking system from outside disruption such as war in 1932 or the balance of payments crisis of the mid-1930s. Politics and the economy are mutually interpenetrating realms, and consideration of one without the other can give only an incomplete picture. Imagining a world of free markets functioning independently of the state simply does not conform with the historical experience of the development of financial systems, in republican China or elsewhere. The question iss not whether the state becomes involved in the operations of markets, but what kind of involvement, what kind of governments, and under what constraints?

The concept of close relations among the economy and the polity would have come as no surprise to Bian Baimei, who had cut his teeth studying political economy under Henry Gardner at Brown University. Later, his experience in Tianjin repeatedly reinforced the message. Over the course of his years in Tianjin, he frequently expressed disdain for political interference in banking, resigning in protest in 1916, labeling warlords "rats" and "scoundrels," and commenting with distaste on the activities of Du Yuesheng during the Nationalist period. Nonetheless, he never denied or opposed close relationships between banking and the state. He worked to find viable ways to lend money to the central and local governments, and he cooperated with the takeover of the banking sector by the Nationalist government in the 1930s.

The careers of many of the other bankers discussed in this book go even farther in demonstrating the close relationships between banking and the state. Wang Kemin represents an extreme example, alternating service as an official with time at the Bank of China. Wang's political ambitions would end tragically, though; he was arrested as a collaborator by the Nationalists in 1945 and died in prison. Many of China's bankers did not go to the same extremes but still showed similar flexibility in moving between state service and banking. Both Zhou Xuexi and Sun Duosen worked as government officials who used their official positions to build corporate empires, including banks. Even Zhang Jia'ao, the putative hero of the Bank of China's long fight for independence, moved between banking and government service several times. He began his career in the Jiangsu provincial government, moved to the Bank of China, and then after being forced out by the bank in 1935 held a number of positions in the Nationalist government.[10] Likewise, Wu Dingchang, head of the Salt Bank, returned to his government roots, serving the Nationalist regime in a number of positions. Zhou Zuomin of Jincheng Bank, for his part, headed up the Beiping-Tianjin Reserve Management Commission after the *fabi* reforms in 1935, and then served on the National Economic Commission of the Wang Jingwei regime.[11]

The rise of this group of professional bankers, along with the institutional development of banks, helped reshape elite roles in state-society relations. The cohort of Tianjin's professional bankers, including Bian Baimei, Zhou Zuomin, Tan Danya, and Wu Dingchang, had much in common. In addition to serving at one or another of the state banks, they all came of age as part of the generation that studied abroad during the first decade of the twentieth century, and many came from the same provinces: Jiangsu, Zhejiang, and Anhui. As outsiders in Tianjin and employees of nationwide banks, they had little interest in the protection of local prerogatives and were inclined to favor state building, so long as state activities did not interfere with the institutional integrity of their banks. In contrast, many members of Tianjin's elites considered themselves natives of the city, and they had a greater interest in protecting their local prerogatives than in building state power. Native elites controlled the powerful Chamber of Commerce, though sojourners began to chip away at this dominance over time, and Nationalist activism attacked elite Chamber leadership in the 1930s by broadening the base of merchant representation. The fact that bankers and local elites often played different roles in state-society relations suggests the need to disaggregate business elites as an analytical category.

Local elite participation in guardianship activities included elements of both government-imposed liturgy and activist elite initiative, though neither of these models sufficiently explains the processes involved. The government offered local elites nothing in return for taking on the guardian role, making elite guardianship more extractive than liturgical. At the same time, elites coordinated their own initiatives with local officials at almost every step; thus, no public sphere or civil society existed separate from the state. Nonetheless, local elites were not powerless, especially when protecting the locality from central force. The actions of local elites to avoid supporting the Beijing branches of the Bank of China and the Bank of Communications in 1916, their opposition to the "H" notes of the Bank of Communications in 1921, and their demand to keep silver reserves in Tianjin in 1935 provide examples of elite activism at its most successful. When faced with outside threats, local elites acted with unity, limiting central state power at key points.

Most important, though, modern banks and bank money changed the institutional context of state-society relations, contributing to a decline in local elite influence. The size and scope of Tianjin's modern banks and the money they issued outstripped local elite capabilities. In addition, local elite organizations were not suited to the demands of guardianship. Their use of ad hoc forms of organization in 1916 and 1927–28 lacked the continuity needed for effective lender of last resort or regulatory activities. As an association of guilds, the Chamber of Commerce itself lacked unity and organizational discipline. Each guild either tried to minimize its own responsibility or remained suspicious of the trustworthiness of others, as with accusations of speculation against the rice and flour merchants in 1927–28.[12] Their failure to develop effective guardianship revealed the weakening position of local elites in regard to monetarization and the increasingly institutionalized financial structures of republican society. Thus, it is a fundamental proposition of this book that forms are as important as functions, and the forms of financial systems play key roles in state-society relations.[13]

The development of "modern" banks and the money they issued introduced powerful new institutions into republican Tianjin. In fact, many officials, bankers, and other members of the elite envisioned banks as having important roles on the front lines in the war for survival among nation-states. That relationship was not nearly as simple, however, as the equation of a strong financial system with a strong state. The government established the patterns for the structure of banks and provided, with more or less success, the regulatory environment in which they operated. At the same time, the need for trust constrained government access to bank resources and pulled local elites into the process, demonstrating the complexity of the environment in which bank-state relations existed. Like all institutions, financial institutions in republican China could "simultaneously empower and control. Institutions present a constraint/freedom duality . . . [T]hey are vehicles for activity within constraints."[14] This dual influence of financial institutions did not end with the Japanese invasion in 1937, as a brief review of subsequent events shows.

In 1938 the Japanese puppet government issued its own nonconvertible currency from its new central bank. Although it was intended at first to be equal in value to the *fabi*, the Japanese puppet government slowly reduced the value of the latter. By December 1938, *fabi* could be exchanged for Federal Reserve notes only at a discount of 40 percent.[15] The new currency rapidly took hold in that part of Tianjin under Japanese control, but at first it traded at a discount in the foreign concessions, which were still controlled by their various foreign governments. By July 1939, however, the *fabi* had fallen in value even in the foreign concessions.[16] After the Japanese occupied the concessions in December 1941, *fabi* disappeared from Tianjin, giving the puppet government considerable scope to print money to finance its activities. The government undermined trust in that currency by printing large amounts of paper money, causing serious inflation during the occupation period. After the war the Nationalist government accelerated the process, printing so much money that it brought on the hyperinflation of the late 1940s. News photos of bank runs and wheelbarrows full of paper money are familiar sights in standard textbooks. Locally in Tianjin, "the enthusiasm that many workers felt for the Guomindang—the feeling that this was a legitimate Chinese government which deserved support—quickly dissipated."[17] Inflation under the Japanese occupation and hyperinflation under the Nationalists in the late 1940s were possible only because of the institutionalization of a nonconvertible currency in 1935. If the Chinese currency had remained exchangeable for silver, bank runs would have brought the banks down long before hyperinflation could have occurred, though possibly with equal devastation.

Gabriel Ardant has noted that the invention of paper money, and the consequent ability of governments to use inflation to finance state projects, was a standard tool in the repertoire of European state-building mechanisms.[18] Likewise, the introduction of the widespread use of paper money in urban centers like Tianjin supported state-building projects in republican China. Whereas Ardant emphasizes a developed economy as a prerequisite for states to use inflationary powers, I have focused on the requirement to promote impersonal trust as a necessary constraint on the use of paper money. Successful strategies to promote impersonal trust in money and banks took many guises, though, and proved flexible enough to exist under a variety of state forms, including the initial years of Yuan Shikai's autocratic centralism, warlord fragmentation, Nationalist activism, and Japanese occupation. Those regimes, in turn, proved unable to exist long enough to provide long-term stability in the regulatory environment for money and banking. In the end, the successful marriage of state power and trust in money and banking would not come in China until after the communist revolution, though the Chinese state today, like all states, still depends on the need for trust in its financial system.

APPENDIX **A**

Currency Circulation of Tianjin's Modern Banks

(000s of yuan)

Year	Bank of China	Bank of Comm.[a]	Prov. Bank	4 Bank Treas.	Other Banks	Total[b]	Growth (1916 = 100)
1916	2,373	2,668	0	0	0	5,041	100
1921	4,450	2,000	1,200[c]	0	—[d]	7,650	152
1923	5,480[e]	2,532	711	3,300	1,211	13,234	263
1925	15,000	4,116	—	—	—	19,116	379
1927	16,500	8,035	5,600[f]	—	—	30,135	598
1928	17,500	15,000	0	6,310[g]	—	38,810	770
1933	21,168	18,425	0	6,930	—	46,523	923

Source: Compiled from information found in *Chamber Collection, 1912–1928* pp. 952, 954, 1044–68, 1112, 1073, 1157–69; Tianjin Bank of China, 161-ZD-510, 161-ZD-620, 161-YB-876; Beijing NCB, 3510; Tianjin Bank Assoc., 129–2–1616–22; *Tianjin jinrong zhi,* p. 148; *Dagong Bao,* 1922; *Chamber Collection, 1928–1937,* p. 866; Wu Shicheng, "Tianjin zhi huashang yinhang," pp. 7–17; BOComm, Main, 398–12065; *Yinhang nianjian,* (1935), pp. F117–126; and *Diary,* April 15 and 17, 1922.

a. Bank of Communications figures do not include the "H" notes, which were Beijing notes issued under the Tianjin name.

b. Wu Shicheng estimated that perhaps only 40 percent of the money issued by Tianjin banks actually circulated within the city of Tianjin, with the rest in Hebei or other North China locations.

c. Uses 1922 figure as estimate.

d. A dash indicates figures unavailable, so total circulation would be even greater for those years.

e. Estimated by averaging the 1922 and 1924 figures.

f. Amount of circulation in June. Later that year circulation reached almost 9 million yuan.

g. Uses 1929 figure as an estimate.

APPENDIX **B**

English and Chinese Names of Banks

Bank of China (Zhongguo Yinhang)
Bank of Communications (Jiaotong Yinhang)
Banque Industrielle de Chine (Zhongfa Shiye Yinhang)
Central Bank (Zhongyang Yinhang)
China and Southsea Bank (Zhongnan Yinhang)
Continental Bank (Dalu Yinhang)
Cultivation Bank (Zhiye Yinhang)
Four Bank Joint Treasury (Sihang Gongku)
Four Bank Savings Society (Sihang Chuxu Hui)
Frontier Bank (Bianye Yinhang)
Hebei Provincial Bank (Hebei Sheng Yinhang)
Imperial Bank of China (Tongshang Yinhang)
National Commercial Bank (Zhejiang Xingye Yinhang)
National Industrial Bank of China (Zhongguo Shiye Yinhang)
Northeast Three Provinces Bank (Dong San Sheng Yinhang)
Salt Bank (Yanye Yinhang)
Shanghai Commercial and Savings Bank (Shanghai Shangye Chuxu Yinhang)
Shanxi Provincial Bank (Shanxi Sheng Yinhang)
Zhejiang Industrial Bank (Zhejiang Shiye Yinhang)
Zhili Provincial Bank (Zhili Sheng Yinhang)

APPENDIX **C**

The Money Scare Vernacular Song

Recently a money scare, Beijing, Tianjin, Shanghai, Hankou all involved
Bonds fell, currency ran, the two banks almost went under.
Half merchant–half government, as the state treasury [the banks] still part of the center
If a bank run really puts them under, the country's markets will stagnate.
Bank of China already restored exchange, probably no obstacle for Communications
Fortunately crisis has been averted, and I have a few things to discuss.
Using paper money is a good thing, easy to carry and easy to save
All of the countries of the world are like this and all have national banks.
If reserves are sufficient, credit is good and people use currency without fear
Paper money is not a silver substitute, it is a vehicle for the circulation of goods.
No country in the world has a dollar of reserves for every dollar of currency
[Economists can attest to this principle]*
If currency were all cashed at the same time, any bank would be hard-pressed.
Too bad our country's people don't understand this principle, all say silver is sweetest
If the wind blows or the grass moves, everyone rushes to cash in paper for silver.
Where are you going to put all that silver, naturally you will want to hoard it
Even more worrisome, deposit your money in foreign banks.
I advise our countrymen to wake up, don't think that only silver is sweet
Currency may be only a piece of paper, but silver has obstructed your vision.
You can't eat it if you're hungry, you can't wear it if you're cold
Silver and paper are the same, they are vehicles for the circulation of goods.
If the markets are in chaos, paper, silver, you'll starve either way
Money is a circulating medium, you shouldn't hoard it.
Like blood circulating in a body, once obstructed illness will result
If every household hoarded ten dollars, all the money in the market would be gone.
Another important matter, don't have superstitious belief in foreign banks
Foreign banks are not completely reliable, sometimes they're empty shells.
For example: the Bank of the Philippines and the Banque Industrielle
Draining your own blood is like helping a fat man gain weight.

* Brackets in the original.

If our money flows to foreign banks, blue-eyed fat-stomached merchants will think it great
When our country has trouble, foreigners will be happy to eat our last bit of grain.
The Boxer Uprising is a good example, could it be that you are not moved?
You need to know that since the European war, money scares all over the world
All countries' finance ruined, not a single one does not depend on paper money.
Fortunately the people have the power, working together all difficulties can be overcome
Truthfully the gold standard is already wrecked, a great fear in the world.
Although our country is poor to the point of starvation, we still have some strengths
America cannot compare, we're stronger than Austria, Germany, France.
If only everyone could understand, unity of the will is our impregnable stronghold
If the country is lost, where will you hoard your silver then?

APPENDIX **D**

Tianjin Bank of China Loans to Governments, 1927

The information that follows is taken from summary report on important events of 1927, Tianjin Bank of China, 161-ZD-734; Tianjin Salt Bank, 213–299.

Zhili Provincial Authorities

1. The Bank of China, Bank of Communications, and each of the Four Banks together guaranteed the purchase of military equipment in the amount of 3.78 million yuan beyond the government's 60 percent deposit.
2. Support for the currency of the Provincial Bank (discussed in Chapter 4).
3. A 1.2 million yuan loan to the Zhili Provincial Finance Bureau made May 11 by the members of the Tianjin Bankers' Association, secured by the 2.5 percent surcharge on customs taxes (Bank of China 250,000, Bank of Communications 250,000, the Four Banks 150,000 each, other twelve member banks 100,000).
4. In May and June a planned loan to the Zhili Provincial Salt Transport Controller for 450,000 yuan was canceled.
5. In June and July the government negotiated a loan to buy arms from a Japanese merchant. The amount was 500,000 yuan with 160,000 from the Bank of China and the remainder from the Bank of Communications and the Four Banks. The government later canceled the purchase agreement.

Army Groups

1. The Third and Fourth Army groups used the Chongwen Gate taxes in Beijing to borrow 1 million yuan from the members of the Beijing Bankers' Association. The Bank of China advanced 300,000 yuan, of which 150,000 yuan came from the Fengtian branch, 100,000 from the Tianjin branch, and 50,000 from the Beijing branch.
2. The Bank of China issued time drafts in American dollars ($250,000), on an overdraft for the Third and Fourth Army groups through the Beijing branch.
3. The Army Office borrowed 30,000 yuan from the Beijing branch for October expenses.

Notes

Abbreviations

Beijing NCB	Archives of the Beijing Branch of National City Bank (Shanghai Academy of Social Sciences)
Beiping-Tianjin RMB	Archives of the Beiping and Tianjin Reserve Management Board (Tianjin)
BOC, Main	Archives of the General Office of the Bank of China (Nanjing)
BOC Collection	Zhongguo yinhang, ed. *Zhongguo yinhang hangshi ziliao huibian* (Collected materials on the history of the Bank of China). Nanjing: Dang'an, 1991. In three volumes with consecutive page numbers.
BOComm Collection	Wang Mingquan, gen. ed. *Jiaotong yinhang shiliao* (Historical materials on the Bank of Communications). Beijing: Zhongguo jinrong chubanshe, 1995. In two volumes with consecutive page numbers.
BOComm, Main	Archives of the General Office of the Bank of Communications (Nanjing)
Chamber Collection, 1912–1928	Hu Guangmin and Lan Changyun, eds. *Tianjin shanghui dangan huibian* (Collection of materials from the Tianjiun Chamber of Commerce archives, 1912–1928). Tianjin: Renmin, 1991. In four volumes with consective page numbers.
Chamber Collection, 1928–1937	Li Jieping and Chen Yimin, eds. *Tianjin shanghui dangan huibian, 1928–1937* (Collection of materials from the Tianjin Chamber of Commerce archives, 1928–1937). Tianjin: Renmin, 1996. In two volumes with consecutive page numbers.
Diary	Bian Baimai's *Diary* (Tianjin)
Diary as reprinted	Bian Baimai's *Diary* as reprinted in *Tianjin wenshi ziliao,* 36 (1986): 1–87.

Financial Laws and Regs.	Zhongquo di'er lishi dang'an guan, Zhongguo renmin yinhang Jiangsu sheng fenhang and Jiangsu sheng jinrong zhi bianweihui, eds., *Zhonghua minguo jinrong fagui dang'an ziliao xuanbian* (Selections of materials from the archives on financial laws and regulations in the Republic of China). No city given, preface dated 1998. In two volumes with consecutive page numbers.
GMD	Guomindang (Kuomintang), or Nationalist Party
HSBC	The Hong Kong and Shanghai Banking Corporation
Monetary Hist. Collection, 1912–1927	Zhongguo renmin yinhang zonghang canshi, ed. *Zhonghua minguo huobishi ziliao, di yi ji, 1912–1927,* (Historical materials on the monetary history of the Republic of China, vol. 1, 1912–1927). Shanghai: Shanghai renmin chubanshe, 1986.
Monetary Hist. Collection, 1924–1929	Zhongguo renmin yinhang zonghang canshi, ed. *Zhonghua minguo huobishi ziliao, di er ji, 1924–1949,* (Historical materials on the monetary history of the Republic of China, vol. 2, 1924–1949). Shanghai: Shanghai renmin chubanshe, 1991.
Shanghai Bank Assoc.	Archives of the Shanghai Bankers' Association (Shanghai)
Tianjin Bank Assoc.	Archives of the Tianjin Bankers' Association (Tianjin)
Tianjin Bank of China	Archives of the Tianjin branch of the Bank of China (Tianjin)
Tianjin Chase Bank	Archives of the Tianjin branch of Chase Manhattan Bank (Shanghai Academy of Social Sciences)
Tianjin Continental Bank	Archives of the Tianjin branch of Continental Bank (Tianjin)
Tianjin Finance Bureau	Archives of the Finance Bureau of the Tianjin Municipal Government (Tianjin)
Tianjin Indig. Bank Assoc.	Archives of the Tianjin Indigenous Bankers' Association (Tianjin)
Tianjin Jincheng Bank	Archives of the Tianjin branch of Jincheng Bank (Tianjin)
Tianjin Salt Bank	Archives of the Tianjin branch of the Salt Bank (Tianjin)

Introduction

1. On the importance of the Chinese modern banking industry, see Thomas G. Rawski, *Economic Growth in Prewar China* (Berkeley: University of California Press, 1989), chap. 3; and Wen-hsin Yeh, "Corporate Space, Communal Time: Everyday Life in Shanghai's Bank of China," *American Historical Review,* 100, no. 1 (February 1995): 97–122.
2. Interview with DTS, 1994.
3. Interview with LSW, 1995.
4. Chang Zhujiu et al., "Dazhong Yinhang yu Sun Zhongshan" (Sun Zhongshan and the Dazhong Bank), *Tianjin wenshi ziliao,* 35 (1986): 171.

5. Tsao [Cao] Yu, *Sunrise,* trans., A. C. Barnes (Beijing: Foreign Languages Press, 1978), p. 156. Tianjin was the likely setting for the play; see Joseph Lau, *Ts'ao Yu [Cao Yu], the Reluctant Disciple of Chekhov and O'Neill: A Study in Literary Influence* (Hong Kong: Hong Kong University Press, 1970), p. 35, n. 4.
6. On bank runs, see Rudiger Dornbusch and Jacob A. Frenkel, "The Gold Standard and the Bank of England in the Crisis of 1847," in Michael D. Bordo and Anna J. Schwartz, eds., *A Retrospective on the Classical Gold Standard, 1821–1932* (Chicago: University of Chicago Press, 1984), pp. 233–273; Roy A. Batchelor, "The Avoidance of Catastrophe: Two Nineteenth-Century Banking Crises," in Forrest Capie and Geoffrey E. Wood, eds., *Financial Crises and the World Banking System* (New York: St. Martin's Press, 1986), pp. 41–73; Harold James, "The Causes of the German Banking Crisis of 1931," *Economic History Review,* 37 (1984): 68–87; Milton Friedman and Anna Jacobson Schwartz, *A Monetary History of the United States, 1867–1960* (Princeton: Princeton University Press, 1963), esp. chap. 7; Charles W. Calomiris, "Contagion and Bank Failures during the Great Depression: The June 1932 Chicago Banking Panic," *American Economic Review,* 87, no. 5 (December 1997): 863–884; Douglas W. Diamond and Philip H. Dybvig, "Bank Runs, Deposit Insurance, and Liquidity," *Journal of Political Economy,* 91, no. 3 (June 1983): 401–419.
7. On balance of payments crises, see Steven Radelet and Jeffery Sachs, "The Onset of the East Asian Financial Crisis," posted on the Asian Crisis Home Page, *http://www.stern.nyu.edu/~nroubini/asia/AsiaHomepage.html.*
8. An early seminal work on financial crises concludes that they are "difficult to define but recognizable when seen"; see the introduction to Charles P. Kindleberger and Jean-Pierre Laffargue, eds., *Financial Crises: Theory, History, and Policy* (Cambridge: Cambridge University Press, 1982), p. 2. Many scholars argue that financial crises occur in recurring patterns; see John Kenneth Galbraith, *Financial Euphoria* (New York: Whittle Books, in association with Viking, 1993); Charles P. Kindleberger, *Manias, Panics, and Crashes: A History of Financial Crises* (New York: John Wiley & Sons, 1996); and Bernice Cohen, *The Edge of Chaos: Financial Booms, Bubbles, Crashes, and Chaos* (Chichester: John Wiley & Sons, 1997). For a contrary view that emphasizes the differences in financial crises and their contexts, see Peter Temin, *Lessons from the Great Depression* (Cambridge, Mass.: MIT Press, 1996). Recent scholarship has tried to distinguish among types of financial crises; see Radelet and Sachs.
9. For a critique of approaches to money that focus on functions and forms, see John Smithin, *Controversies in Monetary Economics* (Cheltenham: Edward Elgar, 1994), chap. 2; Geoffrey Ingham, "On the Underdevelopment of the 'Sociology of Money,'" *Acta Sociologica,* 41, no. 1 (1998): 3–18, and "Money Is a Social Relation," *Review of Social Economy,* 65, no. 4 (Winter 1996): 507–529; Nigel Dodd, *The Sociology of Money: Economics, Reason, and Contemporary Society* (New York: Continuum, 1994), p. 4.
10. Quoted in Ingham, "Money Is a Social Relation," p. 526.
11. Neil T. Skaggs, discussing the ideas of Henry Dunning Macleod, in "Debt as the Basis of Currency: The Monetary Economics of Trust," *American Journal of Eco-*

nomics and Sociology, 57, no. 4 (October 1998): 457. On Macleod, see Joseph A. Schumpeter, *History of Economic Analysis* (New York: Oxford University Press, 1994), p. 1115; and Timothy L. Alborn, "The Moral of the Failed Bank: Professional Plots in the Victorian Money Market," *Victorian Studies*, 38, no. 2 (Winter 1995): 208.

12. Ingham, "Money Is a Social Relation," p. 527.
13. Dodd, p. xxiii.
14. Susan P. Shapiro, "The Social Control of Impersonal Trust," *American Journal of Sociology*, 93, no. 3 (November 1987): 634. For a slightly different view of impersonal trust, see Dorothée Rivaud-Danset, "Trust and Collective Action in Financial Markets," in Nathalie Lazaric and Edward Lorenz, eds., *Trust and Economic Learning* (Cheltenham: Edward Elgar, 1998), p. 78.
15. Niklas Luhmann, *Trust and Power* (Chichester: John Wiley & Sons, 1979), p. 73.
16. Dodd, p. xi.
17. Barbara A. Misztal, *Trust in Modern Societies* (Cambridge: Polity Press, 1996), p. 18. On the importance of future contingency, see Anthony Giddens, *The Consequences of Modernity* (Stanford: Stanford University Press, 1990), p. 33; Shapiro, p. 626; introduction to Lazaric and Lorenz, p. 3; and Luhmann, p. 20.
18. Carol A. Heimer, "Solving the Problem of Trust," *American Bar Foundation Working Papers*, 9804 (1999): 4–6.
19. Charles F. Sabel, "Studied Trust: Building New Forms of Cooperation in a Volatile Economy," in Richard Swedberg, ed., *Explorations in Economic Sociology* (New York: Russell Sage Foundation, 1993), p. 115.
20. Luhmann, p. 89; Oliver E. Williamson, *The Mechanisms of Governance* (New York: Oxford University Press, 1996), chap. 7; Benjamin Coriat and Samira Guennif, "Self-Interest, Trust and Institutions," in Lazaric and Lorenz, p. 50; Mark Granovetter, "Economic Action and Social Structure: The Problem of Embeddedness," *American Journal of Sociology*, 91, no. 3 (November 1985): 489. For Williamson, trust arises for relations among firms, not within them; Oliver E. Williamson, *Markets and Hierarchies: Analysis and Antitrust Implications* (New York: Free Press, 1975), pp. 106–108. My definition of trust includes what Seligman calls confidence and what Lazaric and Lorenz call reputation and confidence. See Adam B. Seligman, *The Problem of Trust* (Princeton: Princeton University Press, 1997), p. 7; introduction to Lazaric and Lorenz, pp. 3–13. On the idea that "trust and calculation are not conflicting principles," see Rivaud-Danset, p. 86.
21. Luhmann, p. 22; Seligman, pp. 6–8.
22. Quote from Giddens, p. 34.
23. Robert D. Putnam, *Making Democracy Work: Civic Traditions in Modern Italy* (Princeton: Princeton University Press, 1993), p. 163.
24. Margaret Levi, "A State of Trust," in Valerie Braithwaite and Margaret Levi, eds., *Trust and Governance* (New York: Russell Sage Foundation, 1998), p. 81.
25. Positive evaluations of personal trust include the discussion in Wellington K. K. Chan, "Tradition and Change in the Chinese Business Enterprise," *Chi-*

nese Studies in History, 31, nos. 1–3 (Spring–Summer 1998): 136–142; and Wong Siu-lun, "Chinese Entrepreneurs and Business Trust," in Gary Hamilton, ed., *Business Networks and Economic Development in East and Southeast Asia* (Hong Kong: Centre of Asian Studies, University of Hong Kong, 1991), pp. 13–29. On the relations between Asian culture and business practices, see Gary G. Hamilton, "The Organizational Foundations of Western and Chinese Commerce: A Historical and Comparative Analysis," in Gary G. Hamilton, ed., *Asian Business Networks* (Berlin: Walter de Gruyter, 1996), p. 47; S. Gordon Redding, *The Spirit of Chinese Capitalism* (Berlin: Walter de Gruyter, 1990). Richard Whitley, *Business Systems in East Asia: Firms, Markets, and Societies* (London: Sage Publications, 1992), p. 23, follows Redding closely for his analysis of Chinese business. Negative assessments, mostly resulting from the Asian financial crisis of 1997, can be found in François Godement, *The Downsizing of Asia* (London: Routledge, 1999), chap. 4; and various denunciations of "crony capitalism"; see Sander Thoenes, "Taking Aim at Asia's Crony Capitalism," *Christian Science Monitor,* January 21, 1988.

26. Kelly Strong and James Weber, "The Myth of the Trusting Culture: A Global, Empirical Assessment," *Business and Society,* 37, no. 2 (June 1998): 159, 167; Levi, p. 82; and Granovetter, p. 483.
27. Sabel, p. 108.
28. Putnam, pp. 165, 166; Douglass C. North, *Institutions, Institutional Change, and Economic Performance* (Cambridge: Cambridge University Press, 1990), p. 15; introduction to Lazaric and Lorenz, pp. 11–13; and Hélène Tordjman, "The Formation of Beliefs on Financial Markets: Representativeness and Prototypes," in Lazaric and Lorenz, p. 97. Agency theory and incentive theories, variations of the rational approach, are equally limited; see Susan Whiting, "The Mobilization of Private Investment as a Problem of Trust in Local Government Structures," in Braithwaite and Levi, p. 173; Bernard Baudry, "Trust in Inter-firm Relations: Multiple Forms of Coordination," in Lazaric and Lorenz, p. 66; and Coriat and Guennif, p. 49. On large gains, see the ideas of James Coleman, as discussed in Whiting, p. 173. On agency costs, see Baudry, p. 66.
29. On transaction cost analysis and authority relations, see Curzio Giannini, "Money, Trust, and Central Banking," *Journal of Economics and Business,* 45 (1995): 217–237. On authority and hierarchy as bases for trust, see Williamson, *Mechanisms,* chap. 10; introduction to Walter W. Powell and Paul J. DiMaggio, eds., *The New Institutionalism in Organizational Analysis* (Chicago: University of Chicago Press, 1991), pp. 4–5; Levi, p. 84; and North, p. 76. For critics of that approach, see Granovetter, p. 499; Baudry, p. 67; and Coriat and Guennif, p. 50.
30. Putnam, p. 174. For different approaches also advocating the importance of social relations, see Francis Fukuyama, *Trust: The Social Virtues and the Creation of Prosperity* (New York: Free Press, 1995), p. 11; and Granovetter, p. 491.
31. Shapiro, pp. 637, 639, 643, quote p. 643.
32. See Kindleberger; also Forrest Capie, "Banking in Europe in the Nineteenth

Century: The Role of Central Banking," in Richard Sylla, Richard Tilly, and Gabriel Tortella, *The State, the Financial System, and Economic Modernization* (Cambridge: Cambridge University Press, 1999), pp. 118–124.

33. Hugh Rockoff, "Walter Bagehot and the Theory of Central Banking," in Capie and Wood, pp. 160–180.
34. See Roy A Batchelor, "The Avoidance of Catastrophe: Two Nineteenth-Century Banking Crises," in Capie and Wood, pp. 41–73; Franco Bonelli, "The 1907 Financial Crisis in Italy: A Peculiar Case of the Lender of Last Resort in Action," in Kindleberger and Laffargue, pp. 51–65; and Alec Cairncross, "The Bank of England and the British Economy," in Richard Roberts and David Kynaston, eds., *The Bank of England: Money, Power, and Influence 1694–1994* (Oxford: Clarendon Press, 1995), pp. 60–61.
35. Shapiro, pp. 648–651, quote p. 651. See also Jocelyn Pixley, "Impersonal Trust in Global Mediating Organizations," *Sociological Perspectives*, 42, no. 4 (1999): 647–671. John Braithwaite suggests that guardianship institutions be arranged in a circle rather than in a hierarchy; John Braithwaite, "Institutionalizing Distrust, Enculturating Trust," in Braithwaite and Levi, p. 354.
36. On encapsulated interest, see Russell Hardin, "Trust in Government," in Braithwaite and Levi, p. 12; Coriat and Guennif, pp. 58–60; conclusion to Braithwaite and Levi, p. 376; and Whiting, p. 175.
37. Geoffrey Brennan, "Democratic Trust: A Rational-Choice Theory View," in Braithwaite and Levi, p. 212.
38. Giddens, p. 113.
39. Charles Goodhart, *The Evolution of Central Banks* (Cambridge, Mass.: MIT Press, 1988), p. 63.
40. Ibid., pp. 63, 64.
41. Introduction to Powell and DiMaggio, p. 14. See also W. Richard Scott, "Unpacking Institutional Arguments," in Powell and DiMaggio, p. 173.
42. Introduction to Powell and DiMaggio, p. 30.
43. I follow North's useful distinction between institutions as the rules and organizations as the players; see North, pp. 3–5.
44. *Zhongguo jinrong shi bianxie zu*, ed., *Zhongguo jinrong shi* (A history of Chinese finance) (Chengdu: Xinan caijing daxue, 1993), p. 139. The role of banks in the economy is a matter of some controversy. The traditional view of banks' reliance on speculation in government bonds has been challenged by Linsun Cheng, "Entrepreneurship, Professional Managers, and the Development of Modern Chinese Banks" (Ph.D. diss., Washington University, 1994), chap. 4. The question of bank involvement in financing industry and commerce must await further research, but as late as 1924, Bian Baimei advised caution when a subordinate advocated increasing ties between the Bank of China and Tianjin's commercial sector. *Diary*, July 2, 1924.
45. Linsun Cheng, p. 60; on Tianjin, see Chapter 5.
46. *Yinhang* was first used to translate the word "bank" into Chinese in the 1860s. See *Zhongguo jinrong shi*, pp. 171, 172. "Indigenous bank," like its alternatives,

"traditional" or "native" bank, is a catchall term that is used to translate a variety of Chinese words for financial institutions, including *qianzhuang, piaohao, yinhao, lufang,* and *qianpu.* On indigenous financial institutions in Tianjin, see Zhang Xiaobo, "Merchant Associational Activism in Early-Twentieth-Century China: The Tianjin General Chamber of Commerce, 1904–1928" (Ph.D. diss., Columbia University, 1995), pp. 90–103. China's state and private modern banks had similar organizational structures, exhibiting what DiMaggio and Powell call "institutional isomorphism"; see "The Iron Cage Revisited: Institutional Isomorphism and Collective Rationality in Organizational Fields."

47. On limited liability, see Yang Guzhi, Tan Zaitang, and Zhang Zhangxiang, "Tianjin qianye shilue" (A brief history of Tianjin's native bank business), *Tianjin wenshi ziliao,* 20 (1985): 99. On the size of Chinese businesses, see William Kirby, "China Unincorporated: Company Law and Business Enterprise in Twentieth-Century China," *Journal of Asian Studies,* 54, no. 1 (February 1995): 43–63. On customer bases, see Linsun Cheng, p. 149, and "Tianjin tongyong huobi ji qi huidui jisuanfa" (Circulating monies in Tianjin and their exchange calculations), *Yinhang zhoubao,* 1, no. 13 (August 21, 1917): 18. In Tianjin, *yinhao* depositors were all known to the firm, and most were connected with the owners; Yang Guzhi, Tan Zaitang, and Zhang Zhangxiang, pp. 107, 108. On collateral, see Linsun Cheng, p. 164. On Shanghai's indigenous banks, see Andrea McElderry, "Shanghai Old-Style Banks (Ch'ien-chuang), 1800–1935," *Michigan Papers on Chinese Studies,* 25 (1976): 1–230.
48. Rawski, pp. 120, 121. Some critics have questioned Rawski's use of statistics; see Dharma Kumar, *The Chinese and Indian Economies from ca. 1914–1949* (London: Development Economics Research Program, London School of Economics, 1992). This criticism does not apply to Rawski's figures on the money supply, though.
49. See Julia C. Strauss, *Strong Institutions in Weak Polities: State Building in Republican China, 1927–1940* (Oxford: Clarendon Press, 1998), chap. 1; D. Eleanor Westney, *Imitation and Innovation: The Transfer of Western Organizational Patterns to Meiji Japan* (Cambridge, Mass.: Harvard University Press, 1987); and Ronald L. Jepperson and John W. Meyer, "The Public Order and the Construction of Formal Organizations," in Powell and DiMaggio, p. 209.
50. See John W. Meyer and Brian Rowan, "Institutionalized Organizations: Formal Structure as Myth and Ceremony," in Powell and DiMaggio, pp. 41–62; Putnam, chap. 6.
51. Scott, "Unpacking," p. 170. See also Walter W. Powell, "Expanding the Scope of Institutional Analysis," in Powell and DiMaggio, p. 183.
52. Rondo Cameron, Olga Crisp, Hugh T. Patrick, and Richard Tilly, *Banking in the Early Stages of Industrialization: A Study in Comparative Economic History* (New York: Oxford University Press, 1967); see also Alexander Gerschenkron, *Economic Backwardness in Historical Perspective* (Cambridge, Mass.: Belknap Press of Harvard University Press, 1962), pp. 11–16.
53. Introduction to Sylla, Tilly, and Tortella, p. 1.

54. David Woodruff, *Money Unmade: Barter and the Fate of Russian Capitalism* (Ithaca: Cornell University Press, 1999), p. 3. See also John Smithin, "Money and National Sovereignty in the Global Economy," *Eastern Economic Journal*, 25, no. 1 (Winter 1999): 49–50.
55. David Glasner, "An Evolutionary Theory of the State Monopoly over Money," in Kevin Dowd and Richard H. Timberlake, eds., *Money and the Nation State: The Financial Revolution, Government, and the World Monetary System* (New Brunswick, N.J.: Transaction Publishers, 1998), p. 40. On free banking, see also George Selgin, "The Rationalization of Central Banks," *Critical Review*, 7, nos. 2–3 (1993): 337.
56. Anna J. Schwartz, "Are Central Banks Necessary?" *Critical Review*, 7, nos. 2–3 (1993): 355–370, quote from abstract p. 355. Separately, Angela Redish, in *Bimetallism: An Economic Analysis* (Cambridge: Cambridge University Press, 2000), p. 4, argues that commodity standards alone cannot provide stability.
57. Banks' role in the issue of bonds is a better-known story, and will be dealt with only indirectly here. On government bonds, see Parks M. Coble Jr., *The Shanghai Capitalists and the Nationalist Government, 1927–1937* (Cambridge, Mass.: Council on East Asian Studies, Harvard University, 1986), esp. chaps. 4 and 5; and Qian Jiaju, *Jiuzhongguo gongzhai shiliao* (Historical materials on public debts in old China) (Beijing: Caizheng jingji chubanshe, 1955).
58. "Society" refers to the disparate groups and individuals who lived and worked in Tianjin. "State" refers to either the central or local government and encompasses a variety of institutions and positions. The most common word for the state in republican-period documents is *dangju*, which I usually translate as "the authorities." In addition, individuals often used words such as *guanfang* (the officials), and *guanting* (official bureaus). On the need to disaggregate the state, see Joel S. Migdal, "The State in Society: An Approach to Struggles for Domination," in Joel S. Migdal, Atul Kohli, and Vivienne Shue, eds., *State Power and Social Forces: Domination and Transformation in the Third World* (Cambridge: Cambridge University Press, 1994), pp. 7–34. For a plea for disaggregation in the case of the Nationalist government in China, see Christian Henriot, *Shanghai, 1927–1937: Municipal Power, Locality, and Modernization*, trans. Noël Castelino (Berkeley: University of California Press, 1991), p. 237.
59. The debate is nicely summarized in Marie-Claire Bergère, "Civil Society and Urban Change in Republican China," *China Quarterly*, 150 (1997): 309–328. For the substance of the debate, see the special April 1993 issue of *Modern China*, in which two proponents, William Rowe and Mary Rankin, restate their case, and one vociferous opponent, Frederic Wakeman, launches his critique. For the empirical evidence supporting the existence of a public sphere, see Mary Rankin, *Elite Activism and Political Transformation in China: Zhejiang Province, 1865–1911* (Stanford: Stanford University Press, 1987); William Rowe, *Hankow: Commerce and Society in a Chinese City, 1796–1889* (Stanford: Stanford University Press, 1987), and *Hankow: Conflict and Community in a Chinese City, 1796–1895* (Stanford: Stanford University Press, 1989); and David Strand, *Rick-*

shaw Beijing: City People in the 1920s (Berkeley: University of California Press, 1989).

60. Marie-Claire Bergère, *The Golden Age of the Chinese Bourgeoisie, 1911–1937,* trans. Janet Lloyd (Cambridge: Cambridge University Press, 1989), pp. 7, 8, 10.
61. Yu Heping, *Shanghui yu Zhongguo zaoqi xiandaihua* (Chambers of commerce and China's early modernization) (Shanghai: Shanghai remnin chubanshe, 1993), p. 366.
62. Susan Mann, *Local Merchants and the Chinese Bureaucracy, 1750–1950* (Stanford: Stanford University Press, 1987), chap. 2; and Margaret M. Pearson, *China's New Business Elite: The Political Consequence of Economic Reform* (Berkeley: University of California Press, 1997), p. 44.
63. Man Bun Kwan, *The Salt Merchants of Tianjin: State-Making and Civil Society in Late Imperial China* (Honolulu: University of Hawaii Press, 2001), p. 6.
64. Ernest P. Young, *The Presidency of Yuan Shih-k'ai: Liberalism and Dictatorship in Early Republican China* (Ann Arbor: University of Michigan Press, 1977), pp. 250, 251; Lloyd E. Eastman, *The Abortive Revolution: China under Nationalist Rule, 1927–1937* (Cambridge, Mass.: Harvard University Press, 1974), pp. 309, 310.
65. Frederic Wakeman Jr., *Policing Shanghai, 1927–1937* (Berkeley: University of California Press, 1995), p. xvii, and "Models of Historical Change: The Chinese State and Society, 1839–1989," in Kenneth Lieberthal, Joyce Kallgren, Roderick MacFarquhar, and Frederic Wakeman Jr., eds., *Perspectives on Modern China: Four Anniversaries* (Armonk, N.Y.: M. E. Sharpe, 1991), pp. 68–102; Prasenjit Duara, *Culture, Power, and the State: Rural North China, 1900–1942* (Stanford: Stanford University Press, 1988), p. 6; and Mann, pp. 2–3. Elsewhere Duara notes that China lacked a strong state but had a strong statist ideology; see Prasenjit Duara, "State and Civil Society in the History of Chinese Modernity," in Frederic Wakeman Jr. and Wang Xi, eds., *China's Quest for Modernization: A Historical Perspective* (Berkeley: Institute of East Asian Studies, University of California, 1997), p. 316. Philip A. Kuhn, "The Development of Local Government," in John K. Fairbank and Albert Feurwerker, eds., *The Cambridge History of China,* vol. 13, *Republican China, 1912–1949,* pt. 2 (Cambridge: Cambridge University Press, 1986), pp. 329–360; "Concluding Remarks," in Joseph W. Esherick and Mary Backus Rankin, eds., *Chinese Local Elites and Patterns of Dominance* (Berkeley: University of California Press, 1990), p. 342; and Xin Zhang, *Social Transformation in Modern China: The State and Local Elites in Henan, 1900–1937* (Cambridge: Cambridge University Press, 2000), p. 271.
66. Marianne Bastid-Brugière, "Currents of Social Change," in John K. Fairbank and Kwang-ching Liu, eds., *The Cambridge History of China,* vol. 11, *The Late Ch'ing, 1800–1911,* pt. 2, pp. 535–602.
67. Ma Min, *Guanshang zhi jian: shehui jubian zhong de jindai shenshang* (Between officials and merchants: the modern merchant-gentry in the midst of dramatic social change) (Tianjin: Tianjin renmin chubanshe, 1995), p. 365.
68. Marie-Claire Bergère, "The Shanghai Bankers' Association, 1917–1927: Mod-

ernization and the Institutionalization of Local Solidarities," in Frederic Wakeman Jr. and Wen-hsin Yeh, eds., *Shanghai Sojourners* (Berkeley: Institute of East Asian Studies, University of California at Berkeley, 1992), pp. 15–34; see also Andrea McElderry, "Confucian Capitalism: Corporate Values in Republican Banking," *Modern China,* 12, no. 3 (July 1986): 401–416.

69. Xiaoqun Xu, *Chinese Professionals and the Republican State: The Rise of Professional Associations in Shanghai, 1912–1937* (Cambridge: Cambridge University Press, 2001), pp. 15, 16.
70. Fukuyama, p. 75.
71. See also Brett Sheehan, "The Persistence and Limits of Localism: State Power, the Public Sphere, and the Money Economy in Republican Tianjin, 1916–1937," in *Guoshishang zhongyang yu difang de guanxi* (Center and locality in Chinese history) (Taipei: Guoshiguan, 2000), pp. 1311–86.

1. Personal Networks and State Needs

1. The Bian family genealogy and Bian's obituary in the *Vallejo Times* list his year of birth as 1884, but his admission record at Brown University says 1886 and his graduation record 1885; see *Jiangdu Bian shi zupu,* Qing Guangxu 25 nian (Genealogy of the Jiangdu [Yangzhou] Bian family), Qing Guangxu year 25 (1899), Family History Center of the Church of Jesus Christ of Latter-Day Saints, Salt Lake City, microfilm, 1904993–995; Brown University archives on deposit with the Hay Library; and Bian's obituary as quoted in Bien [Bian] Bonian, "Xianjun Baimei Gong yu minchu de Zhongguo Yinhang" [My father Mr. Baimei and the Bank of China during the early republican period], *Zhuanji wenxue,* 21, no. 2 (August 1972): 19.
2. See especially Rankin; Rowe, *Hankow: Commerce and Society* and *Hankow: Conflict and Community.*
3. Luo Ming and Wu Yuqing, "Bian Baodi," in Luo Ming and Pan Zhenping, eds., *Qingdai renwu zhuanji* (Collection of Biographies of Qing period personages), 2d ser., vol. 9 (Liaoning: Liaoning renmin chubanshe, 1993), pp. 92–94.
4. Ping-ti Ho, "The Salt Merchants of Yang-chou [Yangzhou]: A Study of Commercial Capitalism in Eighteenth-Century China," *Harvard Journal of Asiatic Studies,* 17, no. 1 (June 1954): 130–168.
5. Luo Ming and Wu Yuqing, p. 92.
6. *Jiangdu Bian shi zupu.*
7. On Li's early activities in Shanghai and Jiangsu, see Kwang-ching Liu, "The Confucian as Patriot and Pragmatist: Li Hung-chang's Formative Years, 1823–1866," in Samuel C. Chu and Kwang-ching Liu, eds., *Li Hung-chang* [Li Hongzzhang] *and China's Early Modernization* (Armonk, N.Y.: M. E. Sharpe, 1994), pp. 17–48.
8. *Jiangdu Bian shi zupu.*
9. Letter from Bien Bonian (Bian Baimei's son) to his daughter, July 26, 1975.
10. On Liu's service for Li Hongzhang, see Kenneth E. Folsom, *Friends, Guests, and*

Colleagues: The Mu-fu System in the Late Ch'ing Period (Berkeley: University of California Press, 1968), p. 137.

11. *Jiangdu Bian shi zupu.*
12. Letter from Bien Bonian, July 26, 1975. Bian Xuchang once served as a judicial official in Anhui Province; letter from Bien Bonian to his daughter, August 24, 1975.
13. *Jiangdu Bian shi zupu.*
14. Like his younger brother, Li Hanzhang held a number of very high positions in the Qing government; see Jia Shucun, "Li Hanzhang," in Luo Ming and Yang Yimao, eds., *Qingdai renwu zhuanji* (Collection of biographies of Qing period personages), 2d ser., vol. 10 (Liaoning: Liaoning renmin chubanshe, 1993), pp. 111–113.
15. Bao Peizhi, "Shouzhou Sun jia yu Zhongfu yinhang" (The Shouzhou [Anhui] Sun family and the Zhongfu Bank), *Tianjin wenshi ziliao,* 35 (1986): 141. Biographical information on Zhou Xuexi from Richard C. Boorman, ed., *Biographical Dictionary of Republican China* (New York: Columbia University Press, 1967–1979); *Minguo renwu da cidian* (Biographical dictionary of republican China) (Shijiazhuang: Hebei renmin chubanshe, 1991); and Hao Qingyuan, *Zhou Xuexi zhuan* (A biography of Zhou Xuexi) (Tianjin: Tianjin renmin chubanshe, 1991), esp. chap. 1.
16. *Who's Who of Returned Students* (Peking: Tsing Hua College, 1917), p. 2, lists the birthplace of Baimei's younger brother, Bian Fusun, as Yangzhou in 1886, but by 1904, Bian had enrolled at Aurora College, and he listed a Shanghai home address on his admission form to Brown University in 1907. On Aurora College, see Chen Lili, ed., *Shanghai zongjiao shi* (A history of religion in Shanghai) (Shanghai: Shanghai renmin chubanshe, 1992), pp. 695–701; and Rev. Peter Lefebvre, S. J., *A Guide to Catholic Shanghai* (Shanghai, 1937), pp. 25–28.
17. "Brown's Versatile Chinese Quartet," *Providence Journal,* October 15, 1911.
18. Ibid.
19. Ibid.
20. On Gardner, see entry in *Who's Who in America,* vol. 9, *1916–1917* (Chicago: Marquis and Co., 1916), p. 903.
21. Henry B. Gardner, *Outlines of Lectures in Elementary Economics, Brown University* (Providence: Continental Printing Co., 1896), pp. 9, 10, 103–121, quotes pp. 113 and 121.
22. "Chinese Student at Brown 'Broke,'" *Providence Journal,* February 12, 1912. The "broke" student referred to in the headline was neither Sun nor Bian.
23. Bian actually spent five years at Brown.
24. Letter from Bien Bonian, July 26, 1975.
25. Bien Bonian, "Xianjun," p. 19.
26. On China's experience with paper money, see Richard Von Glahn, *Fountain of Fortune: Money and Monetary Policy in China, 1000–1700* (Berkeley: University of California Press, 1996), chap. 2; Chao-nan Chen, Pin-tsun Chang, and Shi-kuan Chen, "The Sung [Song] and the Ming Paper Money: Currency Competi-

tion and Currency Bubbles," Sun Yat-sen Institute of Social Sciences and Philosophy, Academia Sinica, Taiwan, Working Paper 92–2 (n.d.); and Gordon Tullock, "Paper Money—A Cycle in Cathay," *Economic History Review*, 9, no. 3 (1957): 393–407. China's experience belies the "normal" progression most economists accept from commodity money (usually precious metals) to fiduciary money (paper money exchangeable into commodity money) to fiat money (tokens of no intrinsic monetary value). The Chinese case is usually treated as what Von Glahn calls "an inexplicable aberration" (p. 43). Walter C. Neale's treatment is typical; see his *Monies in Societies* (San Francisco: Chandler and Sharp, 1976), p. 16.

27. Von Glahn, chaps. 2–5.
28. Both the Spanish and Mexican silver coins were minted in Mexico, the former before Mexican independence in 1821 and the latter after; see *Zhongguo jinrong shi*, p. 107.
29. Von Glahn, p. 210. The official rate was one thousand copper coins for one tael of silver, but the market ratio between copper coins and silver varied over time.
30. Frank H. H. King, *Money and Monetary Policy in China, 1845–1895* (Cambridge, Mass.: Harvard University Press, 1965), esp. pp. 44–45; Eduard Kann, *The Currencies of China: An Investigation of Gold and Silver Transactions Affecting China*, 2d rev. ed. (Shanghai: Kelly and Walsh, 1927).
31. China's indigenous banks served a similar purpose to medieval European money changers; see Robert S. Lopez, "The Dawn of Medieval Banking," in Center for Medieval and Renaissance Studies, University of California, Los Angeles, ed., *The Dawn of Modern Banking* (New Haven: Yale University Press, 1979), pp. 1–24.
32. The *lijin* proved quite successful; Zhou Yumin, *Wan Qing caizheng yu shehui bianqian* (Late Qing period fiscal management and social change) (Shanghai: Shanghai renmin chubanshe, 2000), pp. 164–169. Tax innovation is a topic in itself and is outside the scope of this book.
33. Yao Sui, ed., *Zhongguo jinrong sixiang shi* (A history of finance thought in China) (Beijing: Zhongguo jinrong chubanshe, 1994), pp. 216–256.
34. Zhou Yumin, pp. 169–203.
35. On Li Hongzhang, see Hu Guangming, "Lun Li Hongzhang yu Tianjin jindai zaoqi de chengshihua" (On Li Hongzhang and Tianjin's modern, early urbanization), *Chengshi shi yanjiu*, 3 (August 1990): 64–96; and the essays in Chu and Liu.
36. Linsun Cheng, pp. 1–8.
37. Zhou Yumin, p. 157, chap. 4, and chart on p. 279. The Hong Kong and Shanghai Banking Corporation (HSBC) accounted for about two thirds of foreign loans made to the Qing government between 1860 and 1894; see Zhou Yumin, pp. 282, 283. On HSBC loans to China, see also Frank H. H. King, *The Hongkong Bank in Late Imperial China, 1864–1902: On an Even Keel*, vol. 1 of *The History of the Hongkong and Shanghai Banking Corporation* (Cambridge: Cambridge University Press, 1987), pp. 535–562.

38. Zhou Yumin, p. 449.
39. Wang Yejian, *Zhongguo jindai huobi yu yinhang de yanjin* (Development of money and banking in modern China) (Taipei: Zhongyang yanjiuyuan jingjisuo, 1981), p. 40; Zhuo Zunhong, *Zhongguo jindai bizhi gaige shi* (A history of monetary reform in modern China) (Taipei: Academia Historica, 1986), pp. 49, 50; and King, *Money and Monetary Policy,* pp. 225–228.
40. *Zhongguo jinrong shi,* p. 171; Yao Sui, pp. 272–274.
41. The actual events regarding this plan are a matter of some dispute. In one version, Li was approached by a group of American bankers in the 1870s; see *Zhongguo jinrong shi,* pp. 161–162. In another version, an American syndicate approached Li about railroad and telephone concessions, and Li responded by suggesting that the American syndicate fund a Sino-American bank in Tianjin to finance railroad construction; see Marilyn B. Young, *The Rhetoric of Empire: American China Policy, 1895–1901* (Cambridge, Mass., Harvard University Press, 1968), pp. 38–51.
42. Young, *Rhetoric of Empire,* pp. 43, 46, n. 34, quote p. 43.
43. Norio Tamaki, *Japanese Banking: A History, 1859–1959* (Cambridge: Cambridge University Press, 1995), p. 83.
44. Zhou Yumin, pp. 282–287, 323–334.
45. The Chinese experience echoes that of much of the rest of the world; see Richard Sylla, "Shaping the U.S. Financial System, 1690–1913: The Dominant Role of the Public Finance," in Sylla, Tilly, and Tortella, p. 250; and Charles Tilly, *Coercion, Capital, and European States,* A.D. *990–1992* (Cambridge, Mass.: Blackwell, 1992), p. 85.
46. Yao Sui, pp. 298–321.
47. Ibid., p. 315. See also the 1895 memorial of Hu Yufen, quoted in Zhuo Zunhong, *Zhongguo jindai,* p. 51.
48. The Manchu court official Ronghong later wrote in his diary that his plan for a bank was torpedoed when Sheng Xuanhuai arrived in Beijing with bribes for Qing court officials; Zhou Yumin, p. 364.
49. On the Imperial Bank of China, see *Zhongguo jinrong shi,* pp. 172–176; Shen Danian et al., *Tianjin jinrong jianshi* (A brief history of Tianjin finance) (Tianjin: Nankai daxue chubanshe, 1988), p. 29; Liu Jiazhen, "Zhongguo Tongshang Yinhang jianshi" (A brief history of the Imperial Bank of China), *Tianjin wenshi ziliao,* 48 (1989): 57–71; Huang Jianhui, *Zhongguo yinhangye shi* (History of the Chinese banking industry) (Taiyuan: Shanxi jingji, 1994), pp. 83–89; and Albert Feuerwerker, *China's Early Industrialization: Sheng Hsuan-huai (1844–1916) and Mandarin Enterprise* (New York: Atheneum, 1970), pp. 225–241.
50. On Du Yuesheng, see Brian G. Martin, *The Shanghai Green Gang: Politics and Organized Crime, 1919–1937* (Berkeley: University of California Press, 1996).
51. Zhou Yumin, p. 403. On the dollar equivalency of the indemnities, see Cheng-chung Lai and Joshua Jr-shian Gau, "Fetters or Lifeboat? The Silver Standard and the Chinese Economy, 1900–1937" (Taipei, 1999), p. 10.
52. Ray Ovid Hall, *The Chinese National Banks* (Berlin, 1921), p. 21.
53. Ibid., p. 22; Commission on International Exchange of the United States of

America, *Memoranda on a New Monetary System for China* (Shanghai: Printed at the North-China Herald Office, 1903).

54. Commission on International Exchange, p. 38.
55. Zhuo Zunhong, *Zhongguo jindai*, pp. 58–59, 66–69; and Lai and Gau, pp. 14–15.
56. *Zhongguo jinrong shi*, pp. 176–179.
57. "Lun Hubu Yinhang" (On the Hubu Bank), *Dongfang zazhi*, 1, no. 6 (June 25, 1904): 145–147.
58. The Bank of Communications' currency issue was short-lived during the Qing, and the bank was not given permission to issue paper money again until 1914. On the Da Qing Bank and the Bank of Communications, see Kong Xiangxian, *Da Qing yinhang hangshi* (A history of Da Qing Bank) (Nanjing: Nanjing daxue chubanshe, 1991), p. 67; and *Jiaotong yinhang qi shi wu nian* (Seventy-five years of the Bank of Communications) (Taipei: Jiaotong yinhang, 1983), pp. 97, 98.
59. "Zhongguo jindai huobishi ziliao" (Materials on the monetary history of modern china), in Shen Yunlong, ed., *Jindai Zhongguo shiliao congkan xuji* (Compilation of historical materials on modern China, continued), vol. 68 (Taipei: Wenhai chubanshe, 1974–1983), pp. 1044–73.
60. On the destruction in Tianjin, see Gail Hershatter, *The Workers of Tianjin, 1900–1949* (Stanford: Stanford University Press, 1986), pp. 7, 20; Kenneth G. Lieberthal, *Revolution and Tradition in Tientsin, 1949–1952* (Stanford: Stanford University Press, 1980), p. 30; Yu Shi, "Dong jiqi ju ji shuishi, wubei liang xuetang de huimie" (The destruction of the East Arsenal, Naval Academy, and Army Academy), *Yangwu yundong zai Hedong* (The self-strengthening movement in Hedong area, Tianjin) (Tianjin: Hedong wenshi ziliao, 1994), pp. 73–84; Zhang Xiaobo, pp. 219–226; Shen Danian, p. 3; and Liu Jiazhen, p. 70. The foreign occupation of Tianjin was not entirely destructive. On the civic improvements and infrastructure projects instituted by the foreigners, see Lewis Bernstein, "A History of Tianjin in the Early Modern Times, 1800–1919" (Ph.D. diss., University of Kansas, 1988), chap. 5.
61. Shen Danian, p. 3; Zhang Xiaobo, p. 228; and Kwan, *Salt Merchants*, pp. 107–110.
62. The establishment of *guan yinhao* and *yinqian ju* to manage local monetary problems had a long precedent in China, dating back at least to the 1850s; see Jiang Hongye, *Zhongguo difang yinhang shi* (History of local official banks) (Hunan: Hunan chubanshe, 1991), p. 3. On the Tianjin Official Bank, see Bao Peizhi, "Shouzhou," pp. 140, 141; and Hao Qingyuan, pp. 29–42, 90–109.
63. On the history of local government banks, see Jiang Hongye.
64. Not only were there multiple banks of issue, but also banks could issue multiple kinds of paper money. The Da Qing Bank issued paper money denominated in silver taels, silver yuan, and copper cash, each of which had different local standards; Zhuo Zunhong, *Zhongguo jindai*, p. 78.
65. *Zhongguo jinrong shi*, pp. 179–181.
66. *BOComm Collection*, p. 4.
67. Zhuo Zunhong, *Zhongguo jindai*, pp. 78–84; Frank H. H. King, *The Hongkong*

Bank in the Period of Imperialism and War, 1895–1918: Wayfoong, the Focus of Wealth, vol. 2 of *The History of the Hongkong and Shanghai Banking Corporation* (Cambridge: Cambridge University Press, 1988), pp. 202–205; and Zhou Yumin, pp. 407–412. The possibility that provincial banks contributed to the autonomy of provincial governments and their ability to secede during the 1911 revolution needs further research.

68. *Zhongguo jinrong shi,* pp. 176–181.
69. The actions of the Shanghai shareholders were very controversial; see letter from the Shanghai revolutionary leader Chen Qimei, *BOC Collection,* pp. 7, 8.
70. For biographical information on Wu, see the articles in *Zhuanji wenxue,* 34, no. 3 (March 1979): 31–47, and 4 (April 1979): 66–102; Zhang Boju, "Yanye yinhang yu Beiyang zhengfu he Guomindang zhengfu" (The Salt Bank and the Beiyang and Nationalist Governments), *Tianjin wenshi ziliao,* 13 (1981): 79–84; Wu's entry in Boorman; and Ma Changlin, "Wu Dingchang," in Xu Mao, Gu Guanlin, and Jiang Tianying, eds., *Zhongguo shi yinhang jia* (Ten Chinese bankers) (Shanghai: Shanghai renmin chubanshe, 1997), pp. 225–262.
71. Yuan's first choice for finance minister, Xiong Xiling, had to resign under pressure for relying too much on foreigners during loan negotiations; see Chen Zilai, "Xiong Xiling," in Yang Daxin, ed., *Beiyang zhengfu zongtong yu zongli* (Presidents and prime ministers of the Beiyang government) (Tianjin: Nankai daxue chubanshe, 1989), pp. 250–262. On Liang Shiyi, see Zhang Maopeng, "Liang Shiyi," in Yang Daxin, pp. 352–363. Tenures of the early leaders of the Bank of China can be found in Yao Songling, "Zhongguo Yinhang lijie zhouzhang yilan biao, minguo yuan nian zhi minguo san shi ba nian" (Chart of heads of the Bank of China at a glance, 1912–1949), *Zhuanji wenxue,* 13, no. 4 (October 1968): 61–64. For the Bank of Communications, see *BOComm Collection,* pp. 106–107. During the early months of the revolution, the Bank of Communications also faced a north-south split as its shareholders formed two associations, one for the Beijing-Tianjin area and one in Shanghai; *BOComm Collection,* pp. 38, 39.
72. This account is drawn from Bian's recollections as told to his children and later recounted by his son, Bien Bonian, in "Xianjun," pp. 19, 20.
73. Ralph Sun worked at the Bank of China and then at the Finance Ministry until he resigned to work in his family's flour mills in 1914. See his entry in the 1925 edition of *Who's Who in China,* 3d ed. (Shanghai: China Weekly Review, 1925), reprinted as Jerome Cavanaugh, ed., *Who's Who in China, 1918–1950* (Hong Kong: Chinese Materials Center, 1982), p. 690.
74. On various proposals, see *BOC Collection,* pp. 59–73.
75. Gerard Vissering, *On Chinese Currency: Preliminary Remarks on the Monetary and Banking Reform in China,* vol. 2, *The Banking Problem* (Amsterdam: J. H. Bussy, 1914), pp. 31–42, 204–205, and *On Chinese Currency: Preliminary Remarks on the Monetary and Banking Reform in China* (Batavia, July 1912).
76. *Monetary Hist. Collection, 1912–1927,* pp. 126–129; Young, *Presidency,* p. 217. The 1914 currency law and regulations are reproduced in *Monetary Hist. Collection,*

1912–1927, pp. 88–90, in Chinese, and in H. T. Montague Bell and H. G. Woodhead, eds., *The China Yearbook, 1916* (London: George Routledge and Sons, 1916), p. 348, in English.

77. *Financial Laws and Regs.*, pp. 69–94. For a contemporary review of the debates, see Wang Yike, "Zhongguo bizhi kaolue ji jinshi zhi gaige" (Review of China's monetary system and current reform), *Dongfang zazhi*, 14, nos. 1 and 2 (1917): 23–28 and 85–90.
78. Xu Cangshui, *Minguo chaoquan shi* (History of paper money during the republic) (Shanghai: Yinhang zhoubao, 1924), p. 25; Bell and Woodhead, p. 838.
79. Hall, p. 62; *BOComm Collection*, p. 128.
80. Hall, p. 74.
81. This account is drawn from *Diary*, May 1916.
82. *Zhongguo jinrong shi*, p. 209. The actual amount of Beijing notes is of some dispute. *Tianjin tongzhi: jinrong zhi* (Tianjin gazetteer: finance) (Tianjin: Tianjin shehui kexue yuan, 1995), p. 63, lists the amount as 26 million in May 1916, 46 million by October 1916, and 97 million by the end of 1917. On the early support of the Communications clique for Yuan's presidency, see Stephen R. MacKinnon, "Liang Shih-i [Liang Shiyi] and the Communications Clique," *Journal of Asian Studies*, 29 no. 3 (May 1970): 581–602. On the support of the Communications clique for Yuan's monarchical attempt, see Gu Shoucun, *Beiyang junfa shiqi de jiaotong xi* (The Communications clique during the Beiyang warlord period) (Henan: Henan renmin chubanshe, 1993), pp. 99–112. The problems of the two banks clearly stemmed from excessive loans to the central government; *Diary*, April 12, 1916.
83. Deng Xianhong, "Lun zhongguo yinhang yu beiyang zhengfu de maodun" (On contradictions between the Bank of China and the Beiyang government), *Lishi yanjiu*, 4 (1986): 66. According to Charles Hucker, *duban* is a variation of *zongban*, both of which he translates as "administrator." Since this does not carry the connotation of an official overseeing a joint merchant-official enterprise, I have chosen to translate *duban* as "supervisory official" instead; see Charles Hucker, *A Dictionary of Official Titles in Imperial China* (Stanford: Stanford University Press, 1985), pp. 533, 541.
84. The fact that Zhou Ziqi took control of the Bank of China from its own professional managers is noted by Bian in *Diary*, April 22, 1916; see April 28, 1916, for tensions between the Bank of China and the Finance Ministry.
85. *Zhongguo jinrong shi*, pp. 175–181; "Shiban yinhang zhangcheng" (Charter for the experimental founding of a bank), *Dongfang zazhi*, 1, no. 4 (April 25, 1904): 86–91, quote p. 86. Hall, pp. 34, 35, says that the Hubu Bank regulations were based on those of Japanese banks and that Da Qing regulations were based on those of foreign banks, though he does not say which ones. See also *BOComm Collection*, pp. 1–34; and Kong Xiangxian, esp. chaps. 3–10.
86. Alain Plessis, "Bankers in French Society, 1860s–1960s," in Youssef Cassis, ed., *Finance and Financiers in European History, 1880–1960* (Cambridge: Cambridge University Press, 1992), p. 150; Rondo Cameron, "France, 1800–1870," in

Cameron et al., p. 107; Cameron, "Belgium, 1800–1875," in Cameron et al., p. 136; Sylla, p. 265; Richard Tilly, "An Overview on the Role of the Large German Banks up to 1914," in Cassis, p. 92; P. L. Cottrell and Lucy Newton, "Banking Liberalization in England and Wales, 1826–1844," in Sylla, Tilly, and Tortella, pp. 78, 83, 87, 108.

87. *BOC Collection,* p. 111; *BOComm Collection,* p. 173. On the relationship between banks and Chinese urban networks, see Brett Sheehan, "Urban Identity and Urban Networks in Cosmopolitan Cities: Banks and Bankers in Tianjin, 1900–1937," in Joseph Esherick, ed., *Remaking the Chinese City: Modernity and National Identity, 1900–1950* (Honolulu: University of Hawaii Press, 2000), pp. 47–64.
88. Cameron, "France," p. 109.
89. Cairncross, p. 57.
90. Sylla, p. 258; Larry Schweikart, "U.S. Commercial Banking: A Historiographical Survey," *Business History Review,* 65 (Autumn 1991): 632.
91. Cottrell and Newton, pp. 75–77, quote p. 75.
92. Goodhart, p. 35; François Crouzet, "Politics and Banking in Revolutionary and Napoleonic France," in Sylla, Tilly, and Tortella, pp. 39–43; Hugh T. Patrick, "Japan, 1868–1914," in Cameron et al., p. 252.
93. Forrest Capie, Charles Goodhart, and Norbert Schnadt, "The Development of Central Banking," in Forrest Capie et al., eds., *The Future of Central Banking: The Tercentenary Symposium of the Bank of England* (Cambridge: Cambridge University Press, 1994), p. 2. The Bank of France is an exception, retaining commercial banking functions well into the twentieth century; see Olivier Feiertag and Pablo Martín-Aceña, "The Delayed Modernization of the Central Banks of France and Spain in the Twentieth Century," in Carl-L. Holtfrerich, Jaime Reis, and Gianni Toniolo, eds., *The Emergence of Modern Central Banking from 1918 to the Present* (Aldershot: Ashgate, 1999), p. 40.
94. The initial charter of the Bank of Communications vaguely granted it permission to make all kinds of loans, but more specific limits on operations were imposed by regulations in 1914; see *BOComm Collection,* pp. 173, 190. On the Bank of China, see *BOC Collection,* p. 112.
95. Goodhart, Capie, and Schnadt, p. 5, n. 3, and chart on p. 6.
96. Cairncross, p. 58; Cameron, "France," pp. 102–105; Crouzet, p. 42; Cameron, "Belgium," p. 136; Herman Van der Wee and Monique Van der Wee-Verbreyt, "Belgian Banking in the Nineteenth and Twentieth Centuries: the Société Générale and the Générale de Banque 1822–1997," in Sylla, Tilly, and Tortella, pp. 66–67; Richard Tilly, "Germany, 1815–1870," in Cameron et al., p. 181; Capie, p. 129; Olga Crisp, "Russia, 1860–1914," in Cameron et al., pp. 197–198; Tamaki, pp. 63, 65; and *The Bank of Japan* (Tokyo: Bank of Japan, 1952), p. 1. The United States remained the largest country with multiple banks of issue, but that ended with a monopoly by the Federal Reserve in 1913; see Capie et al., p. 176. Interestingly, Argentina copied the American system of so-called free banking in 1887; see Roberto Cortés Conde, "The Origins of Banking in Argentina," in Sylla, Tilly, and Tortella, pp. 238, 239.

97. An internal history of the Bank of Communications notes that the bank often helped out during crises on an informal basis; reprinted in *BOComm Collection*, p. 15.
98. Capie (p. 118) notes that the monopoly issuer of currency often naturally takes on the role of lender of last resort.
99. Cairncross, pp. 60–61; Capie, pp. 118, 128–130; Van der Wee and Van der Wee-Verbreyt, p. 58; Peter Hertner, "Central Banking and German-Style Mixed Banking in Italy, 1893/5–1914: From Coexistence to Cooperation," in Sylla, Tilly, and Tortella, pp. 202–204; Crisp, "Russia," pp. 212–213; and Pierre L. Siklos, "U.S. and Canadian Central Banking: The Triumph of Personalities over Politics?" in Holtfrerich, Reis, and Toniolo, p. 233.
100. Goodhart, p. 58. Redish (p. 25) points out that large notes receive more scrutiny and thus are also thought to reduce counterfeiting. See also Vissering, 2:194.
101. Cameron, "France," pp. 117–118; Crouzet, p. 42; Cottrell and Newton, p. 83; and King, *History*, 1:370.
102. *Monetary Hist. Collection, 1912–1927*, pp. 129, 130.
103. Regulations from 1913 appear to be lost; see *BOC Collection*, p. 913. On the order to the Bank of Communications, see *Financial Laws and Regs.*, p. 73. On England, see Rondo Cameron, "England, 1750–1844," in Cameron et al., pp. 22, 47; and David Kynaston, "The Bank of England and the Government," in Roberts and Kynaston, pp. 20, 22.
104. *Financial Laws and Regs.*, p. 93. This percentage follows the Qing 1910 currency law that was never implemented; see "Zhongguo jindai huobishi ziliao," pp. 1052–55.
105. H. V. Bowen, "The Bank of England during the Long Eighteenth Century, 1694–1820," in Roberts and Kynaston, p. 16; and E. Victor Morgan, *The Theory and Practice of Central Banking, 1797–1913* (London: Frank Cass & Co., 1965), p. 101.
106. Rondo Cameron, "Scotland, 1750–1845," in Cameron et al., p. 87.
107. Capie et al., p. 176; F. S. Mead, "Bank Reserves in the United States, Canada, and England," *Quarterly Journal of Economics*, 21, no. 3 (May 1907): 452.
108. Conde, pp. 232, 240–241.
109. Tamaki, p. 31; Patrick, pp. 253, 255. The Japanese based their model on the Bank of Belgium, which had no fixed reserve requirement either, but normally kept "a metallic reserve equal to one third of its note issue"; Capie et al., p. 160.
110. Tilly, "Germany," p. 169.
111. King, *History*, 1:372, 381; 2:68.
112. Quoted in Goodhart, p. 44.
113. *BOC Collection*, p. 113; *BOComm Collection*, p. 174.
114. Cameron, "Belgium," p. 136; Tilly, "Germany"; Patrick, p. 252.
115. Bowen, pp. 16, 17; Cairncross, p. 62; Michael Collins and Mae Baker, "Bank of England Autonomy: A Retrospective," in Holtfrerich, Reis, and Toniolo, p. 14;

Elizabeth Hennessy, "The Governors, Directors, and Management of the Bank of England," in Roberts and Kynaston, p. 187; and Crouzet, p. 43.

116. Boris Anan'ich, "State Power and Finance in Russia, 1802–1917: The Credit Office of the Finance Ministry and Governmental Control over Credit Institutions," in Sylla, Tilly, and Tortella, pp. 210–223; Morgan, p. 116.

117. Mead, p. 458.

2. The 1916 Moratorium on Exchange in Tianjin

1. Tianjin's 1848 population of less than 200,000 had grown to almost 425,000 by 1908. Li Jingneng et al., *Tianjin renkou shi* (History of population in Tianjin) (Tianjin: Nankai daxue chubanshe, 1990), p. 82. Before it opened as a treaty port, Tianjin ranked well below the largest cities in China; see G. William Skinner, "Introduction: Urban Development in Imperial China," in *The City in Late Imperial China* (Stanford: Stanford University Press, 1977), p. 29.
2. Although Baoding was technically the provincial capital, Tianjin was the residence of Zhili governors at least half of the year. See Zhang Xiaobo, pp. 123–124; Hu Guangmin, pp. 77–78; and Kwang-ching Liu, "Li Hung-chang [Li Hongzhang] in Chihli [Zhili]: The Emergence of a Policy, 1870–1875," in Chu and Liu, p. 51.
3. The best introduction to Tianjin's history as a trading center is in Tenshin chiikishi kenkyukai, ed., *Tenshinshi: saiseisuru toshi no toporoji* (A history of Tianjin: a topography of the rebirth of a city) (Tokyo: Fukushima showa, 1999), chaps. 2 and 3. See also Lai Xinxia, *Tianjin jindai shi* (Tianjin's modern history) (Tianjin: Nankai daxue chubanshe, 1987). In English, see Zhang Xiaobo, pp. 47–103, and Kwan Man Bun, "The Merchant World of Tianjin: Society and Economy of a Chinese City" (Ph.D. diss., Stanford University, 1990), pp. 57–145. The changes which Li Hongzhang brought to Tianjin are discussed in Hu Guangmin, pp. 64–96. For Yuan Shikai's administration, see Stephen R. MacKinnon, *Power and Politics in Late Imperial China: Yuan Shi-kai in Beijing and Tianjin, 1901–1908* (Berkeley: University of California Press, 1980), chaps. 2–5.
4. Letters of Earle H. Ballou, Yale Divinity Library, CRP—Miscellaneous Personal Papers Collection, Group 8, box 6, folder 1–1.
5. The American Concession, which was never used, remained small, sandwiched between the German and British concessions.
6. Brian Power, *The Ford of Heaven* (New York: Michael Kesend Publishing, 1984), pp. 20, 21, 30, 61.
7. Ibid., p. 39.
8. Hershatter, p. 7; Lieberthal, p. 3; Ruth Rogaski, "From Protecting Life to Defending the Nation: The Emergence of Public Health in Tianjin, 1859–1953" (Ph.D. diss., Yale University, 1996), pp. 218, 219; and Kwan Man Bun, "Order in Chaos: Tianjin's *hunhunr* and Urban Identity in Modern China," *Journal of Urban History,* 27, no. 1 (November 2000): 75–91.
9. Tianjin achieved prefectural status under the Yongzheng emperor in 1731; see

Tianjin tongzhi: zhengquan zhi, zhengfu juan (Tianjin gazetteer: political gazetteer, government volume) (Tianjin: Tianjin shehui kexue chubanshe), p. 124.

10. Clara M. Cushman, *Tientsin Scribbles* (Leominster, Mass.: Boutwell, Owens & Co., 1925), pp. 109, 110. On Zhu Jiabao, see Young, *Presidency*, p. 227.
11. On Yang, see O. D. Rasmussen, *Tientsin: An Illustrated Outline History* (Tianjin: Tientsin Press, 1925), p. 265; and reports of the British Consul in Tianjin, 4th quarter 1918, 3d quarter 1919, and 2d quarter 1922.
12. Yang Guzhi, Tan Zaitang, and Zhang Zhangxiang, p. 112.
13. Kwan, "Merchant World," pp. 285–287; Zhang Xiaobo, p. 90; and Xin Chengzhang, "Tianjin ba da jia" (Tianjin's Eight Great Families), *Tianjin wenshi ziliao*, 20 (August 1982): 39–55.
14. Zhang Xiaobo, pp. 184–218.
15. Ibid., p. 202.
16. Ibid., pp. 315, 316. On Ye Dengbang, see Tianjin wenshi ziliao, ed., *Tianjin renwu lu* (Tianjin personages) (Tianjin: difang shizhi, 1987), pp. 61, 62.
17. On Bian Yinchang, see Zhang Xiaobo, pp. 317–321.
18. *Hebei sheng zhi*, di 42 juan, *caizheng zhi* (Hebei provincial gazetteer, vol. 42, fiscal administration gazetteer) (Shijiazhuang: Hebei renmin chubanshe, 1992), pp. 1–3.
19. Shen Danian, pp. 2–6.
20. In 1905, Tianjin ranked just behind Hong Kong and Shanghai, respectively; Howard Curtis Reed, *The Preeminence of International Financial Centers* (New York: Praeger, 1981), p. 131.
21. Zhang Jia'ao, *Ge sheng jinrong gailue* (Summary of financial matters in China's provinces) (n.p., 1915), p. 9; and Linda Grove, "International Trade and the Creation of Domestic Marketing Networks in North China, 1860–1930," in Shinya Sugiyama and Linda Grove, eds., *Commercial Networks in Modern Asia* (Richmond, Surrey: Curzon Press, 2001), pp. 96–115.
22. Wei Bogang, "Tianjin Hengbin Zhengjin yinhang yu Wei jia liangdai maiban" (Two generations of Wang family compradors and the Tianjin branch of the Yokohama Specie Bank), in Tianjin wenshi ziliao, ed., *Tianjin de yanghang yu maiban* (Tianjin's foreign companies and compradors) (Tianjin: Tianjin renmin chubanshe, 1987), pp. 309–324; Zhang Xiaobo, pp. 151, 152.
23. Shen Danian, pp. 2–6; Ying Fu and Zhu Jisan, "Tianjin qianye yu qianye tongye gonghui" (The indigenous bank business and Indigenous Bank Association of Tianjin), *Tianjin gongshang shiliao congkan*, 7 (1987): 2–3.
24. On the Boxer crisis and the events of 1912, see Zhang Xiaobo, pp. 210–213 and 485–486. For a contemporary view of the decline in Tianjin's finance industry during the first decade and a half of the twentieth century, see "Tianjin zhi jinrong tan" (A discussion of finance in Tianjin), *Dongfang zazhi*, 14, no. 4 (1917): 153.
25. Tianjin Bank of China, 161-ZD-270; Hall, pp. 94–97.
26. "Tianjin zhi jinrong tan," pp. 155, 156.
27. *Chamber Collection, 1912–1928*, pp. 936, 937; and *BOC Collection*, p. 255.
28. *Chamber Collection, 1912–1928*, p. 961. Yang Yide was head of both the Zhili Po-

lice Department and police commissioner of Tianjin. To simplify matters, I refer to him only as chief of police.

29. *Chamber Collection, 1912–1928,* p. 961.
30. *BOC Collection,* p. 255.
31. Ibid., p. 259. Li Chun in Jiangxi made a similar argument for his province; *BOC Collection,* pp. 260, 261.
32. On May 5, Zhu Jiabao transmitted a letter from the Finance Ministry to the Tianjin Chamber of Commerce swearing that there were no plans to discontinue exchange; *Chamber Collection, 1912–1928,* p. 937; Bian noted in his *Diary* as early as May 8, however, that the decision to discontinue exchange was as good as decided.
33. *BOC Collection,* p. 294.
34. *Diary,* May 11, 1916.
35. *Chamber Collection, 1912–1928,* p. 938.
36. Duan had taken control during a cabinet shakeup in late April; Yang Daxin, p. 153.
37. Bao Peizhi, "Xinhai geming yilai wo guo bizhi de bianqian" (Changes in our country's monetary system since the 1911 revolution), *Tianjin wenshi ziliao,* 40 (1987): 171. The figures in this article contradict published figures from the Chamber of Commerce archives and may represent an exaggeration.
38. *Diary,* May 11, 12, and 13, 1916. Bian noted that six of his friends at the Bank of China also resigned; *Chamber Collection, 1912–1928,* p. 963.
39. Since the Chinese name of the association clearly distinguishes between "merchant" and "gentry," I have not translated the term as "merchant-gentry"; see Ma Min, p. 364.
40. The need to keep money and goods circulating was repeatedly brought up by the association's directors during meetings; see *Chamber Collection, 1912–1928,* pp. 994, 998.
41. Ibid., pp. 974, 975.
42. The *North China Herald,* May 20, 1916, p. 394, expressed foreign attitudes about inconvertible banknotes by declaring that "such a situation is intolerable from the foreign standpoint."
43. *Chamber Collection, 1912–1928,* p. 966.
44. This language is found in both the May 15, 1916, announcement, and the May 19, 1916, letter; ibid., pp. 975, 1005.
45. Ibid., pp. 1005, 1006.
46. Ibid., p. 982.
47. The association sent the initial documents to Zhu Jiabao on May 15. He relayed the cabinet's order to include Beijing notes on May 19, and it was on that day that the association issued its list of notes that would be cashed (excluding notes from Beijing) and sent telegrams to officials throughout China; ibid., pp. 974–978, 1005–8.
48. The amount of notes issued was 2,372,600 yuan for the Tianjin Bank of China and 2,667,900 for the Tianjin Bank of Communications.
49. *Chamber Collection, 1912–1928,* pp. 1003, 1004; Zhang Xiaobo, 563.

50. *Chamber Collection, 1912–1928,* p. 1004.
51. Ibid., p. 1010.
52. Zhang Xiaobo, p. 565.
53. *Chamber Collection, 1912–1928,* p. 1016.
54. Ibid., pp. 967, 1000–3.
55. The mid-level group had a fluid composition, but at least forty people both signed the May 15 declaration and attended the May 18 meeting. The number is probably higher, because people are often listed by their given names in one context and their *zi,* or style, in another. More than one thousand people attended the May 22 meeting; *Dagong Bao,* May 23, 1916.
56. *Chamber Documents, 1912–1927,* p. 976.
57. Rowe, *Hankow: Commerce and Society,* pp. 247–248.
58. See Yan's biography in *Tianjin renwu lu,* pp. 131–132; Kwan, *Salt Merchants,* pp. 53–55.
59. Zhang Xiaobo, pp. 559–567.
60. *Chamber Collection, 1912–1928,* p. 982.
61. Ibid., p. 1008.
62. Seventy-nine people attended a May 18 meeting; seventy-three listed their addresses, seventy-two of them in Tianjin.
63. *Chamber Collection, 1912–1928,* pp. 982, 986–987, 993–995, 998, 1015–17.
64. Zhang Xiaobo, p. 207.
65. Ibid., p. 241.
66. Kwan Man Bun points out that salt merchants usually received favors such as increases in the weight of salt bales or tax waivers in return for their large "contributions" to the emperor's treasury; see "Merchant World," pp. 173–187.
67. Zhang Xiaobo, pp. 398–404.
68. *Dagong Bao,* May 23, 1916.
69. *Chamber Collection, 1912–1928,* p. 944. I have chosen to translate without rhyme.
70. *Chamber Collection, 1912–1928,* p. 945. On Wang Zhilong, see Zhou Yu, *Dagong Bao shi* [A history of *Dagong Bao*] (Jiangsu: guji, 1993), p. 22.
71. *Chamber Collection, 1912–1928,* p. 1008, reprints the cable sent to Xu Shichang, minister of the army Wang Shizhen, and Cao Rui, brother of Cao Kun and military governor of Zhili Province from 1918; for the cable to and responses from the Jilin military governor Meng Enyuan, Jiangsu military governor Feng Guozhand, and Jiangxi military governor Li Chun, see pp. 941–942. The responses from Wang Shizhen, Feng Guozhang, and Li Chun were collected and published in *Dagong Bao,* May 23, 1916, under the title "The Preservation Association Gets Telegrams from Fellow Locals [*tongxiang*]."
72. *Dagong Bao,* May 23, 1916.
73. An account of the rally can be found ibid. In the early stages of the bank runs, foreigners had been singled out for participating; see *Yishi Bao* editorial, May 13, 1916.

74. *Dagong Bao*, May 23, 1916.
75. *BOC Collection*, p. 267. The Bank of Communications in Shanghai did not fare as well as the Bank of China and had to shut its doors temporarily; *North China Herald*, May 20, 1916, p. 370.
76. English translation published in the *North China Herald*, May 20, 1916, p. 394. The original Chinese order is reprinted in *BOC Collection*, pp. 264–265.
77. *BOC Collection*, p. 283; *Chamber Collection, 1912–1928*, pp. 947, 1015.
78. Archives of the Foreign Ministry, 3–22–4–4–3.
79. *Chamber Collection, 1912–1928*, p. 1014. This inconsistency was also the main topic of a *Dagong Bao* editorial, May 3, 1916.
80. *Chamber Collection, 1912–1928*, p. 939.
81. *BOC Collection*, p. 267.
82. *Chamber Collection, 1912–1928*, p. 940.
83. Ibid., pp. 942–944.
84. Ibid., pp. 998; for regulations for the Market Protection Bank, see pp. 969–971.
85. Ibid., pp. 907, 968, 972–974, 999, 1000.
86. Ibid., pp. 1018–19, 1022, 1023. This time the organization was called the Representatives of the Zhili Provincial Gentry, Academics, Merchants, and People, an even broader appellation than the recently disbanded association.
87. On the circulation of Tianjin notes in Beijing, see Beijing NCB, pp. 3489 and 3510. On the eventual withdrawal of Beijing notes, see *BOC Collection*, pp. 949, 950.
88. Emily Honig, *Creating Chinese Ethnicity: Subei People in Shanghai, 1850–1980* (New Haven: Yale University Press, 1992), p. 136.
89. Michael Bordo and Eugene White suggest that governments with a history of meeting obligations, such as England in the late eighteenth century, can suspend credibly during crises, while others, such as France at about the same time, cannot; Michael D. Bordo and Eugene N. White, "British and French Finance during the Napoleonic Wars," in Michael Bordo and Forrest Capie, eds., *Monetary Regimes in Transition*, (Cambridge: Cambridge University Press, 1994), pp. 266, 267. During the heyday of the gold standard in the late nineteenth and early twentieth centuries, suspension was common for countries on the periphery; see Martín-Aceña, Reis, and Augustín, pp. 7–10.
90. *Diary*, June 11–July 8, 1916.

3. Local Regulators, Paper Tigers, and Good Citizens

1. Zhang Xianwen, Huang Meizhen et al., *Duan Qirui yu wanxi junfa* (Duan Qirui and the Anhui clique warlords) (Henan: Renmin, 1991), p. 130.
2. On the Nishihara loans, see Madeline Chi, "Bureaucratic Capitalists in Operation: Ts'ao Ju-lin [Cao Rulin] and His New Communications Clique, 1916–1919," *Journal of Asian Studies*, 35, no. 3 (May 1975): 680–683.
3. Zhang Xianwen and Huang Meizhen, chap. 5; Gu Shoucun, pp. 33–37, 53–55.
4. Yang Daxin, pp. 467–470; Andrew Nathan, *Peking Politics, 1918–1923: Factional-*

ism and the Failure of Constitutionalism (Berkeley: University of California Press, 1976), pp. 46, 80, 81, 91, 176; Jerome Chen, *The Military-Gentry Coalition: China under the Warlords* (Toronto: University of Toronto–York University Joint Centre on Modern East Asia, 1979), pp. 42–49.

5. On warlord investments, see Song Meiyun, "Beiyang shiqi guanliao siren touzi yu Tianjin jindai gongye" (Bureaucratic personal investment in modern industry in Tianjin during the Beiyang period), *Lishi yanjiu*, 2 (1989): 38–52; and Wei Ming, "Lun beiyang junfa guanliao de siren zibenzhuyi jingji huodong" (On the personal capitalistic economic activities of Beiyang warlords and bureaucrats), *Jindaishi yanjiu*, 2 (1985): 66–110.
6. Rawski (p. xix) argues for a fairly robust republican-period economy, especially in the so-called modern sector of industry and financial institutions located in or near the treaty ports; see also Liu Foding et al., *Zhongguo jindai jingji fazhan shi* (History of economic development in modern China) (Beijing: Gaodeng jiaoyu chubanshe, 1999), p. 70. China's economy got a boost during the First World War, then declined in the early to mid-1930s, and Tianjin generally reflected these trends. See Liu Foding et al., p. 111; Lai Xinxia, p. 64; Bergère, *Golden Age*, chap. 2; and Sun Dechang and Zhou Zuchang, eds., *Tianjin jindai jingjishi* (The economic history of modern Tianjin) (Tianjin: Tianjin shehui kexueyuan chubanshe, 1990).
7. The one private bank in Tianjin prior to 1916 was the Cultivation Bank, owned by the Li family of salt merchants. For the Chinese and English names of Tianjin Banks, see Appendix B.
8. On the founding of Zhongfu Bank, see Bao Peizhi, "Shouzhou"; *Diary*, July 4, September 19, November 7 and 24, and December 4, 1916; Luo Shuwei, ed., *Jindai Tianjin chengshi shi* (An urban history of modern Tianjin) (Tianjin: Zhongguo shehui kexue, 1993), p. 398; and Tianjin Bank Assoc., 129–2–162. On the National Industrial Bank of China, see Hao Qingyuan, pp. 133–135; and Tianjin Bank Assoc., 129–2–1625.
9. On the Continental Bank and Tan Danya, see Tan Jizhen and Tan Zaitang, "Dalu yinhang de xingshuai jilue" (A brief account of the rise and fall of the Continental Bank), *Tianjin wenshi ziliao*, 13 (1981): 135–138; Yu Yizhen, "Tan Lisun yu Dalu yinhang" (Tan Lisun [Tan Danya] and the Continental Bank), in Shanghai wenshi ziliao, ed., *Jiu Shanghai de jinrong jie* (Finance in old Shanghai) (Shanghai: Shanghai renmin chubanshe, 1988), pp. 180, 181; and Tianjin Bank Assoc., 129–2–1625.
10. Zhou is probably best known to the Western reader through the unflattering portrait of him as a wheeler-dealer in Strand, pp. 102–116. On Zhou and the Jincheng Bank, see Ji Xiaocun; Yang Guzhi, "Zhou Zuomin yu Jincheng yinhang" (Zhou Zuomin and Jincheng Bank), *Tianjin wenshi ziliao*, 13 (1981): 100–105; Xu Guomao and Shao Yidu, "Jincheng yinhang jianshi" (A brief history of Jincheng Bank), in Shanghai wenshi ziliao, p. 161; entries in Boorman and *Minguo renwu da cidian*. On Ni Sichong, see *Minguo renwu da cidian; Tianjin renwu lu;* and Song Meiyun, "Beiyang shiqi," pp. 38–52.

11. Of all Tianjin banks, the most detailed records on shareholders is available for Jincheng; see Zhongguo renmin yinhang (The People's Bank of China), ed., *Jincheng yinhang shiliao* (Historical materials on Jincheng Bank) (Shanghai: Renmin, 1983), pp. 22–34. By 1927, stockholdings were actually quite diversified.
12. On Wei's resignation from the Bank of China, see *Diary*, May 17, 1916. For biographical information on Wei, see *Tianjin renwu lu;* and Wei Bogang, pp. 309–310.
13. Brett Sheehan, "Warlords, Cadres, and Bankers: Private Commercial Banking in the Republican and Post-Mao Periods," *Journal of Asian Business*, 14, no. 1 (1998): 9–12.
14. Nathan, p. 86.
15. Chen, *Military-Gentry Coalition*, p. 99.
16. Chen Guangfu noted that most bank directors had little power in Chinese banks, with day-to-day affairs run by the president (general manager) and chairman of the board; see "Reminiscences of Ch'en Kuang-Fu," manuscript on deposit with the Columbia University Rare Book and Manuscript Collection, p. 67.
17. "Autobiography of Zhang Jia'ao [Chang Kia-ngau, Chang Chia-ao]," pp. 26–29, 37, manuscript on deposit in the Rare Book Room of Columbia University; Bergère, "Shanghai Bankers," pp. 15–34; and the entry in Boorman.
18. Recollections of Zhang's sister as told to her grand-niece in Pang-Mei Natasha Chang, *Bound Feet and Western Dress* (New York: Doubleday, 1996), pp. 67–69.
19. This unfavorable description is in Feng Gengguang, "Wo zai zhongguo yinhang de yixie huihi" (Some memories from being at the Bank of China), *Wenshi ziliao*, 41 (1963): 4–5.
20. "Autobiography of Zhang Jia'ao," p. 38.
21. Feng Gengguang, p. 4. For biographical information on Wang Kemin, see his entry in Boorman.
22. The 1917 charter is reprinted in *BOC Collection*, pp. 119–122.
23. "Autobiography of Zhang Jia'ao," p. 43.
24. *Diary*, April 22, 1921.
25. Ibid., January 17, 1921.
26. Bergère, "Shanghai Bankers," pp. 15–34. On the Shanghai Bankers' Association, see also "Autobiography of Zhang Jia'ao," p. 35; and Xu Cangshui, ed., *Shanghai yinhang gonghui shiye shi* (History of the operations of the Shanghai Bankers' Association) (Shanghai: Shanghai yinhang zhoubao, 1925), pp. 1, 2.
27. On the relationship between native place and institutionalism in the formation of the Shanghai and Tianjin Bankers' Associations, see Sheehan, "Urban Identity," pp. 56–59.
28. On professionalism in banking, see Bergère, "Shanghai Bankers," p. 19; Upton Close [J. W. Hall], "Closeups of China's 'Money Josses," *China Review*, 2, no. 4 (April 1922): 200; and Yeh, pp. 106–107.
29. Tianjin Bank Assoc., 129–2–1612.

30. For the 1915 and 1918 regulations, see *Financial Laws and Regs.*, pp. 313–317. A copy of the 1915 regulations is in the file containing the opening announcement of the Tianjin Bankers' Association; Tianjin Bank Assoc., 129–2–1612.
31. Xu Cangshui, *Minguo*, pp. 44—60.
32. Tianjin Bank Assoc., 161-YB-344.
33. The so-called Laoxikai incident is treated in Zhang Xiaobo, pp. 419–426. Quote from an article in Tianjin's *Dagong Bao* reprinted in Wang Shousong et al., eds., "Tianjin renmin fandui fa diguozhuyi qinzhan laoxikai douzheng" (The struggle of the Tianjin people against the French imperialists' seizure of Laoxikai), *Tianjin lishi ziliao*, 17 (1982): 30.
34. Jin Lüqin, "Qudi waichao wenti" (The problem of suppressing foreign paper money), *Yinhang zhoubao*, 494 (April 1927): 8–12; and Zhongguo renmin yinhang, ed., *Jindai Zhongguo de jinrong shi chang* (Financial markets in modern China) (Beijing: Zhongguo jinrong, 1989), p. 62.
35. The National Commercial, Continental, Dasheng, Jincheng, and Kenye banks all issued paper money through the Bank of China; see *Diary*, February 15, 1917, January 12 and 19, and March 3, 1921; and Tianjin Bank of China, 161-ZD-514, 161-ZD-611, 161-ZD-812.
36. Foreign bank consortiums began lending money to the Qing government as early as 1895; see *Zhongguo jinrong shi*, pp. 166–170, 189–195.
37. Tianjin Bank Assoc., 129-2-1590.
38. Mi Rucheng, "Xin yintuan de zai shenshi" (Another look at the new consortium), paper delivered at the Second International Conference on Modern China and the World, Beijing, September 6–9, 2000.
39. Nathan, pp. 88, 89; and *China Review* (August 1921): 93.
40. Tianjin Bank Assoc., 129-2-1614, 129-2-1616; *Diary*, February 5 and 26, June 24 and 27, 1921. On Bian's meetings with Wang Kemin, see *Diary*, January 19, 20, and 24, 1921, quote from July 21, 1921.
41. *Diary*, January 25, 1921. On bankers' association protests over issuing new 1912 bonds in 1921, see Shanghai Bank Assoc., 173–1–39.
42. *Diary*, Feburary 24, 25, and 28, and March 25, 1921; Tianjin Bank of China, 161-ZD-510, 161-ZD-514. The payments crisis resulted from a decline in the price of silver, which made it hard for Chinese merchants who sold goods in silver to make payments in gold to their foreign suppliers; see Bergère, *Golden Age*, p. 87.
43. *Diary*, September 13 and 14, 1921.
44. *Chen Bao*, November 11, 14, 15, 1921.
45. Han Hongtai, "Beiyang junfa shiqi de jiaotong yinhang" (The Bank of Communications in the time of the Beiyang warlords), in *Jindai yinhangye mixin* (Secrets of the modern banking industry) (Hong Kong: Zhongyuan, 1985), p. 83. On the loans made by the Bank of China, see Tianjin Bank of China, 161-ZD-512.
46. *Diary*, January 8 and August 2, 1921.
47. *Dagong Bao*, November 17, 1921.

48. Ibid., November 18, 1921; the editorial of the same day blames the government but does not mention foreigners.
49. The scholar Ma Yinchu, speaking at Beijing University, made a thinly veiled allegation against Aglen; see Ma Yinchu, "Guochao jidui bu hehu jingji yuanze" (The bank run on national banknotes is not in accordance with economic principles), *Dongfang zazhi*, 18, no. 23 (December 1921): 107–109. See also *Dagong Bao*, November 21, 1921. The alleged foreign plot had been reported a few days earlier in Beijing and Shanghai; see Beijing's *Shuntian Shibao*, November 17, 1921, and Shanghai's *Shenbao*, November 18, 1921. A Tianjin Chamber of Commerce survey published in *Dagong Bao*, November 22, 1921, did indeed indicate that customs was not accepting the paper money of the two banks, but whether the policy predates the crisis is unclear.
50. On Aglen's refusal, see *Dagong Bao*, November 23, 1921.
51. *Chen Bao*, November 19, 1921.
52. Yao Songling, *Zhongguo Yinhang ershisi nian fazhan shi* (Twenty-four years of the development of the Bank of China) (Taipei: Zhuanji wenxue, 1976), p. 76.
53. China's professional bankers held meetings in August to discuss sending their own delegation; see *Diary*, August 21, 26, and 29, 1921.
54. Tianjin Bank of China, 161-ZD-514; *Diary*, July 16, 1924.
55. This account is drawn from reports in Tianjin *Dagong Bao*, November 17, 1921; *Yishi Bao*, November 17, 1921; and *Diary*, November 16, 1921.
56. *Diary*, November 16 and 17, 1921; *Dagong Bao*, November 18 and 21, 1921. The financial report on the Tianjin Bank of Communications is reprinted in *Chamber Collection, 1912–1928*, pp. 1030–36; and the report on the Tianjin branch of the Bank of China can be found in a file marked "confidential records of the manager" in Tianjin Bank of China, 161-ZD-510.
57. *Diary*, December 1, 1921; *Chamber Collection, 1912–1928*, pp. 1040–43.
58. See *Dagong Bao*, November 23, 1921, for a discussion of the role of the bank crisis in the political struggle between Cao Kun and Zhang Zuolin.
59. *Dagong Bao*, November 18, 1921.
60. Newspapers echoed similar localistic sentiments; see, e.g., the November 18, 1921, *Yishi Bao* article informing readers that the Bank of China's Tianjin and Beijing branches had been separate entities all along.
61. *Chamber Collection, 1912–1928*, pp. 1082, 1083.
62. *Dagong Bao*, March 7, 1922.
63. This letter was written in January 1922; *Chamber Collection, 1912–1928*, pp. 1084, 1085.
64. *Diary*, January 17, 1922.
65. Bian's reference to a paper tiger and the response are found in the confidential correspondence between Bian and the main office in Beijing; Tianjin Bank of China, 161-ZD-512.
66. The real bills doctrine held that central banks should discount only those bank assets that arose out of financing commercial transactions, and thus were supposedly self-liquidating when the underlying goods sold. The doctrine played a

significant role in the thinking on central banking in the early twentieth century; for example, see the discussion of the Federal Reserve in Friedman and Schwartz, pp. 191–193.

67. Ma Yinchu, p. 107.
68. After the 1911 revolution, provincial education departments were reorganized into two sections: normal and social. In 1913 the Zhili Education Department reported that its Social Education Bureau was responsible for managing libraries, reforming performances, and overseeing lecture and newspaper reading rooms. Shu Xincheng, *Zhongguo jindai jiaoyushi ziliao* (Historical materials on education in modern China) (Beijing: Renmin jiaoyu, 1961), pp. 312–315. See also Luo Shuwei, p. 480, and Lai Xinxia, p. 291. The bureau's journal was presumably distributed to educational institutions in the province.
69. *Chamber Collection, 1912–1928*, pp. 1024–26. I have not attempted to maintain either the rhyme or the meter of the original, which was written at the end of December when the crisis was mostly past. A translation of the complete text of the song is in Appendix C.
70. Brackets in original.
71. One of the first such movements which had an impact on Tianjin was the 1905 American goods boycott. This was followed by the 1916 protest against the building of the French Cathedral (Laoxikai incident) and of course the May Fourth Movement.
72. Whether or not the "Money Scare Vernacular Song" presented those economic principles accurately is beside the point.

4. The Rules of the Game under Warlord Governments

1. For a summary of the battles fought in and around Tianjin in this period, see *Tianjin jianshi* (Tianjin: Tianjin renmin, 1987), pp. 270–301.
2. *Diary*, April 19, 1924.
3. Tianjin Salt Bank, "Benhang zhengfu jiekuan zhi yanjiu" (Research on this bank's government loans), n.d., unnumbered file.
4. Nathan, p. 87; Arthur Waldron, *From War to Nationalism: China's Turning Point, 1924–1925* (Cambridge: Cambridge University Press, 1995), chap. 6.
5. *Diary*, June 22, 1926.
6. Coble, *The Shanghai Capitalists*, p. 20. On privatization of the Bank of China, see also Cheng, p. 73; "Autobiography of Zhang Jia'ao," pp. 43, 47–48.
7. Bian Baimei reluctantly took on this new responsibility; *Diary*, March 3 and June 4, 1922.
8. The five zones were centered on Shanghai, Hankou, Hong Kong, Tianjin, and Fengtian, the last being the only city completely ruled by Chinese authorities; *BOC Collection*, pp. 952, 953. Internal supervision of the Beijing office and the new currency zones all grew from the 1921 currency crisis; Tianjin Bank of China, 161-ZD-514.
9. *Diary*, October 26, 1924.
10. Du Xuncheng, "Zhongguo jindai liangzhong jinrong zhidu de bijiao" (Compar-

ison of modern China's two kinds of financial systems), in Zhang Weibao and Li Huabiao, eds., *Jindai Zhongguo jingji yanjiu taolunhui 1999 lunwenji* (1999 selection of papers from the modern Chinese economic research conference) (Hong Kong: Xinya yanjiusuo, 1999), p. 231; Bergère, *Golden Age*, p. 133; and *BOComm Collection*, p. 7.

11. *BOComm Collection*, pp. 846–848. Zone headquarters were in Shanghai, Tianjin, Hankou, Fengtian, and Harbin; BOComm, Main, 398–12044.
12. *Diary*, March 11, 1924.
13. *Dagong Bao*, April 16, 1925.
14. *BOComm Collection*, pp. 10, 119–123.
15. Zhang Maopeng, p. 363.
16. The percentages do not tell the whole story. Loans at the bank of China increased throughout the 1920s, so even if the relative percentage of government loans went down, the actual number of loans went up in all years except 1925; Cheng, p. 140.
17. The mere thought of such powerful competition in the paper money business worried Bian Baimei and his colleagues; *Diary*, September 14, 1922.
18. Zhang Boju, p. 76; Ji Xiaocun, p. 106; and Tan Jizhen, p. 140.
19. On the China and Southsea Bank, see Liu Xiaobai, "Qiaoshang Zhongnan yinhang" (The Overseas Chinese China and Southsea Bank), in Shanghai wenshi ziliao, p. 172; Yang Guzhi and Tan Zaitang, "Zhongnan yinhang gai shu" (A brief account of the China and Southsea Bank), *Tianjin wenshi ziliao*, 13 (1981): 159–162.
20. *Tianjin tongzhi: jinrong zhi*, p. 148.
21. The so-called Southern Three banks—the Shanghai Commercial and Savings Bank, the National Commercial Bank, and the Zhejiang Industrial Bank—cooperated but had nothing like the formal organization and risk pooling of the Northern Four. *Zhongguo jinrong shi*, p. 215.
22. In 1922, Bian gave a banquet for the managers of fifteen indigenous banks that had signed agreements to "adopt" Tianjin Bank of China currency; *Diary*, October 24, 1922. A few days later, he noted that ten indigenous banks had already signed adoption agreements with the Four Bank joint treasury; *Diary*, October 30, 1922.
23. Yang Bingde, ed., *Zhongguo jindai chengshi yu jianzhu* (Cities and buildings in modern China) (Beijing: Zhongguo jianshe gongye, 1993), pp. 98, 99; *Tianjin tongzhi: chengxiang jianshe zhi* (Tianjin gazetteer: city planning volume) (Tianjin: Tianjin shehui kexue chubanshe, 2000), pp. 787–790.
24. Jincheng moved into the premises of the former Deutsche Asiatische Bank.
25. Although the most spectacular buildings were in the foreign concessions, Chinese banks also built large and impressive branches in the Chinese part of the city.
26. Yang Bingde, p. 98.
27. Shanghai's National Commercial Bank built a similar building for its Tianjin branch, with fourteen columns encircling its unusual round lobby. *Tianjin tongzhi: chengxiang jianshe zhi*, p. 790.

28. Brendan Gill, introduction to Parnassus Foundation and Museum of Fine Arts, Houston, eds., *Money Matters: A Critical Look at Bank Architecture* (New York: McGraw-Hill, 1990), p. 1; see also Robert Nesbit, "Men and Money: Reflections by a Sociologist," ibid., p. 7.
29. Nesbit, p. 8.
30. YWQ, third meeting with old bankers, Tianjin, 1995. An article translated from a Japanese banking journal published in the Bank of China's internal newsletter in 1931 also made an explicit link between trust and impressive building design; "Yinhang guitai zhi xingshi ji gegu zhi buzhi yu lianluo" (Forms of bank counters and arrangements and connections among departments), *Zhonghang yuekan* (The Bank of China monthly), 2, no. 10 (April 1931): 1. In a similar vein, in *Banking in the American West,* Lynne Pierson Doti and Larry Schweikart found that "more than a merchant background was required to convince depositors to trust a banker with their money: bankers needed other symbols of safety that included first and foremost a safe, a vault, and a relatively elaborate bank building," Quoted in Schweikart, pp. 620–621.
31. Interview with DTS, Tianjin, 1995.
32. YWQ, third meeting with old bankers, Tianjin, 1995.
33. On the use of "front stages" to conceal the workings of expert knowledge, see Giddens, pp. 86–87.
34. See Appendix D.
35. *Diary,* May 17, 1922.
36. Ibid., March 21, 1928.
37. Zhou Xuexi developed many of these enterprises under Yuan Shikai; Hao Qingyuan, chaps. 2–8. Bergère, *Golden Age,* pp. 178–185, discusses official involvement in the Tianjin textile industry.
38. The Zhili government took control of the German and Austrian concessions after the Chinese government entered the First World War on the side of the Allies, and the Soviet Union gave back the Russian Concession after it renounced Russia's unequal treaties with China; Shang Keqiang and Liu Haiyan, *Tianjin zujie shehui yanjiu* (Research on the society of Tianjin's foreign concessions) (Tianjin: Tianjin renmin chubanshe, 1996), pp. 24–28.
39. Tianjin Jincheng Bank, 541–01.
40. *Diary,* December 22, 1924.
41. Tianjin Salt Bank, unnumbered file. On use of Kailan Mining Administration shares for collateral at the Bank of China, see Tianjin Bank of China, 161-ZD-549.
42. Appendix D.
43. Taking deposits or safekeeping funds dates back at least to the Tang dynasty; *Zhongguo jinrong shi,* p. 68. See also Susan Mann Jones, "Finance in Ningpo: The *Ch'ien Chuang,* 1750–1880," in W. E. Wilmott, ed., *Economic Organization in Chinese Society* (Stanford: Stanford University Press, 1972), pp. 50, 63–65.
44. DTS, third meeting with old bankers, Tianjin, 1995, and LSW, second interview, Tianjin, 1995.
45. Brett Sheehan, "The Modernity of Savings," in Madeline Dong Yue and Joshua

Goldstein, eds., *Materializing Modernity* (Seattle: University of Washington Press, forthcoming).

46. *Chamber Collection, 1912–1928,* p. 924.
47. See Appendix A. Population figures from Li Jingneng et al., p. 82.
48. *Diary,* January 24, 1922.
49. Zhongguo renmin yinhang, *Jindai Zhongguo de jinrong shichang,* p. 62.
50. *Dagong Bao,* June 6 and 7, 1925.
51. Ibid., June 11, 1925. The Tianjin banks continued to do business with the foreign banks. Two years later, the Tianjin Bank of China gave the Yokohama Specie Bank a 500,000 yuan overdraft; *Diary,* April 25, 1927.
52. *Zhongguo jinrong shi,* p. 225.
53. Wu Shicheng, "Tianjin zhi pingmin jinrong zuzhi" (The financial organizations of the common people of Tianjin), *Yinhang zhoubao,* 19, no. 46 (November 1935): 7–10.
54. Hershatter, p. 45.
55. *Peking and Tientsin Times,* August 28, 1924.
56. *Dagong Bao,* January 21, 1922. On the same date, the order came out, Bian noted in his diary that "the wording denigrates the Bank of China and the Bank of Communications and promotes the Provincial Bank."
57. *Diary,* April 15 and 17, 1922 and November 11, 1924.
58. In this, Chu Yupu followed the pattern of his patron Zhang Zuolin's Fengtian regime; Ziming, "Gesheng lanchao huomin guan" (Overissue of banknotes by the provinces hurts the people), *Yinhang zhoubao,* 451 (June 1926): 10–12.
59. *Peking and Tientsin Times,* March 27, 1926.
60. *Diary,* March 26 and 27, 1926.
61. Ibid., April 10–20, 1926.
62. *Chamber Collection, 1912–1928,* pp. 1093, 1096, 1097, 1124, 1125; and *Diary,* June 10 and July 7, 1926.
63. *Diary,* September 28 and October 4, 1926.
64. Ibid., November 8 and December 20, 1926, and January 24, February 22, and April 27, 1927; Tianjin Salt Bank, unnumbered file, 1926; Tianjin Continental Bank, 1854–346; and Tianjin Bank of China, 161-ZD-734.
65. *Chamber Collection, 1912–1928,* p. 1112.
66. *Diary.* February 22, 1927. According to *Dagong Bao,* February 23, 1927, the executed men were accused of speculating in the provincial currency.
67. Tianjin Bank of China, 129-3-5378.
68. Tianjin Salt Bank, 213–99.
69. *Chamber Collection, 1912–1928,* pp. 1098, 1099; *Diary,* June 19, 1927.
70. Tianjin Bank of China, 161-ZD-734-02.
71. *Yishi Bao,* August 1, 1927. *Yishi Bao* was well known for criticizing government authorities, and this piece is clearly in such a mode. Nonetheless, the suffering and difficulties faced by the people of Tianjin were real enough.
72. Over several months the exact composition of the Support Association changed, but the Tianjin Bankers' Association, Indigenous Bankers' Association, Chamber of Commerce, and Salt Merchants' Guild provided a core mem-

bership. This list is taken from the October 4, 1927, charter, reprinted in *Chamber Collection, 1912–1928*, pp. 1104–07.

73. *Diary*, June 22, 1927; and *Chamber Collection, 1912–1928*, p. 1155.
74. *Diary*, July 26, 28, and 30, 1927, quotes from July 28 and 30.
75. Ibid., July 30, 1927.
76. *Chamber Collection, 1912–1928*, p. 1139.
77. *Diary*, August 9, 1927.
78. *Chamber Collection, 1912–1928*, pp. 1137–41; and *Diary*, August 1, 9, 17, and 23, October 8, 1927.
79. *Diary*, September 15, 17, 27, and 28, 1927, quotes from September 15 and 17.
80. *Chamber Collection, 1912–1928*, pp. 1157–69.
81. *Diary*, November 12, 13, and 14, 1927. The 1.2 million yuan loan on the customs surcharge made in May had been paid in full shortly before this new loan.
82. *Diary*, December 1, 1927.
83. *Yishi Bao*, December 11, 1927.
84. *Chamber Collection, 1912–1928*, pp. 1115, 1116, 1171; and *Diary*, December 5, 1927.
85. *Chamber Collection, 1912–1928*, pp. 1142–44, 1147.
86. Ibid., pp. 1139, 1141.
87. Zhang Xiaobo, pp. 311–315 and appendixes 5 and 6.
88. *Dagong Bao*, July 31, 1927.
89. Zhang Xiaobo, pp. 286, 451–452.
90. *Diary*, October 19, 1927.
91. For announcements that the crisis was already resolved, see *Dagong Bao*, June 20, 22, and 23, August 10, and October 10, 1927.
92. On changes in legitimacy of the northern regimes in the wake of the 1924 Zhili-Fengtian war, see Waldron, chap. 11.
93. *Dagong Bao*, July 31, 1927.
94. *Chamber Collection, 1912–1928*, pp. 1139, 1141.
95. *Dagong Bao*, November 15, 1927. The five-color flag was the national flag in use in republican China prior to the Nationalist government.
96. Ibid., June 18, 1927.
97. Ibid., February 23, June 17, and October 9, 1927.
98. *Diary*, January 9 and 17, 1928; Tianjin Bank Assoc., 129-2-1585.
99. Tianjin Bank Assoc., 129-2-1585.
100. *Diary*, May 30, 1928.
101. Ibid., June 4, 5, 7, and 14, 1928.
102. Ibid., January 4, 1922.
103. Ibid., title page, 1928.

5. Early Nationalist Rule and a New Environment

1. Coble, *Shanghai Capitalists*, pp. 43–46.
2. *Diary*, October 14 and 16, 1926.

3. At an early meeting, six people were selected to organize the Producers' Association: Li Bozhi (mining), Fan Xundong (chemicals), Tao Lanquan (cotton), Yang Xiyuan (flour), Lu Houting (electricity), and Bian Baimei (modern banking); *Diary*, December 12, 1926.
4. The Tianjin Bankers' Association met to discuss the demands of the Hankou bank workers' union on February 22, 1927; Shanghai Bank Assoc., 173–199. Hankou bank employee demands ranged from cost-of-living increases (necessitated by rampant inflation in Hankou) to control over hiring by unions; see *Peking and Tientsin Times*, April 9, 1927. A labor activist came to see Bian at about this time; *Diary*, March 9, 1927.
5. Yao Songling, *Zhongguo yinhang ershisi nian fazhan shi*, pp. 80–85.
6. *Diary*, February 28, 1927.
7. Ibid., September 17, 1926.
8. Ibid., May 21 and 23, 1927.
9. Report of the American Consulate General for June 1928, pp. 18–23.
10. *Tianjin jianshi*, p. 304. Tianjin was restored to Hebei Province in November 1930.
11. Report of the American Consulate General for June 1928, p. 32.
12. Report of the American Consulate General, November, p. 6; September, p. 17; and July, pp. 10–12.
13. *Diary*, June 9 and 15, 1928.
14. In the summer of 1928, the Finance Ministry under T. V. Soong also took a number of concrete steps to moderate relations between the Nationalists and the business community. Soong convened a National Economic Conference, inviting leading businessmen and officials to discuss China's economic problems. The conference adopted proposals to protect the property of the business class, limit labor agitation, and reduce military spending; Coble, *Shanghai Capitalists*, pp. 49–54.
15. *Tianjin renwu lu*, pp. 301–302.
16. *Diary*, July 1 and 18, 1928; and Tianjin Bank Assoc., 129-2-1585.
17. Ibid., September 9, 1928.
18. Ibid., July 19, 1928. The biographical information comes from *Tianjin renwu lu*. The one businessman who was not a Tianjin native and not a modern banker was Yang Weiyun, a Jiangsu official-manager who had worked with Zhou Xuexi in the reform institutions of the late Qing period.
19. *Diary*, July 21, 1928.
20. The history of GMD activities in Tianjin has yet to be written, in English or Chinese. A detailed examination of the party in Tianjin is beyond the scope of the present project, so by necessity I limit the discussion to generalities.
21. On the relationship between the GMD and the government in Shanghai during the early period of Nationalist rule, see Henriot, chap. 3.
22. Report of the American Consulate General, August 1928, p. 12; and December 1928, quote p. 10.
23. The conflict between the Shanghai merchant associations and the Shanghai Chamber of Commerce is treated in Joseph Fewsmith, *Party, State, and Local*

Elites in Republican China: Merchant Organizations and Politics in Shanghai, 1890–1930 (Honolulu: University of Hawaii Press, 1985), chaps. 5 and 6.

24. On the background of this movement, see ibid., pp. 150–154; and Coble, *Shanghai Capitalists,* 35–36, 60–62. Coble notes that it was indeed the Shanghai Party Committee and not the Nationalist government which benefited from the activities of the anti-Japanese movement.
25. Michael Tsin, *Nation, Governance, and Modernity in China: Canton, 1900–1927* (Stanford: Stanford University Press, 1999), chap. 3.
26. Song Meiyun, "Guomindang zhengfu shiqi de Tianjin shanghui, 1927–1937" (The Tianjin Chamber of Commerce during the time of the Nationalist government, 1927–1937), unpublished paper, p. 8.
27. *Dagong Bao,* August 27, 1928. The theme of "awakening" was a standard one in Nationalist rhetoric; see John Fitzgerald, *Awakening China: Politics, Culture, and Class in the Nationalist Revolution* (Stanford: Stanford University Press, 1996).
28. *Chamber Collection, 1928–1937,* pp. 459, 460.
29. Lin Kaiming and Li Shuying, "Tianjin fanrihui yu dizhi rihuo yundong" (The Tianjin Anti-Japan Association and the movement to boycott Japanese goods), *Tianjin wenshi ziliao xuanji,* 78 (1998): 87–89.
30. *Dagong Bao,* October 21, 1928.
31. *Diary,* October 22, 1928.
32. *Dagong Bao,* October 31, 1928. Ji Hua, "Changlu yanwu de liang da anjian" (Two big incidents of the Changlu salt merchants), *Tianjin wenshi ziliao,* 26 (1984): 131–133, states that the arrests also stemmed from internal divisions among salt merchants, with one Li Tingyu promising revenues to the government in return for furthering his own aims.
33. Song Meiyun, "Guomindang zhengfu," p. 7.
34. *Diary,* October 29, November 2, 7, and 13, 1928, quotes from November 2 and 7.
35. Nine percent of all Japanese goods that moved through Tianjin customs in 1928 would have amounted to more than 6 million yuan.
36. *Dagong Bao,* November 27 and December 2, 1928; and *Diary,* November 26, 1928.
37. Lin Kaiming and Li Shuying, pp. 90, 92.
38. Report of the American Consulate General for January 1929, p. 9. The settlement in Tianjin predates China's accord with Japan over the Jinan Incident by several months, but ongoing negotiations may have played a role as well; see Parks Coble, *Facing Japan: Chinese Politics and Japanese Imperialism, 1931–1937* (Cambridge, Mass.: Council on East Asian Studies, Harvard University, 1991), chap. 1.
39. *Dagong Bao,* December 30, 1928.
40. *Diary,* September 10, 1928; *Dagong Bao,* September 14, 1928.
41. *Chamber Collection, 1928–1937,* p. 477.
42. *Diary,* November 6, 1928. A copy of Zhang Pinti's letter of resignation and the

letters asking him to stay on are reprinted in *Chamber Collection, 1928–1937,* pp. 15–16.

43. On the directors of the Tianjin Chamber of Commerce in 1928 and their native places, see Zhang Xiaobo, appendix 6.
44. *Diary,* November 7, 1928. Biographical information on Wang Wendian from *Tianjin renwu lu.* Wang would later serve on the standing committee of the reorganized Chamber.
45. See Chapter 2; Zhang Xiaobo, pp. 231–238.
46. Fewsmith, p. 154.
47. *Chamber Collection, 1928–1937,* p. 472.
48. Fewsmith, pp. 159–162. The new Chamber of Commerce law is reprinted in *Chamber Collection, 1928–1937,* pp. 19–25. On the reorganization of the Tianjin GMD party branch, see *Tianjin jianshi,* p. 303.
49. *Chamber Collection, 1928–1937,* p. 21.
50. *Diary* as reprinted, May 7 and 11 and June 19, 1930, pp. 4–5; *Tianjin jianshi,* p. 303; and Lin Nengshi, "Yijiusanling nian Tianjin haiguan shijian" (The 1930 Tianjin customs incident), paper presented at the Second International Conference on Modern China and the World, Beijing, September 6–9, 2000.
51. *Diary* as reprinted, July 29 and 30 and August 15, 1930, p. 6.
52. *Chamber Collection, 1928–1937,* pp. 31–36. Interestingly, both Yan's city government and the Chamber seemed to accept the terms of the new Chamber of Commerce law issued by the Nationalist government in Nanjing.
53. Tianjin differed from Shanghai, where the Merchants' Association groups were incorporated into the Chamber of Commerce in 1929; see Fewsmith, pp. 157–158.
54. The southerners Bian Baimei and Wang Wendian played important roles in mediating between the factions of native elites who supported Zhang and Wang. See *Diary* as reprinted, December 10 and 14, 1931, pp. 20–21.
55. A list of the new directors can be found in *Chamber Collection, 1928–1937,* pp. 45–46.
56. Ibid., pp. 229–230; and Tianjin Bank Assoc., 129–2–1002. In fact, Bian did serve four more years; Tianjin Bank Assoc., 129–2–1001.
57. *Financial Laws and Regulations,* pp. 1052–55.
58. *Diary,* April 3, 1921. Zhang's proposal came at a time when he was raising more private capital and trying to make the Bank of China independent from the government; see "Autobiography of Zhang Jia'ao," pp. 43–48.
59. Tan Danya told Zhang Jia'ao that if the Bank of China had a means of making reserves open, then the Four Bank Joint Treasury would go along, but Bian Baimei noted that openness "is not something that will be accomplished in one step"; *Diary* April 3, 1924.
60. Ibid., July 23 and August 12, 1924.
61. Ibid., August 12, 1924.
62. Ibid., January 23, 1926, May 31, 1927, April 3, August 15 and 27, December 24, 1928.

63. Ziming; Luo Congyu, "Wuguo jinri buduihuan zhibi wenti" (The problem of unexchangeable notes in our country today), *Yinhang Yuekan,* (January 1928): 8.
64. Personal communication from Kenneth Pommeranz.
65. Zheng Huixin, *Gaige yu kunrao* (Reform and perplexity) (Hong Kong: Xianggang jiaoyu tushu gongsi, 1998), p. 20.
66. Quoted in Bian's *Diary,* May 31, 1927. In his "Autobiography," p. 51, Zhang Jia'ao implies that the Tianjin branch of the Bank of China had publicized currency reserves throughout the 1920s; all of the archival evidence, however, proves that these attempts were sporadic and less than successful.
67. *Yinhang nianjian, 1934* (Bankers' yearbook, 1934) (Shanghai: Zhongguo yinhang, 1934), p. A33.
68. Tianjin banks began issuing subsidiary or dime notes in the mid-1920s; *Dagong Bao,* April 14, 1925. Dime notes were issued in denominations of copper yuan coins. Theoretically 100 cents in copper coins equaled one silver dollar, but because of the depreciation of copper in relation to silver, by 1930 it took 340 to 350 copper cents (or the equivalent in dime paper notes) to purchase one silver dollar (or a one yuan paper dollar); Chen Youqin, "Zhongguo zhi tongyuan wenti" (China's copper cent problem), *Dongfang zazhi,* 22, no. 13 (1925): 43–53; and *Dagong Bao,* September 25, 1930. A catty of rice cost about 35 copper cents in North China in 1930; see "Retail Prices in Peiping (Feb.–March, 1930)," *Chinese Economic Journal,* 6, no. 6 (June 1930): 712–720.
69. Tianjin Bank of China, 161-YB-876. The 1928 bank runs began with the failure of the Sino-Japanese Huiye Bank, hurt by the ongoing anti-Japanese patriotic campaign, then spread to several other banks. A year later another bank run spread to some Tianjin modern banks after three indigenous banks failed at the same time; Jingru, "Pingjin jinrong fengchao zaiqi ji" (A record of the renewed financial crisis in Beiping and Tianjin), *Yinhang zhoubao,* 13, no. 32 (August 1929): 1–5.
70. Goodhart, p. 43.
71. *Chamber Collection, 1928–1937,* p. 800.
72. *Diary* as reprinted, September 22, 1930, p. 2.
73. *Dagong Bao,* September 25, 1930.
74. Tianjin Bank Assoc., 129-2-1585; and Tianjin Finance Bureau, 54–239.
75. Background information on Quanye Bank is sketchy. In 1923 it had only six branches (Beijing, Tianjin, Jinan, Shanghai, Nanjing, Ningbo), even though it had considerable capital (5 million yuan); Tianjin Bank Assoc., 129-2-1625.
76. *Dagong Bao,* September 24, 1930. The Hebei Provincial Bank had replaced the discredited Zhili Provincial Bank in 1928. On its history and operations, see the two articles published in *Tianjin wenshi ziliao,* 48 (1989): 44–56.
77. *Dagong Bao,* September 25, October 4, 8, 15, and 17, November 22 and 25, and December 2 and 13, 1930; and Tianjin Finance Bureau, 54–359.
78. Audits of reserves became fairly common in this period; *Dagong Bao,* November 22, 1930.
79. Tianjin Finance Bureau, 54–359.

80. Letter dated February 9, 1931, Tianjin Finance Bureau, 54–359.
81. The exchange mechanisms of the gold standard amplified and transmitted the effects of the depression, but China had been shielded in early years by its silver-standard status. On the effects of the depression, see "China during 1931: Report of the General Manager of the Bank of China to Shareholders," *Chinese Economic Journal,* 10, no. 3 (March 1932): 266–274.
82. *Dagong Bao,* January 1, 1931. On the bond market, see Coble, *Shanghai Capitalists,* chap. 4.
83. *Bank of China Collection,* pp. 160–169.
84. Coble, *Shanghai Capitalists,* pp. 78–81, quote p. 80.
85. *Diary,* March 9, 1926.
86. Ibid., January 1 and 6, 1922. On a previous proposal for a central bank, see May 3, 1921.
87. "Autobiography of Zhang Jia'ao," p. 60.
88. *Diary,* June 6, 1928.
89. Coble, *Shanghai Capitalists,* pp. 80, 81; Zheng Huixin, pp. 1–3. Of the 4 million yuan put up by the Bank of China, 2.5 million came from the Shanghai branch, 600,000 yuan each from Tianjin and Fengtian, and 300,000 yuan from Fujian; *Diary,* October 1, 1928. The Hankou branch of the Bank of China had been virtually crippled during Sun Fo's short-lived Wuhan regime and was in no position to help.
90. *Financial Laws and Regs.,* pp. 524–527, 533–538; and *Monetary Hist. Collection, 1924–1929,* p. 84.
91. For a summary of the Kemmerer report, see *Chinese Economic Journal,* 6, no. 4 (April 1930): 470–486; on reaction to the Kemmerer report, see Lai and Gau, pp. 17–19.
92. In the end, the 1931 laws were not enforced in their entirety either (Coble, *Shanghai Capitalists,* p. 172), but the debate they sparked serves to highlight much about the banking industry at that time.
93. A balanced discussion of the law's provisions can be found in Zhu Qinglai, "Yinhang fa pingyi" (Evaluation of the banking law), *Dongfang zazhi,* 28, no. 11 (June 1931): 9–16. Zhu was an educator who studied business in Japan at the end of the Qing dynasty. Later he was an editor of *Banker's Weekly (Yinhang zhoubao),* and was sympathetic to the rules of the game as played by modern bankers; *Minguo renwu da cidian,* p. 1536.
94. *Yinhang nianjian, 1935,* p. 17. The Bank of China Research Department produced the bank yearbooks.
95. Text of the 1924 Banking Law is printed in the 1934 *Yinhang nianjian,* pp. E43–E48.
96. *Yinhang nianjian, 1935* (Shanghai: Zhongguo yinhang, 1935), p. A19; Zhu Qinglai, "Yinhang fa," expresses the differences in almost identical terms.
97. Wu Shicheng, "Tianjin zhi yinhao" (Tianjin's indigenous banks), *Yinhang zhoubao,* 19, no. 16 (April 30, 1935): 17–26, and "Tianjin zhi huashang yinhang" (Tianjin's Chinese banks), *Yinhang zhoubao,* 19, no. 19 (May 21, 1935): 7–16. The financial resources controlled by Tianjin's banks even came

close to the 436 million yuan controlled by the Tianjin offices of foreign banks; see Wu Shicheng, "Tianjin zhi waishang yinhang" (Tianjin's foreign banks), *Yinhang zhoubao,* 19, no. 29 (July 10, 1935): 18.

98. Shuyi, "Tianjin neiguo jinrongye zhi guancha" (Observations on the domestic finance industry in Tianjin), *Yinhang zhoubao,* 12, no. 3 (January 17, 1928): 13.
99. Zhu Qinglai, "Yinhang fa," p. 15. On secrecy, see Wu Shicheng, "Tianjin zhi yinhao," p. 25.
100. *Yinhang nianjian, 1935,* p. A20.
101. Zhu, "Yinhang fa," p. 16.
102. The three new laws promulgated in 1931 are printed in the 1934 *Yinhang nianjian,* pp. E1–28. A general discussion of the controversy over the laws is found in the same work, pp. A17–23. A copy of the opinion paper of the various Bankers' Associations is reprinted in the 1935 *Yinhang nianjian,* pp. E5–15, and the Tianjin Bankers' Association often discussed the laws at meetings; see Tianjin Bank Assoc., 161-YB-873. Correspondence among the various Bankers' Associations can be found in Shanghai Bank Assoc., 173–1–54. For the revised tax rate, see *Financial Laws and Regs.,* pp. 374–375.

6. Trust at a Time of International Crisis

1. *Diary* as reprinted, July 22 and September 13, 1931, pp. 13, 15. Shi Yousan led an unsuccessful rebellion against Chiang Kai-shek and Zhang Xueliang in July; see Coble, *Facing,* pp. 27, 31; and Zang Yunhu, *Qiqi shibian qian de Riben dui Hua zhengce* (Japanese policies toward China prior to July 7, 1937) (Beijing: Shehui kexue chubanshe, 2000), pp. 9, 10.
2. Quoted in Zang Yunhu, p. 2.
3. *Diary* as reprinted, September 19, 1931, pp. 14–15.
4. Coble, *Facing,* pp. 28–29.
5. Ibid., 30–31; Zang Yunhu, p. 9.
6. *Diary* as reprinted, September 21 and 22, 1931, p. 15; *Peking and Tientsin Times,* September 23, 1931.
7. *Diary* as reprinted, September 22, 25, and 26, 1931, pp. 15–16; Tianjin Bank of China, 161-YB-873. At the same time, the bottom had fallen out of the market for government bonds in Shanghai. The financial crisis eventually forced Chiang Kai-shek and T. V. Soong to resign in favor of the Guangdong faction of the Nationalists; see Coble, *Shanghai Capitalists,* pp. 88–103.
8. *Diary* as reprinted, November 9 and 15, 1931, pp. 18–19.
9. Zang Yunhu, pp. 12–15; and Coble, *Facing,* p. 32. For the Nanjing government's view, see "Memorandum on the Disturbances in Tientsin of November, 1931, Submitted by the People of Tientsin to the League of Nations" (1932).
10. *Dagong Bao,* November 18, 1931.
11. Coble, *Facing,* pp. 39–50, quote p. 43; Donald Jordan, *China's Trial by Fire: The Shanghai War of 1932* (Ann Arbor: University of Michigan Press, 2001).
12. *Peking and Tientsin Times,* February 6, 1932; *Dagong Bao,* February 10, 1932.
13. *Peking and Tientsin Times,* February 10, 1932; *Dagong Bao,* February 10, 1932;

and *Diary* as reprinted, February 8, 9, and 29, 1932, pp. 24–26, quote February 29.

14. *Diary* as reprinted, February 13, 1932, p. 25.
15. *Peking and Tientsin Times,* October 13, 1932. Tianjin's banks normally used checks drawn on the Chinese compradors of foreign banks, so-called *fanzhi,* for clearance. Sometimes Tianjin's foreign banks had too much silver, and the only way to get *fanzhi* was to sell drafts on Shanghai banks, called *shenhui.* See Li Zixiang, "Zhongguo de yinhang zhi tezhi" (The special characteristics of Chinese banks), *Dongfang zazhi,* 30, no. 21 (November 1933): 29; YWQ interview, 1995. On the so-called dollar rate in Shanghai during this period, see "The Depreciated Dollar Rate," *Chinese Economic Journal,* 10, no. 4 (April 1932): 304–313. See also Bian Baimei, "Tianjinshi yinhang ji qianye liang gonghui hezu gongku zhi jingguo ji jianglai" (The formation and future of the joint treasury of the Bankers' and Indigenous Bankers' associations in Tianjin), *Zhonghang yuekan,* 5, no. 5 (November 1932): 5.
16. *Diary,* March 7 and April 1 and 6, 1921, quote April 1.
17. Ibid., July 19, 1927; Bian, "Tianjinshi," p. 5.
18. *Diary* as reprinted, February 14, 1932, pp. 25, 26. Plans to found a clearinghouse in Tianjin in 1927 died after the financial crisis weakened the condition of the banking industry; Bian, "Tianjinshi," p. 5.
19. *Diary* as reprinted, July 6 and 23 and October 8, 1932, pp. 30–32; and Wang Shaohua, "Tianjinshi yinqianye gongku jianli shimo" (The founding of the joint treasury of the modern and indigenous bankers of the city of Tianjin from beginning to end), *Tianjin wenshi ziliao,* 70 (1996): 65. Technical difficulties in setting up the joint treasury and in reconciling the views of modern and indigenous bankers ranged from methods of handling deposits and drafts to the question of checks drawn on foreign banks.
20. *Peking and Tientsin Times,* October 13, 1932; *Dagong Bao,* September 18, 1932. The creation of Tianjin's joint treasury followed the founding of a Joint Reserve Association in Shanghai and clearinghouses in both Hankou and Shanghai. Shanghai's joint reserve system differed from Tianjin's in that banks could deposit real estate titles and stocks and bonds as well as specie. See Stonelake Y. P. Young, "China's Banking Progress in the Past Decade," *China Quarterly,* 1, no. 1 (September 1935): 69–71.
21. *Peking and Tientsin Times,* October 15, 1932.
22. *Diary* as reprinted, February 2, 1933, pp. 35–36.
23. Ibid., May 17, 1932, March 21, May 14, and December 21, 1935, pp. 28, 52, 54, 62.
24. Sheehan, "Urban," pp. 53–56. The Salt Bank had moved its office from Beijing to Tianjin during the early Nationalist period.
25. *Diary* as reprinted, April 27, 1932, p. 28. Luo Longji made the suggestion. Luo, a Jiangxi native, graduated from Qinghua University, studied in England and the United States, and worked as general editor of the Tianjin newspaper *Yishi Bao;* see *Tianjin renwu lu,* p. 247.
26. Coble, *Facing,* chap. 3, quote pp. 91–92.

27. *Tianjin jianshi*, p. 331; Coble, *Facing*, p. 111.
28. Coble, *Facing*, pp. 109, 148.
29. *Diary* as reprinted, January 4, 1933, p. 34.
30. Ibid., February 5, 1933, p. 36.
31. Ibid., March 23, 1933, p. 36.
32. *Dagong Bao*, February 15 and 16, 1933; *Diary* as reprinted, February 3 and 14 and April 30, 1933, pp. 36, 40, quote April 30; and Tianjin Bank Assoc., 129–2–1001.
33. *Diary* as reprinted, February 14 and 17, 1933, p. 36.
34. Coble, *Facing*, p. 149.
35. The Chamber of Commerce and Trade Association laws of 1929 are reprinted in *Chamber Collection, 1928–1937*, pp. 19–25 and 188–190.
36. Ji Hua, "Tianjin shanghui tanwang" (Discussion of the past of the Tianjin Chamber of Commerce), *Tianjin wenshi ziliao*, 16 (1981): 52.
37. *Chamber Collection, 1928–1937*, pp. 72–73; *Dagong Bao*, July 3, 4, 5, 6, and 8, 1934.
38. *Diary* as reprinted, July 6, 1934, p. 45.
39. *Chamber Collection, 1928–1937*, pp. 73–77, quote p. 76; *Dagong Bao*, July 10, 1934. In fact, the Chamber leaders had resigned as a group at the time of the Manchurian incident and the "plain-clothes troop incident"; *Diary* as reprinted, December 28, 1931, and January 7 and April 3 and 8, 1932, pp. 21–27.
40. *Diary* as reprinted, July 12 and 19 and November 13, 1934, and January 26, 28, and 30, 1935, pp. 45, 48–50.
41. Ji Hua does not include the soda pop sellers in his factional analysis, but newspaper accounts from the time indicate that they led the insurrection, so I have placed their representative in the new faction. See Ji Hua, "Tianjin shanghui," pp. 52, 53; *Chamber Collection, 1928–1937*, p. 79. Ji confuses the 1934–35 conflict with the establishment of the Merchants' Union, which had been dissolved by government decree in 1929. In fact, the insurgent trade associations had their own organization in 1934–35, but it was called a United Trade Association Office *(tongye gonghui lianhe banshi chu)*, not a Merchants' Union *(shangmin xiehui)*; see *Dagong Bao*, July 27, 1934.
42. *Tianjin renwu lu*, p. 279; Tianjin Bank Assoc., 129-2-1011.
43. *Yinhang nianjian*, 1935, pp. A39, C26–C31; Wu Shicheng, "Tianjin zhi huashang yinhang," p. 13; and Sheehan, "Savings."
44. Appendix A.
45. "Autobiography of Zhang Jia'ao," p. 51.
46. *Dagong Bao*, October 26 and 27 and November 2, 1934.
47. Yao Qingsan, "Zhongguo jinrong wenti zhi huigu yu qianzhan" (The past and future of China's monetary problem), *Dongfang zazhi*, 30, no. 4 (February 1933): 29–36, quote p. 31. Later that year the Chinese state did abolish the tael, making the yuan the sole unit of account for Chinese money; see "The End of the Tael: Dollar as Standard Unit," *Chinese Economic Bulletin*, 22, no. 15

(April 1933): 221–223; and *Diary* as reprinted, April 6 and 7, 1933, p. 38. For a banker's summary of the critiques against banks, see Wang Shumei, "Wo guo muqian yinhang shiye zhi bingtai lunduan" (Theories of the abnormalities of China's contemporary banking industry), *Zhonghang yuekan*, 6, no. 5 (May 1933): 6–9.

48. Li Zixiang, p. 38.
49. Xu Baohe, "Zhongguo jinnian zhi yinhang ye" (This year's banking industry), *Dongfang zazhi*, 30, no. 9 (May 1, 1930): 49–56, and no. 10 (May 16, 1930): 53–65, quotes from the latter, pp. 64, 65. Cheng Linsun's dissertation makes a similar defense of Chinese banks.
50. *Diary* as reprinted, April 10, 1933, p. 39.
51. Ibid., October 20–November 3, 1933, pp. 42–44. Yeh Wen-hsin notes that the turn to the countryside by Chinese bankers at this time also represented a certain disillusionment with urban life (pp. 97–122).
52. On the latter, see Sheehan, "Savings."
53. Fan Ying, "Zhongguo jingji xianzhuang de niaokan" (A bird's-eye view of the current state of the Chinese economy), *Dongfang zazhi*, 30, no. 4 (February 1933): 7; Wu Chengxi, "Minguo ershisi niandu de Zhongguo yinhang jie" (China's banking circles in 1935), *Dongfang zazhi*, 33, no. 7 (April 1936): 75.
54. Lai and Gau, chap. 3. On the gold standard as the transmission mechanism for exacerbating the depression, see Barry J. Eichengreen, *Golden Fetters: The Gold Standard and the Great Depression, 1919–1939* (New York: Oxford University Press, 1992).
55. *Diary* as reprinted, March 7, 1933, p. 37.
56. Coble, *Facing*, p. 158; see also "Public Finance and Money-Market during 1934," *Chinese Economic Journal*, 16, no. 2, (February 1935): 135.
57. Wang Yejian, pp. 51–53; L. Y. Shen, *China's Currency Reform: A Historical Survey* (Shanghai: Mercury Press, 1941), reprinted in Ramon H. Myers, ed., *The Modern Chinese Economy* (New York: Garland, 1980), p. 10.
58. Friedman and Schwartz, p. 699; Brandt and Sargent as quoted in Lai and Gau, pp. 62–63. Brandt and Sargent argue that the major problem in 1934 was a decline in the agricultural sector caused by draught and flood.
59. Lai and Gau, p. 20.
60. Zhuo Zunhong, "Jinrong konghuang yu Zhongyang yinhang de fazhan" (Financial crises and the development of the Central Bank), paper presented at First Conference of Monographs on the History of the Republic of China, Taipei, August 1992, p. 27.
61. Coble, *Facing*, p. 141.
62. Coble, *Shanghai Capitalists*, pp. 161–172. Coble's thesis that T. V. Soong made relatively milder demands on banks may not be entirely true. Even though bond sales decreased in the early 1930s, direct loans from the Salt Bank to the central and local Nationalist governments began to balloon beginning in 1932, when Soong was still finance minister; Tianjin Salt Bank, "Internal Report on Government Dept.," 1927–304.

63. Coble, *Facing*, pp. 202–207.
64. The mayorship of Tianjin became a revolving door for the next two years. In 1935 alone, Tianjin had four different mayors; *Tianjin tongzhi: da shi ji* (Tianjin gazetteer: chronicle of events) (Tianjin: Tianjin shejui kexue, 1994), pp. 238–242.
65. Coble, *Facing*, p. 207. On Song Zheyuan, see Marjorie Dryburgh, "Regional Office and the National Interest: Song Zheyuan in North China, 1933–1937," in David P. Barrett and Larry N. Shyu, eds., *Chinese Collaboration with Japan, 1932–1945: The Limits of Accommodation* (Stanford: Stanford University Press, 2001), pp. 38–55; and Marjorie Dryburgh, *North China and Japanese Expansion, 1933–1937: Regional Power and National Interest* (Richmond, Surrey: Curzon, 2000), pp. 12–15.
66. *Diary* as reprinted, June 8, 1935, p. 55.
67. Ibid., August 22 and 29, 1935, p. 57. Members of the council traveled to Japan in October; see Coble, *Facing*, p. 262.
68. *Diary* as reprinted, October 29, 1934, p. 47. Stores of silver in domestic and foreign banks in Tianjin decreased from 105.2 million yuan at the end of 1933 to 43.6 million yuan at the end of 1934; see Zhuo Zunhong, "Jinrong konghuang," p. 10.
69. *Diary* as reprinted, November 13, 1934, p. 48. On Du's involvement with finance in Shanghai, see Martin, pp. 194–199.
70. Quoted in Zheng Huixin, p. 25 and also p. 8.
71. Ibid., pp. 24, 25; an English translation of the regulations for the loan issue can be found in *Chinese Economic Bulletin*, 26, no. 14 (April 1935): 213–214.
72. "Autobiography of Zhang Jia-ao," p. 84. Coble (*Shanghai Capitalists*, pp. 172–187) provides a good summary of the events of 1935, although he understates the role of coercion in the affair.
73. Zheng Huixin, p. 27.
74. Coble, *Shanghai Capitalists*, p. 199.
75. On the institutional culture of the Bank of China, see Yeh, pp. 97–122.
76. *Diary* as reprinted, March 28, 1935, p. 51; for Bian's take on other aspects of the nationalization process, see March 25, 29, 30, and 31 and April 1, 1935.
77. Zheng Huixin, p. 25.
78. *Diary* as reprinted, April 2, 1935, p. 52.
79. *Dagong Bao*, April 19, 1935.
80. Quoted in Zheng Huixin, p. 35.
81. *Diary* as reprinted, May 1, 8, and 15, 1935, p. 52.
82. Cited in Zheng Huixin, p. 39.
83. Letters of Earle H. Ballou. On silver smuggling, see also Beiping-Tianjin RMB, 129-3-5430. The archives of the Reserve Management Board are now commingled with those of the Tianjin Bankers' Association and thus have the same catalogue number.
84. *Beiyang Huabao*, June 22, 1935.
85. *Diary* as reprinted, October 23, 1934, p. 47.

86. Zheng Huixin, pp. 45–59, 248–266.
87. Coble, *Shanghai Capitalists*, pp. 192–197, summarizes the 1935 *fabi* reforms from the perspective of Shanghai.
88. *Diary* as reprinted, November 4, 1935, p. 59. On implementation, see also November 6, 8, and 9, 1935, pp. 59–60; and BOC, Main, 397–2–613.
89. *Dagong Bao*, November 5, 1935.
90. *Beiyang Huabao*, November 12, 1935.
91. Zheng Huixin, pp. 242–266.
92. Coble, *Facing*, p. 265.
93. Coble, *Shanghai Capitalists*, p. 205.
94. On China's financial situation in mid-1935, see C. S. Yao [Yao Qingsan], "An Economic Survey of China for the First Half Year of 1935," *China Quarterly*, 1, no. 1 (September 1935): 115–129.
95. "Autobiography of Zhang Jia-ao," p. 107.
96. Reserve percentages would be adjusted to a combination of foreign reserves and specie after conclusion of the American loan, but China still agreed to maintain at least 25 percent in silver. Documents on reserve requirements reprinted in *Financial Laws and Regs.*, pp. 415–416, 616–622.
97. Zheng Huixin, pp. 218–241, quote p. 241. On the autonomy movement, see Dryburgh, *North China*, chap. 2.
98. Coble, *Facing*, p. 266.
99. *Diary* as reprinted, November 8, 1935, p. 59.
100. *Dagong Bao*, November 7, 1935.
101. On Bian Shucheng, see Zhang Lansheng, "Dui 'Bian Baimei riji zhaichao' de ruogan buzheng" (Some corrections and additions to 'Selections from Bian Baimei's *Diary*"), *Tianjin wenshi ziliao*, 39 (1987): 228.
102. Beiping-Tianjin RMB, 129–2–1621; see also *Diary* as reprinted, November 21, 1935, p. 60.
103. Dryburgh, *North China*, pp. 101–108; Coble, *Facing*, p. 274; and *Tianjin jianshi*, p. 332.
104. *Diary* as reprinted, December 23, 1935, p. 62.
105. *Dagong Bao*, December 12, 1935.
106. Ibid., December 10 and 14, 1935.
107. Coble, *Facing*, pp. 283–297.
108. *Diary* as reprinted, December 27, 1935, p. 60.
109. Ibid., November 27 and December 6 and 8, 1935, pp. 60, 61. On Japanese attempts to control the money supply in North China, see also Takafusa Nakamura, "The Yen Bloc, 1931–1941," in Peter Duus, Ramon H. Myers, and Mark R. Peattie, eds., *The Japanese Wartime Empire, 1931–1945* (Princeton: Princeton University Press, 1996), pp. 171–186.
110. *Diary* as reprinted, December 10 and 13, 1935, p. 61.
111. Ibid., December 17, 1935, p. 62.
112. Ibid., May 24 and June 15, 1936, pp. 70, 71.
113. *Tianjin Shang Bao*, May 24, 1936.

114. *Diary* as reprinted, July 3 and 6, 1936, pp. 72, 73. See also *Tianjin Shang Bao,* July 5 and 10, 1936.
115. *Diary* as reprinted, February 13, 20, and 21, 1936, p. 64. Xiao Zhenying, for his part, was soon removed as mayor and replaced by another military figure, Zhang Zizhong.
116. *Diary* as reprinted, March 25, 1936, p. 65; Tianjin Bank Assoc., 129-2-1592.
117. At the time, Zhou was pursuing a strategy of preparing his bank to survive in the increasingly Japanese-dominated economy of North China, and the manager of every Jincheng branch in the region was a returned student from Japan; interview with LXH, a former employee of the Jincheng Bank.
118. *Tianjin Shang Bao,* May 14 and July 1 and 4, 1936.
119. *Chamber Collection, 1928–1937,* pp. 87–92.
120. Ibid., pp. 94, 95; *Diary* as reprinted, December 30, 1936, 75. Materials on the 1936 election are extremely scarce, and the reason for the triumph of the old faction remains obscure.
121. *Diary* as reprinted, July 16–20, 1937, pp. 79, 80.
122. Interview with DTS, Tianjin, 1994.
123. Tianjin Bank Assoc., 129-2-1036.
124. *Diary* as reprinted, December 15 and 16, 1937, p. 81.
125. *Diary* as reprinted, December 23, 1937, pp. 82, 83.

Conclusion

1. *Diary* as reprinted, December 24, 1937, and January 5, 8, 10, 12, and 30, 1938, pp. 83–84, quote December 24.
2. Even the small Quanye Bank got help from its Shanghai branch in 1930–31. On the contribution of branch banking to stability in the United States, see Schweikart, pp. 620, 644.
3. Dodd, p. xi.
4. Shapiro, p. 652.
5. Li Chun, cited in Kirby, p. 50.
6. Lai and Gau, p. 33.
7. Sherman Cochran, *Encountering Chinese Networks: Western, Japanese, and Chinese Corporations in China, 1880–1937* (Berkeley: University of California Press, 2000), p. 182.
8. In spite of his support for path dependency, even Putnam (p. 184) admits that organizations may be able to change environmental variables in the long run.
9. Zheng Huixin, pp. 106, 107.
10. After the communist victory, Zhang Jia'ao moved first to Australia and then to the United States. He died in Palo Alto, California, in 1979. His grand-niece has published reminiscences about the remarkable Zhang family; see Chang, *Bound Feet.* See also Chang Kia-ngau, *Last Chance in Manchuria: The Diary of Chang Kia-ngau,* trans. Dolores Zen with the assistance of Donald G. Gillan (Stanford: Stanford University Press, 1989).

11. In 1948, Wu Dingchang resigned because of ill health and moved to Hong Kong, where he died of cancer in 1950. After the defeat of Japan in 1945, the Nationalist government arrested Zhou Zuomin and detained him briefly under suspicion of collaboration, releasing him on the payment of a fine. After 1949 he continued to work for Jincheng Bank and was involved in the efforts of the People's Republic of China to merge and nationalize all of the private banks in China.
12. Zhang Xiaobo (pp. 31–32), too, argues that the ultimate weakness of the Tianjin Chamber of Commerce had an institutional cause: "The Chinese chambers of commerce were legitimized by the state, and their activities were regulated by official guidelines."
13. Charles Tilly, in his seminal work on state building, admitted that he and his colleagues should have examined the forms of state building in addition to the functions. See his essay "Reflections on the History of European State-Making," in Charles Tilly, ed., *The Formation of National States in Western Europe* (Princeton: Princeton University Press, 1975), pp. 49, 50.
14. Ronald L. Jepperson, "Institutions, Institutional Effects, and Institutionalism," in Powell and DiMaggio, p. 146.
15. Tianjin Bank Assoc., 129-3-5047. For a review of the status of the *fabi* currency in China during the early wartime period, see Wu Qiyuan, "The Chinese Dollar: July 1937 to July 1940," *Nankai Social and Economic Quarterly,* 12, no. 1–2 (January 1941): 53–113.
16. Tianjin Chase Manhattan Bank, 3–32.
17. Hershatter, pp. 112, 231. The standard English-language source on the Chinese inflation is by none other than Zhang Jia'ao; see Chang Kia-ngau, *The Inflationary Spiral: The Experience in China, 1939–1950* (Cambridge, Mass.: MIT Press, 1959). The book deals little with state-society relations, and much work on the effects of the inflation remains to be done.
18. Gabriel Ardant, "Financial Policy and Economic Infrastructures of Modern States and Nations," in Tilly, *Formation of National States,* p. 190.

Glossary of Selected Chinese Terms

baoquan guojia zhi lianmian 保全國家之臉面

baoshi yinhang 保市銀行

ben jin renmin 本津人民

Bian Baimei (Shousun) 卞白眉（壽蓀）

chedi zhi pohuai 徹底之破壞

chuxu 儲蓄

cunkuan 存款

dang pai 黨派

dangju 當局

difang 地方

duban 督辦

fabi 法幣

fanzhi 番紙

gongkai 公開

guanfang 官方

guanting 官庭

guofa 國法

guojia 國家

guojia yinhang 國家銀行

helihua 合理化

jiandu 監督

jianren 奸人

jianshang 奸商

jiaopiao 角票

Jicha zhengwu weiyuanhui 冀察政務委員會

jiguan 機關

jiguan zhi shizhi 機關之實質

jingshen 精神

laotou piao 老頭票

liang 兩

lingyong 領用

lufang 爐房

min 民

piaohao 票號

pin min 貧民

qianpu 錢鋪

qianzhuang 錢莊

qu xin yu wairen 取信與外人

sangzi 桑梓

shamgmin xiehui 商民協會

shangjie yi fenzi 商界一分子

shangye 商業

shangye zhi yi fenzi 商業之一分子

shenhui 申匯

shengchan xiehui 生產協會

Shenshang lianhe hui 紳商聯合會

shiye 實業

Tianjin renmin 天津人民

tongfu laoxiang 同父老鄉

tongxiang 同鄉

tongye gonghui 同業公會

tongye gonghui lianhe banshi chu 同業公會聯合辦事處

tongyuan 銅元

wang guo 亡國

weichi difang 維持地方

wulaizhe 無賴者

xianyang 現洋

xiao min 小民

xiaozhong yu jiguan 效忠于銀行

xinyong 信用

yang 洋

yinhang 銀行

yinhao 銀號

Yuan 元

Yuan datou 袁大頭

zhengfuhua er bu danghua 政府化而不黨化

Zhili quansheng shenshang jinrong linshi weichi hui 直隸全省紳商金融臨時維持會

zhiye 植業

zixiang 梓鄉

zongban 總辦

Selected Bibliography

Newspapers

Dagong Bao (Tianjin)
Yishi Bao (Tianjin)
Shen Bao (Shanghai)
Chen Bao (Beijing)
Tianjin Shang Bao (Tianjin)
Peking and Tientsin Times (Tianjin)
Beiyang Huabao (Tianjin)
China Review
Shuntian Shibao (Beijing)
North China Herald (Shanghai)

Archival and Manuscript Sources

See also the sources in the list of abbreviations on pages 195–196.

Reports of the American Consulate General in Tianjin (Tianjin Academy of Social Sciences)

"Autobiography of Chen Guangfu," Columbia University Manuscript Collection (New York)

"Autobiography of Zhang Jia'ao," Columbia University Manuscript Collection (New York)

Archives of Brown University on deposit with the Hay Library

Archives of the Foreign Ministry (Academia Sinica, Taipei)

Jiangdu Bian shi zupu, Qing Guangxu 25 nian (Genealogy of the Jiangdu [Yangzhou] Bian family, Qing Guangxu year 25 [1899]), Family History Center of the Church of Jesus Christ of Latter-Day Saints, Salt Lake City, Utah, microfilm numbers 1904993–995

Letter from Bien Bonian (Bian Baimei's son) to his daughter, July 26, 1975; August 24, 1975

Letters of Earle H. Ballou, Yale Divinity Library (New Haven)

Interviews

In 1994 and 1995 I interviewed a number of men who had worked in Tianjin banks in the 1920s and 1930s. To maintain their confidentiality, I call them LSW, DTS, LXH, and YWQ.

Selected Published Sources

Alborn, Timothy L. *Conceiving Companies: Joint-Stock Politics in Victorian England.* London: Routledge, 1998.

——— "The Moral of the Failed Bank: Professional Plots in the Victorian Money Market." *Victorian Studies,* 38, no. 2 (Winter 1995): 199–225.

Alford, William P. *To Steal a Book Is an Elegant Offense: Intellectual Property Law in Chinese Civilization.* Stanford: Stanford University Press, 1995.

Anan'ich, Boris. "State Power and Finance in Russia, 1802–1917: The Credit Office of the Finance Ministry and Governmental Control over Credit Institutions." In Sylla, Tilly, and Tortella, pp. 210–223.

Ardant, Gabriel. "Financial Policy and Economic Infrastructures of Modern States and Nations." In Tilly, *Formation of National States,* pp. 164–242.

The Bank of Japan. Tokyo: Bank of Japan, 1952.

Bao Peizhi. "Shouzhou Sun jia yu Zhongfu yinhang" (The Shouzhou [Anhui] Sun family and the Zhongfu Bank). *Tianjin wenshi ziliao,* 35 (1986): 137–151.

——— "Xinhai geming yilai wo guo bizhi de bianqian" (Changes in our country's monetary system since the 1911 revolution). *Tianjin wenshi ziliao,* 40 (1987): 169–175.

Bastid-Brugière, Marianne. "Currents of Social Change." In John K. Fairbank and Kwang-ching Liu, eds. *The Cambridge History of China.* Vol. 11. *The Late Ch'ing, 1800–1911.* Part 2. Cambridge: Cambridge University Press, 1980. Pp. 535–602.

Batchelor, Roy A. "The Avoidance of Catastrophe: Two Nineteenth-Century Banking Crises." In Capie and Wood, pp. 41–73.

Baudry, Bernard. "Trust in Inter-firm Relations: Multiple Forms of Coordination." In Lazaric and Lorenz, pp. 64–77.

Bell, H. T. Montague, and H. G. Woodhead, eds. *The China Yearbook, 1916.* London: George Routledge and Sons, 1916.

Bergère, Marie-Claire. "Civil Society and Urban Change in Republican China." *China Quarterly,* 150 (1997): 309–328.

——— *The Golden Age of the Chinese Bourgeoisie, 1911–1937.* Trans. Janet Lloyd. Cambridge: Cambridge University Press, 1989.

——— "The Shanghai Bankers' Association, 1915–1927: Modernization and the Institutionalization of Local Solidarities." In Frederic Wakeman Jr. and Wen-hsin Yeh, eds. *Shanghai Sojourners.* Berkeley: Institute of East Asian Studies, University of California at Berkeley, 1992. Pp. 15–34.

Bernstein, Lewis. "A History of Tientsin in the Early Modern Times, 1800–1910." Ph.D. diss., University of Kansas, 1988.

Bian Baimei. "Tianjinshi yinhang ji qianye liang gonghui hezu gongku zhi jingguo ji jianglai" (The formation and future of the joint treasury of the Bankers' and Indigenous Bankers' associations in Tianjin). *Zhonghang yuekan* (Shanghai), 5, no. 5 (November 1932): 5–9.

Bian Bonian. "Xianjun Baimei Gong yu minchu de zhongguo yinhang" (My Father Mr. Bian Baimei and the Bank of China during the early years of the republic). *Zhuanji wenxue*, 21., no. 2 (August 1972): 19–25.

Bonelli, Franco. "The 1907 Financial Crisis in Italy: A Peculiar Case of the Lender of Last Resort in Action." In Kindleberger and Laffargue, pp. 51–65.

Boorman, Richard C., ed. *Biographical Dictionary of Republican China*. New York: Columbia University Press, 1967–1979.

Bordo, Michael D., and Anna J. Schwartz, eds. *A Retrospective on the Classical Gold Standard, 1821–1932*. Chicago: University of Chicago Press, 1984.

Bordo, Michael D., and Eugene N. White. "British and French Finance during the Napoleonic Wars." In Bordo and Capie, pp. 241–273.

Bordo, Michael D., and Forrest Capie, eds. *Monetary Regimes in Transition*. Cambridge: Cambridge University Press, 1994.

Bowen, H. V. "The Bank of England during the Long Eighteenth Century, 1694–1820." In Roberts and Kynaston, pp. 1–18.

Braithwaite, John. "Institutionalizing Distrust, Enculturating Trust." In Braithwaite and Levi, pp. 343–375.

Braithwaite, Valerie, and Margaret Levi, eds. *Trust and Governance*. New York: Russell Sage Foundation, 1998.

Brennan, Geoffrey. "Democratic Trust: A Rational-Choice Theory View." In Braithwaite and Levi, pp. 197–217.

"Brown's Versatile Chinese Quartet." *Providence Journal*, October 15, 1911.

Cairncross, Alec. "The Bank of England and the British Economy." In Roberts and Kynaston, pp. 56–82.

Calomiris, Charles W. "Contagion and Bank Failures during the Great Depression: The June 1932 Chicago Banking Panic." *American Economic Review*, 87., no. 5 (December 1997): 863–884.

Cameron, Rondo, Olga Crisp, Hugh T. Patrick, and Richard Tilly. *Banking in the Early Stages of Industrialization: A Study in Comparative Economic History*. New York: Oxford University Press, 1967.

Capie, Forrest. "Banking in Europe in the Nineteenth Century: The Role of Central Banking." In Sylla, Tilly, and Tortella, pp. 118–133.

Capie, Forrest, Charles Goodhart, and Norbert Schnadt. "The Development of Central Banking." In Capie et al., 1–231.

Capie, Forrest, Charles Goodhart, Stanley Fischer, and Norbert Schnadt, eds. *The Future of Central Banking: The Tercentenary Symposium of the Bank of England*. Cambridge: Cambridge University Press, 1994.

Capie, Forrest, and Geoffrey E. Wood, eds. *Financial Crises and the World Banking System*. New York: St. Martin's Press, 1986.

Cassis, Youssef, ed. *Finance and Financiers in European History, 1880–1960.* Cambridge: Cambridge University Press, 1992.

Chan, Wellington K. K. "Tradition and Change in the Chinese Business Enterprise." *Chinese Studies in History,* 31, nos. 1–3 (Spring–Summer 1998): 127–144.

Chang Kia-ngau [Chang Chia-ao, Zhang Jia'ao]. *The Inflationary Spiral: The Experience in China, 1939–1950.* Cambridge, Mass.: MIT Press. 1959.

——— *Last Chance in Manchuria: The Diary of Chang Kia-ngau.* Trans. Dolores Zen with the assistance of Donald G. Gillan. Stanford: Stanford University Press, 1989.

Chang, Pang-Mei Natasha, *Bound Feet and Western Dress.* New York: Doubleday, 1996.

Chang Zhujiu et al. "Dazhong Yinhang yu Sun Zhongshan" (Sun Zhongshan and the Dazhong Bank). *Tianjin wenshi ziliao,* 35 (1986): 162–177.

Chen, Chao-nan, Pin-tsun Chang, and Shi-kuan Chen. "The Sung [Song] and the Ming Paper Money: Currency Competition and Currency Bubbles." Sun Yat-sen Institute of Social Sciences and Philosophy, Academia Sinica, Taiwan, Working Paper 92–2, n.d.

Chen, Jerome. *The Military-Gentry Coalition: China under the Warlords.* Toronto: University of Toronto–York University Joint Centre on Modern East Asia, 1979.

Chen Lili, ed. *Shanghai zongjiao shi* (A history of religion in Shanghai). Shanghai: Shanghai renmin chubanshe, 1992.

Chen Youqin. "Zhongguo zhi tongyuan wenti" (China's copper cent problem). *Dongfang zazhi,* 22., no. 13 (1925): 43–53.

Chen Zilai. "Xiong Xiling." In Yang Daxin, pp. 250–262.

Cheng, Linsun. "Entrepreneurship, Professional Managers, and the Development of Modern Chinese Banks." Ph.D. diss., Washington University, 1994.

Chi, Madeline. "Bureaucratic Capitalists in Operation: Ts'ao Ju-lin [Cao Rulin] and His New Communications Clique, 1916–1919." *Journal of Asian Studies,* 35, no. 3 (May 1975): 675–688.

"China during 1931: Report of the General Manager of the Bank of China to Shareholders." *Chinese Economic Journal,* 10., no. 3 (March 1932): 258–285.

"Chinese Student at Brown 'Broke.'" *Providence Journal,* February 12, 1912.

Chu, Samuel C., and Kwang-ching Liu, eds. *Li Hung-chang* [*Li Hongzhang*] *and China's Early Modernization.* Armonk, N.Y.: M. E. Sharpe, 1994.

Coble, Parks. *Facing Japan: Chinese Politics and Japanese Imperialism, 1931–1937.* Cambridge, Mass.: Council on East Asian Studies, Harvard University, 1991.

——— *The Shanghai Capitalists and the Nationalist Government, 1927–1937.* Cambridge, Mass.: Council on East Asian Studies, Harvard University, 1986.

Cochran, Sherman. *Encountering Chinese Networks: Western, Japanese, and Chinese Corporations in China, 1880–1937.* Berkeley: University of California Press, 2000.

Cohen, Bernice. *The Edge of Chaos: Financial Booms, Bubbles, Crashes, and Chaos.* Chichester: John Wiley & Sons, 1997.

Collins, Michael, and Mae Baker. "Bank of England Autonomy: A Retrospective." In Holtfrerich, Reis, and Toniolo, pp. 13–33.

Commission on International Exchange of the United States of America. *Memoranda on a New Monetary System for China.* Shanghai: Printed at the North-China Herald Office, 1903.

Conde, Roberto Cortés. "The Origins of Banking in Argentina." In Sylla, Tilly, and Tortella, pp. 224–248.

Coriat, Benjamin, and Samira Guennif. "Self-Interest, Trust, and Institutions." In Lazaric and Lorenz, pp. 48–63.

Cottrell, P. L., and Lucy Newton. "Banking Liberalization in England and Wales, 1826–1844." In Sylla, Tilly, and Tortella, pp. 75–117.

Crisp, Olga. "Russia, 1860–1914." In Cameron et al., pp. 183–238.

Crouzet, François. "Politics and Banking in Revolutionary and Napoleonic France." In Sylla, Tilly, and Tortella, pp. 20–52.

Cushman, Clara M. *Tientsin Scribbles.* Leominster, Mass.: Boutwell, Owens & Co., 1925.

Deng Xianhong. "Lun zhongguo yinhang yu beiyang zhengfu de maodun" (On contradictions between the Bank of China and the Beiyang government). *Lishi yanjiu,* 4 (1986): 65–80.

"The Depreciated Dollar Rate." *Chinese Economic Journal,* 10, no. 4 (April 1932): 304–313.

Diamond, Douglas W., and Philip H. Dybvig. "Bank Runs, Deposit Insurance, and Liquidity." *Journal of Political Economy,* 91., no. 3 (June 1983): 401–419.

DiMaggio, Paul J., and Walter W. Powell. "The Iron Cage Revisited: Institutional Isomorphism and Collective Rationality in Organizational Fields." In Powell and DiMaggio, pp. 63–82.

Dodd, Nigel. *The Sociology of Money: Economics, Reason, and Contemporary Society.* New York: Continuum, 1994.

Dornbusch, Rudiger, and Jacob A. Frenkel. "The Gold Standard and the Bank of England in the Crisis of 1847." In Bordo and Schwartz, pp. 233–273.

Dryburgh, Marjorie. *North China and Japanese Expansion, 1933–1937: Regional Power and National Interest.* Richmond, Surrey: Curzon, 2000.

——— "Regional Office and the National Interest: Song Zheyuan in North China, 1933–1937." In David P. Barrett and Larry N. Shyu, eds. *Chinese Collaboration with Japan, 1932–1945: The Limits of Accommodation.* Stanford: Stanford University Press, 2001. Pp. 38–55.

Du Xuncheng. "Zhongguo jindai liangzhong jinrong zhidu de bijiao" (Comparison of modern China's two kinds of financial systems). In Zhang Weibao and Li Huabiao, eds. *Jindai Zhongguo jingji yanjiu taolunhui 1999 lunwenji* (1999 selection of papers from the Modern Chinese Economic Research Conference). Hong Kong: Xinya yanjiusuo, 1999. Pp. 229–250.

Duara, Prasenjit. *Culture, Power, and the State: Rural North China, 1900–1942.* Stanford: Stanford University Press, 1988.

——— "State and Civil Society in the History of Chinese Modernity." In Frederic Wakeman Jr. and Wang Xi, eds. *China's Quest for Modernization: A Historical Perspective.* Berkeley: Institute of East Asian Studies, University of California, 1997. Pp. 300–324.

Eastman, Lloyd E. *The Abortive Revolution: China under Nationalist Rule, 1927–1937.* Cambridge, Mass.: Harvard University Press, 1974.

Eichengreen, Barry J. *Golden Fetters: The Gold Standard and the Great Depression, 1919–1939.* New York: Oxford University Press, 1992.

"The End of the Tael: Dollar as Standard Unit." *Chinese Economic Bulletin,* 22, no. 15 (April 1933): 221–223.

Esherick, Joseph W., and Mary Backus Rankin, eds. *Chinese Local Elites and Patterns of Dominance.* Berkeley: University of California Press, 1990.

Fan Ying, "Zhongguo jingji xianzhuang de niaokan" (A bird's-eye view of the current state of the Chinese economy). *Dongfang zazhi,* 30, no. 4 (February 1933): 7–18.

Feiertag, Olivier, and Pablo Martín Aceña. "The Delayed Modernization of the Central Banks of France and Spain in the Twentieth Century." In Holtfrerich, Reis, and Toniolo, pp. 37–68.

Feldman, Gerald. *The Great Disorder: Politics, Economics, and Society in the German Inflation, 1914–1924.* New York: Oxford University Press, 1993.

Feng Gengguang. "Wo zai zhongguo yinhang de yixie huihi" (Some memories from being at the Bank of China). *Wenshi ziliao,* 41 (1963): 1–19.

Feuerwerker, Albert. *China's Early Industrialization: Sheng Hsuan-huai (1844–1916) and Mandarin Enterprise.* New York: Atheneum, 1970.

Fewsmith, Joseph. *Party, State, and Local Elites in Republican China: Merchant Organizations and Politics in Shanghai, 1890–1930.* Honolulu: University of Hawaii Press, 1985.

Fitzgerald, John. *Awakening China: Politics, Culture, and Class in the Nationalist Revolution.* Stanford: Stanford University Press, 1996.

Folsom, Kenneth E. *Friends, Guests, and Colleagues: The Mu-fu System in the Late Ch'ing Period.* Berkeley: University of California Press, 1968.

Friedman, Milton, and Anna Jacobson Schwartz. *A Monetary History of the United States, 1867–1960.* Princeton: Princeton University Press, 1963.

Fukuyama, Francis. *Trust: The Social Virtues and the Creation of Prosperity.* New York: Free Press, 1995.

Galbraith, John Kenneth. *Financial Euphoria.* New York: Whittle Books in association with Viking, 1993.

Gardner, Henry B. *Outlines of Lectures in Elementary Economics, Brown University.* Providence: Continental Printing Co., 1896.

Gerschenkron, Alexander. *Economic Backwardness in Historical Perspective.* Cambridge, Mass.: The Belknap Press of Harvard University Press, 1962.

Giannini, Curzio. "Money, Trust, and Central Banking." *Journal of Economics and Business,* 45 (1995): 217–237.

Giddens, Anthony. *The Consequences of Modernity.* Stanford: Stanford University Press, 1990.

Gill, Brendan. Introduction to Parnassus Foundation and Museum of Fine Arts, Houston, eds. *Money Matters: A Critical Look at Bank Architecture.* New York: McGraw-Hill, 1990. Pp. 1–6.

Glasner, David. "An Evolutionary Theory of the State Monopoly over Money." In Kevin Dowd and Richard H. Timberlake, eds. *Money and the Nation State: The Financial Revolution, Government and the World Monetary System.* New Brunswick, N.J.: Transaction Publishers, 1998. pp. 21–45.

Godement, François. *The Downsizing of Asia.* London: Routledge, 1999.

Goodhart, Charles. *The Evolution of Central Banks.* Cambridge, Mass.: MIT Press, 1988.

Goodman, Bryna. *Native Place, City, and Nation: Regional Networks and Identities in Shanghai, 1853–1937.* Berkeley: University of California Press, 1995.

Granovetter, Mark. "Economic Action and Social Structure: The Problem of Embeddedness." *American Journal of Sociology,* 91, no. 3 (November 1985): 481–510.

Grove, Linda. "International Trade and the Creation of Domestic Marketing Networks in North China, 1860–1930." In Shinya Sugiyama and Linda Grove, eds. *Commercial Networks in Modern Asia.* Richmond, Surrey: Curzon, 2001. Pp. 96–115.

Gu Shoucun. *Beiyang junfa shiqi de jiaotong xi* (The communications clique during the Beiyang warlord period). Henan: Henan renmin chubanshe, 1993.

Hall, Ray Ovid. *The Chinese National Banks.* Berlin, 1921.

Hamilton, Gary G. "The Organizational Foundations of Western and Chinese Commerce: A Historical and Comparative Analysis." In Gary G. Hamilton, ed., *Asian Business Networks.* Berlin: Walter de Gruyter, 1996. Pp. 47–65.

Han Hongtai. "Beyang junfa shiqi de jiaotong yinhang" (The Bank of Communications in the time of the Beiyang warlords). In *Jindai yinhangye mixin* (Secrets of the modern banking industry). Hong Kong: Zhongyuan, 1985. Pp. 66–93.

Hao Qingyuan. *Zhou Xuexi Zhuan* (A biography of Zhou Xuexi). Tianjin: Tianjin renmin chubanshe, 1991.

Hardin, Russell. "Trust in Government." In Braithwaite and Levi, pp. 9–27.

Hebei sheng zhi. Di 42 juan. *Caizheng zhi* (Hebei provincial gazetteer. Vol. 42. Fiscal administration gazetteer). Shijiazhuang: Hebei renmin chubanshe, 1992.

Heimer, Carol A. "Solving the Problem of Trust." *American Bar Foundation Working Papers,* 9804 (1999): 1–55.

Hennessy, Elizabeth. "The Governors, Directors, and Management of the Bank of England." In Roberts and Kynaston, pp. 185–216.

Henriot, Christian. *Shanghai, 1927–1937: Municipal Power, Locality, and Modernization.* Trans. Noël Castelino. Berkeley: University of California Press, 1991.

Hershatter, Gail. *The Workers of Tianjin, 1900–1949.* Stanford: Stanford University Press, 1986.

Hertner, Peter. "Central Banking and German-Style Mixed Banking in Italy, 1893/5–1914: From Coexistence to Cooperation." In Sylla, Tilly, and Tortella, pp. 182–209.

Ho, Ping-ti. "The Salt Merchants of Yang-chou [Yangzhou]: A Study of Commercial Capitalism in Eighteenth-Century China." *Harvard Journal of Asiatic Studies,* 17, no. 1 (June 1954): 130–168.

Holtfrerich, Carl-L., Jaime Reis, and Gianni Toniolo, eds. *The Emergence of Modern Central Banking from 1918 to the Present.* Aldershot: Ashgate, 1999.

Honig, Emily. *Creating Chinese Ethnicity: Subei People in Shanghai, 1850–1980.* New Haven: Yale University Press, 1992.

Hu Guangming. "Lun Li Hongzhang yu Tianjin jindai zaoqi de chengshihua" (On Li Hongzhang and Tianjin's early period modern urbanization). *Chengshi shi yanjiu,* 3 (August 1990): 64–96.

Huang Fu-Ch'ing. *Chinese Students in Japan in the Late Ch'ing Period.* Trans. Katherine P. K. Whitaker. Tokyo: Center for East Asian Cultural Studies, 1982.

Huang Jianhui. *Zhongguo yinhangye shi* (History of the Chinese banking industry). Taiyuan: Shanxi jingji, 1994.

Hucker, Charles. *A Dictionary of Official Titles in Imperial China.* Stanford: Stanford University Press. 1985.

Hummel, Arthur W., ed. *Eminent Chinese of the Ch'ing [Qing] Period, 1644–1912.* Taipei: SMC Publishing, 1991.

Ingham, Geoffrey. "Money Is a Social Relation." *Review of Social Economy,* 65, no. 4 (Winter 1996): 507–529.

——— "On the Underdevelopment of the 'Sociology of Money.'" *Acta Sociologica,* 41, no. 1 (1998): 3–18.

James, Harold. "The Causes of the German Banking Crisis of 1931." *Economic History Review,* 37 (1984): 68–87.

Jepperson, Ronald L. "Institutions, Institutional Effects, and Institutionalism." In Powell and DiMaggio, pp. 143–163.

Jepperson, Ronald L., and John W. Meyer. "The Public Order and the Construction of Formal Organizations." In Powell and DiMaggio, pp. 204–231.

Ji Hua. "Changlu yanwu de liang da anjian" (Two big incidents of the Changlu salt merchants). *Tianjin wenshi ziliao,* 26 (1984): 127–218.

——— "Tianjin shanghui tanwang" (Discussion of the past of the Tianjin Chamber of Commerce). *Tianjin wenshi ziliao,* 16 (1981): 41–60.

Ji Xiaocun and Yang Guzhi. "Zhou Zuomin yu Jincheng yinhang" (Zhou Zuomin and Jincheng Bank). *Tianjin wenshi ziliao,* 13 (1981): 100–134.

Jia Shucun. "Li Hanzhang." In Luo Ming and Yang Yimao, pp. 111–113.

Jiang Hongye. *Zhongguo difang yinhang shi* (History of local official banks). Hunan: Hunan chubanshe, 1991.

Jiaotong yinhang qi shi wu nian (Seventy-five years of the Bank of Communications). Taipei: Jiaotong yinhang, 1983.

Jin Lüqin, "Qudi waichao wenti" (The problem of suppressing foreign paper money). *Yinhang zhoubao,* 494 (April 1927): 8–12.

Jingru. "Pingjin jinrong fengchao zaiqi ji" (A record of the renewed financial crisis in Beiping and Tianjin). *Yinhang zhoubao,* 13, no. 32 (August 1929): 1–5.

Jordan, Donald. *China's Trial by Fire: The Shanghai War of 1932.* Ann Arbor: University of Michigan Press, 2001.

Kann, Eduard. *The Currencies of China: An Investigation of Gold and Silver Transactions Affecting China.* 2d rev. ed. Shanghai: Kelly and Walsh, 1927.

"Kemmerer Currency Reform Project: A Summary." *Chinese Economic Journal,* 6, no. 4 (April 1930): 470–486.

Kindleberger, Charles P. *Manias, Panics, and Crashes: A History of Financial Crises.* New York: John Wiley & Sons, 1996.

Kindleberger, Charles P., and Jean-Pierre Laffargue, eds. *Financial Crises: Theory, History, and Policy.* Cambridge: Cambridge University Press, 1982.

King, Frank H. H. *The Hongkong Bank in Late Imperial China, 1864–1902: On an Even Keel.* Vol. 1 of *The History of the Hongkong and Shanghai Banking Corporation.* Cambridge: Cambridge University Press, 1987.

——— *The Hongkong Bank in the Period of Imperialism and War, 1895–1918: Wayfoong, the Focus of Wealth.* Vol. 2 of *The History of the Hongkong and Shanghai Banking Corporation.* Cambridge: Cambridge University Press, 1988.

——— *Money and Monetary Policy in China, 1845–1895.* Cambridge, Mass.: Harvard University Press, 1965.

Kirby, William. "China Unincorporated: Company Law and Business Enterprise in Twentieth-Century China." *Journal of Asian Studies,* 54, no. 1 (February 1995): 43–63.

Kong Xiangxian. *Da Qing yinhang hangshi* (A history of Da Qing Bank). Nanjing: Nanjing daxue chubanshe, 1991.

Kuhn, Philip A. "The Development of Local Government." In John K. Fairbank and Albert Feurwerker, eds. *The Cambridge History of China.* Vol. 13. *Republican China, 1912–1949,* Part 2. Cambridge: Cambridge University Press, 1986. Pp. 329–360.

Kumar, Dharma. *The Chinese and Indian Economies from ca. 1914–1949.* London: Development Economics Research Program, London School of Economics, 1992.

Kwan Man Bun. "The Merchant World of Tianjin: Society and Economy of a Chinese City." Ph.D. diss., Stanford University, 1990.

——— "Order in Chaos: Tianjin's *hunhunr* and Urban Identity in Modern China." *Journal of Urban History,* 27, no. 1 (November 2000): 75–91.

——— *The Salt Merchants of Tianjin: State-Making and Civil Society in Late Imperial China.* Honolulu: University of Hawaii Press, 2001.

Kynaston, David. "The Bank of England and the Government." In Roberts and Kynaston, pp. 19–55.

Lai, Cheng-chung, and Joshua Jr-shian Gau. "Fetters or Lifeboat? The Silver Standard and the Chinese Economy, 1900–1937." Taipei, 1999.

Lai Xinxia. *Tianjin jindai shi* (Tianjin's modern history). Tianjin: Nankai daxue chubanshe, 1987.

Lau, Joseph. *Ts'as Yu [Cao Yu], the Reluctant Disciple of Chekhov and O'Neill: A Study in Literary Influence.* Hong Kong: Hong Kong University Press, 1970.

Lazaric, Nathalie, and Edward Lorenz, eds. *Trust and Economic Learning.* Cheltenham: Edward Elgar, 1998.

Lefebvre, Peter S. J., Rev. *A Guide to Catholic Shanghai.* Shanghai, 1937.

Levi, Margaret. "A State of Trust." In Braithwaite and Levi, pp. 77–101.

Li Jingneng et al. *Tianjin renkou shi* (A history of population in Tianjin). Tianjin: Nankai daxue chubanshe, 1990.

Li Zixiang. "Zhongguo de yinhang zhi tezhi" (The special characteristics of Chinese banks). *Dongfang zazhi*, 30, no. 21 (November 1933): 28–39.

Lieberthal, Kenneth G. *Revolution and Tradition in Tientsin, 1949–1952*. Stanford: Stanford University Press, 1980.

Lin Kaiming and Li Shuying. "Tianjin fanrihui yu dizhi rihuo yundong" (The Tianjin Anti-Japan Association and the movement to boycott Japanese goods). *Tianjin wenshi ziliao*, 78 (1998): 87–89.

Lin Nengshi. "Yijiusanling nian Tianjin haiguan shijian" (The 1930 Tianjin customs incident). Paper presented at the Second International Conference on Modern China and the World, Beijing, September 6–9, 2000.

Liu Foding et al. *Zhongguo jindai jingji fazhan shi* (History of economic development in modern China). Beijing: Gaodeng jiaoyu chubanshe, 1999.

Liu Jiazhen. "Zhongguo Tongshang Yinhang jianshi" (A brief history of Tongshang Bank). *Tianjin wenshi ziliao*, 48 (1989): 57–71

Liu, Kwang-Ching. "The Confucian as Patriot and Pragmatist: Li Hung-chang's Formative Years, 1823–1866." In Chu and Liu, pp. 17–48.

——— "Li Hung-chang in Chihli: The Emergence of a Policy, 1870–1875." In Chu and Liu, pp. 70–109.

Liu Xiaobai. "Qiaoshang Zhongnan yinhang" (The overseas Chinese China and Southsea Bank). In Shanghai wenshi ziliao, pp. 172–179.

Lopez, Robert S. "The Dawn of Medieval Banking." In Center for Medieval and Renaissance Studies, University of California, Los Angeles, ed. *The Dawn of Modern Banking*. New Haven: Yale University Press, 1979. Pp. 1–24.

Luhmann, Niklas. *Trust and Power*. Chichester: John Wiley & Sons, 1979.

"Lun Hubu Yinhang" (On the Hubu Bank). *Dongfang zazhi*, 1, no. 6 (June 25, 1904): 145–147.

Luo Congyu. "Wuguo jinri buduihuan zhibi wenti" (The problem of unexchangeable notes in our country today). *Yinhang yuekan* (Beijing), (January 1928): 8.

Luo Ming and Pan Zhenping, eds. *Qingdai renwu zhuanji* (Collection of biographies of Qing period personages). 2d ser. Vol. 9. Liaoning: Liaoning renmin chubanshe, 1993.

Luo Ming and Wu Yuqing. "Bian Baodi." In Luo Ming and Pan Zhenping, pp. 92–94.

Luo Ming and Xu Che, eds. *Qingdai renwu zhuanji* (Collection of biographies of Qing period personages).2d ser. Vol. 7. Liaoning: Liaoning renmin chubanshe, 1992.

Luo Ming and Yang Yimao, eds. *Qingdai renwu zhuanji* (Collection of biographies of Qing period personages). 2d ser. Vol. 10. Liaoning: Liaoning renmin chubanshe, 1993.

Luo Shuwei, ed. *Jindai Tianjin chengshi shi* (An urban history of modern Tianjin). Tianjin: Zhongguo shehui kexue, 1993.

Ma Changlin. "Wu Dingchang." In Xu Mao, Gu Guanlin, and Jiang Tianying, pp. 225–262.

Ma Min. *Guanshang zhi jian: shehui jubian zhong de jindai shenshang* (Between officials and merchants: The modern merchant-gentry in the midst of dramatic social change). Tianjin: Tianjin renmin chubanshe, 1995.

Ma Yinchu. "Guochao jidui bu hehu jingji yuanze" (The bank run on national banknotes is not in accordance with economic principles). *Dongfang zazhi,* 18, no. 23 (December 1921): 107–109.

Ma Yongshan. "Yiketanga." In Luo Ming and Xu Che, pp. 108–111.

MacKinnon, Stephen R. "Liang Shih-i [Liang Shiyi] and the Communications Clique." *Journal of Asian Studies,* 29, no. 3 (May 1970): 581–602.

——— *Power and Politics in Late Imperial China: Yuan Shi-kai in Beijing and Tianjin, 1901–1908.* Berkeley: University of California Press, 1980.

Mann, Susan. *Local Merchants and the Chinese Bureaucracy, 1750–1900.* Stanford: Stanford University Press, 1987.

Mann Jones, Susan. "Finance in Ningpo: The Ch'ien Chuang [Qianzhuang], 1750–1880." In W. E. Wilmott, ed. *Economic Organization in Chinese Society.* Stanford: Stanford University Press, 1972. Pp. 47–77.

Martin, Brian G. *The Shanghai Green Gang: Politics and Organized Crime, 1919–1937.* Berkeley: University of California Press, 1996.

Martín-Aceña, Pablo, Jaime Reis, and Aguatín Llona Rodríguez. "The Gold Standard in the Periphery: An Introduction." In Pablo Martín-Aceña and Jaime Reis, eds. *Monetary Standards in the Periphery: Paper, Silver, and Gold, 1854–1933.* New York: St. Martin's, 1999. Pp. 1–17.

McElderry, Andrea. "Confucian Capitalism? Corporate Values in Republican Banking." *Modern China,* 12, no. 3 (July 1986): 401–416.

——— "Shanghai Old-Style Banks (Ch'ien Chuang), 1800–1935." *Michigan Papers in Chinese Studies,* 25 (1976): 1–23.

Mead, F. S. "Bank Reserves in the United States, Canada, and England." *Quarterly Journal of Economics,* 21., no. 3 (May 1907): 449–462.

"Memorandum on the Disturbances in Tientsin of November, 1931, Submitted by the People of Tientsin to the League of Nations." 1932.

Meyer, John W., and Brian Rowan. "Institutionalized Organizations: Formal Structure as Myth and Ceremony." In Powell and DiMaggio, pp. 41–62.

Mi Rucheng. "Xin yintuan de zai shenshi" (Another look at the new consortium). Paper presented at the Second International Conference on Modern China and the World, Beijing, September 6–9, 2000.

Migdal, Joel S. "The State in Society: An Approach to Struggles for Domination." in Joel S. Migdal, Atul Kohli, and Vivienne Shue, eds. *State Power and Social Forces: Domination in the Third World.* Cambridge: Cambridge University Press, 1994. Pp. 7–36.

Minguo renwu da cidian (Biographical dictionary of republican China). Shijiazhuang: Hebei renmin chubanshe, 1991.

Misztal, Barbara A. *Trust in Modern Societies.* Cambridge: Polity Press, 1996.

Morgan, E. Victor. *The Theory and Practice of Central Banking, 1797–1913.* London: Frank Cass & Co., 1965.

Nakamura, Takafusa. "The Yen Bloc, 1931–1941." In Peter Duus, Ramon H. Myers, and Mark R. Peattie, eds. *The Japanese Wartime Empire, 1931–1945*. Princeton: Princeton University Press, 1996. Pp. 171–186.

Nathan, Andrew. *Peking Politics, 1918–1923: Factionalism and the Failure of Constitutionalism*. Berkeley: University of California Press, 1976.

Neale, Walter C. *Monies in Societies*. San Francisco: Chandler and Sharp, 1976.

Nesbit, Robert. "Men and Money: Reflections by a Sociologist." In Parnassus Foundation and Museum of Fine Arts, Houston, ed. *Money Matters: A Critical Look at Bank Architecture*. New York: McGraw-Hill, 1990. Pp. 7–13.

North, Douglass C. *Institutions, Institutional Change, and Economic Performance*. Cambridge: Cambridge University Press, 1990.

Patrick, Hugh T. "Japan, 1868–1914." In Cameron et al., pp. 239–289.

Pearson, Margaret M. *China's New Business Elite: The Political Consequence of Economic Reform*. Berkeley: University of California Press, 1997.

Pixley, Jocelyn. "Impersonal Trust in Global Mediating Organizations." *Sociological Perspectives*, 42, no. 4 (1999): 647–671.

Plessis, Alain. "Bankers in French Society, 1860s–1960s." In Cassis, pp. 147–160.

Powell, Walter W. "Expanding the Scope of Institutional Analysis." In Powell and DiMaggio, pp. 183–203.

Powell, Walter W., and Paul J. DiMaggio, eds. *The New Institutionalism in Organizational Analysis*. Chicago: University of Chicago Press, 1991.

Power, Brian. *The Ford of Heaven*. New York: Michael Kesend Publishing, 1984.

"Public Finance and Money-Market during 1934." *Chinese Economic Journal*, 16, no. 2 (February 1935): 135–148.

Putnam, Robert D. *Making Democracy Work: Civic Traditions in Modern Italy*. Princeton: Princeton University Press, 1993.

Qian Jiaju. *Jiuzhongguo gongzhai shiliao* (Historical materials on public debts in old China). Beijing: Caizheng jingji chubanshe, 1955.

Radelet, Steven, and Jeffery Sachs, "The Onset of the East Asian Financial Crisis." Posted on the Asian Crisis Home Page, *http://www.stern.nyu.edu/~nroubini/asia/AsiaHomepage.html*.

Rankin, Mary. *Elite Activism and Political Transformation in China: Zhejiang Province, 1865–1911*. Stanford: Stanford University Press, 1987.

Rasmussen O. D. *Tientsin: An Illustrated Outline History*. Tianjin: Tientsin Press, 1925.

Rawski, Thomas G. *Economic Growth in Prewar China*. Berkeley: University of California Press, 1989.

Redding, S. Gordon. *The Spirit of Chinese Capitalism*. Berlin: Walter de Gruyter, 1990.

Redish, Angela. *Bimetallism: An Economic Analysis*. Cambridge: Cambridge University Press, 2000.

Reed, Howard Curtis. *The Preeminence of International Financial Centers*. New York: Praeger, 1981.

"Retail Prices in Peiping (Feb.–March, 1930)," *Chinese Economic Journal*, 6, no. 6 (June 1930): 712–720.

Rivaud-Danset, Dorothée. "Trust and Collective Action in Financial Markets." In Lazaric and Lorenz, pp. 78–93.

Roberts, Richard, and David Kynaston, eds. *The Bank of England: Money, Power, and Influence, 1694–1994*. Oxford: Clarendon Press, 1995.

Rockoff, Hugh. "Walter Bagehot and the Theory of Central Banking." In Capie and Wood, pp. 160–180.

Rogaski, Ruth. "From Protecting Life to Defending the Nation: The Emergence of Public Health in Tianjin, 1859–1953." Ph.D. diss., Yale University, 1996.

Rowe, William. *Hankow: Commerce and Society in a Chinese City, 1796–1889*. Stanford: Stanford University Press, 1987.

——— *Hankow: Conflict and Community in a Chinese City, 1796–1895*. Stanford: Stanford University Press, 1989.

Sabel, Charles F. "Studied Trust: Building New Forms of Cooperation in a Volatile Economy." In Richard Swedberg, ed. *Explorations in Economic Sociology*. New York: Russell Sage Foundation, 1993. Pp. 104–144.

Schinz, Alfred. *Cities in China*. Berlin: Gebruder Borntraeger, 1989.

Schumpeter, Joseph A. *History of Economic Analysis*. New York: Oxford University Press, 1994.

Schwartz, Anna J. "Are Central Banks Necessary?" *Critical Review*, 7, nos. 2–3 (1993): 355–370.

Schweikart, Larry. "U.S. Commercial Banking: A Historiographical Survey." *Business History Review*, 65 (Autumn 1991): 606–661.

Scott, W. Richard. "Unpacking Institutional Arguments." In Powell and DiMaggio, pp. 164–182.

Selgin, George. "The Rationalization of Central Banks." *Critical Review*, 7, nos. 2–3 (1993): 335–354.

Seligman, Adam B. *The Problem of Trust*. Princeton: Princeton University Press, 1997.

Shang Keqiang and Liu Haiyan. *Tianjin zujie shehui yanjiu* (Research on Tianjin's foreign concessions). Tianjin: Tianjin renmin chubanshe, 1996.

Shanghai wenshi ziliao, ed. *Jiu Shanghai de jinrong jie* (Finance in old Shanghai). Shanghai: Shanghai renmin chubanshe, 1988.

Shapiro, Susan P. "The Social Control of Impersonal Trust." *American Journal of Sociology*, 93, no. 3 (November 1987): 623–58.

Sheehan, Brett. "The Modernity of Savings." In Madeline Dong Yue and Joshua Goldstein, eds., *Materializing Modernity*. Seattle: University of Washington Press, forthcoming.

——— "The Persistence and Limits of Localism: State Power, the Public Sphere, and the Money Economy in Republican Tianjin, 1916–1937." In *Guoshishang zhongyang yu difang de guanxi* (Center and locality in Chinese history). Taipei: Guoshiguan, 2000. Pp. 1311–86.

——— "Urban Identity and Urban Networks in Cosmopolitan Cities: Banks and Bankers in Tianjin, 1900–1937." In Joseph Esherick, ed. *Remaking the Chinese City:*

Modernity and National Identity, 1900–1950. Honolulu: University of Hawaii Press, 2000. Pp. 47–64.

——— "Warlords, Cadres, and Bankers: Private Commercial Banking in the Republican and Post-Mao Periods." *Journal of Asian Business,* 14, no. 1 (1998): 5–22.

Shen Danian et al. *Tianjin jinrong jianshi* (A brief history of Tianjin finance). Tianjin: Nankai daxue chubanshe, 1988.

Shen, L. Y. *China's Currency Reform: A Historical Survey.* Shanghai: Mercury Press, 1941. Reprinted in Ramon H. Myers, ed. *The Modern Chinese Economy.* New York: Garland, 1980.

Shen Yunlong. "Qing mo min chu de Wu Dingchang xiansheng" (Wu Dingchang during the late Qing and early republican periods). *Zhuanji Wenxue,* 34, no. 3 (March 1979): 31–34.

Sheng Xuanhuai "Tiaochen ziqiang daji zhe" (Memorial on the general plan for self-strengthening). In Zhang Youhui. *Yinhang ye zai Zhongguo zhi faren* (Origins of the banking industry in China). Taipei: Fumei, 1974. P. 35.

Shi Lei. "Qian Xinzhi." In Xu Mao, pp. 8–114.

"Shiban yinhang zhangcheng" (Charter for the experimental founding of a bank). *Dongfang zazhi,* 1, no. 4 (April 25, 1904): 86–91.

Shu Xincheng. *Zhongguo jindai jiaoyushi ziliao* (Historical materials on education in modern China). Beijing: Renmin jiaoyu, 1961.

Shuyi. "Tianjin neiguo jinrongye zhi guancha" Observations on the domestic finance industry in Tianjin). *Yinhang zhoubao,* 12, no. 3 (January 17, 1928): 21–23.

Siklos, Pierre L. "U.S. and Canadian Central Banking: The Triumph of Personalities over Politics?" In Holtfrerich, Reis, and Toniolo, pp. 231–278.

Skaggs, Neil T. "Debt as the Basis of Currency: The Monetary Economics of Trust." *American Journal of Economics and Sociology,* 57, no. 4 (October 1998): 453–467.

Skinner, G. William, ed. *The City in Late Imperial China.* Stanford: Stanford University Press, 1977.

Skocpol, Theda. "Bringing the State Back In: Strategies of Analysis in Current Research." In Peter B. Evans, Dietrich Rueschemeyer, and Theda Skocpol, eds. *Bringing the State Back In.* Cambridge: Cambridge University Press, 1985. Pp. 3–37.

Smithin, John. *Controversies in Monetary Economics.* Cheltenham: Edward Elgar, 1994.

——— "Money and National Sovereignty in the Global Economy." *Eastern Economic Journal,* 25, no. 1 (Winter 1999): 49–61.

Song Meiyun. "Beiyang shiqi guanliao siren touzi yu Tianjin jindai gongye" (Bureaucratic personal investment in modern industry in Tianjin during the Beiyang period). *Lishi yanjiu,* 2 (1989): 38–52.

——— "Guomindang zhengfu shiqi de Tianjin shanghui, 1927–1937" (The Tianjin Chamber of Commerce during the time of the Nationalist government, 1927–1937). Unpublished paper, n.d.

Strand, David. *Rickshaw Beijing: City People in the 1920s.* Berkeley: University of California Press, 1989.

Strauss, Julia C. *Strong Institutions in Weak Polities: State Building in Republican China, 1927–1940.* Oxford: Clarendon Press, 1998.

Strong, Kelly, and James Weber. "The Myth of the Trusting Culture: A Global, Empirical Assessment." *Business and Society,* 37, no. 2 (June 1998): 157–183.

Sun Dechang and Zhou Zuchang, eds. *Tianjin jindai jingjishi* (The economic history of modern Tianjin). Tianjin: Tianjin shehui kexueyuan chubanshe, 1990.

Sylla, Richard, Richard Tilly, and Gabriel Tortella. *The State, the Financial System, and Economic Modernization.* Cambridge: Cambridge University Press, 1999.

Sylla, Richard. "Shaping the U.S. Financial System, 1690–1913: The Dominant Role of the Public Finance." In Sylla, Tilly, and Tortella, pp. 249–270.

Tamagna, Frank M. *Banking and Finance in China.* New York: International Secretariat, Institute of Pacific Relations, 1942.

Tamaki, Norio. *Japanese Banking: A History, 1859–1959.* Cambridge: Cambridge University Press, 1995.

Tan Jizhen and Tan Zaitang. "Dalu yinhang de xingshuai jilue" (A brief account of the rise and fall of the Continental Bank). *Tianjin wenshi ziliao,* 13 (1981): 135–158.

Temin, Peter *Lessons from the Great Depression.* Cambridge, Mass.: MIT Press, 1996.

Tenshin chiikishi kenkyukai, ed. *Tenshinshi: saiseisuru toshi no toporoji* (A history of Tianjin: a topography of the rebirth of a city). Tokyo: Fukushima showa, 1999.

Thoenes, Sander. "Taking Aim at Asia's Crony Capitalism." *Christian Science Monitor,* January 21, 1988.

Tianjin jianshi. Tianjin: Tianjin renmin, 1987.

"Tianjin tongyong huobi ji qi huidui jisuanfa" (Circulating monies in Tianjin and their exchange calculations). *Yinhang zhoubao,* 1, no. 13 (August 21, 1917): 18–22.

Tianjin tongzhi: chengxiang jianshe zhi (Tianjin gazetteer: city planning volume). Tianjin: Tianjin shehui kexue, 2000.

Tianjin tongzhi, dashi ji (Tianjin gazetteer, chronicle of events). Tianjin: Tianjin shehui kexue, 1994.

Tianjin tongzhi, fuzhi, zujie zhi (Tianjin gazetteer, foreign concessions). Tianjin: Tianjin shehui kexue, 1996.

Tianjin tongzhi, jinrong zhi (Tianjin gazetteer, finance). Tianjin: Tianjin shehui kexue, 1995.

Tianjin tongzhi: zhengquan zhi, zhengfu juan (Tianjin gazetteer: political gazetteer, government volume]. Tianjin: Tianjin shehui kexue, 2000.

Tianjin wenshi ziliao, ed., *Tianjin renwu lu* (Tianjin personages). Tianjin: Difang shizhi, 1987.

"Tianjin zhi jinrong tan" (A discussion of finance in Tianjin). *Dongfang zazhi,* 14, no. 4 (1917): 153.

Tilly, Charles. *Coercion, Capital, and European States,* A.D. *990–1992.* Cambridge, Mass.: Blackwell, 1992.

Tilly, Charles, ed. *The Formation of National States in Western Europe.* Princeton: Princeton University Press, 1975.

Tilly, Richard. "Germany, 1815–1870." In Cameron et al., pp. 151–182.

——— "An Overview on the Role of the Large German Banks up to 1914." In Cassis, pp. 93–112.

——— "Public Policy, Capital Markets, and the Supply of Industrial Finance in Nineteenth-Century Germany." In Sylla, Tilly, and Tortella, pp. 134–157.

Tordjman, Hélène. "The Formation of Beliefs on Financial Markets: Representativeness and Prototypes." In Lazaric and Lorenz, pp. 97–123.

Tsao [Cao] Yu. *Sunrise.* Trans. A. C. Barnes. Beijing: Foreign Languages Press, 1978.

Tsin, Michael. *Nation, Governance, and Modernity in China: Canton, 1900–1927* Stanford: Stanford University Press, 1999.

Tullock, Gordon. "Paper Money—A Cycle in Cathay." *Economic History Review,* 9, no. 3 (1957): 393–407.

Upton Close [J. W. Hall]. "Closeups of China's 'Money Josses." *China Review,* 2, no. 4 (April 1922): 200.

Van de Ven, Hans J. "Public Finance and the Rise of Warlordism." *Modern Asian Studies,* 30, no. 4 (1996): 829–868.

Van der Wee, Herman, and Monique Van der Wee-Verbreyt. "Belgian Banking in the Nineteenth and Twentieth Centuries: The Société Générale and the Générale de Banque, 1822–1997." In Sylla, Tilly, and Tortella, pp. 53–74.

Vissering, Gerard. *On Chinese Currency: Preliminary Remarks on the Monetary and Banking Reform in China.* Batavia, July 1912.

——— *On Chinese Currency: Preliminary Remarks on the Monetary and Banking Reform in China.* Vol. 2. *The Banking Problem.* Amsterdam: J. H. Bussy, 1914.

Von Glahn, Richard. *Fountain of Fortune: Money and Monetary Policy in China, 1000–1700.* Berkeley: University of California Press, 1996.

Wakeman, Frederic Jr. "Models of Historical Change: The Chinese State and Society, 1839–1989." In Kenneth Lieberthal, Joyce Kallgren, Roderick MacFarquhar, and Frederic Wakeman Jr., eds. *Perspectives on Modern China: Four Anniversaries.* Armonk, N.Y.: M. E. Sharpe, 1991. Pp. 68–102.

——— *Policing Shanghai, 1927–1937.* Berkeley: University of California Press, 1995.

Waldron, Arthur. *From War to Nationalism: China's Turning Point, 1924–1925.* Cambridge: Cambridge University Press, 1995.

Wang Shaohua, "Tianjinshi yinqianye gongku jianli shimo" (The founding of the joint treasury of the modern and indigenous bankers of the city of Tianjin from beginning to end). *Tianjin wenshi ziliao,* 70 (1996): 65–70.

Wang Shousong et al., eds. "Tianjin renmin fandui fa diguozhuyi qinzhan laoxikai douzheng" (The struggle of the Tianjin people against the French imperialists' seizure of Laoxikai). *Tianjin lishi ziliao,* 17 (1982): 30.

Wang Shumei. "Wo guo muqian yinhang shiye zhi bingtai lunduan" (Theories of the abnormalities of China's contemporary banking industry). *Zhonghang yuekan,* 6, no. 5 (May 1933): 6–9.

Wang Yejian. *Zhongguo jindai huobi yu yinhang de yanjin* (Development of money and banking in modern China). Taipei: Academia Sinica Economics Institute, 1981.

Wang Yike. "Zhongguo bizhi kaolue ji jinshi zhi gaige" (Review of China's monetary system and current reform). *Dongfang zazhi*, 14, nos. 1 and 2 (1917): 23–28, 85–90.

Wei Bogang. "Tianjin Hengbin Zhengjin yinhang yu Wei jia liangdai maiban" (Two generations of Wei family compradors and the Tianjin branch of the Yokohama Specie Bank). In *Tianjin wenshi ziliao*, ed. *Tianjin de yanghang yu maiban* (Tianjin's foreign companies and compradors). Tianjin: Tianjin renmin chubanshe, 1987. Pp. 309–324.

Wei Ming. "Lun beiyang junfa guanliao de siren zibenzhuyi jingji huodong" (On the personal capitalistic economic activities of Beiyang warlords and bureaucrats). *Jindaishi yanjiu* 2 (1985): 66–110.

Westney, D. Eleanor. *Imitation and Innovation: The Transfer of Western Organizational Patterns to Meiji Japan*. Cambridge, Mass.: Harvard University Press, 1987.

Whiting, Susan "The Mobilization of Private Investment as a Problem of Trust in Local Government Structures." In Braithwaite and Levi, pp. 167–193.

Whitley, Richard. *Business Systems in East Asia: Firms, Markets, and Societies*. London: Sage Publications, 1992.

Who's Who in America. Vol. 9. *1916–1917*. Chicago: Marquis and Company, 1916.

Who's Who in China. 3d edition. Shanghai: China Weekly Review, 1925. Reprinted as Jerome Cavanaugh, ed., *Who's Who in China, 1918–1950*. Hong Kong: Chinese Materials Center, 1982.

Who's Who in China. Shanghai: China Weekly Review, 1931.

Who's Who of Returned Students. Peking: Tsing Hua College, 1917.

Williamson, Oliver E. *Markets and Hierarchies: Analysis and Antitrust Implications*. New York: Free Press, 1975.

——— *The Mechanisms of Governance*. New York: Oxford University Press, 1996.

Wong, Siu-lun. "Chinese Entrepreneurs and Business Trust." In Gary Hamilton, ed. *Business Networks and Economic Development in East and Southeast Asia*. Hong Kong: Centre of Asian Studies, University of Hong Kong, 1991. Pp. 13–29.

Woodruff, David. *Money Unmade: Barter and the Fate of Russian Capitalism*. Ithaca: Cornell University Press, 1999.

Wu Chengxi. "Minguo ershisi niandu de Zhongguo yinhang jie" (China's banking circles in 1935). *Dongfang zazhi*, 33, no. 7 (April 1936): 75–88.

Wu Qiyuan. "The Chinese Dollar: July 1937 to July 1940." *Nankai Social and Economic Quarterly*, 12, no. 1–2 (January 1941): 53–113.

Wu Shicheng. "Tianjin jinrong jie zhi tuanjie" (Unity in Tianjin's financial circles). *Yinhang zhoubao*, 19, no. 32 (August 20, 1935): 17–23.

——— "Tianjin jinrong jijie zhi yanjiu" (Research on the seasons of Tianjin finance). *Yinhang zhoubao*, 19, no. 42 (October 29, 1935): 19–23.

——— "Tianjin zhi huashang yinhang" (Tianjin's Chinese banks). *Yinhang zhoubao*, 19, no. 19 (May 21, 1935): 7–17.

——— "Tianjin zhi pingmin jinrong zuzhi" (The financial organizations of the common people of Tianjin). *Yinhang zhoubao*, 19, no. 46 (November 1935): 7–12.

——— "Tianjin zhi waishang yinhang" (Tianjin's foreign banks). *Yinchang zhoubao*, 19, no. 29 (July 10, 1935): 2–18.

——— "Tianjin zhi yinhao" (Tianjin's indigenous banks). *Yinhang zhoubao*, 19, no. 16 (April 30, 1935): 17–26.

Xin Chengzhang. "Tianjin ba da jia" (Tianjin's Eight Great Families). *Tianjin wenshi ziliao*, 20 (August 1982): 39–55.

Xu Baohe. "Zhongguo jinnian zhi yinhang ye" (This year's banking industry). *Dongfang zazhi*, 30, no. 9 (May 1, 1930): 49–56; no. 10 (May 16, 1930): 53–65.

Xu Cangshui. *Minguo chaoquan shi* (History of paper money during the republic). Shanghai: Yinhang zhoubao, 1924.

Xu Cangshui, ed. *Shanghai yinhang gonghui shiye shi* (History of the operations of the Shanghai Bankers' Association). Shanghai: Yinhang zhoubao, 1925.

Xu Guomao and Shao Yidu. "Jincheng yinhang jianshi" (A brief history of Jincheng Bank). In Shanghai wenshi ziliao, pp. 161–171.

Xu Mao, Gu Guanlin, and Jiang Tianying, eds. *Zhongguo shi yinhang jia* (Ten Chinese bankers). Shanghai: Shanghai renmin chubanshe, 1997.

Xu, Xiaoqun. *Chinese Professionals and the Republican State: The Rise of Professional Associations in Shanghai, 1912–1937*. Cambridge: Cambridge University Press, 2001.

Yang Bingde, ed. *Zhongguo jindai chengshi yu jianzhu* (Cities and buildings in modern China). Beijing: Zhongguo jianshe gongye, 1993.

Yang Daxin, ed. *Beiyang zhengfu zongtong yu zongli* (Presidents and prime ministers of the Beiyang government). Tianjin: Nankai daxue chubanshe, 1989.

Yang Guzhi and Tan Zaitang. "Zhongnan yinhang gaishu" (A general account of the China and Southsea Bank). *Tianjin wenshi ziliao*, 13 (1981): 159–162.

Yang Guzhi, Tan Zaitang, and Zhang Zhangxiang. "Tianjin qianye shilue" (A brief history of Tianjin's native bank business). *Tianjin wenshi ziliao*, 20 (1985): 90–154.

Yao, C. S. [Yao Qingsan]. "An Economic Survey of China for the First Half Year of 1935." *China Quarterly*, 1, no. 1 (September 1935): 115–129.

Yao Qingsan, "Zhongguo jinrong wenti zhi huigu yu qianzhan" (The past and future of China's monetary problem). *Dongfang zazhi*, 30, no. 4 (February 1933): 29–36.

Yao Songling. *Zhongguo yinhang ershisi nian fazhan shi* (Twenty-four years of the development of the Bank of China). Taipei: Zhuanji wenxue, 1976.

——— "Zhongguo Yinhang lijie zhouzhang yilan biao, minguo yuan nian zhi minguo san shi ba nian" (Chart of heads of the Bank of China at a glance, 1912–1949). *Zhuanji wenxue*, 13, no. 4 (October 1968): 61–64.

Yao Sui, ed. *Zhongguo jinrong sixiang shi* (A history of finance thought in China). Beijing: Zhongguo jinrong chubanshe, 1994.

Yeh, Wen-hsin. "Corporate Space, Communal Time: Everyday Life in Shanghai's Bank of China." *American Historical Review*, 100, no. 1 (February 1995): 97–122.

Ying Fu and Zhu Jisan. "Tianjin qianye yu qianye tongye gonghui" (The native bank business and Native Bank Association of Tianjin). *Tianjin gongshang shiliao congkan*, 7 (1987): 1–28.

Yinhang nianjian. (Bankers' yearbook). Shanghai: Zhongguo yinhang, 1934, 1935.

"Yinhang guitai zhi xingshi ji gegu zhi buzhi yu lianluo" (Forms of bank counters and arrangements and connections among departments). *Zhonghang yuekan*, 2, no. 10 (April 1931): 1–8.

Young, Ernest P. *The Presidency of Yuan Shih-k'ai [Yuan Shikai]: Liberalism and Dictatorship in Early Republican China.* Ann Arbor: University of Michigan Press, 1977.

Young, Marilyn B. *The Rhetoric of Empire: American China Policy, 1895–1901.* Cambridge, Mass.: Harvard University Press, 1968.

Young, Stonelake Y. P. "China's Banking Progress in the Past Decade." *China Quarterly,* 1, no. 1 (September 1935): 65–80.

Yu Heping. *Shanghui yu Zhongguo zaoqi xiandaihua* (Chambers of commerce and China's early modernization). Shanghai: Shanghai remnin chubanshe, 1993.

Yu Shi. "Dong jiqi ju ji shuishi, wubei liang xuetang de huimie" (The destruction of the East Arsenal, Naval Academy, and Army Academy). In Tianjin Hedong wenshi ziliao, ed. *Yangwu yundong zai Hedong* (The Self-Strengthening Movement in Hedong area, Tianjin). Tianjin: Hedong wenshi ziliao, 1994. Pp. 73–84.

Yu Yizhen. "Tan Lisun yu Dalu yinhang" (Tan Lisun [Tan Danya] and the Continental Bank). In Shanghai wenshi ziliao, pp. 180–186.

Zang Yunhu. *Qiqi shibian qian de Riben dui Hua zhengce* (Japanese policies toward China prior to July 7, 1937). Beijing: Shehui kexue chubanshe, 2000.

Zelizer, Viviana. "Fine Tuning the Zelizer View," *Economy and Society,* 29, no. 3 (August 2000): 383–389.

——— *The Social Meaning of Money.* New York: Basic Books, 1994.

Zhang Boju. "Yanye yinhang yu Beiyang zhengfu he guomindang zhengfu" (The Salt Bank and the Beiyang and Guomindang governments). *Tianjin wenshi ziliao,* 13 (1981): 69–99.

Zhang Jia'ao, *Ge sheng jinrong gailue* (Summary of financial matters in China's provinces). N.p., 1915.

Zhang Lansheng, "Dui 'Bian Baimei riji zhaichao' de ruogan buzheng" (Some corrections and additions to "Selections from Bian Baimei's *Diary*"). *Tianjin wenshi ziliao,* 39 (1987): 225–228.

Zhang Maopeng. "Liang Shiyi." In Yang Daxin, pp. 352–363.

Zhang Xianwen, Huang Meizhen et al. *Duan Qirui yu wanxi junfa* (Duan Qirui and the Anhui clique warlords). Henan: Renmin, 1991.

Zhang Xiaobo. "Merchant Associational Activism in Early-Twentieth-Century China: The Tianjin General Chamber of Commerce, 1904–1928." Ph.D. diss., Columbia University, 1995.

Zhang, Xin. *Social Transformation in Modern China: The State and Local Elites in Henan, 1900–1937.* Cambridge: Cambridge University Press, 2000.

Zhang Youhui. *Yinhang ye zai Zhongguo zhi faren* (Origins of the banking industry in China). Taipei: Fumei, 1974.

Zheng Huixin. *Gaige yu kunrao* (Reform and perplexity). Hong Kong: Xianggang jiaoyu tushu gongsi, 1998.

"Zhongguo jindai huobi shi ziliao" (Materials on the monetary history of modern China). In Shen Yunlong, ed. *Jindai Zhongguo shiliao congkan xuji* (Compilation of historical materials on modern China, continued). Vol. 68. Taipei: Wenhai chubanshe, 1974–1983.

Zhongguo jinrong shi bianxie zu, ed. *Zhongguo jinrong shi* (A history of Chinese finance). Chengdu: Xinan Caijing daxue, 1993.

Zhongguo renmin yinhang [The People's Bank of China], ed. *Jincheng yinhang shiliao* (Historical materials on Jincheng Bank). Shanghai: Renmin, 1983.

——— *Jindai Zhongguo de jinrong shichang* (Financial markets in modern China). Beijing: Zhongguo jinrong, 1989.

Zhou Yu. *Dagong Bao Shi* (A History of Dagong Bao). Jiangsu: Guji, 1993.

Zhou Yumin. *Wan Qing caizheng yu shehui bianqian* (Late Qing period fiscal management and social change). Shanghai: Shanghai renmin, 2000.

Zhu Qinglai. "Yinhang fa pingyi" (Evaluation of the banking law). *Dongfang zazhi,* 28, no. 11 (June 1931): 9–16.

Zhuo Zunhong. *Zhongguo jindai bizhi gaige shi* (A history of monetary reform in modern China). Taipei: Academia Historica, 1986.

——— "Jinrong konghuang yu Zhongyang yinhang de fazhan" (Financial crises and the development of the Central Bank). Paper presented at the First Conference of Monographs on the History of the Republic of China, Taipei, August 1992.

Ziming. "Gesheng lanchao huomin guan" (Observations on the harm to the people of irresponsibly issuing currency in various provinces). *Yinhang zhoubao,* 451 (June 1926): 10–12.

Index

www.ingramcontent.com/pod-product-compliance
Lightning Source LLC
LaVergne TN
LVHW091517200926
848483LV00005B/442/J